# Vital Souls

# THE ANTHROPOLOGY
# OF FORM AND MEANING

# VITAL SOULS

Bororo Cosmology,
Natural Symbolism, and
Shamanism

Jon Christopher Crocker

Foreword by
David Maybury-Lewis

The University of Arizona Press
Tucson, Arizona

*About the Author*

Jon Christopher Crocker received his B.A. in sociology and in French from Duke University in 1960. As a Fulbright scholar, he spent the next year in Paris, attending the courses of Gurvitch, Leroi-Gourhan, and Lévi-Strauss. He then went to the Department of Social Relations at Harvard University, where he specialized in social anthropology and sociology and worked with David Maybury-Lewis on the Central Brazil Project. His first fieldwork was among the Ramah Navajo Indians in New Mexico during the summer of 1962. From 1963 to 1965 and again in 1967, he lived among the Bororo Indians of Brazil. He received his Ph.D. from Harvard in 1967 and has taught at Duke University and the University of Virginia. He has also been a visiting professor at New York University, the University of North Carolina at Chapel Hill, and the Université de Paris X (Nanterre).

THE UNIVERSITY OF ARIZONA PRESS

Copyright © 1985
The Arizona Board of Regents
All Rights Reserved

This book was set in 10/12 Linotron Bembo.
Manufactured in the U.S.A.

Library of Congress Cataloging in Publication Data

Crocker, Jon Christopher.
Vital Souls.

Bibliography: p.
Includes index.
1. Bororo Indians—Religion and mythology.
2. Indians of South America—Brazil—Religion and mythology. 3. Shamanism—Brazil. I. Title.
F2520.1.B75C76   1985      299'.8      85-1003

ISBN 0-8165-0877-1

*For All My Parents*
*and*
*for My I-Edaga*
*Bernardo Xiwabore*

# Contents

## Reference Material

# Illustrations

# Tables

# Foreword

The Gê- and Bororo-speaking peoples have lived on the high plateau of Central Brazil since time immemorial. The Portuguese came upon them in the eighteenth century, as they explored the heartland of the continent, and brought back stories of nomadic Indians who possessed superhuman qualities of courage, strength, endurance, and celerity. This aura has not been entirely dissipated to this day, even after centuries of warfare, disease, and encroachment have decimated the Indians and trapped them in enclaves on the lands which they once so freely roamed. Yet the legend of the Gê and the Bororo was one-sided. They were well known for their great circular or horseshoe-shaped villages, laid out like paradigms on the open savanna; for their hunting skills and their gruelingly athletic rituals. What was not so well known until recently was the marvelous complexity of their social institutions and their social thought.

Curt Nimuendajú and the Salesian fathers Colbacchini and Albisetti started to explore these topics in the 1920s, but it was not until twenty years later that the full richness of Bororo philosophy became apparent. Colbacchini and Albisetti's monograph on the Eastern Bororo (1942) and the monumental (if almost unusable) Bororo encyclopedia, which started coming out in the 1960s, made Bororo thinking accessible at least to a scholarly audience. By this time the Indian peoples of Central Brazil had attracted considerable anthropological attention because of the dual organization that characterized their societies. Claude Lévi-Strauss had already published influential articles on them which have come to be held up as classic examples of the application of his structuralist method to the analysis of social systems. Lévi-Strauss also had first-hand knowledge of the Bororo, whom he visited on an expedition to Mato Grosso during his early days as a young professor at the University of São Paulo. The experience seems to have influenced him profoundly, for he returns to them again and again in his work and writes of them movingly in the most personal of all his books, *Tristes Tropiques.*

The very richness of social and cosmological invention which fascinates Lévi-Strauss has tended to daunt other scholars. The Bororo seem unusually difficult to encompass. The Salesians undertook the Sisyphean task of putting everything about them into an encyclopedia, which is understandably not yet complete. Lévi-Strauss comes back to them again and again, now writing about their social structure, now about their ethos, now elucidating their myths, but nowhere does he put these analyses together to give us a full account of Bororo thought as it relates to Bororo institutions.

This is the ambitious task which Christopher Crocker undertakes in the present volume. I like to think that it could not have been accomplished except as part of the Harvard–Central Brazil Project, which I had the privilege of directing in the 1960s. In the course of that project my students (now colleagues) and I studied four Northern Gê societies, two Central Gê peoples and the Bororo, and we have been discussing the comparative implications of our work ever since. Since the Bororo differ more, linguistically and culturally, from the Gê-speaking peoples than any of these do among themselves, Christopher Crocker often felt that his data and his concerns were tangential to our energetic discussions of what we hoped were pan–Central Brazilian topics. I remember reassuring him that in time the close relationship between his materials and ours would be so strikingly demonstrated as to seem obvious. The present volume is a vindication of that faith and of Dr. Crocker's research skill.

*Vital Souls* does indeed develop themes which were adumbrated in *Dialectical Societies,* the volume put out jointly by the members of the Central Brazil project, but it does much more than that. It offers for the first time an extended exegesis of Bororo ideas, supported by full ethnographic detail. It also relates these ideas to Bororo social institutions and social action, so that we learn about individual shamans as well as Bororo cosmology, about the spiraling divorce rate as well as Bororo theories of society, about present crises and conflicts as well as the ideology developed for earlier and less desperate times. Above all, this book provides a lengthy and systematic elucidation of Bororo cosmology. It examines the contrast between two categories of spirit—*aroe* and *bope*—and shows how this governs Bororo thinking about life and death, structure and process, essence and entropy. It thus lays bare the philosophical underpinnings of Bororo dual organization, which is one of the most elaborate in a part of the world already noted for dual organization. It enables us to understand the reasoning which leads Bororo to posit that, in a most important sense, a person only exists in terms of the other moiety of the society and only possesses what has been given away to it.

After this sensitive discussion of Bororo culture it may come as a shock to some readers to learn that Dr. Crocker believes the Bororo must abandon their way of life or die clinging to it. Perhaps he is too pessimistic. Other Central Brazilian societies (including the Bororo's immediate neighbors, the Shavante) have so far managed to adapt to the most dramatic changes while maintaining a sense of themselves and their traditions. Yet some Bororo at least appear to share Crocker's pessimism, for they have on occasion made plans to phase out their communities by ceasing to have children rather than to give up being themselves. Are these simply Bororo zealots who would rather die than change, or is it the very richness and elaboration of Bororo culture which makes change so difficult? I prefer to think that the powerful tradition of the Bororo way could also serve as a source of strength for those Bororo who must live as Bororo in a different but not distant future. This volume, then, could turn out to be either a monument to the Bororo past or a signpost for their future. Either way it is a worthy tribute to the genius that is theirs.

DAVID MAYBURY-LEWIS

# Vital Souls

jaguar

# Prologue:
# Why the Bororo?

There is a certain romantic view of anthropologists that we adventure around the world, settling down among whatever people happen to catch our interest. Indeed, we can even choose to study a nonpeople: a band of monkeys. This view seems linked to an assumption that most academic specialities do not "pay" in the same way as brain surgery or corporate law. So the selection of a society to study seems at once the freest and most nonprofitable of human choices. But the truth is different. The tortuous circumstances that lead each professional anthropologist to settle on one place or topic are characterized by at once fortuitous accident and self-interested pragmatism. Moreover, these circumstances very directly affect the kind of research we do, the schedule of our publishing, and the topics of what we write. Hence, a few personal and professional details of the background of this study are presented so that the reader can grasp the significance of the contingencies that brought it about. They are not a matter of self-indulgence but are intended to explain why I have found the Bororo so very profitable, intellectually and personally.

I was drawn to anthropology as an undergraduate first by the writings of Ruth Benedict and then by the dynamism of my first teacher, Weston La Barre. He was, and continues to be, one of the best practitioners of psychoanalytic anthropology in the history of the discipline. I think now that I was initially attracted to his theoretical perspectives because of their systematic coherence but particularly because they almost uniquely in my undergraduate experience dealt with the nonpragmatic, even incoherent aspects of human behavior, those we now label "symbolic." In my senior year I decided to go on to graduate studies at Harvard's School of Social Relations, which at that time strove for an integration among the social sciences, focusing on their intermittent concern with the human activities that have traditionally been the domain of the humanities: religion, literature, the arts, history. It seemed to make sense, before I went, to spend some time in the cradle of Western civilization, but I could not afford a ticket to Europe, let alone a month of food and hotels. Fulbrights to England were even then hotly sought, and so, drawing on my undergraduate background in French, I asked La Barre if there were any French anthropologists who might merit an American pilgrim. His response was enthusiastic; it was the first mention I had heard of Claude Lévi-Strauss. Even, then, vague quotas seemed to be established in Washington: at any rate, as a southern sociology major I got a Fulbright to go to France.

My year there was initially baffling. My French was dreadful, especially in comparison to otherwise silly twits from Sarah Lawrence; my living conditions were deplorable; and especially I found the French social scientists, above all Lévi-Strauss himself, literally incomprehensible. I had been intellectually reared, apart from La Barre, by sociologists and psychologists committed to logical positivism, the "scientific method," and who had an optimistic regard for the fate of technological civilization. I knew very little of linguistics, clearly of great methodological significance to the French, and even less of Durkheim, to whom Lévi-Strauss dedicated his first seminal work. Two things saved me: La Barre is an Americanist, and so I had some acquaintance with the ethnographies Lévi-Strauss used in his lectures; next, I fell in with another American anthropologist, Nicholas Hopkins, who had just received his B.A. from Harvard. Through our talks and the readings he suggested, I began to have some dim idea about what all the fuss was about. There came to be, in fact, a "group" or, better, a loose network of English-speaking young graduates nearly all from the humanities who focused themselves upon the emerging idea of "structuralism." The epicenter of this group was Renata Adler, who was exceedingly generous in providing space in which we could all gather and very able at summing verbally for us "what it was all about." On the other hand, it should be noted that part of my initial bafflement was due to the subjects of Lévi-Strauss's seminars, which were given over at that time to the last sections of the two books he was finishing, *Le Totémisme Aujourd' hui* and *La Pensée Sauvage* (1962a and 1962b). Although both these works continue to demand critical reinterpretation,

Renata and Nicholas seem in memory's recall to have anticipated all the later criticisms and nuanced interpretations. Or perhaps we all did. It turned out to be a magical year.

When I arrived at Harvard, I was "somebody who had studied with Lévi-Strauss," whose works the graduate faculty and advanced students were pursuing with avidity but some perplexity. I shared this last quality but, fortunately, soon encountered someone who actually understood Lévi-Strauss's theories about primitive kinship systems, the nature of "savage thought," totemism, and so on. This was David Maybury-Lewis, who had just arrived at Harvard, fresh from a distinguished graduate degree at Oxford; he had done his fieldwork among the Akwẽ-Shavante in Brazil. These Indians live just to the north of the Bororo, among whom Lévi-Strauss had done fieldwork in the mid-thirties. The Akwẽ-Shavante speak a variant of Gê, a language family widely distributed in central Brazil. The Gê-speaking societies have long intrigued anthropologists owing to the apparent contrast between their very simple hunting-gathering economies and the remarkable complexity of their social and religious organizations. Furthermore, while each society has its own unique institutions, all of the Gê share a number of characteristics: they inhabit circular or semi-circular villages and contrast the central ceremonial place, associated with masculinity, and the surrounding huts, a peripheral, domestic sphere conceptually female. Upon marriage men move from their parents' home to those of their wives, in what is known as uxorilocal residence. Each household thus contains a "core" of related women, mothers, daughters, sisters, and their immature children, together with the in-married fathers and husbands. But above all, the Gê conduct their lives through a variety of "dual organizations."

Anthropologists have been familiar with this type of social institution since almost the beginning of the discipline in the latter half of the nineteenth century. While it assumes a variety of forms, essentially a dual organization assigns all members of a society to one of two categories, which have certain obligatory rights and duties toward one another. Very often they must intermarry, producing a system of "exogamous moieties" (exogamy means to "marry out" of some specific group or category, and moiety derives from the French term for "half"). They may be required to carry out various economic services for one another, exchanging food or collaborating in building various structures, in farming, hunting, fishing, and gathering. Political activities such as warfare also demand the collaboration of both divisions. But above all dual organizations direct the religious lives of their members. The two divisions may impersonate each other's ancestors or totems; each buries the dead of the other. They complement one another's roles in ceremonies dedicated to renewing the cosmic order, re-creating natural and social fertility, or displaying the eternal verities.

Lévi-Strauss's earlier work (1949c, 1958) stressed the essential importance of the study of dual organization to the comparative understanding of human societies for one reason: they represent the translation into social forms and practices and religious beliefs of certain fundamental categories of the human mind. Central among these are classification through opposition and the necessity of mediating between such contrasted pairs, through such social devices as reciprocity (illustrated by marriage between the moieties) and by various symbolic devices such as inversion and reversal (in which a thing "becomes" its logical opposite). But he also noted a major problem with this hypothesis. Dual organizations often express their social logic in startlingly similar ways. Those that prescribe intermarriage often do so by praising the advantages of a brother and sister in one division marrying a brother and sister in another. The granting of a spouse in almost all human societies involves an asymmetrical relationship between the spouses' social groups, logically expressed through such obligations as bride-price or dowry or political fealty. (Just what factors cause the brides' or the husbands' group to be regarded as "superior" or "inferior" continues a hotly debated issue among anthropologists.) Exogamous moieties resolve this problem of asymmetry by the simple reciprocal trade of a sibling for a spouse.

But Lévi-Strauss also showed that the "natural" logics of these societies, the ways in which they associate aspects of the perceptual world with one or another of the two divisions, vary in startling ways. For example, sometimes the sun and moon are considered an elder and a younger sibling, and so "belong with" a single social unit. Or they are represented as "brothers-in-law," symbolizing the complementarity of the two divisions. Furthermore, the basic social mechanisms of dual organizations vary dramatically: some base a child's membership in a division on the fathers, others on the mothers, while others (including, it developed, the Gê) on a variety of complex but partially "arbitrary" or voluntary mechanisms, such as adoption or divination. The rule concerning postmarital residence is just as varied: many of the famous examples among American Indians are uxorilocal, but the Australian cases tend to be virilocal (residence with the husband's family). Then too, these societies seemed preoccupied with issues of hierarchy, either of actual political authority or symbolic prestige, a strange concern when social life appears to be based on complementary reciprocity. Finally, these systematic variations appear not in just any worldwide survey but precisely within those ethnographic regions that are characterized by dual organizations. That is, if one society recruits its division through the principle of fatherhood, their neighbors do so through that of motherhood. The issue then is obvious: could these differences in social practice and natural symbolism be systematically related? That is, does a dual organization based on recruitment through males, for instance, experience more power struggles concerning relative position in a hierarchy and represent the celestial bodies as older and younger brothers or as father and son?

The only possible answer is just as obvious: one has to study a number of historically related dual organizations and seek that lasting criterion of scientific verity, concomitant variation. The rub was that modern research techniques require the anthropologist to spend at least a year, and preferably two, among a particular society. Further, the Gê languages are generally mutually unintelligible. Before studying the Shavante, Maybury-Lewis first worked among another Gê group, the Sherente, who had already been studied by the great German–Brazilian ethnographer Kurt Nimunendaju in the thirties. Even though Sherente and Shavante are more closely cognate than is usually the case among the Gê, he still had to learn an almost new language. So he proceeded to seek funds for a novel research project: to place a graduate student, well versed in the traditions of social anthropology and in Lévi-Strauss, among every understudied Gê society, as simultaneously as possible, and to investigate the systematic relations between variations in social institutions and modes of categorization. His efforts were successful, and the story of what became the Central Brazil Project as well as our initial conclusions can be found in *Dialectical Societies* (Maybury-Lewis 1979).

## The Bororo and Anthropology

One of the lures of social anthropology is its tantalizing promise that under its aegis one might have the opportunity to live with a people totally uncontaminated by the ways of modern civilization. I had grown up with romantic images of the American Indian, but a summer seminar in fieldwork methods among the Navajo and Zuñi in 1962, following my first year at Harvard, soon convinced me just how very tragically contaminated they are. I decided to continue with African studies, or should those societies prove too acculturated, with learning about New Guinea, with its then "authentic" cultures. But Maybury-Lewis invited me, in the early fall of 1962, to join his seminar on Lévi-Strauss and the Gê. He also suggested I work on a newly published work, the first volume of the *Enciclopedia Bororo* (Albisetti and Venturelli 1962). Lévi-Strauss (1958) had published several controversial papers suggesting, on the basis of earlier Bororo ethnography, that "dual organizations" do not in fact exist but are a sort of conceptual falsification of a more stratified political reality. Maybury-Lewis's (1960) criticism of his arguments occasioned one of

Lévi-Strauss's (1960) most lucid commentaries on the relation of ethnography to his own developing theories.

I was flattered by the invitation but horrified. The *Enciclopedia* is largely in Portuguese, the reference headings in Bororo; I am a poor linguist, and French was not that cognate with Portuguese. I barely grasped the theoretical issues involved and had to prepare for my M.A. exams which would cover not just anthropology but a great deal of the recent work in psychology and sociology. Nor was Maybury-Lewis sure that his emerging project would include the Bororo: their linguistic affiliations were (and are) disputed; at best, they were very distantly related to Gê. As the months wore on, though, I found myself increasingly fascinated by this society, a seduction common to nearly all Westerners who encounter them. They turned out to have a unique place among all native peoples in South America and, perhaps, in the world, for both extrinsic historical reasons and their own idiosyncrasies.

A very cursory history of the Bororo is given in the last chapter of this book. Briefly, it hinges around the ways that Portuguese occupancy of the hemisphere was far earlier and much less thorough than that of the Spanish and British. It is also almost impossible to verify, for not only were the Portuguese less interested in sorting the various kinds of native inhabitants they encountered but they faced a somewhat more homogeneous cultural mass than did their Spanish counterparts. For example, feather headdresses are one of the principal cultural items defining "Lowland South America." These are either the hatlike relatively short "crowns," similar to those worn by Sioux and other Plains Indians, but more usually feather "diadems," a horizontal row of plumage worn across the apex of the skull stretching down in front of the ears, tied beneath the chin. It resembles, then, a sort of irridescent halo, since it consists largely of red, yellow, and blue macaw feathers. The early Portuguese referred to all Indians wearing such headdresses as "os coronodos," "the crowned ones." Of all the Brazilian tribes, the Bororo make the largest and (in my view) most spectacular "diadems." There is no way to identify in the colonial sources themselves which of the many "coronodos" were Bororo, but fortunately there is other evidence.

Brazilian explorers reached the homeland of the Bororo in west and north Mato Grosso toward the end of the seventeenth century. They established an important gold-mining center at Cuiaba, a traditional Bororo village site, early in the first decade of the next century. Exceptionally large Indians wearing "coronodos" are reported as visiting São Paulo during the same time (the Bororo are perhaps the physically largest lowland Indians). Indians identified as "Bororo" joined the militaristic bands of Portuguese who explored and exploited much of Brazil during the first half of the eighteenth century, but I suspect that many of these were Gê or those tribes who had adopted some Gê cultural styles (Hemming 1978). The initial positive relations soon broke down, for a variety of reasons (see below), and a state of mutual warfare broke out which lasted for well over a century.

The first systematic Western observer of the Bororo was the German explorer Steinen (1942), who visited the first "pacified" (or "conquered") Bororo in the late 1880s. His accounts of their beliefs and social ways were enhanced when the French philosopher Levy-Bruhl utilized many of his Bororo data in arguing the profound differences between "primitive" and "modern" thought (1919). But modern ethnography received one of its greatest benefits when members of the Italian Catholic teaching order, the Salesians, established themselves among the Bororo in the last decade of the nineteenth century. It is largely thanks to their efforts that this society has made such an impact on modern anthropology, for the Salesians have meticulously provided the dream of every ethnographer: reliable, thoroughly documented accounts of the ways an indigenous people construe the world. They did so first through a number of traditional ethnographic accounts (e.g., Colbacchini and Albisetti 1942) but more recently in a remarkable series of works known as the Enciclopedia Bororo (Albisetti and Venturelli 1962, 1969, 1976). The first volume, with which Maybury-Lewis confronted me, focuses on material culture, social organization, and ceremonial life. As mentioned earlier, the headings are in Bororo, followed by definitions and descriptions in Portuguese. It is copiously illustrated with photographs of most of the artifacts described, a feature of importance during my fieldwork. One reason for its excellence is that the Bororo are enormously proud of their civilization and keenly aware of the challenges it faces. They are eager to have it accurately recorded before it disappears. So the Salesians had a series of able collaborators, but one remarkable man in particular, Akiro Bororo Kejwu (Albisetti and Venturelli 1962: 0.14–0.16). He had received the equivalent of a university education, was literate in Portuguese, Italian, and French, and devoted to his native culture. Thus, the Enciclopedia is something like a permanent, exceptionally able informant.

## Fieldwork Among the Bororo

I based my master's thesis on the first volume, but, when my wife, Eleanor, and I set off for Brazil in the spring of 1964, our intended society was not the Bororo but the Suyá, definitely a Gê-speaking group. They had avoided all contact with Brazilian society until the summer of 1963. That decided me: here was an ethnographer's dream, a truly uncontaminated society. But when we arrived in Rio de Janeiro, where the Gê project was affiliated with the Museu Nacional, I was utterly dismayed to find that the entire Suya population consisted of twelve individuals! The museum's director, Robert Cardoso de Oliveira, suggested that in view of my past work I might try the Bororo instead. Maybury-Lewis agreed, for, even if the Bororo were not Gê speakers, their society shared many characteristics with those of the Gê. This decision, though, meant that we would have to become fluent in Portuguese, since the vast majority of Bororo were bilingual. I had also to read all the museum's documents on the Bororo, which were extensive. We settled down for several months of work in Rio.

During this period we were enormously helped by the generous hospitality of Robert da Matta and his wife Celeste, who were also members of the Gê project, and of his parents and brothers. We also came to know the then director of the Brazilian division of the Summer Institute of Linguistics, Dale Kitzman. This organization is engaged in translating the Bible into indigenous languages all over the world. It sponsored a family team among the Bororo, George and Ester Huestis, who were willing to assist us in getting settled among the Bororo and help us in learning the language. Dale became a true friend, who at one point in our stay in Brazil shared the most awful car trip I have ever endured, from Rio to Cuiabá. Through his good offices we were allowed to use the Institute's group house in Cuiabá for a "base." George and Ester proved to be marvelously helpful throughout fieldwork, both in helping us learn about the Bororo and in the mechanics of daily life. The relationship between missionaries and anthropologists is often portrayed as one of mutual antagonism. I am happy to report that ours with the members of the Institute and with Fathers Albisetti and Venturelli were quite the reverse.

We began fieldwork in August of 1964, settling first in an abandoned building near the small Bororo village of Pobojari. This community was on the outskirts of a very small Brazilian settlement which employed most of the adult Bororo men as day laborers. They spent an unfortunately large amount of their wages on the local sugar cane rum, and traditional village life suffered greatly. Quarrels and fights were daily events, and most efforts at the collective ceremonials so essential to the Bororo were a shambles. But the chief of the village, Bernardo Xiwabore, was acknowledged by all to be the most learned in traditional lore in that whole area of Bororoland, perhaps among all living Bororo. Bernardo was well into his seventies, if not eighties, crippled by arthritis and dim of vision. It rapidly became evident, though, that he would define the terms of our relationship: no passive "informant" role for him. I was, in his view, woefully immature and ill-equipped emotionally as well as intellectually for life as a man. We soon developed that magical rapport which characterizes the most favored "anthropologist-informant" pairs, transforming them into a unique human experience which perhaps alone makes the discipline possible at all.

All my life I have been a night person, quite capable of sleeping till noon. But Bernardo appeared at daybreak and brooked no sleeping in whatsoever. He told me what I had to learn, in the proper order for it to be learned: myths, the details of ceremony, the rules of proper social conduct. If it had not been for my grounding in Bororo ethnography, thanks in large part to the Enciclopedia, I would have been totally lost. But I must have made some progress as an anthropologist and a human being, for in mid-November Bernardo abruptly announced that I was to be his *i-wagedu,* "name-receiver," usually a real or classifactory "sister's son." Anthropologists often appear to be boasting when they report their "adoption" into a primitive society. But such responses are not very surprising, given that these societies are based on intense, multifaceted "kinship" relationships. Given a strange outsider living in their midst, struggling to learn and practice their social ways, situating him or her in the systems which direct their own lives is simple common sense. Still, there is often an aspect of "play" in such adoption: the stranger is clearly just that, and certain to leave eventually. But Bernardo clearly took his position as name-giver with the utmost seriousness. He had no sons, and his available "sisters' sons" were all either immature children or young men largely disinterested in his vast erudition. Bororo chiefs are obliged by the strongest traditional morality to transmit their knowledge but are allowed latitude in deciding just which of their possible heirs to instruct. So, when Bernardo said, "You are my *true i-wagedu,*" I took him very literally. This book is one part of my efforts to fulfill the obligations of that status. I have tried to have it speak Bernardo's wisdom, not my own.

Despite our bond, Bernardo and I agreed that Pobojari was just not the place to learn about traditional Bororo society. The neighboring village, Korugedu Paru, about 25 kilometers downstream, was universally considered the most conservative of all Bororo villages. So in early March of 1965 we moved there, paying for a hut to be constructed on Eleanor's clan's site. (She had been given a Bororo name by Bernardo's wife.) Although I never again encountered anyone like Bernardo, I did come to have other friendships that transcended professional roles. Ugo, of the Bado Jeba Xobugiwuge clan, and Kano Jo, of the Bokodori Ex-erae, became especially close mentors. Many of the shamans described later were helpful, and one in particular, Celilo, took what I can only describe as a scholarly care that I learn the details of Bororo cosmology.

Among the younger men, of roughly my own age, Americo, Garcia, and Arvoro were patient in teaching me the details of Bororo hunting and fishing, as well as in sharing their understanding of the nuances of Bororo esoterica. My own clan sister Margarita and the formidable Dita, our neighbor, became close friends of both Eleanor and myself. Finally, the aged Maneomaru, of the Paiwoe clan, Bernardo's counterpart in Korugedu Paru, was always available for confirmation of obscure details, and he often took pains to ensure my instructors were themselves correct. Not that I should be too romantic: many Bororo were unhelpful and a few were downright hostile, but there is no point in naming them.

Thanks to the civil generosity of its inhabitants, fieldwork in this village was an ethnographer's delight. For reasons explained earlier, most adults were eager that I "get things right." Eleanor and I fulfilled, as much as our abilities enabled it, the obligations of our respective statuses in Bororo society and in the daily routine of subsistence. For her, far more than for me, this required constant labor: never again have we taken drinking water and firewood for granted. Moreover, she had to endure the boredom and occasional pains of life in the tropics without the stimulus of a professional job. Eleanor did so with unfailing good humor, so much so that our Bororo friends, themselves constantly troubled by conjugal strife, used to ask me, "What is your American secret of a happy marriage?" Especially they, and I, like to remember her medical adroitness, especially during the flu epidemic described in the text. Perhaps the best evocation of the quality of our life in the village is this: when we left in February 1966, we and the village wept uncontrollably. When I returned, in early June of 1967, everyone asked, "But where is Eleanor?" And when I left, no one cried.

## The Book's Plan

This work is intended as an ethnography in the old-fashioned sense: that is, I want it to be accessible to non-anthropologists. For this reason I do not explicitly compare the Bororo to the Gê, nor do I elaborate the theoretical implications of the material examined in terms of the recent literature in the discipline. But the bibliography contains many works not directly cited in the text; the professional reader can there find the background for much of my argument. For the same reason I do not address other interpretations of the Bororo data brought forward by other anthropologists, notably Lévi-Strauss. While much of my material confirms his hypotheses, some, in my view, does not; but I have thought it better to present the data as objectively as possible. Finally, I do not incorporate here the work of ethnographers who followed me into the field. To do so would make an already lengthy book much too extensive and, again, of interest only to a few specialists. The last are able to pursue the different works and draw their own conclusions.

Just how an anthropologist presents an understanding of another society used to be straightforward. A volume on the practical verities of economic and politics, another on the intricacies of domestic life, and a final effort to explain the "religion," a progression from the "necessary" to the "possible" to the "imaginary." Now that we have understood just how thoroughly each of these domains permeates the other, no such facile divisions seem possible. The Bororo seemed especially difficult to present in terms of a technology-to-ideology format, because, as will become evident, the latter permeates the former just as much as the inverse. The Bororo live their daily, momentary existences very much in the domains of what can only be called the "really imagined," for they understand perceptual reality in terms of a philosophical antithesis they term *bope* and *aroe*. The first involves the processes of physical change, exemplified by the growing of vegetables and the killing of animals, while the second dwells on the immutability of physical reality in its "givenness" as the regularity of night and day, the seasons, natural species. For the Bororo, human life requires the harmonious coordination of both principles, achieved as much by symbolic action as technical knowledge. The domestic household, for example, attempts to regulate itself by rules ordering its members' conduct which derive in almost even measure from both their understandings of the *aroe* and of the *bope*. My first effort to describe how they integrated these two principles was over a thousand pages long, and I decided two books were clearly necessary.

This first book dwells on how the Bororo understand the flux of individual lives in terms of what they call the *bope*. Consequently, it considers how they deal with those crises in personal existence brought by the private afflictions of illness and accident, by those more regular transformations of personal and social being caused by the birth and death of relatives, above all children and parents, and how they articulate the human life cycle to "natural" processes. It examines how they do so through two agencies, one a human being, the other the resources of symbolic thought. The first is the shaman, the human intermediary between Bororo society and that power they deem *bope*. The second identifies those forms and conditions in nature which are particularly endowed with crucial meaning about the *bope*, both as a cosmological reality and as life-changing events. Therefore, the Introduction briefly surveys the current anthropological understanding of shamanism and "animal symbolism." Since the *bope* can only be understood in relation to their antitheses, the *aroe*, it concludes with a description of the whole of Bororo cosmology and its integration into daily social life. The first section of the book deals with how the Bororo utilize the idea of the *bope* to comprehend and deal with the dynamics of conjugal life. The second describes the ways they employ various natural creatures to negotiate their collective as well as individual relation with the *bope*. The third examines the symbolic and social powers of the shaman of the *bope,* and the fourth attempts to complete the system through an examination of that shaman's counterpart for the realm of the *aroe.* In brief, the book is organized by the categories through which the Bororo understand their own idiosyncratic lives and their society, which are indeed brought into being by these categories.

In more abstract terms, I have tried to write this book to address certain questions posed by colleagues, students, and the general tenor of recent anthropological inquiry. Many of these issues have been skillfully addressed by my colleagues on the Central Brazil Project. But here I feel obliged to mention what I construe them to be, since the following is at least partially intended as an answer. First, and basic, what does life in what Lévi-Strauss describes as an "elementary society" really *feel,* as well as think, like? Second, how is it that such a society can be so concerned about matters of prestige and rank, both about individuals and the groups they represent, and yet so "egalitarian"? Or, in a related vein, why could it be that Bororo villages seemed never to have been possessed by that pervasive factionalism which seems so endemic to their northern neighbors, the Akwẽ-Shavante and the Kayapo? Why have they never (apparently) warred against each other? And third, why should the Bororo try so thoroughly and relentlessly to integrate their cosmology and their society? This relates very directly to the central issue of the book: the Bororo once had ritual specialists who mediated between them and those powers they call the *aroe:* such persons have disappeared from Bororo life. I will argue that they can only be understood if we consider that such a personage was vital to their life as a society. Why, then, has he, and correspondingly they, apparently accepted his demise, and with what consequences?

I am not in the least convinced that I have *the* answer to these questions. Rather, a series of answers are presented cumulatively, so that they are completely revealed only at the end. I did not intend to make the narrative a "mystery story." The data are complex and the analytical relationships among them even more so. I have tried to set forth a coherent narrative in which each chapter builds upon the preceding chapters but also points toward material yet to be presented. One difficulty will be the numerous use of Bororo terms. I have tried to minimize these as much as possible, yet constantly faced the ethnographer's dilemma that most translations are inaccurate, with connotations that mislead the reader. The Bororo, for example, gloss the term *aroe* as "alma," "soul" in Portuguese. It is true that *aroe* designates some immaterial essence which is the metaphysical dimension of a human being, but it also refers to a great many more ideas, some exceedingly nuanced and subtle. Another problem has been the large number of natural species unfamiliar to most readers from outside South America. I have tried to be as precise as possible in identifying each species so standard references can be used (e.g., Walker 1968, Schauensee 1970). Finally, although I have tried to be as comprehensive as possible about certain Bororo institutions and practices mentioned in the text, some self-referencing has been necessary when I have described these more fully in other publications.

Some final acknowledgments. Had Dick Diebold not given me wise counsel at a critical moment in my graduate days, I never would have met the Bororo at all. Fred Adler, Patrick Menget, and Catherine Perlés provided inspiration and helpful criticism at crucial phases in the book's gestation. I am obliged to the National Institute of Mental Health both for the funding of the original fieldwork and for a summer grant that allowed me to complete much of the manuscript. Several generations of loyal student typists labored with critical intelligence over earlier versions of this book. I owe a great deal to the professionalism and the efficiency of its final typist, Ms. Donna Walts.

Finally, if it had not been for my friends, colleagues, and editors Peter Metcalf and David Sapir, this book would never have been published. I can only hope they take as much pleasure in its physical existence as I do. As for my family, Eleanor, Jarle, and Darcy: if it had not been for you, this would have been finished years and years ago. But it certainly would not have been the same book, and I think in almost every way it would have been much worse.

armadillo

# Introduction:
# Shamanism and Society

Shamanism is among those classic themes in social anthropology which, like "totemism" and "magic," were neglected for many years until they suddenly and recently revived. This work is part of the reawakening. It concerns ritual specialists among the eastern Bororo Indians of Mato Grosso, Brazil. There persons regularly enter into intimate contact with supraordinary powers through trances and dreams. This contact enables them to cure illness, to predict the future, to secure game animals, and to defend the community from all manner of harm. As archetypical "shamans," they dramatically relate to their cosmos and thereby to their society, in its aid. But they do so in ways that are singularly Bororo. I intend to show just how much this is so, by setting them in the whole context of Bororo society, considered both as a cosmological system and as mode of individual life. Also, I want to illuminate that terrible and wonderful concern of anthropology—the relation between the private, magical trance and the collective vision.

Many studies of the first great period in anthropology, from about 1920 to 1940, were either devoted to the topic of shamanism or featured it as basic to "primitive religion."[1] Amerindian specialists particularly agreed that shamanism was a fundamental ethnographic trait of their culture area (Lowie 1948: 173–74; Hultkrantz 1963: 86–87; Metraux 1967a: *passim*). Although Eliade's encyclopedic study of 1951 should have focused professional attention on the subject, it was neglected for almost two decades. Slowly, during that same time, other aspects of "primitive religion" came to be intensively investigated in the field and theoretically elaborated. Topics central to shamanism, such as animal symbolism, trance, food codes reflecting analogies between the body and society, relations between individual afflictions and social processes, the "sociology of knowledge," all developed without corresponding attention to what might be regarded as the parent phenomenon.

There were some partial exceptions to this neglect, almost all of them continuations of the American anthropological interest in psychological aspects of culture, especially as they manifest themselves in psychocognitive dimensions of "folk healing." These studies varied in the degree they considered the social and symbolic matrix of the shaman, but usually they focused on his or her personal "deviancy" from what that matrix defined as normal human conduct and belief. This was entirely consistent with what anthropologists have classically viewed as the theoretical conundrum of shamanism: the apparently inextricable mix of idiosyncratic psychic elements with purely sociological ones. The problem was recognized almost simultaneously with the identification of the shaman as a unique ritual specialist. Eliade's definition of shamanism as "an archaic individual technique of ecstasy" is a relatively modern version of the paradox, but shortly after the turn of the century Goldenweiser (1918: 290) described the shaman as "being at once overwhelmingly psychological in his means, and purely sociological in his ends." The unique element of the role, the one that differentiated it from other forms of religious specializations, seemed to be its stress on individuated mystical experience. Correspondingly, investigators tried to understand the psychological reasons why some persons whose talk and actions were definitely abnormal if not "mad" in their own societies' judgments, were not only tolerated but credited with a vast range of mystical power.

Beginning in the late 1960s, anthropological interests in shamanism began to revive, or at least be publicly expressed. This was no triumph of the free will of academic inquiry. Public interest in such matters as the "higher truths" that drugs and mysticism might reveal legitimated and stimulated fieldwork on such "supernatural experts" as shamans. Although the resulting publications have been copious, the great bulk of analysis appears to me to be headed in the wrong direction. In explaining why, I will give the reasons for the method employed in this ethnography.

# Shamanism and Witchcraft

A broad definition of "shaman," such as Eliade's or Goldenweiser's, includes a wide variety of mystical specialists in almost every inhabited part of the world, among societies at every level of socioeconomic complexity, who are variously integrated with or opposed to other specialists. Shamans, in this sense, are also called mediums, faith healers, prophets, seers, or simply mystics. Yet they are by no means universal among human societies, regardless of how generously defined. About as many cultures take a negative as a positive attitude toward individual "trance" or "possession" (Bourguignon 1976), and such attitudes often vary dramatically through time in a single culture. The Christian churches, for example, have changed their minds dozens of times about the very possibility of trance. More than one anthropologist has attempted to explain the social correlates of shamanism, its institutional, ideological, or psychological "causes"; yet none of their theories has met any general acceptance (Douglas 1973, Firth 1975, Lewis 1971, Crapanzano and Garrison 1980). In contrast, anthropological investigations of another widely distributed spiritual agent, the witch, have been largely successful in explaining his or her social origins, the varying specifics of his symbolic attributes, and his temporal and geographic distribution. Until recently, most of these studies were carried out in sub-Saharan Africa, where the witch is usually portrayed as unconscious of his or her mystical powers. To explain why many people believed in a being anthropologists knew to be purely imaginary, we had to assume that witchcraft beliefs were in some sense "true," though not in the ways believers assert. That is, anthropologists were compelled to examine the witch as a symbol. The problem with studies of trance is that its practitioners are all too real and all too articulate about the reality of their mystical experiences. Often these are discordant with the standards of truth, above all symbolic truth, held by all other members of the mystic's society. Deciphering the idiosyncratic symbolic world constructed by an individual trance specialist can be ethnographically done, as Zamplani (1980) has brilliantly demonstrated.

Fortunately, the classic examples of shamans require no such laborious case-by-case approach. The shaman's mystic experiences concord with his society's perception of the truth-of-things, with their collective representations. Even his "means" turn out to be far more sociological than Goldenweiser thought. Thus, shamanism can be investigated sociologically, as witches have been, but this raises another problem, central to the comparative study of the shaman: In his classic form this specialist seems very largely if not entirely found only among American Indians and in Siberia.

Any survey of shamans in the Western Hemisphere reveals a series of detailed and interlocking attributes. These include "fasting, purification, skeletonization, symbolic death and resurrection after a trance, dismemberment, gashing, shamanic trees, celestial ascent by rainbows, replacement of internal organs and introduction of magic power into the shaman's body in the form of pebbles, rock crystals and so forth; killing of the neophyte by initiatory demons, travel on flying animals, sexual abstinence, magical arrows of sickness, sucking, blowing, tutelary spirits, cannibalistic tests, animated 'pains' as sources of power and causes of illness" (Wilbert 1972: 81, summarizing Eliade 1964). To this might be added, again from Eliade, metamorphoses into regionally characteristic animals and birds (in South America, jaguars and eagles); vertical ascent and descent to cosmological poles (the "sun" and "bottom of the sea"), where earthly fertility and health is regained or assured; trances achieved through plant narcotics (above all tobacco) and hallucinogens; the narrow and deadly "gate" (clashing rocks, moving trees) which must be passed on the initiatory or subsequent mystic journeys; prediction of the future and control of the weather; assurance of game and/or hunting success; aggressive combats with the assistance of "familiars" against malign powers, "an essential role in the defense of the psychic integrity of the community" (Eliade 1964: 509); the inevitable utilization of trance in the diagnosis and treatment of affliction; "secret languages" and other hidden knowledge, often gained in apprenticeship to an expert; seances at night with an assistant-interpreter present; instruments of percussive "din" used in entering trance; a quest for solitude, meditation, and the joyful terror of ecstatic experience for its own sake.

Some of these attributes appear among trance specialists in other parts of the world. In the Americas, however, they almost invariably accompany one another, in much richer detail than outlined above. Further, the similarity of shamans in different societies within the hemispheres' separate culture areas is even more striking. Thus, my initial argument is that to proceed with understanding these specialists we ought to begin by examining their subtypes in one culture area: here, shamans in the indigenous Americas. This strategy, however, may seem ill-suited to my sociological aims. Amerindian societies are vastly different in their organizations and cosmologies: how could they generate such similar mystical specialists? Again I will use as a model the history of anthropological exploration of African witchcraft, which confronted precisely the same problem. It proceeded by utilizing the analogy between the human body and society, as initially developed in the social sciences by Durkheim and his associates. They had the acumen to assume its validity as a code for a remarkable variety of institutions and behaviors. Their interpretations of sacrifice, totemism, taboo, funerals, divination, magic, among others, either proceeded directly from this assumption or incorporated it as a self-evident axiom. Later generations of anthropologists, most notably perhaps Evans-Pritchard, have amply demonstrated the utility of "the somatic metaphor." But of all the ethnological domains investigated in this tradition, none depends more on its central assumption than practices concerning mystic human causation of affliction, that is, the anthropology of witches, magicians, sorcerers, and the like.

Illness and death are understood in many "primitive" societies through symbolic systems which draw parallels between human suffering, social pathology, and cosmic laws. Disruptions in the moral order of society threaten the organic well-being of its members and destroy the equilibrium of the natural universe. Such willful individual acts as incest and murder are hideous evils because they wreck a single structural physiology that animates the relations among men, groups, animals, plants, ancestors, and spirits. Effective diagnosis and treatment of disease thus require a reestablishment of that single moral universe, through a cleansing of the pollutions brought about by the transgression of categorical imperatives. A sick person implies a diseased cosmos; by the same logic, irregularities or disruptions of nature, in such phenomena as eclipses and droughts, do not bode well for human welfare. Underlying this body-society-nature analogy is an assumption that all organic irregularity is fundamentally wrong. Disturbances in what are assumed to be the self's or nature's normal functioning are "bad" not just because they hurt or disgust or disappoint expectation, but above all because they just should not be. Death, in these social traditions, is itself the ultimate moral affront to the individual person, a lethal betrayal of all principles of right and order. Particular afflictions are small deaths, almost as unjust, whether they result from some clumsy accident or leprosy or sterility. Since natural rhythms are generally consistent, in contrast to humans' constant violations of their moral codes, it is logical to blame human malevolence or inobedience for organic disruptions both among human beings and in nature. Hence the near universality of witches, sorcerers, and "sinners."

The immorality of human suffering and death, and its explanation through one or another variant of the organic analogy, seem ancient and universal to Indo-European society (Onians 1951: 426–66; Tillyard n.d.). It appears to be shared by other cultural traditions, such as those of Bantu

Africa, the Malayo-Polynesian world, and east Asia. But its commonality should not persuade us of its universality. Our own Western tradition has now convinced us that people fall sick or suffer accidents through, most often, no "fault" of their own. (We do retain a certain predilection for assuming that immoral behavior leads to physical disaster; tobacco and alcohol are punitive substances.) My argument will be that Amerindians also base their systems of healing and mystical specialties on something other than the body-society analogy, something akin to our "modern" understanding. The shaman operates in a universe as determinedly mechanistic as those inhabited by osteopaths and ophthalmologists. He removes pathogenic substances with all the assurance of a surgeon cutting away a malign tumor but can offer no more precise explanation for its existence than can that sophisticated barber. He cannot help those suffering from the subtle diminishments of age, provides no aid for the infertile, and counts as of no account those who die after his ministrations. In his rigid and self-guarding professionalism, he can be as blindly protective of himself and his own kind as the most selfish member of the American Medical Association. No wonder that his public mistrusts his motives and doubts his techniques; he would as eagerly embrace no-fault insurance as any doctor. But he too doubts his powers and wonders why his magical tricks heal the suffering. He does transcend, for himself and his public, in his nonhealing mystical experiences, the limits of the human condition, and endures the mad horrors of Boschian hells. He is helpless when seized by his spirits, who shake and worry his body and wrest his very soul from him. As he shudders his way through miracles, his audience regards him with an awed pity, revolted and mystified. Yet the next day they depend on him to find game or avert the catastrophe of an eclipse. It is just this combination of mystical technologist and helpless "seer" which makes the shaman unique among mystical specialists. This paradox can only be understood if we forsake all prior assumptions about the "moral" character of affliction and the "private" truth revealed in possession.

Most explicit Amerindian ideas about shamans contain very little reference to the social system or to the idiosyncrasies of individual behavior. They are not members of a specialized caste or clan. The afflictions they treat are seldom understood as due to human culpability or volition, even that unconscious version of malign will found so often in African versions of witchcraft. The usual example is something known as "soul loss," perhaps the most common affliction shamans (in any definition) are asked to cure. This occurs when an individual is startled by an unusual event, or in a bad dream, or forgets a traditional magical warning, a "taboo." Even in the last circumstance, soul loss is seldom considered as due to any sort of moral laxity on the victim's part. Its shamanistic treatment is flatly mechanistic: the soul has to be retrieved and united with its owner. This is done during the shaman's trance or while he sleeps. It requires no overt modification in the patient's social relationships, and often his or her physical being is almost ignored during the "cure." In short, Amerindian soul loss seems a peculiarly amoral "thing."

Other aspects of Amerindian epidemiology are just as a-sociological. The pathogenic substances, so often the object of the shaman's sucking, blowing, and massage, come to reside in the victim's body for, typically, no very good reason. They may be the malign darts of spirits who delight in capriciously tormenting humans. Or they could be the projectiles of some hostile shaman, an ally of a distant political unit opposed to the victim's own, or even a member of an enemy society. Such a person may be credited with malignant intentions and lethal powers, but he selects his victims at random (Rivière 1970: 248–49). Or the pathogenic agents can also be acquired by unhappy accident, the Amerindian version of pollution, through chance encounter with some mystically surcharged bit of nature. This might be a tree blasted by lightning, a corpse, an unusually potent animal or plant, the organic substances of otherwise ordinary creatures, including man himself, or just, simply, a "bad" place. The excision of the substances acquired in these ways usually has little explicit reference to the patient's moral condition or his social relationships. The shaman removes them with a surgeon's deftness, and the victim may or may not recover.

The most common association between affliction and prior human volition in this culture area involves the breaking of "taboos" concerning human behavior toward game animals and the general preparation of food. Perhaps the best known example is the Eskimo, as described by the early ethnographer Knud Rasmussen. He characterized the "taboos" very aptly as "rules of life," which one of his informants explained in a way that approximates Bororo concepts.

> The greatest peril of life lies in the fact that human food consists entirely of souls. All the creatures that we have to kill and eat, all those that we have to strike down and destroy to make clothes for ourselves, have souls, like we have, souls that do not perish with the body, and which must therefore be propitiated lest they should revenge themselves on us for taking away their bodies. (Rasmussen 1929: 56)

This "propitiation" means following elaborate rules dictating almost every aspect of human behavior toward the game, before and after its death. The rules are based on the dyadic seasonal variation in Eskimo social ecology made famous by Mauss and Beuchat (1906), on, in other words, the principle that the animals and practices of the winter months should never come into contact with those of the summer. Creatures of the land (sought during the winter) and of the sea (those pursued in summer) must be kept separate, or mixed only with elaborate ritual precautions. Something more than "pollution" is involved here, for the animals' souls are credited with powers of revenge, as the informant states. Furthermore, at least among the Iglulik Eskimo, neglect of the rules provokes the wrath of Takanakapsaluk, the "Mother of Sea Beasts," who controls the reproduction and migrations of all creatures who live in the ocean. "Because she was their mother . . . human beings had to observe all the numerous and difficult rules of taboo, the purpose of which was to ensure that the thoughts and hands of unclean human beings should never come in contact with the 'sacred' food" (Rasmussen 1929: 68). She can afflict the guilty party and his fellows either by epidemics or by withholding game; to mend the offense a possessed shaman must journey down to the house of Takanakapsaluk at the bottom of the sea to beg her forgiveness. This is only granted when the malefactor (or more commonly, malefactors) confess some breach of the rules, in a collective "seance" directed by the shaman's incisive questioning.

Rasmussen's dramatic accounts of the "seances" he witnessed make clear the precision, great number, and especially the nonsocial quality of the "rules of life": eating certain foods (especially seal and caribou) at the wrong season or when ritually unclean, working at seasonally inappropriate tasks, or when clothed wrongly, even combing the hair when impure (Rasmussen 1929: 132–41). Yet violating a picayune rule is the immediate cause of serious illness. The gravity of the affliction seems completely out of proportion to the infraction. The audience's responses appear to reflect this very directly: "It is such a slight offense, and means so little, when her life is at stake. Let her be released from this burden, from this cause, from this source of illness" (Rasmussen 1929: 134).

Although the ethnographic details vary, the association between shamanism and violations of elaborate rules about game animals and food seems almost axiomatic in the Americas. Other societies also dictate how humans should avoid mixing substances of logically different natures, in what are termed "pollution beliefs." Mary Douglas has shown that these are expressions of a fundamental moral order that is beyond issues of social ethics. In discussing the ancient Hebrew idea of holiness, she says,

> Holiness means keeping distinct the categories of creation. It therefore involves correct definition, discrimination and order. Under this head all the rules of sexual morality exemplify the holy. Incest and

adultery are against holiness, in the simplest sense of right order. Morality does not conflict with holiness, but holiness is more a matter of separating that which should be separated than of protecting the rights of husbands and brothers. (Douglas 1966: 53)

Ethnographic analyses have shown the logic of bizarre dietary rules and their profound associations with moral prescriptions for behavior in crucial social relationships, above those between men and women (Bulmer 1967, Leach 1964, Lévi-Strauss 1969, Tambiah 1969, Turner 1974). However, the immediate problem is that most if not all of this work has been done in societies which have some variant or other of the organic analogy, which might be regarded as fundamental to ideas about pollution. How else could an "impure body" or filthy cooking threaten the moral order of the cosmos? But Amerindians reject this assumption. A central issue in this book, then, is to clarify just how they regard "pollution," how they symbolize it to order both human relations with the natural world and with other human beings. Any study of shamanism among Amerindians, I propose, must focus on analyses of the natural symbolism they employ to understand and regulate pollution, rather than the inaccessible psychic experiences of "trance."

The book's theme, then, is how shamanism and food codes relate to canons of human morality. The social ethics of Amerindians have, in fact, puzzled many observers almost as much as shamanism itself. They seem to have very little in the way of sanctions, social or mystical, to punish human wrongdoing. Generations of anthropologists working with reasonably traditional American Indians have been constantly surprised at how very much willful individuals can "get away with." Acts thought criminal by other human groups—murder, incest, sacrilege—are often punishable only through the uncertain mechanisms of self-help, or by remote, unreliable supernatural forces. Theft, a threat to the integrity of the self often considered almost as grave as soul loss, is regarded as just a simple tort, correctable by restitution. Adultery, rape, and unprovoked assault are again matters for the aggrieved parties to punish, although they typically have little obligatory assistance from kinsmen or authorities. Even political rivalry, which may lead to murderous feuds, is weakly controlled, except when it involves the alleged use of "illegitimate" means of attack—poisons, sorcery, or treachery. According to certain ethnographers (Clastres 1974, Lévi-Strauss 1944b), this "looseness" of the legal system seems related to the lack of hierarchic political organization and of legitimate authority (save in the "high civilization" areas of Meso- and Andean America). Even the "social emotions" (sloth, greed, pride, envy, and so on) and petty foibles (gossip, rancor), which so often gnaw away at the smooth flow of collective life, seem often not even to be recognized, let alone condemned. The comment of my name-giver Bernardo strikes me as typical of the Bororo attitude toward such failings. When I grumbled about a malingering troublemaker, Bernardo, himself a model of human rectitude, said, "We must be patient with him—perhaps some day he will learn."

Yet for centuries observers have been impressed by the general orderliness of Amerindian societies. The "noble Red Man" is no romantic stereotype but an ethnographic reality (at least historically), one which I certainly found among the Bororo. Persons treat one another with courtesy and genuine kindness, and village life flows with a harmonious dignity. Certainly there were moments of general anger and recrimination; some individuals were notorious for their immoral or even criminal conduct. But homicide is almost unheard of, theft exceedingly rare, factional disputes mild and short-lived. There is no recorded or remembered instance of Bororo villages warring with one another. Only in one area, marriage, was there recurrent, disruptive conflict, and even then it did not lastingly affect relations with children or relatives.

Such an orderly human world does not occur without excellent sociological reasons. I will argue that these reasons are to be found in the synthesis of the social order founded on what the Bororo term the *aroe* with the elaborate behavioral code regulating human relations with the antithetical cosmological principle, the *bope*. Compliance with the code, it will be seen, leads the Bororo to do things rather less than "noble." They are exactingly fastidious about the minutiae of ceremonies, horrified by some nearly imperceptible fault in cooking, and remarkably prudish about all human organic functions. The value they place on checking body appetites cannot be unrelated to the fact that they have what must be among the world's worst cuisines. Public flatulence is thought so embarrassing that persons of social standing daily consume acid berries thought to control it. Husbands and wives constantly bicker over the most trivial aspects of domestic life. But the *bope,* and their shaman, also provide the ways of understanding and controlling, if not overcoming, these human failings.

## An Outline of Bororo Cosmology

The Bororo call themselves *Orari Mogo-doge,* "Those Who Dwell Near the Surubim." Surubim are gigantic catfish of the family Pimelodideos, species of which are found in all large Brazilian rivers. *Orari* refers to the species *fasciatum,* which is often called in Portuguese "pintado" ("painted") for the vertical black stripes which run irregularly down its iridescent gray sides. These fish are common in the São Lourenço river of

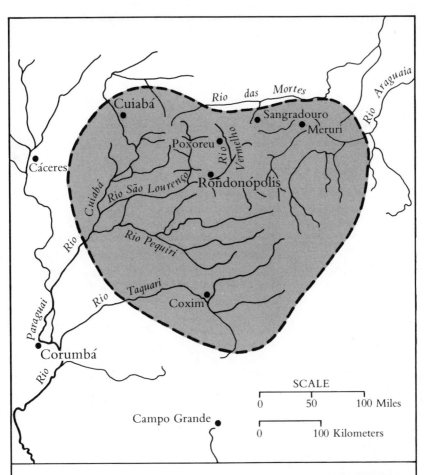

*Area of Greatest
Bororo Expansion
(circa 1850)*

From Albisetti and
Venturelli 1962:0.25−0.26

 Area of Bororo Expansion

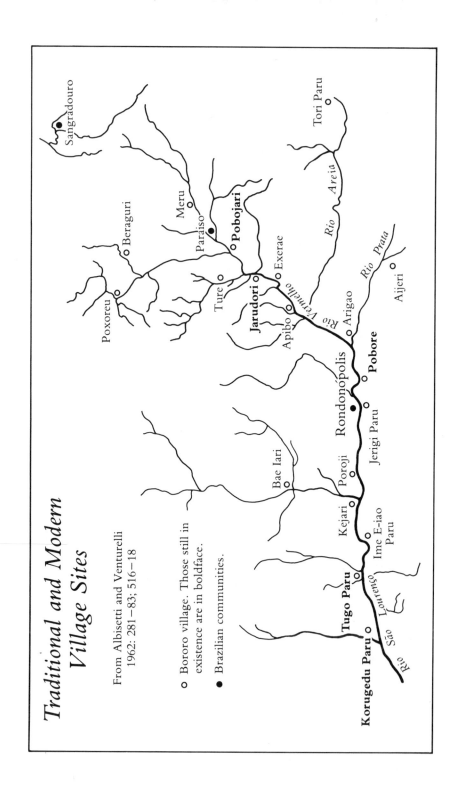

# Traditional and Modern Village Sites

From Albisetti and Venturelli 1962: 281–83; 516–18

○ Bororo village. Those still in existence are in boldface.

● Brazilian communities.

Sangradouro

Tori Paru

Beraguri

Meru

Paraíso

**Pobojari**

Poxoreu

Ture

**Jarudori**

Exerae

Apibo

Arigao

Aijeri

*Rio Areia*

*Rio Prata*

*Rio Vermelho*

Rondonópolis

**Pobore**

Bae Iari

Poroji

Jerigi Paru

Kejari

Ime E-iao Paru

**Tugo Paru**

*Rio São Lourenço*

**Korugedu Paru**

central Mato Grosso and in its larger tributaries; thus, the Bororo define their homeland in terms of this hydrological system.[2] It drains a large section of the southwestern corner of the central Brazilian plateau, between 15 and 18 degrees latitude and 53 and 57 degrees longitude. Traditionally, this large area supported a total Bororo population estimated to have been at least 50,000 gathered into villages of a thousand or more: today it has about 500 Bororo, living in eight villages, five of which are on the banks of the São Lourenço.[3] In some of these communities the Bororo have managed to conserve most of their indigenous institutions and customs.

Aboriginally the Bororo were hunters and gatherers who cultivated maize, which seems to have been a ceremonial food rather than a daily staple. As their name for themselves hints, they were above all fishermen, taking a wide variety of species both from rivers and shallow ponds. Their traditional village sites were always near the confluence of the São Lourenço or other large river with a smaller stream. Their exploitation of different ecological zones was facilitated by the natural diversity of Bororo land. It ranges from the thick jungle edging the São Lourenço to the gallery forests along the smaller rivers and streams, through the brushy savannah typical of the Brazilian highlands, to the rocky cliffs at the edge of the plateau. Consequently this region was immensely rich in a great variety of flora and fauna, as the edge-zone theory in ecology would predict (Allee et al. 1961:476–78). Bororo utilization of it was facilitated by the organized collective nature of their subsistence techniques. Even today in the traditional villages there is a daily division of labor, so that small groups are fishing, hunting, and gathering in a dozen or more different locales. Further, about once a week a collective ritual hunting or fishing expedition integrates the labor of all the community's able-bodied men. In the dry season this foray may be a game drive or poisoning of small lakes with timbo, the woody vine whose sap reduces fish's ability to process oxygen. The Bororo also collectively build elaborate fish weirs, traps, and nets, mostly in the rainy season. Women's subsistence labor is more loosely organized above the domestic group level, but it still features cooperation and reciprocal exchanges between households.

So effective are these techniques in such a favored environment that the Bororo were able to support communities of well over a thousand, and the overall population density, especially in the middle São Lourenço, seems to have been high. But Brazilian expansion into the São Lourenço basin since 1900, and especially after 1950, has severely depleted the fauna. Further, crude mining techniques and intensive swidden agriculture polluted the rivers to such an extent that many traditional fishing methods, which depended on clear water, are no longer practicable. Partly as a result, the Bororo have adopted a number of Brazilian cultigens, especially manioc and beans, but also rice, sugar cane, and oranges. These plants and maize now make up the bulk of Bororo diet, about 60 to 70 percent over the annual cycle. Wild vegetables, fruits, and nuts (tubers, pequi, various coconuts, quince, and so on) supply about 10 to 20 percent of the year's food. But protein in some form, at least in the traditional village where I did most of my fieldwork, appears at least once a day in every household. The Bororo, like other hunting peoples, do not consider a meal to be complete without meat, and they have very definite preferences about just what kind of meat it is. Generally, the flesh of the larger mammals, birds, and fish is the most highly esteemed, but it is just this food which is subject to elaborate rules requiring the intervention of the shaman. Small mammals, reptiles, birds, and fish (probably eaten twice as often as the larger creatures) are thought quite ordinary stuff, suitable perhaps for persons in weakened conditions, or as side dishes. After two or three days of such fare, people begin to complain that they "have not eaten anything at all for a week." In Parts I and II, I consider the Bororo culinary code in detail, relating it to assumptions about the functioning of the human body through time and to the social relationships which food mediates.

Bororo ecology, as nearly all other aspects of their society, is inextricably meshed with the plan of the village, a true indigenous paradigm for social organization. The elaborate details of this plan are familiar to every Bororo over the age of ten, and every traditional community attempts to replicate the plan to the fullest extent that its social demography and topography permit.[4] The village is bisected by an east-west line paralleling the path of the sun and, in most of Bororoland, the course of the São Lourenço. It is assumed that the land slopes gradually from east to west, so that buildings to the east are physically higher than those to the west, although practically such a difference is usually imperceptible. This east-west line marks the division between the moieties of Exerae (to the north) and Tugarege (to the south). Each moiety is composed of four groups which the Bororo literature calls "clans," although they have only some of the attributes of "unilineal descent groups." Each clan is again divided into five to ten named household groups comparable to (but different from) lineages. In some contexts these units are regarded as forming "subclans," contrasted usually by reference to the presumed east-west slope. The easterly subclan is known as the "upper" (Xobugiwuge) and the westerly as the "lower" (Xebegiwuge).[5] The distinction refers only to the assumed topographical contrast and not to any difference in social status (Crocker 1969a).

Recruitment to all these social units is based upon a system of personal names. Each of the household groups is associated with a set of names which refer, in Bororo theory, to "totemic" attributes of the clan,

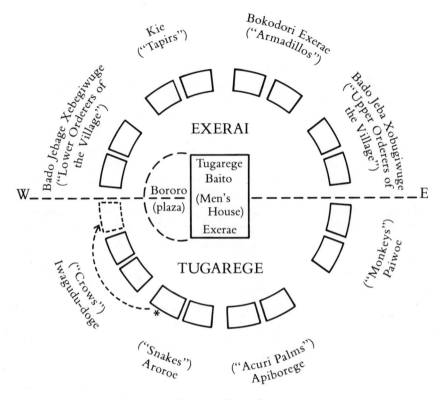

Bororo village plan

and the Bororo term for these groups is, *i-e,* literally, "my name." A child is ceremonially given several names selected from those controlled by its mother's group. The person conferring the name is the *i-edaga* (literally "my name-giver"), normatively the mother's eldest uterine brother. He is assisted by the *i-maruga,* normatively a close agnatic female relative of the father. The child does not socially exist until he or she has received these names, which are usually conferred eight months to a year after birth. All rights of corporate membership in the name-group, sub-clan, clan, moiety, and tribe are conveyed with the name, and only in that way. In adoption, the head of the name-group selects names with the advice and consent of the rest of the clan and formally bestows these on the adopted individual. His closest uterine female relative becomes the adoptee's *mater,* the assisting *i-maruga* provides a set of agnatic relationships, and the individual acquires at once a titled status, corporate membership, and a network of classificatory kinspeople. Adoption, which is increasingly rare, indigenously occurs either within the clan or between neighboring clans of the same moiety. However, most recent field-workers among the Bororo (and their consorts and offspring, if any) have been adopted in this fashion, and all Bororo treat the statuses, memberships, and relationships so formed with utmost seriousness.

For these reasons the Bororo can be considered as functionally but not ideologically matrilineal. They do not regard members of the same "clan" as "blood relatives," nor do they posit descent from a single ancestress as relating the persons of any social unit, including the household groups.[6] Genealogies are not used to differentiate or integrate groups. Instead, organizational emphasis is upon the names and the cosmology to which they refer. On the other hand, blood relationships are recognized in both uterine and agnatic lines. Terminology, normative prescriptions, and behavior all express a distinction between such "true" (*remawu*) relatives and those based on corporate memberships, to the extent that the Bororo can be viewed as organizing their life through two relationship systems (Crocker 1979). The two are integrated in a variety of ways which center around the categorical bonds of prescriptive alliance, actual marriages, ceremonial prestation, and the ties of agnation which proceed from these.

The Bororo state that the Exerae must marry only the Tugarege, and the Tugarege only the Exerae. Conceptually marriage cannot exist between members of the same moiety. Although examples of such incestuous unions are found even in the most traditional villages, notably among the younger, somewhat acculturated Bororo, the majority of adults deplore these roundly. "No one knows how to act toward such people: how can someone be at once a brother and a brother-in-law? a daughter and a niece? It is not possible." The other categorical imperative of marriage is that residence must be uxorilocal, but here there is a certain flexibility. Although nearly every couple eventually builds a house on the wife's name-group's site in the village circle, most have lived with a variety of each spouse's relatives before then. The high rate of divorce, the frequency with which residence is changed from one village to another, and other factors combine to make the Bororo developmental cycle of the domestic group an extremely complex and unpatterned affair. I consider the topic at length in Chapters 2 and 3.

In the center of the village stands the men's house, or *baito*. It should be oriented on a north-south axis, with a doorway on each end opening out to the moieties. A cleared semi-circle to the immediate west constitutes the dance plaza and men's meeting place, the *bororo* proper. In traditional times the men's house was a dormitory for all the community's bachelors and a place of refuge for the married men. Today most adult males spend most of their leisure time inside the *baito* or, in the evening, out in the plaza. The men's house is also the domain of Bororo ceremony. These rites are often forbidden to women and the uninitiated; they tend to be organized around bonds of alliance and the particularistic ties of agnation. As Lévi-Strauss (1967: 138 [1956]) presciently noted in the 1950s, the Bororo village expresses a concentric dualism: the male-dominated sacred center over against a feminine, domestic, profane periphery. Through this center pass all the symbolic and material transactions uniting the social categories differentiated around the village circle. These prestations include all the game and other food secured during the collective expeditions described at the beginning of this section. The concentric dualism thus establishes and mediates an ecological process (Crocker 1977c, 1979, and below, *passim*). Just how requires a brief consideration of Bororo cosmology.

For this society, the village plan maps out the principles which organize the relations of all beings and processes, sentient or inanimate, perceived or imagined. Its divisions do not merely order the flux of human sentiment or structure their institutionalization; they reflect and impose the laws whereby the whole cosmos is regulated. Where other social traditions see the human organism as a microcosm for the universe, the Bororo perceive the village as *the* manifestation of transcendent reality. For them, any category of physical thing has another modality of being, which they identify as *aroe*. This is an essence, or soul, or, sometimes, a name—for the Bororo often assume a nominalist posture. Such a being exists primarily in an underworld otherwise inhabited by the ancestors of the Bororo. In their thought, furthermore, every human being constitutes, by reason of the unique conglomeration of attributes gathered in his or her idiosyncratic name, a sort of single species, a non-replicable thing. At death the essence of this immortal form, also termed *aroe,* goes to dwell in the place consecrated to such modalities of being. All the *aroe* are spatially organized into moieties each with four divisions, oriented by the cardinal points.

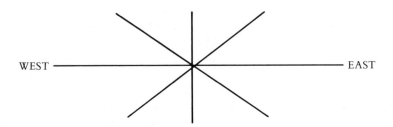

On this basis of symbolic geographics, the localized corporate groups are associated with eight fixed sets of *aroe*.[7] The names of the groups, their internal segments, and finally personal names themselves, refer to attributes of their conjoined *aroe.*

Next, all public Bororo ceremony has for its end the representation, through costumes, dance, and song, of the *aroe.* Each group sponsors the representation of its *aroe,* but it is a fundamental element in Bororo society that its members never themselves represent their *aroe.* Instead they decorate, with elaborate body paintings and ornaments, members of clans in the other moiety, thus enabling them to represent or, in the native view, to become the transcendental essences of animals, fish, birds, plants, rocks, the heavenly bodies—"All," said one man, "that there is." The identity of the performers is as firmly set by tradition as that of the sponsors, so that for every *aroe* representation (and I collected descriptions of over a hundred) there is an owning group and a performing group (or subunits thereof). This honor of becoming an *aroe* is considered the greatest prestation one human group can bestow upon another. As a result, the Bororo say, the male members of the sponsoring group may marry into the performing group "without shame." Each group has about a dozen such prestational bonds with subunits of groups in the other moiety. These ties of ceremonial performance, preferential marriage, and all the derived exchanges are called "roads," *utawara,* by the Bororo, who draw spiderweb-like diagrams showing how these categorical prescriptions result in paths being worn between the prestating units (cf. Albisetti and Venturelli 1962:450, for an example of such a diagram).[8] Often the gifts of *aroe* representation are reciprocal, with the performers of one later enabling its sponsors to portray *their aroe* in another ceremony. But the Bororo think particularistically of each transaction in itself asymmetrically, and consider the system to achieve symmetry only at the inclusive level of the moieties.

I must stress that the relationship between the group and its spatially joined *aroe* can be considered "totemic" only in the analogic sense established by Lévi-Strauss (1963b). There is no predicated descent from the *aroe,* no mystical connection involving rites of increase or sense of guardianship, no "sacrificial" meal of a species named by the *aroe.* There is no prescribed behavior for group members toward their *aroe* species, save in one derived respect. They have the right to wear ornaments made from the skin, plumage, teeth, nails, and beaks of these creatures, or woven designs reproducing their markings and forms. These decorations are just those which, when used as a total ensemble with body paintings, represent the *aroe* essence of the species. But as a person bears personal names reflecting only a few attributes of his corporation's *aroe,* so too he wears only partial refractions of their being.

The "clan" is exceedingly jealous of its rights over these ornaments and traditionally would punish severely illegal use of them. But such is no simple matter to determine, for the inventory of Bororo ceremonial property is enormous. There are dozens of different kinds of labretes, bracelets, necklaces, woven belts, headdresses, earrings, gourd rattles and whistles, and somatic designs, each varying only slightly in form and colors from others in its type. Additionally, certain utilitarian items (baskets, clubs, penis sheaths, mats, pottery, bows and arrows) are decorated and used in ceremonial prestations. Rights over each one of these items are associated with a particular group of households (or "name-group"). The *Enciclopedia Bororo* takes roughly two hundred pages to describe this system, yet it is known to most adult Bororo men. When a strange Bororo arrives in the village, they can soon tell his name-group, subclan, clan, and moiety just from the particular labrete he wears. These ornaments, then, define personal and social identity almost as closely as does the idiosyncratic set of personal names, and all this differentiation is generated by the *aroe* (Crocker 1977b, 1977c). At the same time these symbolic materials are the currency for social transactions which reflect and institute enduring relationships between the constituent units of Bororo society. With a natural abundance and no technical divisions of labor, the Bororo have created an organic solidarity which is no less real for being symbolic. Not that the system lacks material referents, for the game collectively obtained and much of the vegetable food privately produced follow the prestational roads of the *utawara*. As the Bororo say, "Where the *aroe* representations go, there also goes the food to nourish the children there."

The *aroe* provide the Bororo with what Douglas (1973:84) terms "high grid–high group," an elaborate, shared classificatory system and an intensively differentiated social structure in which ego is "controlled by other people's pressure."

> In such a system, the purity code has set up a strong distinction between the private and the public, and its wider implications are irresistible. Here the eruption of the organic into the social domain is most dangerous, to be purified with ritual. The individual in transition from one social status to another is like matter out of place, impure, and to be ritually re-integrated. Rituals have the function of celebrating the transcendence of the whole over the part. (Douglas 1973:174)

Douglas goes on to characterize such a system as dominated by moral regulators modeled after human figures—ancestors or culture heroes—and positively valuing wealth and social pomp, exulting in self-control. All of this describes the Bororo rather well, if certain redefinitions are made. First, the usual focus of "purity" and "pollution" on the human body and its processes does not occur among the Bororo, as might be expected in a society which does not employ genealogies as a model for individual and group relations (the "organic analogy"). Instead, the "eruption of the organic into the social domain" is represented by a cosmological principle antithetical to that order expressed through the *aroe*. Second, these last figures of transcendent nominalism do include ancestors and culture heroes but also embrace all distinguishable things, natural and unreal; they are the very spirits of classification. Further, their function as "moral regulators" is complemented if not preempted by that other cosmological principle. Contemporary Bororo shamanism deals only with the forces of this last principle, mainly through an elaborate code of rules prescribing human conduct toward wild game. How these shamanistic practices express and sanction the principles of Bororo social morality is one subject of this book.

The Bororo term for the non-*aroe* elements in the universe is *bope*. The *bope*, like the *aroe*, are manifest in natural phenomena, particularly in rain, the daily cycle of light and dark, thunder and lightning, heat and cold. The Bororo say that the *bope* cause all things to reproduce[9] and to die. They are therefore the principle of all organic transformation, of fructification, growth, death and decay, the spirits of metamorphoses. Hence they oppose and complement the *aroe,* the representatives of immutable categorical form. As with the *aroe,* there are classes of *bope* associated with particular natural things and processes. The titular chief of all the *bope*, Meri, manifests one dimension of himself in the sun, while his younger brother, Ari, shows forth as the moon. One type of *bope* brings rain, another lightning. But many sorts of *bope*, including the lowest variety known as *maereboe*, are not so tangibly personified. They invisibly inhabit the lower heavens and this earth, and they attend all human behavior with great interest. In this they contrast with the *aroe*, who dwell in the remote underworld and rarely venture from it and who ignore most human activity. But the Bororo are daily made aware of the *bope's* presence about them, through the workings of the physical universe, unusual natural events ("omens"), and other less tangible ways.

As the principle of the *aroe* manifests itself in each human being's immortal names, his or her transcendent soul, so too the *bope* show forth in the human body, and in the organic being of all living creatures. Their manifestation is in the *raka,* the "blood," that *élan vital* which animates every being and enables it to accomplish those actions appropriate to its kind. By virtue of *raka* men hunt and women gather, birds fly and jaguars kill their prey. But above all through *raka* organic life is able to reproduce itself. The gradual expenditure of *raka* through all these activities brings about aging, the diminishment of powers to sustain and create being. The end of *raka* is death and, for humankind at least, the liberation of the transcendent *aroe* from the decaying body. But death, say the Bororo, never just comes: the *bope* actively bring it about. And so too they cause all unnatural perturbations in organic processes, all illnesses, and many injuries. Indeed, the omnipotent *bope* would long ago have destroyed all human existence, were it not for two things: a class of persons who are able in some measure to defend human society against them, the shamans, and a food code that prescribes orderly relationships between men and *bope*.

This code has the nature of a contract or covenant in which, if human society carries out its obligations to the *bope,* they in turn will ensure fertility, natural plenty, and long untroubled life. These obligations center on behaving in certain ways toward a large set of animals and plants, and especially on conveying to the *bope* their rightful share of these foods, through the intermediary of the shaman. But if persons fail to honor these prescriptions, the *bope* punish them by all manner of afflictions and, ultimately, kill them. Contemporary Bororo interpret nearly every injury, illness, or misfortune befalling individuals, and all human deaths, as due to infractions of this food code. Human malign volition as a cause of affliction does exist in Bororo theory; they recognize the possibility of witchcraft and sorcery. And traditionally, the *aroe* were sometimes identified as causing a particular illness, in retribution for offenses against them through improper conduct of the ceremonial representations. But among modern Bororo these agencies of human suffering are only rarely adduced as hypothetically responsible for a particular misfortune, and each one, whether it terminates in a return to health or in death, is ultimately found to be caused by the *bope*.

Human offenses against the *bope,* as revealed by the shaman, have all that quality of picayune neglects and unwilled accidents found in so many food codes used to explain individual affliction. Also, perfectly innocent persons, children or a spouse, can be struck down for something a parent or husband or wife has done. This is understood as due to the way that sexual partners and their immature offspring share, in a sense, a single organic being, one *raka*. I say "in a sense" because the Bororo stress that every animate being has a unique life-force. But they also acknowledge that in its very manifestations of willed action, this force merges with others through the organic processes of eating, eliminating, and copulating. This intermingling of *raka* is simultaneously potent and dangerous; unless disciplined by human will, it can lead to the suffering and death of one or all participants in the merged *raka*. The idea of *raka* and the intense human relationships it expresses are the Bororo version of pollution. Since *raka* is at once very similar to but yet quite different from our Western traditional understanding of pollution, the first chapter is devoted to this fundamental Bororo concept.

# PART I

⁊⋙⋘⋔⋙⋘

# The Conceptual and Social Contexts of Affliction

We are borne ruinous: poore mothers crie,
That children come not right, nor orderly,
Except they headlong come, and fall upon
An ominous precipitation.
How witty's ruine? how importunate
Upon mankinde? It labour'd to frustrate
Even God's purpose; and made women, sent
For mans reliefe, cause of his languishment.
They were to good ends, and they are so still,
But accessory, and principall in ill.
For that first marriage was our funerall:
One woman at one blow, then kill'd us all,
And singly, one by one, they kill us now.
We doe delightfully our selves allow
To that consumption; and profusely blinde,
We kill our selves to propagate our kinde.
And yet we do not that; we are not men. . . .

John Donne, "An Anatomy of the World"

macaw

# 1

⟨〰⟩

# Vital Humors

The Bororo term for the source of
life and well-being is *raka,* associated generally with all natural vigor and
fructification. *Raka* is the animating force which endows living things
with the capacity to continue their existences. It empowers the rains to
fall, jaguars to kill, men and women to work, sing, and procreate. It is
animate, yet insentient. While intimately tied with the *bope,* it is neither
their agent nor their exclusive possession. For *raka* drives the soul, *aroe,*
whose connection with the material body swells and diminishes with the
growth and loss of *raka.* In warm-blooded creatures[1], *raka* is considered a
property of the entire organism, existing in concentrated form at the
joints and in organic fluids. These vehicles of *raka,* most especially blood
and its derivatives, semen and mother's milk, are considered unclean,
polluting substances to all beings save their owner. Thus, the Bororo try
to avoid contact with animal blood and excreta, especially those produced by creatures considered unusually potent in *raka.* The immediate
paradox of these ideas is that persons who dwell together, particularly
husband and wife, must nourish and participate in one another's *raka.*
They necessarily enter, therefore, into endangering contact with one another's and with other beings' *raka.*

Nearly all Bororo health practices, whether prescribing or prohibit-
ing, are intended to conserve individual *raka* and protect it against threats

41

to its vigor and integration with the *aroe*. Meat, for example, is thoroughly boiled to the point of tastelessness to ensure that the slightest trace of blood is removed. *Raka* can be diminished in a host of ways so numerous that the Bororo catalog them in terms of their effects rather than their causes. That is, sickness, the infirmities of age, and death itself are attributed *ipso facto* to the temporary or permanent loss of *raka*. To be *rakakare*, "without blood," is to be simultaneously old, dangerously ill, and liable to progressive deterioration. Those in such a condition fail in the hunt; they cannot form new life; nor can they carry out those duties which ensure the continued health of others. But Bororo ideas about the attributes and functions of *raka* itself are not very precise. It is not so much a set of widely known dogmas as the final logical step in a series of empirical inferences. At the most, one might say that the Bororo regard *raka* as an almost hydraulic mechanism, explaining the vicissitudes of physical being, and as an abstract cosmological principle whose power is manifested in the transformations of the visible physical universe. They do have definite ideas about the characteristics of *raka* in human beings, however, which correlate with certain aspects of the social system and domestic group.

Men and women share qualitatively the same *raka,* save for its different transformation in each sex into semen or menstrual blood and milk. Yet quantitatively, through time, the sexes generally and individuals of each sex tend to contrast in the absolute amounts they severally possess. Each person is born with a certain finite capacity for the development of *raka,* determined generally by the relative and absolute amounts possessed by the parents during conception and the early months of life. One of the few unquestioned elements in the Bororo *raka* dogma is that every individual must expend his or her limited stock of *raka* after adolescence: in copulation, in physical labor, in dancing and singing. Although this degenerative process may be slowed by conscientious adherence to sundry ritual interdictions and practices designed to allay the mechanical results of physical appetite, it can never be completely checked. Generally, the older a person is, the less *raka* he or she has. The Bororo also maintain as dogma that the parents' *raka* determine the physical, moral, and spiritual characteristics of their children. Gossip points out the pastiche of such elements in individuals, attributing moral laxity to a maternal grandfather, a prominent nose to a paternal uncle, a certain ability in the retention of myths to an older aunt.

The most immediate application of these notions has to do with their synthesis: the more aged, or the less *rakare,* any parent, the more diminished their determination of any offspring's total characteristics. The firstborn of a young couple must be a vigorous creature who reflects its parents' attributes almost perfectly. But to be the last-born of an aged

couple is to enter life impoverished of its most essential element. Moreover, matters are seldom so symmetric: Bororo males tend to be older
than their consorts, sometimes by as much as twenty or thirty years.
Although the opposite is sometimes true, the Bororo can usually empirically confirm their doctrine that children are more "like" their mothers than their fathers. Although some authorities on the Bororo urge this
habit as a "proof" for the matrilineality (Albisetti and Venturelli 1962:
434–35), the indigenous logic has nothing to do with notions about descent and its attendant rights. One proof of this involves a logical corollary of Bororo dogmas regarding human conception: that more than one
male may contribute his *raka* to an infant's development and that young
men are prone to use up this substance with a certain abandon. An aged
pater, and putative genitor, is quite apt to discover this corollary cast up
to him in his neighbors' sniggering remarks regarding the obvious physical resemblances between his infant's body and that of various young
men. In sum, then, their ideas about *raka* provide the Bororo with almost
limitless possibilities of verifying their cosmological doctrines and of relating the nuances of unique individual identity to a set of existing social
perceptions of historical personalities.

The degree to which a child attains to the absolute amount of pre-
determined *raka* depends both on its consumption of *rakare* substances,
initially mother's milk and subsequently certain meats and vegetables,
and on its parents' care in obeying various ritual prescriptions involving
the care of the *raka* now shared between the three of them.[2] After adolescence and during adulthood, men and women are usually approximately
equal in terms of their relative *raka,* depending always on each individual's legacy of this fluid from its multiple parents. Yet it seems that
men tend to "spend" more of this substance than do women. They age
more rapidly and are more vulnerable to affliction. The Bororo are vague
as to why this should be so. Men generally are more endangered during
their lifetimes than are women. A male infant is perceived as a more
constitutionally fragile creature than his sister, even if she should be
formed much after him and thus, in theory, have much less *raka* in her
constitution. The Bororo say that men must confront the dyadic threats
of the jungle and of the ceremonial *aroe,* which are dangerous to physical
and psychic well-being. Some informants seemed to feel that men lost
more *raka* during coitus than did women. Others stressed a certain willingness in males to defy the traditional prescriptions for the preservation
of *raka,* especially those dictating restraint in all forms of sexual activity.
Often all these vague notions were summarized in the dictum, heard
from men and women alike, that males tended to be "hotter" than
females, and by implication more prone to waste that substance which
endows animate being with "heat," with passion and fleshly appetites.

Such an observation concords with certain social differences between the sexes' life cycles and with attendant contrasts in the genitor's and genitrix's participations in their child's *raka*.

## *Raka* and Gender:
## Sexual Differences in Pregnancy

The Bororo believe that a new existence, an *aroe,* can only be formed from the commingling of the *rakare* substances from each sex in the womb of the mother. Theoretically, each copulation after the birth of one child contributes some portion of *raka* to the developing fetus. If the mother's and her lovers' *raka* is strong, she quickly begins to show the signs of pregnancy. If she, and especially her partners, tend to be *raka-kare,* with "little blood," it might require half a dozen years or more to accumulate the amount of *raka* needed to engender new life. These notions mesh neatly with the indigenous observation that young parents, or promiscuous young wives with older husbands, tend to have children closely together, while older Bororo find their offspring spaced more widely. The occasional empirical contradictions to this pattern are easily explained by postulating an unusually large stock of *raka* to the fertile person. Besides, the Bororo are not as physiologically mechanistic as the crude outline of their theory of reproduction might imply. They stress that, regardless of the quantity and quality of the *rakare*-laden sexual fluids, the *bope* still must intervene to animate these substances with life. Just how or why the *bope* accomplish this, the Bororo regard as a mystery; but the close association between the genesis of physical life, the *bope,* and *raka* is a critical element in the general symbolic structure.

Semen is directly equated with menstrual blood, and both are derivatives of blood itself. Semen is termed literally "white blood," while the testicles of all mammals are recognized as the organ responsible for the transformation of one fluid into the other. I thought at first this meant that while the male may require years of copulation to furnish the amount of *raka* necessary to engender new life, the female only begins to contribute her *raka* with the cessation of her menses, during the months of recognized pregnancy. But this was a novel deduction for the Bororo to whom I advanced it, and they tended to deny its value as an explanation for the differences in the sexes' amounts of *raka*. Instead, they reemphasized the usual age discrepancy between father and mother. A young man could engender a child (with *bope* assistance) with only a few months of copulation, they said, and, besides, the feminine secretions during intercourse might well be derivatives of blood and embued with *raka*. And finally, men were simply more sexually active than women. Just regard the *i-pare* (bachelors). . . .

Traditionally, Bororo males delayed marriage until their late twenties. Since male initiation occurs shortly after puberty and since adultery is a serious, although allegedly common, offense, the society might appear to have constrained its bachelors to a *raka*-sustaining, if frustrating, celibacy. But a unique yet typically Bororo institution intervened, that of the *aredu baito,* or men's house associate (Crocker 1969b). Although no longer practiced, for demographic reasons and Brazilian negative attitudes, most mature informants had participated enthusiastically in this custom during their youth. Women informants were especially nostalgic about its disappearance.

After initiation, which formally endows males with sexual rights over women of the other moiety, young men were required to live in the men's house (*bai mana gejewu,* or *baito*). They, the *i-pare,* formed a kind of age class, collectively disposable for activities needed by the community and comparable to similar groups among the Akwẽ-Shavante (Maybury-Lewis 1967: 105–14). But, uniquely, the Bororo *i-pare* had the right to choose several young unmarried girls to be their companions in the men's house. Rules of moiety exogamy were scrupulously obeyed, with the *i-pare* of one moiety having only girls from the other as their consorts. There had to be an absolute parity in the number of girls given over by each moiety to the *i-pare.* Each girl was shared in common by all the *i-pare* of the moiety opposite her own. She was compensated for her services by gifts of ornaments and of food. The custom might well be regarded as an authentic case of group marriage, save for one thing: as soon as a men's house associate became pregnant, she had to resign her status and return to her maternal home. But she had the right to choose any one of the *i-pare* she desired to be her husband and the child's pater, and the young man had to accept this marriage, albeit with great reluctance. When asked for an explanation for this unwillingness to be wed, the Bororo said, "No man wants to be called father." But Bororo men seem to find their children very rewarding, and fatherhood is essential both to Bororo criteria of a "good" life and to the assumptions of the social system, which dictate the social and cosmological necessity of offspring.

The answer to this paradox involves again the consequences of Bororo ideas about *raka.* In this society, to be a father is to be old, marked by the physical signs of senescence and of decay. Any parent must irrevocably lose a substantial amount of his or her *raka* in engendering a new life. Consequently, he or she manifests physical signs of such loss: white hair, wrinkled skin, a diminishment of perceptual faculties, a failing of physical élan. In recompense there is the child, who replicates its genitors' material and spiritual characteristics and who in turn will transmit these to a new generation, losing its *raka* in the process. In this way the force of *raka* itself is never diminished but runs through time in an unbroken stream of pure fructifying energy. Its very possession, however, is lethal in the end to its individual possessors, causing them by its very power to spend and transmit it, and to grow old and die. The Bororo have good reason to treat the physical agencies of *raka* as the most potent and dangerous substances in the universe. The ironic and ambiguous complexity of this metaphor is thus an exceptionally powerful generative paradigm for Bororo assumptions and practices regarding the maintenance of natural order and well-being.

Sociologically, the *aredu baito* institution is the key to the different quantitative functioning of this force in men and women. The former, as *i-pare,* use up their *raka* in nonfertile couplings with their companions, who represent but a small proportion of the village's unmarried girls, while all men must pass through the *i-pare* stage. Traditionally, women married shortly after puberty, with men who were often twice or more their age. Their husbands, with already depleted stocks of *raka,* were the more inclined to restrain their sexual activities. Even among contemporary Bororo, who usually lack *aredu baito* and whose males tend to marry a few years after initiation, the average interval between siblings is 6.3 years.[3] Another element in this pattern involves the proscription on coitus for the parents of a newborn, which theoretically is absolutely binding for three or four years after birth.

But informants indicated that fathers often recommended moderate sexual activities when their child was around two years old, while the mothers tended to obey the prohibition much longer. The consequence of all these practices is that for traditional Bororo, fatherhood was empirically associated with middle age, whereas motherhood began with early adolescence. The traditional perception that men "age" more rapidly than women, that they lose their *raka* sooner and more completely, derives from the fashion in which the birth of successive children tend to be the crucial markers of sexually differentiated stages in the mature life cycle. A man with four or five children is inevitably over fifty, sociologically and physically ancient, but his wife, his categorical peer, is just entering early middle age. Bororo males have ample reason to dread being addressed as "father." But they realize the very *raka* which animates their youthful vitality and checks the course of time must, by its own nature, flow from them and congeal into a son or daughter. Further, only fathers can enter the prestige system of Bororo politics and ceremonial. In a matrilineal culture, men prove their ultimate worth only as self-abrogating producers of "others."

Bororo women regard birthing children in a less institutionalized way. Their attitudes express the idiosyncrasies of personal character and particular conjugal situations. Some women are noted for their love of large families, while others seem cheerfully resigned to sterility, a condition almost literally unthinkable for a man. At most, there is a general assumption that the bearing of children is as natural a part of women's identity as the killing of animals is that of a man's. To be sure, older informants, both male and female, sometimes castigated young women in their late teens or early twenties for failing to have offspring, implying that such production is a feminine moral obligation. A male transvestite of the middle São Lourenço, who had permanently adopted female dress and behavior, was regarded as comically anomalous just because "he/she" had adopted a role which precluded all possibility of parenthood. But all of these institutionalized attitudes, as well as the individual sentiments of fertile women, have been strongly influenced by the very high infant mortality of the past few decades. Women who have one or two living children out of eight or ten born are almost the norm among mature Bororo. Persons of all ages who have survived all their progeny are not rare. In these circumstances it is not surprising that many women declare their wish not to have any more children, most often justifying this with the phrase, "I do not want to see the child die."

Traditionally vegetable contraceptive techniques and self-induced abortion were known but vaguely disapproved by the Bororo. The latter is still considered, at least by senior men, to be cause for divorce, and the former must be consented to by the husband and senior matrilateral relatives. However, there seemed to be a general consensus that a woman had the final right to decide either action (Albisetti and Venturelli 1962: 762). Most informants claimed both techniques were widely utilized by women other than those of their immediate family. Only one female informant admitted that she herself had once induced abortion, and then under extenuating circumstances, having broken with the fetus's putative genitor, but she claimed that nearly all other fertile women in the village routinely practiced both methods. Elder women and men, those heading households and subclans, privately agreed to this, but publicly urged the tumbling population decline as a paramount reason for unchecked fecundity.

At one village, Pobojari on the Rio Vermelho (cf. Appendix C), these contradictions between private sentiment and social opinion have been resolved in the favor of private sentiment. There the residents told me in the spring of 1964 that they had collectively decided to have no more children. Brazilian settlers had occupied all the lands surrounding the community, oppressing it ecologically and politically. No more game or fish were to be found in the vicinity, and whenever they attempted to hold one of the public rituals so vital to Bororo life, jeering Brazilians would appear to mock and to disrupt their activities. The omnipresence of cachaca (sugar-cane rum) in the village, and its impact upon traditional norms, seemed also a critical factor in the village's assessment of its ability to maintain itself (Z. Levak, personal communication). For these reasons, the inhabitants told me, "Because our children will soon be no longer able to be Bororo, but must become Brazilian, we have decided to have no more children." In my hasty census of the village, I could find no child under the age of five. When I and the Bororo with whom I was traveling returned to the middle São Lourenço, this decision became a public issue, and I heard it used by two or three young women in at least semi-public contexts as a justification for avoiding pregnancy.

While recognizing the legitimacy of such a self-genocidal decision, most Bororo of the middle São Lourenço formally denied its relevance for their lives, collective or private. In such a muddle of conflicting opinions beset by irreversible historical processes, I received the impression that the great majority of fertile women, however they might have sought to avoid pregnancy, did not seek to terminate it once they had become aware of its existence. I have no empirical way to demonstrate this intuition, no explanation other than the traditional attitudes concerning childbirth to explain its existence. The central point is the problematic quality of pregnancy for women, and the existence of traditional modes of denying its progress, which contemporary forces may have exacerbated but certainly did not produce. For males, the issue simply does not arise on an individual level, although it may very well take precedence over traditional understandings on the level of group decision. All these elements cannot be analyzed until the entirety of Bororo experiences and interpretations of the life cycle have been surveyed; hence, the subject will be addressed again in the concluding chapter.

The sociological and cosmological dangers of parenthood are symbolized in the mass of interdictions and prescriptions binding on parents during pregnancy, birth, and early childhood. Analysis of these provides additional understanding of Bororo assumptions about *raka* and how these relate to the actual dynamics of conjugal roles. That is, the threats of childbirth provide us with an index to indigenous perceptions of how those who must participate in each others' *raka,* the nuclear family, guard against these challenges to the integrity of self. A woman recognizes her pregnancy both by the cessation of menstruation for at least two months and by the onset of such physical signs as morning sickness, tenderness in the breasts, and so forth. She must immediately advise her husband and all others who have had sexual contact with her, so that they may begin following those rules of conduct and diet which ensure their own health and that of the fetus.

The most cited and apparently most consistently followed regulation demands the absolute celibacy of all those who have participated in the infant's formation. This prohibition extends from the onset of recognized pregnancy to at least after the child has received a social personality, through the name-giving ceremony at between six months and a year after birth. The extent to which this rule is obeyed and prolonged after the minimal interval depends on how much a man believes himself to be the child's genitor. During pregnancy disobedience to this rule threatens the fetus and not the adult parent. The Bororo say that the "smell" (*jerimaga*) of semen and feminine sexual fluids infects the fetus, causing it to be born weak and with a much reduced potential *raka*. They also say that repeated coition after pregnancy is liable to form twins, which are regarded as such thorough anomalies that the Bororo cannot cite any living examples. (That is, one of the twins is put to death secretly just after birth and the surviving child is presented as completely normal.)[4] This interdiction applies to all forms of sexual activity, including those a potential father might have with women other than his pregnant wife. The rule is not thus purely mechanistic: it does not assume some kind of physical antipathy between the fetus and those fluids which originally brought about its existence. It is rather that from the onset of pregnancy the parents' *raka* continues to sustain mystically the growth of the infant in the womb, so much so that its expenditure elsewhere diminishes the unborn's frail stock. The association between twins and copulation after pregnancy is consistent with this interpretation. Informants pointed out that "those born together" tend to be mutually small and weak, eminently *rakakare;* they have "stolen" one another's *élan vital*.

More abstractly, this rule instructs parents that, if they have created a new being through the free vent of their passions, they now must exercise self-control if this creation is to become socially real, which is to say subject to the abstract and self-denying rules of social order. To persist in copulation would result in an "over-determination" of the parents' relationship not only to the fetus but to one another as well, for just the same prohibition applies after childbirth. Having begun a new life, the parents must now channel their *raka* into ensuring its material well-being, the husband indirectly by his attentive hunting and fishing, and the mother directly through her gardening and collecting. Thus, children's participation in their parents' physical beings is far more than a simple sharing of the organic stuff of their bodies; it involves the nourishment and security produced by these beings' *raka*-sustained actions. This last element, which becomes the dominant theme in the relationship after the child's birth, lies behind the Bororo equation of fosterage with parentage, as well as their view of the residential group as an organic entity.

The other restrictions of pregnancy involve two types: those governing behavior and those concerning diet. The latter are more emphasized, even if tending to lack the universality and specificity of proper collective representations which characterize the basic rule, the injunction against copulation during pregnancy. Behavior restrictions are neither lengthy nor complex. Future mothers must not jump from heights or engage in other violent movements, such as those involved in gathering and cutting firewood. Such actions risk jarring the developing embryo from its maternal host. A pregnant woman should also avoid sleeping on her back, else the sexual fluids might divide and form twins. (All post-adolescent women sleep on their sides in any case, so as to hinder the *bope*'s sexual access to them during the night. Since all *bope* are considered completely licentious and lustful creatures, ungoverned by any moral principles, there is a certain consistency in this account of the origin of twins and their accreditation to the father's inability to control his desire. Some informants did not distinguish between the *bope* and a man whose sexual responses are ultimately due to his *bope*-derived *raka*.) But the father may go about his normal activities, even redoubling his efforts in the hunt to ensure that his wife's vagrant cravings for various dishes may be satisfied—desires that the Bororo, as well as nineteenth-century Victorians, consider a normal element of pregnancy. He is, though, forbidden to make fires outside the village to cook a meal during the hunt. If he does this, red and black stains (or "birthmarks") will pass from the fire to his unborn child. In other terms, the potential father is prohibited from exercising his self-sufficiency, his ability to survive outside the conjugal context.

The regulations about diet, although far from being held in universal consensus, are nonetheless regarded as much the more important insurances for a normal pregnancy. Unlike the preceding rules governing conduct, nearly all of them are indifferently binding on mother and father alike. In descending order of their frequency and stress among informants, there are four major prohibitions. The first is a prohibition against eating the young of any species, especially those of large mammals. Such creatures, informants said, were likely not to be parents themselves; therefore, they caused the infant they nourished to be maladroit during the process of birth.[5] Furthermore, these animals tended to be surcharged with *raka*, as are the young of any species, including man. While expectant mothers needed to have reasonable infusions of such energy, this could be easily overdone. As with coitus after pregnancy, too much *raka* tends to threaten the baby's own unique development of this vital fluid, in a sort of short-circuit effect. Second, neither parent should consume a beast lacking a limb or in any other way incomplete in its organic form, nor should they eat a fruit or vegetable some of which had already been eaten by an animal or bird. Their offspring would otherwise be born with the corresponding organic lack or wound. Third, neither father nor mother should consume the marrow of an animal or partake of any being considered as especially bony, such as piranha. These objects physically bar the infant from an easy exit from the mother's body. Fourth, both parents must avoid consuming a variety of ground-nesting birds, especially the *kuo* (jawo, *Tinamideus crypturus noctivague*), the *nabul* (inarmbu, *Tinamideus crypturus* sp.), and various kinds of wild turkeys (Cracidos). If eaten, the souls of the dead birds peck at the child in the womb, which causes it, especially after birth, to be extremely fretful and complaining. This condition is the only one of the prenatal proscriptions whose disobedience can be alleviated by shamanistic intervention. Correlatively, it is one of the least known and most often ignored.

The simplest explanation of these regulations would be to regard them as unsystematic metonyms, rather crude examples of what was once called homeopathic magic. The obvious (apparently) characteristic of the interdicted item either reproduces itself in the child itself or hinders the process of birth and postnatal development. The general vagueness and lack of consensus surrounding these rules, several of which are not usually known by younger Bororo, would seem to enhance their status as *ad hoc* perceptions, to be followed in the degree that an individual finds their particular associational logic compelling. And yet, these rules cannot be so lightly dismissed. Some are common to societies both close to and distant from the Bororo; others are unique to this society, while many common among lowland Indian groups are not recognized by the Bororo.[6] Further, some of these prohibitions apply only during pregnancy, while others recur in all situations when persons are menaced by the bonds of mutually shared *raka*. That is, a pattern must be assumed operative here, consistent with Bororo practices regarding *raka* in other situations and consonant with their assumptions about the nature of this force.

This pattern might be abstractly described as the assumption that expectant parents must seek a kind of homeostasis in which the relation of form to animating force is neither over- nor under-determined. Just as the young of a species have a surfeit of *raka,* those of its members who bear an organic defect have failed to accomplish an integration of two essential conditions of being: a categorizable physical state and a controlled life drive. An excess to one side or the other risks the integration of these two principles in the developing fetus. The last two proscriptions are consistent with this interpretation, although they also involve more complex Bororo assumptions about the proper nature of animate form. In the third prohibition (against consumption of "bony" creatures by the parents), Bororo ideas about the proper relation of "hard" to "soft" elements in physical constitutions are operative. Creatures such as the piranha are considered to be unreasonably bony, and to nourish oneself on bone marrow rather than cooked flesh likewise tilts the dietary balance to one side. As for the fourth proscription, which forbids the consumption of ground-dwelling birds, it involves more than an appreciation that such creatures are anomalous in terms of general avian attributes. The various calls of these birds seem to the Bororo to be replicas of human language, but in a distorted way. All are omens of the *bope,* which is why shamans are able to treat the affliction. Although the Bororo recognize a large variety of avian omens, most birds are regarded as unfit for consumption, except for the ground-dwellers which, on the contrary, are pursued and eaten with great enthusiasm. The symbolic character of these birds, as well as the other omen species, reflects nuances of their association with both the *bope* and the *aroe,* a topic discussed in Part II. More generally, Lévi-Strauss discovered that the genus *Tinamideus* and its North American counterpart play crucial medial roles in the mythic system of both continents. These roles hinge on the species' status as beings that are eminently vulnerable yet mockingly elusive, and, hence, in Bororo terms, most ambiguous in their *raka* (Lévi-Strauss 1971:481–86). They possess either far too much or much too little to be safe elements in an infant's diet.

The further operations of *raka* in the generation and development of a human being are revealed in Bororo practices during and after childbirth. Since these continue the logic of their prepartum customs, it is necessary to explore these customs in their symbolic and sociological detail before a final analysis is attempted.

## *Raka* and *Aroe:*
## The Production of "Souls"

All the regulations during pregnancy protect the infant. Neither of the parents is the least threatened by the developing fetus and may lead perfectly normal existences. But all this changes dramatically with birth: the mother, father, and baby now mutually endanger one another, and the strictest precautions must be taken to avoid permanent damage to the triad's health and even premature death. This section attempts to explore these precautions in order to illuminate further the idea of *raka.* In doing so, I must confront the general problem of the couvade, those practices which insist that during and after birth the father's actions materially affect the well-being of the infant.

Generally these postpartum rules are observed with decreasing rigor until the child is about three or four years old, or until, as the Bororo say, "he is able to shoot his toy bow." The most critical periods are the birth process itself and the time from birth to the naming ceremony, which occurs at six to eight months. If an infant dies before this, the corpse is interred privately by the parents and consanguines, in the same way as for dead household pets rather than with the extremely complex Bororo funeral. Since this rite accomplishes the transition of the deceased's soul and its integration with the souls of the ancestors, as well as a certain rebirth of that same soul in the social system, it seems that unnamed infants are assumed to lack a soul. And underlying the various precautions of the first six months of life seems to be the notion that during this period the integration of infant's *raka* with its soul (*aroe*) and physical envelope is extremely frail. Simultaneously, the very formlessness and fluidity of this *raka* can pollute its creators, the parents, in the same way that all body products once issued from the body constitute a contamination for their producer and all those who physically participate in his or her organic processes. In this sense, babies are shit (the metaphor is not randomly chosen, as shall become apparent).

As soon as a woman feels labor pains, she immediately informs a certain relative, who seeks out the husband so that he can at once go to the men's house. She and the prospective mother then repair to the nearest jungle shelter. This relative should normatively be the husband's father's mother or, in her absence, the husband's father's sister. Since the Bororo emphasize the intimacy of ties between children and their father's clan and since they hold that these ought to be reaffirmed by marriage with a woman of that clan, it often occurs that this relative is a member of the wife's clan, and conceivably even her own mother's mother. Contemporary Bororo women usually prefer their own mothers, if alive, to the husband's father's mother, if the two are not matrilineally related. But women who have no close senior female kin in the village obey the traditional prescription.

This specification of the midwife's relation to the parents is crucial for a number of symbolic and sociological reasons. First, birth is considered a very shameful as well as dangerous affair. The midwife's presence creates or reaffirms a life-long bond of intimacy between her, the mother, and the child, as those who have shared the most intensive contact with the powers of *raka* possible in the Bororo life cycle. Second, the midwife must destroy any child born with obvious physical defects or as one of twins. She does so by pinching the nostrils together with thumb and forefinger while pressing upward with her palm against the jaw, so as to close the mouth, as soon after birth as possible. Since the Bororo associate the soul with breath, it can be said that in this way the midwife prevents the union of *raka* with *aroe* from even beginning to occur. The dead thing has not even been "born," and may be disposed of as are all other body wastes. The third obligation of the midwife is considered by far the most crucial. She must ask both mother and father if they have dreamed during labor, and, if so, what was the subject of their dreams. If this was in any way negative, the child must be ritually killed to avoid the fulfillment of the dream.[7]

The Bororo consider dreams as the experience of the soul (*aroe*) during sleep, with only marginal relevance to normal existence. To be sure, the dreams of shamans are often prophetic, since their souls can travel through time and space, but they reveal rather than cause the dreamed-of event. The Bororo can offer no explanation for this terrible potency of the parents' dreams during labor other than to say it has to do with *raka*. Now, *raka* is the sustaining force in historical, nonreversible time. Its gradual loss causes the degenerative physical transformations of aging, and its complete disappearance brings about a socially unique moment, death, the disappearance of a human personality. It is also responsible for the complementary and equally singular temporal marker, the birth of a child. During birth the *raka* of each parent is so powerfully alive and creative that it endows the mother's and father's *aroe* with the capacity to transcend historical time, during those moments when their infant is crystalizing a segment of local social history.

If a man and woman can so alter the organic flow as to introduce into it a new being, they are capable of bringing about other changes in the sensate world. The examples of these dreams cited by informants are consistent with this interpretation: positive dreams during childbirth are always of spectacular success in hunting and fishing, while negative ones feature signs of massive epidemics. One of the most central tenets of Bororo cosmology is, thus, that the sustenance of any organic life requires the diminution of other life and that those who create new life from their own bodies are endowed with the awesome capacity to destroy existing forms, through the most ephemeral projections of their spirits during those moments when their creation assumes animate independence.

As soon as the child is born, the midwife buries the afterbirth and burns any mats, apparel, and other items which may have been soiled by the birth fluids, for these are extremely polluting to men, children, and women alike. The husband at the same time, having been informed of the sex and condition of his child when the midwife sought him out with questions about his dreams, takes a very thorough bath, so that the smell of birth will pass from him. If he does not do this, he will be weary and listless through his life, that is, *rakakare*. Other than this, he remains quietly at home or in the men's house. To engage in any of his usual masculine activities would involve him in a series of lethal dangers described below, to which his spouse is also subject. The father is as unobtrusive as possible in complying with this rule, as the midwife, mother, and infant return surreptitiously from the jungle to the maternal hut.

So effectively is the fact of birth concealed, that in each of the three nativities during my fieldwork, the village was not generally aware of the event until a week or longer after its occurrence. I learned of one instance of an alleged stillbirth six months later, although most village members seem to have known of it long before me. One reason for this reticence is the intense curiosity a newborn arouses, owing to its capacity to witness physically the sexual activities of its parents, especially the mother. Another reason is that an offspring transforms the relations of its mother and father with their affines and, to a lesser degree, with their consanguines, especially in the case of the firstborn to a union. The Bororo consider, with some reason, that marriages lacking an offspring are unstable, and the wife's relatives in particular are apt to treat the husband more as a casual visitor in the household than as an affine, who nominally is subject to various duties for his wife's relatives. But all of this changes with the birth of a child, and, as the Bororo say, the parents whose most secret acts have been made irreversibly and ostentatiously public, are apt to be "shy."

During the first critical weeks, the midwife acts as the mediator between the couple and the social world. She is likely to be the one who first publicly displays the infant. She tends to the wants of the parents, who are effectively restrained by the precautions of birth from carrying out any of their normal life-sustaining activities. Her critical role is institutionally recognized in the name-giving ceremony, in which she and the mother's brother play the crucial roles. One consequence of this is that the child enters into a highly ambiguous and symbolically surcharged relationship with this woman, whom he or she calls *i-maruga*. She, who as the agent of society exercised the power of life and death during his birth and who must collaborate in the ritual production of his *aroe,* is the generative mediator in many myths where she accomplishes the passage of the hero from a deathlike sterility to an achievement of his vitality, thus reintegrating him into historical time (cf., for instance, the following myths and their analyses in Lévi-Strauss 1969: M1, M5, 35–65). The relationship of this status and that of the equally important mother's brother to the healthful integration of the Bororo *persona* are discussed later. For the moment, the more direct physical connections of *raka* between parents and child deserve attention, for they give rise to a series of ritual precautions which reveal some fundamental Bororo assumptions about the nature of physical substance and the consequences of its co-participation.

The parents continue to obey the interdiction on all sexual activity. The smell of sexual fluids would pass directly to the child and make it very thin and weak, liable to disease, an early death, or at best an extremely delicate childhood. Just how this smell might be transmitted, Bororo could not say: some opined that it would be conveyed through the mother's milk, while others said merely that the constant physical association of parent and child gives ample opportunity for the debilitating effects of copulation to be transmitted between them. The Bororo generally regard the effects of coitus as physically transferable through the slightest of contact. A man who has just had intercourse avoids sitting in the men's house, so that his polluted condition may not pass to someone who may occupy the same site just after him. The men's house is the scene of preparation for and reception of *aroe,* the souls of the ancestors, who punish those who mystically contact them and *raka* at the same time in dreadful fashions. If someone who has just impersonated an ancestor, or an *aroe,* were to sit down in the men's house in a place recently vacated by a contaminated man, it would be much the same as if one threw an electrical appliance into another's bathtub. The actual agency of contact, the pollution/smell of *raka,* is termed *jerimaga* by the Bororo.

For at least two or three weeks after delivery of their child, the parents must not work, hunt, take baths, sleep a great deal, or even pass their hands over their faces, as one does when sleepy, wet their hair, or scratch their bodies with their fingernails. A man should not even touch his bows, arrows, nets or other instruments of the chase; a woman cannot draw water, prepare food, or make pottery. Neither parent can occupy any ritual role. Their diet should avoid the same species as during pregnancy, but with the addition of all creatures surcharged with *raka* (the *bope ure* animals which are the topic of Chapter 4), all varieties of turtles, and many varieties of wild honey. Generally the restrictions on conduct are intended to protect the parent, whereas the rules on diet apply to the baby's well-being. The former are almost identical with the rules pertaining to husband and wife during menstruation, whereas the latter are unique to childbirth. Finally, the first series governs behavior only during several weeks after delivery, save for the enduring prohibition on intercourse, while the second set concerning diet persists with slowly diminishing force until the child has achieved a certain plateau of development thought to manifest independence from its parents' state of physical being. Thus, if the precautions are designed to protect parents from the maleficence contained in the sheer physical presence of their offspring (couvade), they are operative over a far shorter period than those regulations intended to shield a vulnerable child from its parents' physical activities, especially those involving the ingestion of certain threatening substances (postpartum taboos).

This asymmetry should permit us to decipher various unvoiced Bororo attitudes toward the operation of *raka* in the natural world. The first conclusion of such a rereading must be that the physical presence of a child, like that of menstruation, negates and suspends the "natural" capacity of each sex to accomplish its inherent abilities.

This society regards the physical world as ripe with menaces to the well-being and comfort of human persons. Constantly in songs, myths, and verbal formulas,[8] there are endless lists of the natural agencies which hurt mankind: thorns that pierce the flesh, stinging insects, venomous snakes, beasts that tear with teeth and claws, even rocks that bruise and wound the feet. The Bororo seem to consider all such injuries as fundamentally wrong, as damages wantonly and capriciously inflicted upon an innocent humanity. Consequently, one of their most important social institutions is dedicated to redressing these crimes of nature against society. Called *mori-xe,* it involves the rule that, whenever a Bororo is injured by a natural element, another Bororo is obliged to kill or destroy the culprit (or a member of the same species). The avenger gives the dead creature to the victim, who must reciprocate with an ornament belonging to his social group. The avenger, who is always a member of the opposite moiety, has the right to wear this style of ornament for the rest of his life. Thus, the moieties socially collaborate to rectify threats to the balance between culture and nature, just as they unite naturally to create new social beings. As might be suspected, all such processes of mediation and creation involve the operation of *raka* and also those forces ultimately responsible for it, the *bope.* Part II discusses these relationships in detail. Here only those aspects of *mori-xe* relevant to the rules of couvade are considered.

The Bororo assume a link between *raka* and a person's capacity to fulfill his various roles, especially those defined by sex. Skill in hunting, which is practically the essence of Bororo criteria for masculinity, is *ipso facto* evidence of powerful *raka.* Feminine industry in cooking and gardening is likewise proof of ample "blood." In contrast, those deficient in *raka,* the sick, aged, and very young, are by definition sexless and *rakakare,* not so much exempt from the usual expectations for males and females as manifestly and tragically unable to be and act as they naturally should.

Once an old man known as Domingo, halting, feeble, and mostly blind, had managed to struggle along after the other men on a collective hunting expedition. Quite by accident he literally stumbled over a small alligator and, as much to his own surprise as everyone else's, managed to kill it. Alligator meat is not especially esteemed by the Bororo, and as the collective hunt had been productive of preferred game, poor Domingo had a hard time in getting people to accept portions of his prey. Nonetheless, the feat was widely celebrated by the entire village, with numerous wry remarks that appearances were often deceiving, and Domingo was enormously proud of himself. But the witticism in widest circulation was that Domingo would next become a father.

One possible reason for the extreme importance of *mori-xe* among the Bororo is that, in injuring persons quite properly engaged in accomplishing their sexual roles, nature betrays its own logic, is a traitor to the principles of that force which is just as much its own animating force as it is man's. *Raka* allows each species to be its specific self: by its power jaguars can kill their prey, deer can reproduce, plants can grow and bear. But it also enables these entities to damage man's *raka,* usually by the direct loss of its agency, human blood, and this, the logic of Bororo institutions implies, is simply not fair. For one thing, such injuries incapacitate the victims and prevent them from fulfilling their proper sexual roles, which include the sustenance of those whose own lack of *raka* makes them dependent on this force in others, both human and animal. By killing the guilty party, the sufferer's lost *raka* is not restored, but at least the principle of symmetry has been reaffirmed, and society has demonstrated its own capacities to nature.

There is another element here which is symbolically important: usually men avenge other men's injuries, and women, women's. This is pragmatically reasonable, since most working parties from the village are exclusive to one sex or the other. Since the revenge is nearly always accomplished immediately, men simply are not physically present to avenge a woman's injury, or vice versa. But on another level there is a certain consistency in having each sex protect the integrity of the unique abilities with which *raka* endows it.

In this connection it is difficult to determine the comparative ratio of natural injuries between men and women. Certainly men, owing to the fact that their hunting brings them into contact with animals well able to defend themselves, tend to suffer much more serious and incapacitating wounds than do women. For example, one traditional fishing technique involves stalking fish in the shallows with bow and arrow or spear. The freshwater stingray (*Potamotrygon histrix*) unfortunately is accustomed to lie motionless in these same shallows, partly covered with sand and almost invisible. When stepped upon by a naked foot, it lances the foot with its barbed and possibly poisonous tail. Inevitably, in my experience, such wounds become infected and require several months to heal; they are so painful that the victim cannot walk during this time. But on the other hand, women, whose activities of gardening, collecting, and fire-wood-gathering take them in parties of two to six daily into the jungle, tend to encounter the less debilitating but annoying bites of insects, snakes, and other small creatures. For them, *mori-xe* is almost a daily affair, while among men it arrives perhaps semi-weekly. Nor can I decide if the Bororo are ethnographically unusual in the degree they view nature as a lethal force, or if they are especially maladroit. Certainly their attitudes do not lack empirical experience: during fieldwork my wife treated over twenty cases of incapacitating injuries, in a population of one hundred and fifty, over a period of fourteen months. However, even such an incidence does not explain the Bororo elaboration of *mori-xe,* nor the idea of *raka.*

In this context the rules surrounding the behavior of parents during and after birth are particular to themselves and even bizarre. Disobedience of these rules brings about the physical signs of old age. The general interdiction on hard physical labor is justified by the claim that such labor causes a good deal of sweat, the odor of which would not leave the parent but would infect him or her with a certain listlessness the Bororo equate with *rakakare.* Baths normally cleanse the body and purify it from the physical/mystical consequences of expending *raka,* whether in sex or in other kinds of physical labor. But for the parents of a newborn, baths, other than the one taken by the father immediately after birth, merely seal in for the rest of life the smells and incapacities of physical fatigue. Furthermore, the Bororo say, if one bathed in this condition, one's hair might accidentally become wet, and then it would soon turn white. They also cite this consequence for the prohibition of sexually appropriate labor, on the grounds that a parent might be surprised by a sudden rain squall while in the jungle. Also, if he or she were engaged in such normal activities as hunting or gardening, the wind could blow in their eyes and make their vision dim. Or they might walk into a spider's web while passing along a jungle trail, and this, falling across their eyes, would blind them, or make them as nearsighted as the oldest of living Bororo. If they scratch with their nails, their skins become wrinkled and creased, hanging from their bodies in scabrous folds. Parents must use a deer femur to scratch with, or at least a bit of pointed wood.

No more can a new father or mother even so much as touch any of the implements necessary to the discharge of their sexually determined roles, let alone engage in the manufacture of these items. If a man were to pick up his bow or his fishing net, it would never succeed again in killing living creatures. Any pottery a woman might make during this period would crack in the fire and be worthless. Further, food prepared in it would make people sick, although not fatally. A new mother, and a woman during her menses, contaminates all food and drink she contacts. The Bororo are scrupulous in adhering to this rule, throwing away dishes prepared by a woman just before these natural conditions have befallen her. The consequences of eating such polluted food involve a general loss of *raka,* especially among males and young children. Informants tended to stress connections of direct contiguity in discussing this point. If a woman in a contaminated condition makes food or draws water for others, the stench of her pollution passes directly through the agency of the substance to those who consume it, destroying permanently their "blood." Such women seem to be especially dangerous to masculine implements, which they may render impotent by the slightest contact. Their unclean power is even so great as to menace the abilities of male shamans, whose abilities to intervene with the supernatural world can be permanently destroyed by accidental contact with such persons. A new father also contaminates food prepared even in his physical presence, thereby threatening shamanistic powers. Finally, neither parent can occupy a ceremonial role for similar reasons of direct contagion. Just as persons must not engage in sexual activity before or after entering into contact with the *aroe,* which is what such roles involve, so the parents of a newborn or those intimately connected with menstruation cannot perform those duties incumbent on them. "The *aroe* do not like it," say the Bororo, "and besides, it makes you ill."

The logic of this antithesis between the physical manifestation of *raka* contained in an infant, and the danger of its parents' carrying out the obligations imposed upon them by their sexual characters, can be related to more general Bororo attitudes toward the natural world. These stress the inamicability, the pain inflicted by nature upon man, or rather, nature's capacity to prevent human beings from working their will upon nature. The striking element in the prescriptions is their careful delineation of the menaces contained in things which could not, on the face of it, be less dangerous, or physically more harmless. The wind or spider web which blinds or the water which makes hair white are the most innocuous of elements, which even otherwise cleanse the body from *raka*'s noxious effects.[9] Scratching with the nails, an action normally casual and "natural," is now lethal, in a sort of direct mechanical fashion as the skin lightly furrowed by the passing nails becomes permanently wrinkled. The interdiction on sleeping or even rubbing one's face is somewhat more complex, although the logic remains the same. I must first explain that Bororo tend to nap a great deal, in periods of one or two hours, during the day, and are awake a great part of the night. One of the symptoms of powerful *raka* is, on the contrary, the ability to forego sleep. Too much sleep, as too much coitus and self-indulgence in food and tobacco, has a dual cause-effect relationship with *raka:* it is at once the expression in the individual of its weakness, and a contributing factor to its continued decline. The implicit assumption then is that, since *raka* is the finite energy driving man to accomplish his biological and sexual goals, man must restrict his satisfaction of certain "natural" desires in order that he might conserve enough *raka* to achieve other, socially beneficial needs.

We encounter again the fundamental paradoxical irony in the idea of *raka:* the very force which brings the capacity to enjoy physical life, is permanently lost in its satisfaction. The Bororo concept has certain parallels with Freud's elaboration of the libido, including his conclusion that the ultimate drive of this force was toward thanatos, or death. In the context of birth precautions, the Bororo logic seems to be that the normally delicate balance between desires fulfilled and those denied is far more precarious when one (or two) created a child. In accomplishing this massive expenditure of *raka* which is the infant, the mother and father have so enfeebled themselves that they cannot risk letting their remaining blood compel them to any satisfaction of its normal desires. It is as though with the birth a dam has broken, through which *raka* threatens to pour unchecked. As the infant gradually becomes less of a fluid thing, losing its character as a sack of uncongealed pure energy, and begins to control its own imperious needs, it represents less and less a danger for the parents. It must not be forgotten that exactly the same prohibitions on behavior apply to a couple when the wife is menstruating as to the parents of a newborn. In both cases the operations of *raka* have taken on external, visible form, greatly polluting in themselves and necessitating the suspension of all *raka*-induced activity until they have congealed, as it were, until the intimacy of contact with the bodies that produced them has faded.

A somewhat different rationale pervades the restrictions on diet, which is consistent with their intended aim of protecting the infant. The reasoning behind the species prohibited during pregnancy has already been explained. The prohibitions on animals and plants thought to be especially inbued with *raka* mirror the same assumptions as the postpartum sex taboo. The Bororo say quite explicitly that for the parents to eat any of these species would be equivalent to their having intercourse: the surcharge of *raka,* transmitted through the mother's milk, or by the smell (*jerimaga*) such meat produces in persons, causes the infant to be sickly and is likely even to kill him. As mentioned before, during the first six or eight months of life, the child's *raka* is very weak and, more crucially, not fully integrated with its soul (*aroe*). It should be nourished on vegetable gruels and the meat of such innocuous, *raka*-lacking creatures as small fish and birds. Its parents should also limit themselves to such foods during the first month after birth. Mother's milk is considered an especially vital part of its diet, being the agent of direct *raka* but in a safe, "pasteur-ized" fashion. For similar reasons cow's milk is given to sick persons of any age, and, in fact, afflicted individuals usually follow the same rules of diet as do the parents and the newborn. In their case, too, the individual *raka* is menaced, subject to more intensive loss, and weakened by those *raka*-imbued substances which usually sustain it. These substances in-clude not only the *bope ure* species, but certain tubers, corn, various wild fruits, and many varieties of wild honey, all of which are considered to have extraordinary amounts of *raka*.[10]

The only prohibited species not so endowed or subject to the meto-nymic logic of the foods tabooed during pregnancy are turtles and al-ligators. Informants could offer no reasons for the parents and infant to avoid eating these animals or their eggs, nor were they very precise about the consequences for the child if they did. Efforts to narrow the problem by specifying just which species of turtle were prohibited elicited re-sponses that were initially just as ambiguous. Several informants agreed that the turtles known to them as *jerigigi* and *upe* were interdicted, while those called *ato* and *boigabe* were permissable and even preferable food for any Bororo, no matter their condition. Identifying these was something of a problem. They were glossed as "tartaroga" and "cágado," respec-tively. Bororo and local Brazilians agreed that the contrast between the two sets was simply that between riverine and land turtles. But my Por-tuguese dictionary defined "cágado" as "common name of several fresh-water *and* land turtles, a long-necked turtle," while "tartaruga" applies only to aquatic turtles, whether freshwater or saltwater (Nôvo Michaelis 1961:209). The *Enciclopedia Bororo*, normally exceedingly reliable in its identification of Bororo ethnozoological taxonomies, further confused the issue by identifying the *ato* as a "jabuti" ("*Testudo tabulata*") but the *boigabe* as a "cágado," although specifying "*Testudo lutaria*." "Jabuti" is the vernacular term for the very large land tortoise found throughout lowland South America, quite precisely the "*Testudo tabulata*" (Ihering 1968: 367) but very different from the long-necked, riverine *cágado*.

My perplexity was finally resolved by a passage from Lévi-Strauss. "As a matter of fact, in the dialects of the Mato Grosso the terms jaboti and cágado are used with a certain latitude and occasionally overlap (cf. Ihering, "Cágado" entry; EB, Vol. I, p. 975: in the sacred language, the jabuti is called "great cágado")" (Lévi-Strauss 1969: 228). Ihering is in fact more definitive, stating that in Mato Grosso the animal known elsewhere as jabuti is called cágado (Ihering 1963: 113; 1968:180). The Salesians appear to alternate between regional and national idioms in their work, although not scientifically misidentifying, as their rendering of *boigabe* shows.

So, then, the interdiction is consistent and comprehensible. Land tur-tles such as *ato* and *boigage* are not prohibited; the parents of a newborn child are forbidden to eat the flesh or eggs of such water turtles as *jerigigi* and *upe*. Since these species were always mentioned together with alligator, one might suspect some form of association between these reptilian forms. The Bororo treat alligators with a certain symbolic ambivalence, as will be seen later. As carrion eaters, they seem to be rather like marine vultures, but as carnivores, a kind of watery jaguar. The flesh of at least certain members of the species is regarded as *"bope* food," to be consumed only after shamanistic intervention (cf. Chapter 3), and several informants said alligators generally were *"bope* of the water." For both reasons they would be too potent in *raka* for the parents of a newborn to consume. I suspect that "cágado," river turtles, are simply guilty by association, owing to their long snaky necks, preference for a diet of rot and decay (which they share with their dry land cousins, in Bororo myth), and liminal habitat. They seem to be, for the Bororo, a kind of sub-*bope* species, although I must admit I never heard anyone make the explicit identification.

## Double Inversions: Cross-Siblings and "Naming"

The postpartum rules are generally terminated when the child is ritually given a name. The parents, however, are generally cautious in their resumption of normal life and, in particular, continue to limit intercourse, at least in principle, until the child is three or four. They may eat of the formerly prohibited species, but in a cautious, experimental fashion, watching to see if their new diet has any adverse effects on their offspring. While the name-giving ceremony is thus not an absolute symbolic marker of a definitive transformation in the child-parent relationship, it has a very marked impact. Since I have described its details and logic elsewhere (Crocker 1977b, 1977c) only an outline is given here.

The child's names are chosen from a stock of personal names "owned" by the mother's lineage, by her matrilateral relatives. For the ceremony, the child is heavily ornamented with the sticky red paste of urucu berries, and coated with *Kido guru,* a resinous glue made from the sap of certain plants, powdered charcoal, and animal fat. An elaborate design owned by the mother's group is traced on its face, and its body covered with white duck down. A very elaborate "skull cap," *boe etao bú,* made from macaw breast feathers according to a design again associated with the mother's groups, is affixed to its head (see Albisetti and Venturelli 1962: 392–94, 624–26, for illustrations of these decorations). The child may also be provided with bracelets, necklaces, and other ornaments, although this is not strictly necessary. The materials for the ritual ensemble, themselves rare and valuable, are contributed by the women of the father's clan, who also make the skull cap. This ensemble is utilized only in the name-giving ceremony, initiation, and funeral. It symbolizes a passage from one status to another, and is always contributed by the agnatic relatives of the person undergoing the transition.

For the naming ritual the father himself makes a *baragara,* a "dagger," from a deer's femur and decorates it according to a fashion owned by his clan (Albisetti and Venturelli 1962: 222–27). An infant cannot be named without this ornamentation and this implement; therefore, to receive a soul-name, a social personality, requires a social father, a pater. Generally the Bororo prefer that the genitor, who infused this new being with *raka,* and his female relatives be the ones to provide it with a name, for not only is this symbolically symmetrical, but, too, they think a genitor and his relatives are apt to be more conscientious in fulfilling the myriad duties of paterhood during a person's lifetime. Should the genitor be unable or unwilling to be the pater, the mother's father provides some member of his own clan, usually a brother or sister's son, as the child's pater.

The Bororo emphasize the intimate association between proper names and that immaterial aspect of being termed *aroe,* "soul." All such names are derived from the natural and supernatural entities associated with each clan, which I term for convenience's sake its totems (Crocker 1975a). These entities are called the clan's *aroe.* The name-giving confers upon the child its nominal participation in these beings which literally define all collective and individual identity. As noted earlier, after this ritual a dead child must be buried with the complete funeral rites, which serve to incorporate its *aroe* with those of the ancestors. But the Bororo do not assert that the name-giving ritual is the origin of the soul. All existence must have form, a categorical being—hence, nominal essence. All living things thus necessarily possess, in their view, an *aroe.* The permanent departure of this element is death. Since a newborn obviously lives, even without a name, it must *ipso facto* possess a soul, or at least a kind of one. Informants said that the *aroe* in any creature was most directly and completely manifested in its breath, just as *raka,* although a general organic condition, has blood as its principal agency. When the souls of the ancestor return to the village they are sometimes felt by human beings as gusts of cold air. When the midwife suffocates an ill-omened baby, she prevents it from ever having an *aroe;* it is born "dead."

Although proper names cannot be equated with souls, we have seen that the connection between the *aroe* and the *raka* of a newborn is most tenuous up until the naming ritual. The Bororo regard having a soul as a distinct form of being, as implying membership in a category of similar beings. The possession of a proper name is the badge, if not the condition, of such membership (cf. Crocker 1977b, 1977c, and 1979 for extended discussion of these points). When I asked who or what "named" animals, the Bororo were much amused. Natural beings, they said, were born what they were, with *aroe*. By this they seemed to imply that even the young of natural species were recognizably members of their species. But human beings manifest no physical signs of belonging to any certain one of the eight kinds of humanity incorporated in the Bororo social system, the eight clans. Hence they had to be named, and thus they came to possess separate yet classifiable souls.

Although this acquisition of a definite *aroe* demands the collaboration of the mother's and father's groups, this is a symbolic conjunction, inverted and complementary to the biological union responsible for the child's physical form. The principal roles in the naming ceremony are played not by the father and mother, but by a close male relative of the mother, preferably her brother, and by an agnatic female ascendant of the father. These persons cannot have had any sexual contact prior to the ceremony. The father's relative should be, in fact, the midwife. It will be remembered that she is nominally the father's father's sister or mother. As a member of the same moiety as the mother and her relatives, she has been normatively barred from sexual relations with the mother's brother, the *i-edaga*. However, she is reckoned as an *agnatic* female ancestor of the child. As such, the child will address and refer to her as *i-maruga,* the same term used always for senior women of the father's clan, including those (the "father's sisters") who have created the ornamental ensemble essential to the naming. This sort of playing off of categorical and lineal relationships to achieve a certain kind of dyadic symmetry is as common in Bororo ceremonial transformation of kinship relations as it is in their cosmologic classifications. In modern circumstances, the midwife must nowadays be some immediate uterine ascendant of the wife's, most often her mother, or perhaps an elder sister.

Regardless of what the biological relationship between the infant and the midwife actually is, the last will be an *i-maruga* for all the child's life. It is characteristic of Bororo symbolic patterns that the person who had the capacity to give or deny the breath of life, to bestow *aroe* in its crudest form, now in the naming ceremony is empowered to bestow the *name-aroe,* thus bringing the new life into full sociological and cosmological existence. The participation of the mother's brother, who is termed *i-edaga* by the child, is likewise essential to this second birth. The *i-edaga* actually bestows the name, taking the feather-covered child from the arms of the *i-maruga* and calling out the name four times, as he moves counterclockwise to face each of the cardinal points successively beginning at the north and concluding eastward. If the child is male, the *i-edaga* next uses the *baragara* "dagger" to make a small hole in the lower lip, which will enable the boy to wear labretes. The Bororo take great pride in this masculine ornament, which also serves as a mark of tribal identity and which, almost as much as the names themselves, is basic to the foundation of the male social persona. The male child's father may have his septum pierced by the *i-edaga,* so that he can wear various nasal ornaments reserved for those who have fathered men (cf. Albisetti and Venturelli 1962: 329–34). Neither female babies nor their mothers are subject to any physical operations at the naming ceremony, although girls have their ears pierced in a minor ceremony a year or two before initiation.

The name-giving ritual is a merry event, full of laughter and good humor among all the participants. It is usually accompanied by a collective hunt and a village feast in the evening (*Aroe Emeru;* see below and Crocker 1979). The general tone is one of rejoicing that a new person has joined the collectivity, along with recognition of the parents' new status, especially marked if this is their first child. Up to this point the birth has continued to be semi-surreptitious, ignored by most village members and never alluded to publicly by the parents or their relatives. Now people can express their general relief that the delicate period between the natural and social births has been negotiated successfully, with no evil consequences for parents or their child. After this ritual no crisis or affliction, that is, threats to the individual's *raka,* will be publicly affirmed or provided with so extensive a set of rules for its resolution until his or her death. Masculine initiation does present a series of comparable dangers, but in a much attenuated form, with few restrictions on diet and behavior. Menstruation likewise represents a marked period of threat to both husband and wife but is entirely a private matter, shared only between conjugal partners.

Never again after birth does the sharing of *raka* among consanguines mutually endanger one another during times of personal affliction. One consequence of this is the exclusive focus of all Bororo rites of affliction upon the sick person and his "natural" contacts with the extrasocial domain of *raka.* There is now at least the beginning of an answer to, the question of why Bororo shamans should be so thoroughly mechanistic and asocial.

Bororo childbirth practices bear on one of the oldest and most debated topics in social anthropology, the explanation of couvade. While this is not the appropriate context to survey all the possible implications of the Bororo material for the comparative and theoretical aspects of the problem, one recent work on couvade does present an appealing hypothesis especially relevant to the Bororo situation. Rivière asserts that many anthropologists have assumed that the couvade had to do with bonds of physical substance between the child and its parents. On the contrary, he says, it would appear that in at least some South American Indian societies the enjoined actions and avoidances of both parents have to do with the creation of the infant's soul. "In those societies at least, the couvade is a ritual relating to the spiritual creation of a newborn child. Insofar as the couvade is a spiritual birth, its relationship to physical birth can be expressed thus: Birth : Couvade :: Natural : Spiritual" (Rivière 1974: 423–35). He thus compares couvade, which holds the biological parents responsible for the creation of both aspects of being, body and soul, with *compadrazgo* (godparenthood), in which the spiritual dimension of parenthood is entrusted to non-natural parents.

Unfortunately, it appears that the Bororo think of all their postpartum regulations as concerned exclusively with protecting and furthering the natural development of the infant. To be sure, one reason for its precarious existence during the early months of life is the tenuous attachment between *raka* and *aroe,* and the parents' diet might be interpreted as intending to preserve and strengthen this connection. But the suspension of all their normal sex roles (usually cited as indicative of couvade), has nothing to do with the protection of their own *raka,* as the absolute replication of this suspension during pregnancy demonstrates. Moreover, the Bororo reasoning behind the forbidden foods and the interdiction on sexual intercourse stresses over and over the direct, mechanical, metonymic danger of these substances and actions for the infant's own delicate *raka.* Finally, it is those symbolic inverted complements to the natural parents, his sister and her brother, who directly and clearly engender ritually the child's name-soul.

In this way, the Bororo case is much closer to the godparent situation, although without the complete antithesis between natural and spiritual parenthood that seems to characterize the latter (Gudeman 1972, as cited by Rivière 1974: 432). By utilizing cross-sex siblings of the biological parents, and by restricting the ceremonial roles to those who have not had sexual contact with one another, the Bororo at once invert and connect the two sets of relationships. This disjunction between those collaborations which produce and maintain the natural self, the *raka,* and those which originate and nourish the social self, the *aroe,* is basic to all Bororo ritual involving the preservation and renewal of the individual. On a larger sociological plane it is mirrored in the relationships between persons and the households with which they share at once a common *raka* and definitional essence, or *aroe.* The contradictions between these bonds, and the Bororo effort to control them through the same kind of symbolic and social structures as that between *i-maruga* and *i-edaga,* are the cosmological source of physical affliction and all modes of its treatment.

tapir

# 2

ᘓᘏᘓ

# The Wheel of Life

Traditionally the Bororo ·occupied a large section of north central Mato Grosso, an area they regarded as autochthonously their own. The boundaries were somewhat loosely defined by the Rio dos Mortes on the north, the Araguia on the east, the Cuiabá on the west, and the Taquari on the south (see map, page 27). Across the Cuiabá River to the west lived a distinct section of the tribe differentiated by dialect and perhaps by certain contrasts in the details of social and ceremonial organization (Montenegro 1958). (The Bororo living at the confluence of the Cuiabá and São Lourenço rivers are termed by the rest of the society Utugo-Kuri-doge, and are regarded as variant in their dialect and in certain rituals. They may represent an amalgamation between eastern and western elements, an interpretation volunteered by several informants.) This division had in any case either died out or been absorbed by the turn of the century.

The Bororo defined their lands less by reference to the external "boundary" rivers than by reference to the São Lourenço and its tributaries. This riverine system constituted the central "spine" or geographical axis of their territory. It figures crucially in myths and in the cosmology of Bororo villages and the afterlife. The largest and traditionally most important villages were found along both north and south banks of this river, while the outer limits of Bororoland tended to coincide with the headwaters of its tributaries. Even today, save for the sizable propor-tion of Bororo now gathered at the Salesian missions near the Araguiya, the remaining Bororo villages are found only along the banks of the São Lourenço.

The river's symbolic importance accords with its natural attributes and the uses made of them by the Bororo. Draining a sizable portion of the western Central Brazilian massif, the São Lourenço falls very pre-cipitously with a narrow deep channel (around 15 by 5 meters), except in its lower reaches. Its upper course is marked by rapids and even falls among the ignaceous rock cliffs and pillars characteristic of the massif's edge; its middle ranges by a wide shallow valley where its course is still deep and swift; only in its last 50 kilometers or so before entering the Plate does it become the broad shallow marsh usual for the Plate's and the Amazon's tributaries. It is a very rapid river, marked by strong eddies and currents, and regarded as very dangerous by the local Brazilians, who sometimes drown in it. For most of its length, the São Lourenço is also characterized by geological and biological extremes. The gallery for-est it sustains is usually narrow with soils of great fertility, a result of extensive flooding during the wet season.

At the same time, the savannah with its unique array of faunal and floral resources is seldom more than 2 or 3 kilometers away from its banks. The river itself supports a surprisingly large variety of fish species and marine animals. Apparently, it was one of the major spawning beds for fish living in or ascending the Plate system. Netting these spawns has proved a very lucrative enterprise for Brazilians living around Cuiabá and lower down the São Lourenço. But their activities, combined with the river's pollution due to mining operations and the sewage of Brazilian towns along its banks, have resulted, at least according to the Bororo, in very marked declines in the spawning runs and in the general number of fish. The general fertility of all natural resources in the São Lourenço valley has led to its intensive colonization since 1950, with extremely pernicious ecological, political, and epidemiological consequences for the Bororo.

Bororo males traditionally define themselves as fishers, gatherers, and hunters, and they concentrate most of their activities on and around the river. During the period of fieldwork the bulk of the protein con-sumed in two villages was riverine in origin. Although agriculture has come to be the major subsistence activity since Brazilian occupancy of the area, it is regarded as an activity appropriate for women and for men who can no longer gather, fish, or hunt. Recently, some healthy males have begun more intensive cultivation for the sake of cash crops, but they spend the greatest part of their profits on guns, ammunition, and fishing nets. Because of the richness of the alluvial soils and the limited demands

placed upon them by the reduced Bororo populations, there is no short-
age of cultivable soils in spite of the extensive Brazilian incursions on
their lands. And although the Bororo bitterly complain about the increasing scarcity of wild game and fish, they succeed in obtaining more
than adequate amounts of both, especially in the dry season. Traditionally, the richness of the various econiches exploited by the Bororo,
together with the highly efficient division of labor and distribution afforded by their social organization, supported very large villages, of at
least a thousand in the pre-contact era.[11] As far as the total natural environment is concerned, the Bororo might reasonably fear their own
abilities to cope with it, or the harm it might do them, but they can never
doubt its constancy and abundance.

The traditional Bororo village was a corporate unity in its own right,
identified by a permanent name and by usufruct rights over a well-de-
fined geographical area. However, members of other Bororo communities are freely granted rights to hunt or fish over its domain. Villagers
attach much more importance to its mythical associations and the vigor
and completeness with which it fulfills traditional norms than they do to
its material resources. Generally the boundaries between contiguous villages were marked by tributaries of the São Lourenço, although in its
upper reaches rock outcroppings appear to have been used as markers.
These natural phenomena often appear in myths, as do various singular
geographical features in each village's area. Since myths have nearly always to do with the exploits of culture heroes, the clans' ancestors, and of
the totemic species associated with each social group, the landscape is
completely socialized in a pan-Bororo system of symbolic meaning.
While each village was politically and ecologically autonomous, there
have always been extensive ceremonial cooperation and exchange of prestige goods between communities. Such ties especially characterized the
villages within each of the six regions in which Bororoland was divided
(Crocker 1979), although less systematic contacts existed between
regions.

Traditionally the villages of a region apparently collaborated in warfare against other Indians and against the Brazilians, whom the Bororo
fought vigorously for at least a century until they were "pacified" in the
last decades of the nineteenth century. But the modern Bororo insist that
violence never occurred between villages or regions of their society, and
available historical accounts, admittedly limited and inaccurate, indicate
nothing to the contrary (Montenegro 1958; Albisetti and Venturelli 1962:
217–21, 280–93).[12] Such internal pacificity is almost unique to the Bororo among the indigenous societies of lowland South America and is all
the more remarkable in the absence of supra-village political institutions.
It can be understood only through the formal plan of the Bororo village

and the attributes of the clans arranged there. Indeed, Lévi-Strauss feels that the details of these distinctively Bororo organizations can themselves only be the result of a self-conscious political evolution striving for internal harmony (Lévi-Strauss 1974). No actual community, to my knowledge, succeeds in reproducing this plan, for always some subclans and even entire clans are not represented in the village population. A space is then left in the circle, and both daily and ceremonial life can proceed "as if" the missing groups were present. In many ceremonies, however, the participation of all eight clans, and even all sixteen subclans, is essential, and then members of the lacking groups travel from other villages so that the ritual may proceed. Traditional villages attempt to lure these visitors into remaining, and often they accept. Contrarily, when a clan has more than two closely related resident households, one of them usually leaves to reside in a community where that clan is under- or non-represented. Thus, the purely formal requirements of the village model entail major consequences for the development and mobility of domestic units and the larger social units they represent.

This process is facilitated by the way in which the Bororo define the clan and subclan as residential unities, as the social category common to those who occupy huts in a certain segment of the village, and not as a group of consanguines. The clans, their subdivisions, and their associated named status, ceremonial paraphernalia, rituals, totemic *aroe,* and the whole complex system of esoterica are common to all Bororo, just as much as the scheme for their integration, the village model. This, in addition to the little attention given genealogical criteria in social relationships, means that any Bororo can easily change his village of residence. Each community, save for its unique demographic configuration, is just like all the others. I have seen a Bororo enter a completely foreign village and proceed immediately to the homes of his clansmen. The bonds of corporate membership, of affinal and patrilineal relationships, are defined by social categories and not by genealogies, so that each Bororo has preexisting "brothers," "mothers," "affines," and "fathers" in all Bororo villages, with all the rights and duties such ties carry. The village plan and the clans serve as a timeless and immutable grid by which individuals may define themselves and each other, without reliance on the restricting particularities of descent lines and localities.

Given such conditions, high rates of intervillage mobility are not surprising, even if many contemporary moves are attributable to the disappearance of natal villages, epidemics, and other results of Bororo demographic collapse. Young men traditionally wandered about from village to village, often marrying and residing uxorilocally. They were in no sense obliged to do this, since Bororo marriage involves no concept of bride service. Instead, they were encouraged to leave their parents' villages for a variety of political and social factors discussed in the early pages of the next chapter. After marriage, the young couple seemed often to drift about from village to village, usually settling where one or the other of their parents were resident. Divorce, which is exceedingly frequent among the Bororo, is still often followed by the migration of one spouse from the village, usually the husband. Even after children are born to the union, the couple is extremely mobile. Entire extended family groups freely move from one community to another. Nearly always these dislocations have initially a very indefinite character. The newcomers are said to be "visiting." During the dry season, the usual time for such displacements, as much as a third of the village population may be comprised of visitors. While the majority of such visitors eventually return to their villages, some remain, and others, after vacillating for two or three seasons, eventually settle down in their turn.

The Bororo do attach considerable emotional importance to their natal village, or at least to the one in which they spent their childhood. If parents continue to reside there, or close consanguines with whom they share affection, they attempt to remain in or to return to it. Bororo also speak with nostalgia, even with "homesickness," of places rich in personal and mythical associations. Some appear to feel a continuity with the generations of their ancestors who lived on a particular site. The traditional village of *Jaru dori* has a total population of one man. He maintains the village circle, a small men's house, and the hut of his own clan. When I asked him why he remained, when he would have been welcomed at any other community, he replied, "The bones of my mother and father are here, the bones of my grandparents, my wives and children. As long as I am here, the village of *Jaru dori* exists. When I die it will be over." But this was a unique case. For nearly all other Bororo, the values of traditional life are far stronger than such sentimental ties, and such a life can only be conducted in a proper Bororo village.[13] After all, it is easy enough to take aged parents or other close relatives with one to a new community.

There can be no doubt that the severe demographic decline of the Bororo during the past one hundred years has profoundly affected patterns of individual and family mobility, and thus the character of the domestic group through time. Entire villages have disappeared; the demise of all close relatives has allowed individuals an increased freedom from responsibility to parents and consanguines. The constitution of villages is thus determined more by the disappearance of entire clans than by the dynamics of indigenous political and domestic processes. Nonetheless, it appears that contemporary problems have exacerbated rather than created the forces urging intervillage mobility. The shallow genealogies I was able to gather reflect an overwhelming preponderance of village exogamy. In two villages on the middle São Lourenço each adult over twenty had lived in over three communities for more than a year. Persons and family groups float from community to community in bewildering succession. Village membership is almost as easily acquired as it is renounced, and at any given moment informants disagree as to who could "now" be considered a "part" of the village. But they were unanimous in asserting that such mobility was thoroughly traditional, at least in quality if not in degree. This fluidity, and the village-corporate group attributes which foster it, are one source of the pacificity within Bororo society. For not only are all manner of relatives, agnates, and affines apt to reside in other communities, but these are a mirror replica of one's own village. There are no "foreign" elements within the Bororo system.

Still, if the Bororo have managed to integrate their society, they have done so at the price of the domestic group's stability. Divorce is frequent, stepparents the norm rather than the exception. Siblings are seldom coresident, and often find it necessary to live in different villages. Although the parent-child bond, especially between mother and daughter, often forms the nucleus of the domestic group, it too is subject to rupture during the middle years of the younger generation's lives. While the residential unit is the crucial unity of production and consumption among the Bororo, its internal processes are marked by continual disruption and conflict. Relations between members of the same corporate group tend to be equally strained. Clan members unite only in face of their collective obligations toward groups of the other moiety. Affines, especially fathers, are formally obliged to bring peace among their wives' people. If the historical development of Bororo domestic groups reflects the general structural attributes of the village plan and the clan, these groups are also subject to intense social tensions and to the idiosyncratic changes these generate.

## Conjugality and Clans: The Domestic Group Through Time

To establish definitive residence in a Bororo village one must build a house in it. The Bororo hut is now generally constructed in Brazilian peasant fashion, in a long rectangle with walls of woven palm leaves and a thatched roof of the same material. Its size depends equally upon the number of people it must shelter and the industry of those who build it. The last are always the in-marrying males, who are obliged to construct a home for their wives and their wives' matrilineal relatives. They must also build the dwelling on that portion of the village circle allocated to their affines' social unit. In a very few instances a man may have the right to construct his wife's house in her father's subclan area, which is to say within his own moiety and perhaps within his own clan's area. I know of only one instance in which a husband actually began such a construction, and he was a shaman, a rather aberrant one even by shamanistic standards. The unequivocal right of a woman to have her own hut built on the appropriate spot belonging to her social unit, and the husband's equally undeniable obligation to build it for her, provide some of the basic dynamics in marriage and intervillage mobility. Most men are loath to undertake the fairly extensive labor a hut requires if they have reason to suspect the permanence of the union or of the new residence.

More often than not their suspicions are well founded. A majority of Bororo in the middle São Lourenço live in dwellings constructed by males no longer married to women of the household. Whether newlyweds or visitors, men attempt to postpone the definitive commitment implied by house construction as long as possible. This makes initially for crowding in existing huts and, over the long term, leads to an exacerbation of domestic tensions. The classic resolution of the problem was for the husband to build a home for his wife directly behind that of her parents. Although some men still accept this solution, very often they drift on to another village, living with one set or other of real or categorical relatives until their marital and residential situation is resolved. Most usually this is through the birth of a child.

The stable core of most Bororo households is a matrilineage—a grandmother, mother, and daughter, together with their husbands and immature or unmarried offspring. Although married sisters may coreside for a time, they seldom remain in the same dwelling after both have children. There is no normative barrier to their doing so, quite to the contrary. The Bororo celebrate the image of a *pater et mater familias* surrounded by their coresident descendants. But they admit that, owing to the rivalry of mature siblings (above all sisters), such a happy situation seldom occurs. "Not only do the sisters fight each other about their children," informants said, "but their husbands do not understand one another," which is a light euphemism for their mutual suspicion and hostility. Many households manage to include clan or moiety "sisters," their children and spouses in relative harmony for a time. But in these cases one couple and their offspring have accepted the position of dependent, whose position in the group hangs upon the sufferance and sense of corporate obligation of its senior members. Often the husband within these units is a transitory or retiring figure. Should he seek a more prominent role, he manifests it by constructing a new dwelling for his family, either alongside or behind that of his wife's "adoptive" family. Or he simply moves them to a new village altogether.

Further, the Bororo household nearly always includes persons related to the matrilineal core in highly variable ways. Some are uterine consanguines, such as matrilateral parallel cousins. Others are simple classificatory co-clan members, frequently "visitors" by informal title. A surprisingly large percentage are agnatic relatives of either the matrilineal core or of the in-marrying males. This comes about through a combination of intervillage visiting and high divorce. Most visitors to a community dwell "temporarily" with the closest blood relative living there. A visiting daughter or son, together with their families, will stay with a father of either spouse if the mothers are dead or live in another village. Parents or grandparents move in with their lineal descendants rather than with affines or collaterals. Normatively, if such interlopers wish to remain in the village, they must construct a hut on that segment of the village circle assigned to the wife's social group. But often a mother or father is not married, or the former's spouse is so feeble as not to be able to accomplish his duty of house-building. Even though they may live with a son or daughter for a time, in all defiance of the rules of matrilateral-uxorilocal residence, they seem finally to move in with classificatory matrilineal clan relatives. The case of old Maneomaru is illustrative. Even though he had two sons' daughters in the village, he made it a point of honor to divide his life between the men's house and the hut of a senior classificatory clanswoman. In such cases lineal descendants contribute a major portion of an aged parent's subsistence, but they do not actually shelter him or her.

Contemporary Bororo residential patterns also reflect the horrible mortality rates of the last five and six decades. Many aged persons have lost all their lineal descendants, so that the traditional practice of an old mother and her husband living with her mature daughters cannot be maintained. Clan members are formally obliged to provide shelter and subsistence for these old "mothers" and "mother's brothers," and nearly all Bororo do so with no external signs of resentment or hostility. In one village, Korugedu Paru, two-thirds of all dependent aged individuals resided with unrelated clanswomen (cf. Appendix B). Only two of them (one being Maneomaru) had agnatic relatives in the village, but both lived with their matrilineal clans. At one period, there were six elderly "visitors" in the same community, of whom four were staying with agnatic relatives of one spouse or the other, and two with uterine descendants. Of the four, two said that if they remained in the village they would go to live on the wife's matrilineal clan site, and one of the other two was the aberrant shaman who began building a house on his wife's father's clan area.

In short, it appears that while the high mortality levels have exacerbated the importance of corporate bonds as determining residential affiliation, as over against consanguineal and lineal ties, the mere lack of living children does not account for the consistent tendency of categorical clanship to prevail ultimately over the ties of a shared *raka*. While the Bororo feel strongly obligated to provide for and shelter an aged parent, and even for his or her siblings, in the end the normative prescriptive that one must live with one's clan (or one's wife's clan) determines residence. But if the Bororo household is based more on its corporate affiliations than on unities of shared blood, the opposition between the two forms of solidarity is reflected in other aspects of its composition.

Besides the old and infirm, the other large class of unrelated domestic dependents is orphans and abandoned children. Again, the mortality rates are responsible for a portion of this phenomenon. The death rate among women of child-bearing age is high, partly as a result of attempts to bring on abortions. But of the motherless children in two villages over half had mothers living in other villages. To be sure, some of these mothers were regarded (or regarded themselves) as temporary "visitors" to the other community, who would eventually reclaim their offspring. In my experience, such reunions were comparatively rare. Both male and female informants said that often young women found it easier to begin a new marriage by following their husband to another village, unencumbered by the results of previous unions. Bororo stepfathers are not noticeably hostile to their wife's children; rather, they are conscientious in fulfilling their duties as substitute paters. However, women appeared reluctant to subject the very fragile relations of a new marriage to the added stress of a squalling infant from an earlier liaison. Further, mothering is shared among nearly all the adult female members of a household in any case. Leaving a child "for a time" in the care of a mother or sister simply involves the prolongation of a daily pattern. Then too, a divorce should not, and in practice practically never does, alter the relation between a father and his child. When the genitor-pater is resident in the village, he may well encourage his former wife to leave the child behind her when she moves. Indeed, the Bororo warmly endorse marriage between a father and a wife's sister, consanguine or classificatory, "so that they may raise the children." There are three such marriages at Korugedu Paru, and many others appear in the genealogies. Gossips, on the other hand, attributed this spirited compliance with traditional norms as due to women's adroitness in seducing their sisters' husbands. But even in the case of orphans who have no or very distant relatives in the village, classificatory clanswomen and their husbands comply cheerfully with their corporate obligation to rear the children of their matrilineal relatives. The relationship between Jerigi Otojiwu and the nine-year old son of his wife's classificatory sister was often cited as a model of the ideal father-son relationship and as disproving the adage that genitors make the best paters. (Cynics noted that Jerigi's apparent life-long sterility might well have had something to do with the situation.)

Among the nonrelated personages found within the household, and often a more transitory figure than even the visitors, is the in-dwelling husband, or "friend," of one of the household's clanswomen. In effect, most Bororo marriages begin as liaisons, lasting at most six months or a year. The sociological and ideological reasons for their fragility will be briefly reviewed later in this chapter. For the moment, the frequency of "divorce" only rounds out this description of the Bororo household as a heterogeneous and rapidly changing flux of personalities. The notion of the developmental cycle of the domestic group, as useful as it may be in other ethnographic contexts, is simply inapplicable to the Bororo. The analytical utility of this notion depends on the correlation between social practices (marriage and residence) and the processes of individual biological maturation (Crocker 1979). The lack of such correlation among the Bororo indicates that their households are not based on "natural" bonds, on consanguinity. Although these are not irrelevant to the groups involved, the relationships between social bonds and the domestic group's structural transformations through time are highly variable and subject to numerous extrinsic forces. Among the last are the results of high village mobility, which lead to the unpredictable inclusion of all manner of consanguineal and classificatory relatives within the household. Even if one excludes such accidental additions on the grounds they do not affect the basic dynamics of marriage, birth, and aging within the household's core, there remains the problem that in-marrying males are quite capable of drifting out as casually as they drifted in, even if they leave children behind them. Moreover, as already mentioned, sisters seldom dwell together after they begin families, and even aged mothers are able to wander off to visit sons or daughters in a nearby community.

None of this should be taken to indicate any lack of solidarity within the Bororo household cum institution. Nor should it cloud the central importance of the matrifocal residential group as the fundamental social unity among the Bororo. The absence of individual continuity and of structure associated with biological relationships simply reflects the fact that this social unit is based on the sharing not of blood but of common symbolic properties, which define its differentiation from other units just as efficiently as any reckoning of lines of descent might do. The Bororo household is a corporation, disposing of rights over scarce property, immortal, with a single political head and a single moral personality. But it has these attributes because it is part of a single cosmological unity, a Bororo clan, whose unique identity is expressed through its relationships with the "souls" of things rather than with their *raka*, their physical being. The Bororo deny any suggestion that clan members may be descended from a single human ancestress. Their union derives from the way their individual and corporate names (or "souls") derive from a common and circumscribed stock of possible nominal forms (Crocker 1977b) rather than from any hypothetical "common blood." At the same time, the household does nourish relationships formed from the imperishable facts of birth and of the sharing of physical substance. The mediation between these two modes of corporateness comes not from the internal developments within the domestic group but through its continuous transactions with other analogical units within the village.

The household's corporate attributes are most readily visible in its economic and ritual enterprises, two activities which are in this society virtual facets of a single undertaking. The members of the residence group participate in a single domestic economy, rationally dividing their labor to function most effectively as a unit in all phases of production, distribution, and consumption. The Bororo consciously develop this cooperation as at once a normative (the household should be one entity) and a pragmatic (it can produce more thus) goal. They often contrast their own practices with those of Brazilian peasants, among whom each nuclear family tends to strive toward economic independence. In contrast, the Bororo overtly claim that a domestic group cannot be truly viable unless it includes at least two nuclear families, of different generations if possible. In fact, the great majority of their residential groups are focused on extended families united by classificatory bonds as often as consanguineal ones. Moreover, they insist that the units gathered under one roof integrate their subsistence efforts. As a common saying goes, "There should be but one cooking fire in the home." In this, if not in other aspects of domestic life, the Bororo agree with their indigenous neighbors, among whom co-residence also implies a co-economy (cf., for example, for the Bororo's northern cousins, the Shavante, Maybury-Lewis 1974: 85–96). True, both in theory and in custom the Bororo prefer that each conjugal unit assume responsibility for its own maintenance. Traditionally, such self-reliance is manifested by a garden that husband, wife, and children alone develop and maintain. The establishment of such a plantation usually precedes a man's construction of a house for his wife, or follows after some months the birth of their child. By both undertakings he signals his acceptance of a certain permanency in his conjugal life. Consequently, affines commonly bring considerable pressure to bear on in-marrying males to achieve at least an independent garden.

But such disjunction of productive activity does not imply any independence of the couple from the household, quite the opposite. The explicit motive is that only a separate garden can permit a couple to contribute its manifest share to the maintenance of the household. The garden plots of co-residents are usually contiguous, and reciprocal labor on each other's fields is a widely followed norm. The household's males help each other to fell and to burn the covering trees and brush. They assist one another's wives to clear and plant, while the women of a single household scarcely seem to differentiate between their own and their housemate's cultivations, in terms of tending, weeding, and harvesting. Even the type and proportion of crops raised in each garden are intended to complement those planted by co-residents. After food is produced thus independently, it is almost invariably pooled within the household for common consumption and distribution. The only major exception to such collectivization involves couples with extensive ritual obligations for food prestations, who reserve a part of their own harvest or maintain a separate garden to fulfill their ceremonial duties. Several aged widows in Koredu Paru even attempt to have such plots in order to be self-sufficient in their prestations. In fact, labor and food from the common stock are contributed surreptitiously by their co-residents, so that they can afford themselves the illusion of independence. Even when an individual is required to transact relationships with other domestic units personally, he or she is apt to find the household has acted with them.

While the corn, rice, beans, manioc, plantains, and other cultigens raised in the gardens compose the major part of Bororo diet,[14] game, fish, and wild vegetables are much preferred foods. Bororo ideas of a proper meal focus around protein as the central dish, with vegetables as a kind of condiment. Furthermore, they have decided ideas about the relative value of kinds of protein. Generally, those rich either in fat or in assumed *raka* are highly esteemed. Such foods are almost exactly those loved by the *bope,* who protect the species which provide them and demand a share when they are consumed by the Bororo. The shamanistic practices which accompany these beliefs are described in Part II. The relevance of such gastronomic habits here is that dishes featuring these wild species are obligatory in the food prestations between different households. Such exchanges are so common that, for some domestic groups in Koregedu Paru, their joint production during the dry season provided only 20 percent of their total consumption. They received the remainder of their sustenance from other groups. Nearly all these prestations follow from the individual obligations of household members. Husbands are required to send a portion of their game, and the produce of their garden, home to parents and elder siblings. Women give their brothers' affines cooked dishes. Even agnatic relatives, if only classificatory ones, deserve to receive gifts of food.

But by far the most usual motive for interhousehold exchanges of food involves ritual relationships in which members of one moiety have become symbolic "children" of certain household members (Crocker 1977b, 1979). All such transactions explicitly involve only couples and individuals; in fact, the entire household cooperates in the production of foods designated for prestation, just as it shares in the consumption of dishes rendered its individual members. Indeed, this sharing of foods rich in *raka,* in symbolic connotations of the general social control over life, death, and natural processes, defines—even creates—the household's quality as a natural entity, a congregation of persons who share not just a categorical and residential being, but a common substance.

The premises of *raka* ensure that only persons who actively come into contact with each other's vital fluids—husband, wife, and newborn child—actually participate in one another's substance to the degree necessitating rules to control the dangers thus generated. After the child becomes a moral personality, around three or four, his own state of being no longer affects nor can be menaced by that of others sharing the same historical *raka,* parents or siblings. In this limited sense, the married couples within each household form private islands of shared *raka.* But the Bororo also feel that persons who live together over the years come eventually to partake of a single organic identity. They have, first of all, "eaten from the same pot," and, further, the foods they have jointly consumed are above all those laden with *raka,* crucial to individual and collective well-being. Next, co-residents also participate in one another's biological processes "at second hand." For example, behind each hut a network of paths leads out into the savannah, the forest, and to the nearest stream. These paths are "private" to the household's members, for along them people make love, urinate, and defecate. Because all bodily functions are shameful and should be concealed, Bororo etiquette requires nonrecognition of whatever may be going on in a neighbor's private zone. The way that housemates are obliged to conduct their private lives more or less jointly brings about a sort of reduced cosubstantiality. This does not give rise to the kind of mutual dangers generated by the much more intensive participation in each other's *raka* of a husband and wife. To be sure, an individual's polluting body wastes tend to menace his co-residents much more than other persons. A menstruating woman and her husband threaten the rest of the household almost as much as they do themselves and each other. But these dangers do not define the residential group as a single organic unit, as they do the married couple.

They operate sheerly by contiguity and hence extend beyond the limits of the hut.

The symbolic expressions of the Bororo household's common substance occur in domains other than that which utilizes *raka* as its idiom. The sharing of *rakare* foods and of a common privacy is as much an expressive consequence of this identity as a cause. This mixture of elements comes about because the Bororo household is the mediating institution between the historical processes of *raka,* its manifestations in sexuality, birth, illness, and death, and the timeless social categories which order such changes.

If the household shares in the production, distribution, and consumption of natural goods, it is much more a single unity in the creation and exchange of non–utilitarian wealth. In effect, the Bororo residential group is responsible as a nondifferentiated totality for the ceremonial activities required of the clan and subclan to which it belongs, and for the ritual obligations its individual members have contracted. All these obligations require the expenditure of what the Bororo regard as symbolic wealth: scarce feathers, shells, animal skins, teeth and claws, paints and dyes, plant materials, and the knowledge and skill necessary to combine these into ornaments. These resources are regarded as individual property and are the subject of the only jural concepts of ownership developed by the Bororo. But persons are morally bound to supply their co-residents and the clan with such goods as are necessary for a particular ceremony or material prestation. Just as couples maintain gardens to themselves but share their harvest within the hut, so too any prestige items they hold are at the disposition of the larger group.

The duty to fulfill ceremonial obligations falls upon the in–marrying males. They, especially after they have become fathers, are required to render all kinds of service to their affines, for the Bororo consider a wife-taker father as permanently indebted to his wife's relatives, or rather, to her corporate category. The most usual form of this service is the actual manufacture of ritual objects and the ornamentation of the dancers who represent the clan's *aroe* totems. Such work often requires a considerable amount of skill, as well as time, to execute, and may take up a major portion of the husband's productive efforts. In–marrying males are also expected to contribute most of the raw materials needed, but, as these are very difficult to amass, other house members often furnish the rest.

The most utilized material in Bororo ornaments is macaw feathers, which are a kind of symbolic currency in all ritual transactions (Crocker 1977b). Nearly all traditional households possess a pair of domesticated macaws. These provide at once the feathers with which the household relates to other like units, a mode of contact between the residential group and its departed members,[15] a badge of its self-sufficiency as a unit, and a symbol of the dependency of its personnel upon its continued existence. The macaws are regarded almost as household members, who give up their feathers in exchange for food and protection. They are formally owned, and in practice usually cared for, by the active female head of the group. When Bororo men say that they are macaws, they allude to the analogic roles they as husbands and fathers, and macaws as captive, valued dependents, play in the sustenance of the household. But the macaws, and the ceremonial transactions their plumage facilitates, have nothing to do with *raka*, but instead stand for souls, the group's identity as *aroe*.

## Household and Category: The Timelessness of *Aroe* Homes

The relationships between a Bororo residential group, the subclan and clan, and the totemic forms are in principle very complex and are in practice further subject to elaborate permutations following from local demographic, sociological, and political situations.[16] Briefly, each of the eight corporate categories (or "clans") recognized by the Bororo is associated with about thirty to fifty *aroe* forms. These are the ideal or nominal essence of floral and faunal species, natural phenomena, semi-divinized culture heroes, and certain monsters, already described in the introduction. Each *aroe* is thought of as two forms, contrasted in size, sex, color, and occasionally markings. The relation between them is variously described as that between brother and sister, elder and younger, or simply "one" and "the other." It is as if Bororo thought proceeds in such totally dyadic terms that it cannot conceptualize the essence of any categorical form except by dualities, which between them exhaust the range of contrasts inherent in actual participants in the form. Each of the forms is attached to a subclan, which bears among its titles a reference to that form. In other words, these are "subspecies."

The Kie (Tapir) clan, for example, recognizes among its *aroe* totems the Kie Kujagureu ("Red Tapir") and the Kie Xoreu ("Black Tapir"). The first is associated with the Kie Xobugiwuge, the easterly Kie subclan, and the second with the Kie Xebegiwuge, the westerly Kie subclan. There are further differentiations within each subclan and *aroe* form, which particularize types of being within each dyadic form. There are, for example, "Fat Tapir," "Slender Tapir," "Running Tapir," "Sleeping Tapir," and so forth. It is this particular form which is associated with the domestic group, as providing the names of its individual members.

Examples of "clan" ornamental assemblages

Generally, although with some exceptions, each residential unit among the Bororo is regarded as a "name group," insofar as children born to its female members have the right to titles reflecting some of the specific ramifications of *aroe* forms connected to the mother's group. Each clan recognizes from six to ten such name groups, more or less evenly divided between its component halves, the subclans. Each group is responsible for the representation of those particularized *aroe* forms which define its unique identity, and so it has rights over all the ornaments, body paintings, chants, and dances necessary to that representation.

The household, then, is at once the context for the continuation of physical existence, for the consequences of serial time, and the unit which must provide the materials and skills to represent its timeless *aroe*. Failures to comply with the latter duty are punished by the *aroe*,[17] just as perturbations in its organic existence are inflicted by the *bope*. Generally, when any Bororo has ceremonial contact with the *aroe*, all sexual activity must be halted for several days before and after this contact. When the entire household collaborates in activities involving the *aroe,* all its members are subject to this rule. If it is broken, any one or a number of them, not just the guilty party alone, are afflicted by the *aroe*. These spirits are also angered by errors in the manufacture of ornaments and in the ritual performance itself. But, according to informants, the greatest dangers incurred by the residential group in its dealings with the *aroe* occur in the preparation of food for the spirits and for the dancers who impersonate them. Such food is limited to boiled vegetables, especially corn and palm fruits, boiled fish, and sweetened water. The *aroe* detest the *raka*-imbued game associated with the *bope,* and indeed their diet is the same as that prescribed for parents of a newborn child and sick persons, all of whom have very fragile *raka*. As this implies, the *aroe* are considered to lack *raka* almost completely: their usual appearance as cold transparent winds reflects this absence of the warm blood which gives substance and power to other beings.

Food for the *aroe* must be very carefully prepared, with no hint of dirt or undercooking. The fruits and vegetables have to be whole and ripe, the fish properly scaled and dressed. So exigent are the *aroe* that, informants said, in the past women were constantly sick as a result of some small error in the cooking of *aroe* food. Their husbands, on the other hand, actually represent the *aroe* and are thus apt to be afflicted for mistakes in ornamentation or ritual performances. If there are grave faults in the household's duties toward the *aroe,* the spirits are entirely capable of punishing, even killing, the entire group, infants and aged persons included. The Bororo explain the extinction of various name-groups (equated with households) as due to the *aroe*'s vengeance for some injury done them by members of those groups.

So, if the concept of *raka* (and its associated dangers) expresses the character of conjugal relationships, that of the *aroe* and their powers serves to define the unique identity of the household and the dependency of each member upon the others' correct fulfillment of their symbolic duties. Just as *raka* enables each sex to carry out its sociobiological roles, at once complementing and threatening each other, so the *aroe* provide the ground of differentiation by which each household maintains its unique and vital position within the village. Through the *aroe,* every residence is dependent upon all the others for the continuation of communal life. As every infant needs a *pater* in order to receive names and membership in its maternal group, every household needs the collaboration of others in the opposite moiety to realize the *aroe* representations necessary to transform sexless boys into mature men and to change a dead man into a soul. The reciprocity which binds men and women comes from the contrasting operation of *raka* in them; that which unites the village, from the definitional system of the *aroe*. In each sphere there are dangers for those who enter into exchange with each other, which serve as codes for the governance of the relationships and as expression of their sociological powers. It can now be seen that the common substance of the Bororo household is not a genealogically defined element but the feathers and paint and skins used to incarnate the *aroe*. The way in which people who live together come to share in each other's categorical being, and the threats to their health thus incurred, are given symbolic form in these substances. The afflictions visited upon the household by the *aroe* employ them as pathogenic agencies: when the shaman treats an illness caused by the *aroe,* he sucks out a bit of feather.

Although the Bororo might seem to contradict the traditional anthropological wisdom that consanguinity or descent must be the basis for all enduring socialities in tribal cultures, their use of diet, residence, and ritual as the substantive ground for collectivities has various functional consequences which explain various idiosyncratic features of their society. First, it is difficult to see how a society which insisted on genealogies as the foundation of corporate groups could attain the residential mobility with structural continuity which so characterizes the Bororo. By restricting the operations of physical substance (*raka*) to a married couple and, for a very limited time after birth, their offspring, the Bororo can use the idiom of common symbolic substance (*aroe*) to form nonrelatives into a household. Second, the requirement that the residential unit as a totality be economically integrated and responsible for the ritual duties of its members means that families cannot establish little self-sufficient enclaves within it. Further, since the group's ceremonial obligations are embedded within a historical series of categorical prestations and continuing corporate relationships, any newcomer soon finds his own self-interests quickly merging with those of his household. And finally, the absolute necessity for households to be ritually and ceremonially interdependent on each other ensures peace both within and between villages.

But in thus utilizing a symbolic and residential code rather than a genealogical one for the structuring of personal and corporate relations, the Bororo set an enormous problem for themselves: that of the integration and regulation of consanguineal and conjugal units, which *do* rest on shared physical substance. This they have failed to do. Indeed, by the very stress on the importance of nominal forms they so undermine the unities of blood as to nearly destroy them. Conflicts between husband and wife, and between siblings, are endemic, intense, and frequent. So negative are these relationships that people become sick and even die of them—that is, in Bororo idiom, problems in the management of *raka* cause nearly all affliction. The social characteristics of these problems are the subject of the next section.

# Elder, Younger, Other:
# The Politics of Household
# Economy Through Time

Every Bororo household has one dominant woman who exercises normative control over all its other female members, and a fair amount of influence over its men. Often she is the mother of some of the younger women and the immature children. Usually the hut has been built for her by her husband, and she is regarded as its owner. But occasionally she is the daughter of that owner, now old or enfeebled, or a sister's daughter, or sometimes just a classificatory clanswoman. Some female heads have no children, or only immature ones, nor do they need to be married. In one case the female household head is a young girl of about twenty-five, living quite improperly in her husband's maternal hut. In sum, genealogical position, here no more than in other Bororo realms, has little to do with authority. The female head is the woman who assumes responsibility for ensuring that the household accomplishes its corporate and particular ritual obligations, and for coordinating its resources, including the physical labor of its members. To the former end she sometimes maintains a private garden, the produce of which goes uniquely to the nourishment of the *aroe*. Such women are apt to be dynamic personalities, almost as fluent as men in ritual esoterica and as insistent on their own prerogatives. Often they dominate, privately if not publicly, their husbands. They tend to be moralistic insofar as they follow the traditional canons for proper behavior which set the interests of the name-group and subclan over those of individuals and family units. Their influence and even power in village affairs is therefore considerable, even if implicit and seldom publicly recognized.

The titular head of the household, and of the name-group/subclan it represents, is normatively the senior active male consanguine resident in the village. Stereotypically, he is the brother of the female head, although his actual relationship with her varies as much as her own connections with other household members. His position, even more than hers, depends upon the interplay of all manner of contingent and normative factors. Generally, the position of subclan and name-group head (*emijera,* or "chief") is supposed to be transmitted by its incumbent to a younger brother, and thence to a consanguine sister's son. Once again, mortality rates have severely affected this system. Very often senior males have difficulty in locating any other senior male member of the name-group, much less a consanguine. But even traditionally the dominant component in authority was more achieved than ascribed.

The *emijera*'s duties are preeminently ceremonial ones. They involve singing the chants essential to the household's fulfillment of its *aroe* responsibilities, a minute knowledge of the esoteric lore not just of the household's own social groups but of most of the other clans and name-groups in the village, and, of course, the ability to make the several hundred artifacts required of the clan. Such knowledge is regarded as the most precious good in the Bororo system, and as such is jealously guarded. It is conveyed from one man to another only in private, and then only if its possessor has deemed the other morally worthy of receiving it. Further, each owner of knowledge is required to transmit his lore to *some* member of the next generation. Since knowledge is quite literally power in this society, the choice of an intellectual heir is a grave and anxious undertaking, all the more acute since young Bororo men are regarded as unprincipled, dissolute idiots seduced by Brazilian manners, hopeless traitors to the traditional system.[18]

The actual choice of a male household head involves still other considerations than esoteric competency, which is a precondition rather than a qualification. For the Bororo, knowledge of the traditions brings about moral behavior consonant with the principles embedded in them. Over and over they excused the rash conduct of a young man on the grounds that "he did not know enough yet," and the offender was treated to an interminable series of myths and legends. Since knowledge and morality are mutually self-defining, anyone who acts in ways which deny standards of conduct is clearly ignorant. By the same logic, a decent man who fulfills his obligations and acts with self-restraint is assumed to be knowledgeable. Such assumptions are frequently contradicted by the experience of individuals who, by their performance in rituals, reveal their considerable familiarity with traditional forms but whose behavior toward others is consistent maltreatment.

Such a personage is Jose Kadegare, a member of the prestigious Bado Jebage Xebigewuge Xobugiwuge subclan. The name-groups of this unit provide the incumbent of the ritual office of Noapayepa, second in ceremonial importance only to Bakorokudu, who comes from the clan's other division. Noapayepa may even, as the Bororo put it, "go in the place of Bakorokudu" on some occasions. The participation of these two ceremonial personalities is essential to nearly all major ceremonies. The men who fulfill the roles enjoy considerable prestige which, if they are adroit politicians, can be translated into effective villagewide authority. But both offices demand very considerable knowledge, since they, and especially that of Bakorokudu, demand the singing of numerous long chants and the formal direction of the ceremonies that these songs accompany.

No one in the village doubted that among the men of both subclans of the Bado Jebage Xebigewuge, Kadegare was the most versed in traditional lore. But at the same time, his conduct led to widespread mistrust of his personal morality. He had married a woman of his own moiety, a Bokodori Exerae, and had built her a house some 50 meters outside the village (but in direct line with the position occupied by her subclan in the village circle), an almost unknown aberrancy. He was constantly embroiled in quarrels with his fellow clan and moiety members, generally over money and other Brazilian artifacts he lent them. He had an explosive temper, quite against the Bororo norm for masculine self-restraint and dignity, and was reputed to be pathologically jealous of his wife. Finally he was a shaman, a bizarre one at that, as I show in later chapters. So the village was thoroughly ambivalent about his playing the role of Noapayepa. Their compromise was to let him do this about half the time, giving the status alternately to a young man who, even if completely incompetent ritually, was at least generally obedient to the canons of Bororo morality.

The decision on who is to be the ritual subclan chief (*emijera*) is actually made not by members of the group but by persons in the other moiety. They designate whom they wish to play the relevant ceremonial role by giving him the necessary ceremonial equipment. Of course, they respect the sentiments of the group members, who confidentially make their preferences known to their close relatives in the other moiety. Indeed, the men married into the subclan—its "fathers," categorically and empirically—are the crucial mediators between their own social groups and their wives' clans, and often exercise effective control over which of their affines is to be formal head of the household in which they dwell. This power constitutes in an informal but effective way the return for all the services they render their wife's clan and partly explains the great cordiality between masculine affines. Since, as the case of Kadegare demonstrates, the selection of an *emijera* is not permanent and does not confer, in itself, any increment of moral authority, the Bororo have considerable latitude for playing out a series of complex, subtle political games. Perhaps the most surprising aspect of the system is that in the majority of cases at Korugedu Paru the choice of subclan chiefs and male household heads was very easy, there being one man in each group so clearly qualified on both moral and symbolic grounds that his selection was almost automatic.

The chiefs and all the other nonresident male members of the subclan/household have a series of obligations toward their parents, sisters, sisters' children, and all other residents. The most consequential of these is to ensure that the group's ceremonial obligations are carried out. They themselves, especially the chiefs, must perform the principal ritual roles in these, always assisted by their sisters' husbands. They must ensure that the household has sufficient materials and vegetable foods for the prestations, although in practice most households are self-sufficient in this regard. Outside of ceremonial contexts, they should collaborate with the female head and her husband to ensure adequacy of food and the means necessary to produce it. Brothers especially must provide for their unmarried sisters and their dependents. This is the source of numerous conflicts between spouses and between siblings, since a man's labor and its products must be shared between two households, with both sister and wife usually claiming to receive less than they deserve. Toward his sister's children a man has a number of important ritual and pragmatic duties, symbolized in the relationship of name-giver (i-edaga). As he provides the corporate membership and the social "soul" conveyed in the proper names, the mother's brother is constrained to ensure that the child grows up properly instructed in Bororo ways and that his material well-being is assured. He acts, in short, something like a spiritual godparent. As we have seen, the mother's brother/i-edaga should pass along his esoteric knowledge to his sister's son, his name-receiver (i-wagedu). In return for this care, the sister's children owe their i-edaga respect and material support in his old age. It would be a falsification of Bororo thinking, however, to say that the mother's brother has jural authority over his sister's children, or over the junior members of his matrilineal subclan. Depending on personalities and historical circumstances, he may at most come to have a certain moral influence over them. Even then, men are far more likely to heed their fathers, and girls their mothers, than they are their maternal uncles. The relationship is not especially prone to conflict, quite the contrary. This is due principally to the way in which the Bororo locate jural responsibility and authority within the generation, rather than between it.

The relations between siblings and parallel consanguines are complex both normatively and in practice, as has already been indicated. First, the Bororo hold that birth order and relative age provide the structure for all relationships between clan members of the same generation, considerably outweighing degrees of consanguinity. The eldest born has complete moral responsibility and formal authority over all younger siblings, real and classificatory, within the subclan. In principle, his position applies throughout the clan and even the moiety, but, in fact, his peers in other social units are jealous of their own spheres of authority, to the extent that there is bitter although covert rivalry between the senior members of social groups in the same moiety. The elder brother is obliged for the delicts of his younger siblings, no matter now minor or grave these might be. In the most extreme and rare case, that of murder within the clan and moiety, he should kill the murderer, even if it should be his own younger brother. More usually, he must see to it that material debts and indemnities incurred by his siblings are paid, even if he must use his own resources to do so, which is common. He should superintend the marriages of his brothers and sisters, even having the authority to terminate a sister's marriage should the husband be cruel to her. His brothers' wives bring their grievances against their husbands to him, and he is obliged to carry out the pater's role for their children if this should be defaulted. And, of course, he must perform all the personal and categorical ritual duties his siblings and their social group are responsible for. In theory, then, the elder brother is the subclan/household's legal guardian and tutelary *emijera*.

Actually many Bororo males find the position of elder brother to be so onerous and demanding that its rewards of public prestige do not begin to compensate for its burdens. As with the position of *emijera,* criteria of personal ability and willingness are at least as important in determining the identity of the public "elder brother" (*i-mana*) as relative age. The status is consequently very mobile. An additional reason for this inconstancy results from the Bororo lack of any institutionalized age-set system. Theoretically the children of one's mother's siblings within the subclan constitute one's generation, but the general Bororo vagueness about genealogical details is fully operative in the age context. The crux of the system lies in the distinction between elder brother and mother's brother (*i-edaga*), which designate very different relationships indeed. The contrast is nearly always subject to historical modification as the actors' social roles change through time. A man who is an *i-edaga* during childhood fades into an *i-mana* with young adulthood and the acquisition of personal political and ritual status, only to become an *i-edaga* again as he becomes enfeebled and unable to carry out his various duties. In most households the individual recognized by an older brother as *i-mana* is likely to be his younger brother's *i-edaga*. As usual with the Bororo, the precision and apparent rigidity of the formal scheme is merely a flexible guide for the shifting flux of personal relationships through time, with actual positions of formal authority as much determined by these subtle temporal processes as determining them. The system of relative age only barely controls the competition among siblings. Indeed, by affirming that there must be an absolute ranking among them, it might even be said to foster conflict.

The Bororo equation of age with authority has to do with their assumptions about the mechanics of time, knowledge, and *raka*. Their usual response when asked why the elder brother should "go first," why he was considered to have the wisdom and resources necessary for his role, was that having been born first, he had had simply more time to acquire

A clan chief (who was often a village chief)

these capacities than his siblings. Further, the firstborn son of the union of young parents is considered to be munificently provided with *raka,* which endows him with the physical capacity to excel in all activities a man must perform, including intellectual ones. As the nominal heir to the subclan's *emijera* at the time of his birth, he would have received special instruction in traditional knowledge throughout his childhood. Recognizing his favored position, his father and subclan chiefs in the other moiety would make special efforts toward his moral and ritual education. The siblings who came after him would be less and less imbued with *raka,* decreasingly treated with special attention, unable in any wise to regain the temporal ground lost in their later birth. Actually, Bororo expectations with regard to seniority and ability act as a self-fulfilling prophecy; thus, in spite of various outstanding individual cases disproving these assumptions, they are in the main confirmed.

Most *emijera* (chiefs) are among the firstborn of their generation within the clan; they tend to be extraordinary personalities marked by dignified self-confidence and great intelligence. Their characters and abilities have impressed generations of Western observers (Baldus 1937; Lévi-Strauss 1936; Albisetti and Venturelli 1962: 0:12–0:17). The consistency and thoroughness with which Bororo society produces such men is not at all mysterious. The entire system is based on the assumption that intellectual attainments, personal morality, and administrative abilities are indissoluble elements of a single characterological whole, and it devotes its energies to validating this assumption. Younger brothers have thus some reason to be bitter, cantankerous individuals; as one informant said, "Envy stops up their ears, they do not listen to their *i-mana*'s counsels, and they go on from one stupidity to another."

The position of the in-married male, he who is at once a husband, a father, a daughter's husband, has been alluded to piecemeal and must now be summarized. Far more than other sexual and social roles, this one undergoes a series of historical transformations through time. Initially, his public attitude and even physical participation in the marriage is apt to be a denial that it exists at all. No public ceremony attends Bororo marriages, which are initiated (outside of the men's house associates) by a woman's gift of food to a bachelor. If he accepts it, they are considered married. For some time he may join his wife in her hut only late at night, disappearing before dawn. He does owe her, and her housemates, almost the entirety of his production, which amounts to all game and fish he kills. Gradually the village becomes aware of the union, and slowly he begins to participate in the daily life of the household. Unions are so fragile that many do not even reach this stage. Of those that do, a substantial number are terminated within a year or two. When the first child is born there is a marked tendency for the marriage to stabilize. After a man has made a child for his wife's clan, his obligations and his rights toward his affines markedly increase (Crocker 1969b). He is now expected to take a very active responsibility in assisting his affines in the performance of their ritual duties. He and his spouse are apt to contract particular ceremonial duties toward members of the other moiety (that is, the husband's own) who represent deceased members of her clan. These involve frequent prestations of cooked food and ornaments, nearly all of which he must provide.

As his children mature, the husband is treated with increasing respect by his wife's brothers, whose political-ritual status he begins to determine. All the while he develops a special relationship with his wife's father, whom he terms *i-edaga*. As one might suppose, the explicit norms for this connection are the same as those for the mother's brother/name-giver. But in this case the social distance and focus on ritual abilities which mark the matrilineal tie are transformed by the close association of daily living and mutual responsibility inherent in the affinal one. Nearly all stable wife's father–daughter's husband relations among the Bororo are marked by a warmth and mutual trust found otherwise only in the father-son bond. The two men collaborate in their economic affairs, assisting one another in their gardens, hunting together, and ensuring that the household be able to supply the raw materials needed for the rituals it sponsors. Together they assume responsibility for elderly members of their wives' subclan and for its orphans, often coming to act effectively as father and grandfather for these last. Owing to their close association in discharging the household's ceremonial duties, the son-in-law often comes to supplant effectively his *i-edaga*'s proper sister's son as the heir to his esoteric knowledge. As the older man becomes less able to hunt and to farm, the younger gradually assumes both his economic and symbolic duties, but with no sense of acceding to his authority within the domestic group. He continues to defer to the *i-edaga*'s judgments until the latter's demise, or until senility has made them inconsequential.

The character of this relationship is linked to a number of factors. First, the two members are definitionally of different generations, so that there is no element of moral authority in it; nor does the position of wife's father contain any elements of creditor, which are entirely held by the wife's brothers.

Second, the *i-edaga* is only exceptionally a member of his daughter's husband's clan. Unlike the Shavante, who prefer that co-clansmen marry into the same household (Maybury-Lewis 1974: 100), the Bororo seek actively to avoid such duplication of affinal ties, especially within generations but also between them. A matrilateral cross-cousin is classed in the kinship term which contains daughters and brothers' daughters (*aredu*), toward whom one has the obligations of a father. The more usual category for a potential wife is *i-maruga,* a term which is applied to all female members of the father's clan, as well as to the wife's mother. Actually, the statistics available on marital choice reflect only a very slight predominance of the patrilateral cross-cousin (Crocker 1967). Usually the wife's father and daughter's husband are of different clans, or at least different subclans. Consequently, they have no reason to compete for the same scarce resources of prestige and symbolic goods, access to which are confined to clan members.

Thirdly, the relationship is strongly marked by the position of intruder into a closed matrilineal world which both men occupy, even after the passage of many years and their procreation of members of this world. The categorical opposition between male and female, as well as the obstacles more specific to the conjugal relationship discussed at the beginning of the section, unite the in-married males against the collective menace presented by their wives and children. If the substances of symbolic identity and shared privacy set aside the household as a unique organic and cosmological group, it is divided within itself through the different consequences this organic unity implies for male and female members. Such a division is expressed during the funeral ceremony or during birth, when the in-married males are apt to move collectively but temporarily to the men's house until the dangers contained in the matrilineal home have passed.

Finally, both the wife's parents realize that their well-being in old age depends largely upon the goodwill of their son-in-law. It is to their interest to integrate him into the household, and their frequent failure to do so, as represented by the constant divorce of "fathers," is a reminder of the tact and forbearance necessary to its achievement.

If relationships between parents-in-law and their daughter's husband tend to be characterized by goodwill and lack of conflict, those between members of the same generation within the household could hardly be worse. The tendency of sisters and female collaterals to have separate residences has already been described. Actually, in some cases, when disparate in age or very differently related to the household heads, women of the same generation and the same subclan manage to coexist relatively peacefully under the same roof for some years. This is especially true when one or the other is divorced or childless and when both parents remain married and co-resident, since father, mother, and elder brother together exert a considerable amount of control over their female relatives' actions. But even such "sisters" tend to drift apart with increasing age. There is really practically nothing of mutual concern to motivate their co-residence, save sentimental ties with the parents, and these are soon overridden by the perception that their self-interests are implacably opposed. This is due to the way they must compete for their parents' and brother' preference and to the structured opposition between their children. After all, one of them must be chosen at least tentatively as the potential heir of the household's *emijera,* one of the sisters' brothers or mothers' brothers. Although a woman's status is not in the least tied to that of her brother or son, no more than that of her husband, she is sensible of the rules of male competition, and reluctant to see her sister gain even such a secondhand victory over her.

Clan sisters find one another an especial threat to the solidarity of their marriages. Given the fragility of most unions, the normative approval of sororal succession in marriage, and the intimate propinquity afforded by the household, their fears are not in the least unfounded. Of some fifteen divorces during fieldwork, ten were occasioned by the wife's accusation of her co-resident real or classificatory sister as her husband's paramour. Or, as a male informant said, with at once sheepishness and sly pride, "Children born in the household look like all the men who live there," implying that all the in-marrying males contribute their idiosyncratic *raka* to its genesis.

As this might imply, men married to sisters affinally co-resident in the same household have very troubled relationships indeed. Not only do their wives and wives' relatives invidiously compare them, they discover that their wives' father, structurally their only ally within the group, is judging their abilities with an equally critical eye. Or else one husband is a much younger and later arrival, thoroughly disadvantaged by his predecessor's secure position in the residential group. So much is the relationship contradictory to the household's practices, that a term for "wife's sister's husband" was given with difficulty by most informants. While the Bororo do not explicitly prohibit men of the same subclan marrying "sisters," such an occurrence is rare; even the most naive Bororo male would not compound his problems with his elder brother by becoming co-resident with him. But to the extent that their wives occupy different structural positions in the residential group, the relation of their husbands is eased. Such difference in the wives' relative status may be brought about by contrasts in age, or by an extremely distant collaterality, or simply through one woman's accession to the other's dominance. The relative ages and potentials of previously born children may also affect these relations. Even though such factors may mitigate the actual relationships of the household's in-married males, ultimately they seem to find it necessary to change their residence or to terminate their marriage. Once again, there are few constraints to either action. The enduring relationships resulting from the union are those with its offspring, the wife's brothers, and their parents, and these endure beyond the marriage itself. The structural conditions facilitating intervillage mobility have already been discussed. In brief, it is not surprising that over 80 percent of Bororo households include no more than one in-married male of the same generation.

So goes the development of the Bororo household. Once established within its feminine dominion, men find themselves menaced by cosmological dangers and caught up in social strife. Obliged by the principles of Bororo structure and by political self-interest to maintain cordial relations with their male affines, they must undertake the economic maintenance of the entire household, including its aged and young dependents and the unmarried adult sisters of their spouse. They must accomplish the bulk of the work necessary for the group's fulfillment of its ceremonial duties, using up in the process their own scarce non-utilitarian wealth. The natal household continues to demand their active participation in its affairs and a share of their productive effort.

Their performance of these manifold obligations is roundly criticized on all fronts. Their wives deceive them facilely with their own brothers, and then complain about the husband's inadequacy as a provider of food and of such goods as dresses, cooking pots, and blankets. In return for all their efforts they receive, finally, a child, and see in it the reproduction of their organic selves and the sign of their own aging mortality. Little wonder that in one of the most important *aroe* representations, that of the *Aije,* the men attack the women's huts with balls of white mud and threats of physical violence. Nor is it surprising that most men cannot long endure their conjugal situations; they return to the men's house, only to commence a new marriage some months later. It is not that males cannot survive economically without a wife, quite the opposite. But the social system is predicated on the necessity of having affines, an *i-edaga,* and above all sons. And the Bororo define human nature in such a way that marriage is the only way to achieve personal integration (Crocker 1969b, 1977c). No matter that this integration is flawed by its internal contradictions; it still must be pursued. Finally, marriage provides the only set of rules by which the actions generated by *raka,* and the dangers to the self which result from them, can be safely controlled. The inevitability of marriage is as much inherent in Bororo structure as its strifes and fraility.

capuchin monkeys

# 3

꥟

# Sexual Dialectics

In this section Bororo life stages are outlined, with emphasis on their crises and social stresses, in order to show the diachronic aspect of matters which until now have been described synchronically. My intention is to show how the dynamics of these stages reflect principles of metonymy, or relations of contiguity in time and space, as expressed through the logic of *raka*.

After it has received a name, the Bororo child is fully integrated into the household's activities. He accompanies his mother and her sisters on gathering expeditions into the forest and is taken along by his parents when they go to work on their gardens. He is apt to spend much time in the company of his grandparents and to be cared for by all the mature women of the household. As he becomes older and begins to imitate in play behavior appropriate to his sex, he becomes increasingly the responsibility of his older same-sex siblings within the household. By the time she is eight or nine, for example, a girl is likely to be occupied all day long with the three- to seven-year-old daughters of her mother and aunts. Even at these young ages children are constantly given small household tasks: bringing water from the stream, helping in the preparation of vegetable food, gathering dead wood for the fire, weeding in the garden. By seven or eight most boys are able to hunt and fish for the smaller prey, and their contributions to the household's food supply are much praised and encouraged. But from infancy on, children are constantly taught to remain within their own household's area, never venturing onto the neighboring space, let alone into other residences. If they cause some small problem there—interfering with cooking, perhaps—severe recriminations will follow from its resident women. Children are explicitly forbidden to play with neighboring children, for if they hurt them, their mother's brother or their own elder adult brother will have to pay an indemnity to the victim and his or her parents. This is not a serious affair economically, but it does bring shame upon the household, which is always being invidiously compared to and by its neighbors. Only after ten or so, when both boys and girls begin to manifest their personalities independently from their maternal residences, do children of the same moiety begin to associate frequently.

Given the very high incidence of childhood illness, Bororo children quickly and frequently experience the household's handling of individual affliction. A sick child, even an orphan, is the center of solicitous concern. The customary Bororo response to any hurt or unhappiness in a child is to hold him or her while pressing gently with both hands over the body and limbs. A sick child is passed from one adult member of the residence to the next for this treatment all day long. The father seeks out the services of a shaman and spends his days gathering wild medicines. This attention not only reflects the general Bororo love for children but also is based on the assumption that the child is sick through no fault of its own. It has so little *raka* yet that the illness cannot be self-pollution. Nor do the *bope* directly attack children, whom they know are not yet fully responsible for their actions.

Nearly always the child's illness comes from some misdeed by one of the household's adult members. They may have offended the *bope* in some manner, and these spirits do not hesitate to punish a parent by afflicting his or her child, or any child resident in the offender's household. Or a married couple in the household may have been careless during the wife's menstrual period, so that food and drink were contaminated and caused the child to be sick. Or the illness might be caused by the child's accidental consumption of game surcharged with *raka* and improperly treated by the shaman or badly cooked. Generally, then, the adult-child vectors of affliction are direct physical pollutions, coming about through failure to observe all the rules for the safe handling of *raka* and through the sharing of a common place and substances which characterizes the household. This also means that siblings as such represent no mystical danger for the child, at least until puberty. After the beginnings of sexual life, their *raka* has the same menace for an ego as that of other co-residents, but for the same reasons of immediate contact, not for any bond reflecting the mystical connections of consanguinity.

Very occasionally a child will be afflicted by either the *bope* or the *aroe* not as a punishment but as a mode of spiritual experience. The most dramatic case of this during fieldwork occurred when the four-year-old son of Kahojo suddenly collapsed one day in a nervous fit. He remained unconscious, cold, and clammy for over an hour. Medically he exhibited all the symptoms of a grand-mal epileptic seizure and responded to treatment for it. Socially, the Bororo interpreted his seizure as due to the *aroe* taking away his soul in order that they could initiate it to the spirit world. This is the first sign of an individual's selection as a shaman of the *aroe*. His household was one of the most traditional in the village. His father, Kanojo, and grandfather, Ugo, were both subclan *emijera,* well-informed about the *aroe* and frequently in contact with them. It was, in short, precisely the kind of household that might be expected to produce a shaman of the *aroe*. The village was extremely pleased that one of these specialists might be produced among them. The parents and close relatives were, however, terrified, fearing especially that the child was too young for such violent contacts with the spirits. In sum, then, neither *bope* nor *aroe* inflict a child volitionally save as a positive act, to communicate to them some special power. The symbolic associations between childhood, lack of *raka,* and the *aroe* will be set out in Chapters 10 and 11.

In all the general innocuousness of children's contact with the *aroe* and the general permissiveness with which they are raised, there is one glaring exception, the rite of the *barae etawuje,* or "representation of the civilized one." This ceremony occurs about once a month in the traditional villages of the middle São Lourenço, and it is anticipated by children, even those nearing puberty, with marked emotional ambiguity in which pure terror predominates. The *barae etawuje* is said by adults to be the appearance in the village of an old, evil Brazilian who lives alone off in the mountains or in the distant forests, who is a kind of ogre that eats up children who fail to obey their parents and near relatives. This monster is an *aroe,* one of the totems of the Bokodori Exerae clan, but its representation occurs outside all other ritual contexts and may be performed by anyone. The explicit purpose of the *barae*'s appearance in the village is to frighten the children into good behavior. The performer is nearly always a woman of the Exerae moiety, who dresses up in old castoff Brazilian male clothes with her face completely masked. She, or "it," hobbles around with a staff, falls over things, and generally acts like a buffoon. It chases the children, demanding if they have been good, and their parents relate whatever mischief and disobedience they have committed since the *barae*'s last visit. Older children laugh hysterically and tease the *barae,* but younger children are terrified. Their mothers, to whom they run screaming for protection, hand them over to the *barae*

The "old Brazilian" terrifying children

when it approaches. Adults generally regard the whole farce, including the children's reactions, as exceedingly comical. Between the visits of the *barae* naughty children are told they will be given to the monster upon its next visit, and such threats obviously frighten them very much.

The rite is an anomaly in many respects. The ludicrous behavior of the *barae* itself is not unique, for the actors in other *aroe* representations (that of the "Meridabo Etawuje," "Wild Dogs," for example) also act comically. However, the inevitable transvestism of the actor is limited to the *barae etawuje* and is regarded as essential to it. Women never represent *aroe* other than in this case. In all other contexts the Bororo are very gentle and kind to children, never punishing them physically. I think this is one element in the sexual inversion and use of a Brazilian figure: such behavior toward children is so thoroughly un-Bororo that it can only come from a thing which is completely opposite normal social categories. The extreme old age of the figure and its comic feebleness reflect Bororo views of age as physically disgusting and ludicrous. The clumsiness of old people is very funny, and Bororo anecdotes often are stories of some especially maladroit behavior coming from physical decrepitude (or lack of *raka*). But children are noted for their grace and agility. There seems to be a structural opposition between youth and age, then, and the *barae etawuje* employs this for the sake of social morality, always the concern of the *aroe* and of men. The transvestism reflects this last association, in expressing the complementary roles of males and females in the rearing of children. Men, whether fathers or mothers' brothers, are morally responsible for the public conduct of their younger relatives, whereas women must care for the child's growth and physical well-being. But there is also an element of sexual antagonism in the inversion, an assertion that only a member of the sex opposite that of the actor's would behave so horribly toward a child, tempered by the fact that "it" is, after all, a *Brazilian* man.

Aside from these visits, and the recurring crises of sickness, Bororo spend what appear to be happy and uncomplicated childhoods. If the relationship with the mother is unstable and likely to rupture, the mother's sisters and their husbands are willing and adroit stepparents. The crucial relationship with the father is only lightly affected if he divorces the mother. In most cases the genitor-pater has an extremely intimate bond with his son which endures through the lives of both men, and is a much more important factor in determining village residence than marriage. If the father is dead or otherwise unable to carry out his role, the mother's brother/name-giver takes over the pater's duties in addition to those incumbent on his own relationship. Further, both the *i-edaga* and the *i-maruga* of the birth-naming ritual have a special moral responsibility and a certain authority over the child. These derive from their relationship to the child's soul; thus, they must ensure that he or she develop proper standards of Bororo morality, which, as we have seen, are themselves associated with knowledge of the *aroe*—that is, of the myths, rituals, chants, and ornaments concerning these spirits.

The pater and mater in their turn are more obligated to ensure the child's abilities in utilitarian activities appropriate to its sex. A father instructs his son in hunting and fishing techniques and in the construction of bows, arrows, nets, traps, and so forth.[19] The daughter learns cooking, gathering, and farming from her mother. There is consequently no conflict in the parent–cross-sex sibling relationship to the child. Mother's brother and father collaborate on different aspects of the sister's son/son's developing social personality, just as their ritual and practical duties to his clan are differentiated and complementary. As one informant said, "The father makes a bow for his son, and the mother's brother gives him his dance bracelets." The only cause of difficulty in these relationships occurs when there is more than one son: brothers must compete for the attention both of father and of mother's brother. The Bororo often attempt to mitigate this in advance by having different maternal relatives serve as successive name-givers for a woman's children, but the father is still left with divided responsibilities.

As children begin to participate early in the household's economic life, so they are included in its ceremonial activities. When, for example, the members of a subclan are invited to be decorated as *aroe* by the members of a group in the other moiety, the children, even toddlers of one or two years old, are included. Very great pains are taken with the children's decoration, and they are considered very beautiful when the painting is completed, the objects of villagewide pride and admiration. Further, one of the most lauded and common acts of a father is to send his son or daughter to be decorated in his place, when his own maternal subclan or he himself should receive some *aroe* painting. Mother's brothers, especially when they have no children of their own, do the same. Both men also have the right to ornament their children with the paintings and decorations of their own maternal clans. Thus, a child can represent the *aroe* of all clans in both moieties: those of the father that he himself gives it; those of other clans in the opposite moiety when they decorate the child's subclan; those of its own subclan, thanks to the mother's brother; those of other units in its own moiety when they give an *aroe* presentation to the father and/or his subclan. This point has considerable significance, because adults practically never represent the *aroe* of their own moiety and never those of their own maternal clan or subclan. By substituting for their father, children enter into intimate contact with the entities that

A mother's brother ornamenting a sister's son

define the symbolic character of those neighboring households and sub-clans which they are otherwise forbidden to enter. This use of agnatic ties to facilitate relations in the moiety is a fundamental element in Bororo society and will be encountered in later chapters (cf. also Crocker 1977b, 1977c, 1979). The other, more general implication of these ornamentations is that before puberty, children's contacts with the domain of mystical forces, the *bope* and the *aroe,* is essentially limited to the *aroe.*

In other terms, until sexual life has begun, until *raka* begins its most characteristic functioning, the *bope* are irrelevant to one's existence. Since these forces, and their agency *raka,* control all aspects of serial change, of "natural" time, children inhabit a timeless, immortal, and static world of pure form. It is consistent for them to represent the *aroe,* the principles of this world, so frequently and to be otherwise so closely associated with them. There is one exception to this: the immature young are not allowed even to see the most powerful of the *aroe,* the *aije,* when they are impersonated by men. But neither are women, for these spirits are associated with masculine vitality and the opposition of male to female. It is, in fact, introduction into this mystery of the *aije* that constitutes Bororo initiation. The Bororo life cycle thus is marked by the very sharp transition of puberty. Childhood, existence within the maternal households with limited contacts with other social units, is a period dominated by the nominal, transcendental forms of the *aroe,* of only random external contact with the dangers of pollution and self-injury contained in *raka.* In the Bororo scheme children do not "grow up"; they are ageless. But with adolescence all this changes; personal time begins with the operation of *raka,* the commencement of sexual life. The residential group changes its character; from the purity and beauty of the *aroe,* to the blood and death and corruption of the *bope.* For girls the natal household itself is thus transformed; for boys, the change is accompanied by a physical transition to the huts of the other moiety. The question is why, and it must be answered in terms consistent with the logical patterns and conceptual systems already analyzed in this chapter.

# Initiation:
# The Redoubling of Self

As soon as a boy begins to show the physical signs of puberty, his uncles and father begin to prepare for his initiation. Formerly this was a year-long process, much of it passed with the initiates in seclusion in a forest camp. Nowadays it is considerably abbreviated but always includes a period of intensive instruction in myths and rituals involving the *aroe* given by all the chiefs of the village. The terminal ceremony features the initiate's introduction to the *aije,* which until now he is supposed to have considered actual monsters that visit the community at the end of the funeral cycle. He is shown the bullroarers which imitate the cries of these monsters and which the Bororo explicitly compare to giant phalluses. Finally, he is given a penis sheath by a previously initiated father's sister's son, who has sustained and encouraged him through the ceremony. He and this agnatic relative, a masculine counterpart to the *i-maruga* of initiation, call each other *i-orubadari* ("sponsor").

The ritual relationship marked by this term is one of the most important in adult male life. It is considered extremely suitable to marry the sponsor's sister (i.e., a father's sister's daughter for the initiate, a mother's brother's daughter for the initiator). Indeed, the sponsor calls the penis sheath he gives "*a-tawuje,*" "your wife." With it he conveys not just marital rights over his sister but rights to the sexuality of all women in his own moiety, that opposite the initiate's (Crocker 1969b). For after initiation the young man can join the bachelors of his own moiety in abducting any young girl of the opposite moiety and installing her as their sexual companion in the men's house. Marriage with the sponsor's sister, if it occurs at all, comes much later, at least traditionally. Actually, few Bororo seem to have married genealogical patrilateral cross-cousins, and marriage into the father's clan is only slightly more common than unions with members of the other three clans in the opposite moiety. Thus it seems that the *i-orubadari*'s gesture and statement convey general sexual rights over a socially defined class of women rather than over those belonging to a specific social group or a genealogically defined category.

Furthermore, the reciprocity inherent in the sponsoring relationship is much more imbued with the symmetry of cross-moiety *aroe* relationships than with the asymmetry of affinal ones. Sponsors decorate each other with the *aroe* designs and ornaments of each other's clans (that is, A decorates B as A's own maternal *aroe*). They may even sleep together in the men's house, for after initiation neither can pass the night again in his own natal household.[20] Finally, when one dies, the other becomes his ritual replacement, or "new soul," *aroe maiwu.* As such he assumes certain aspects of his dead friend's social personality, most especially his filial obligations to support his aged parents. The intimacy of this relationship, above all the way each man literally and symbolically becomes the other, synthesizes into a single bond the varied characteristics of both the relationships with the father and with the mother's brother. It consequently is the focus of numerous myths and much personal commentary on historic examples. In practice the bond is a very real and important one in the lives of Bororo men. It stands in almost complete opposition to the jealousies and bitterness of relations with brothers and members of one's own moiety. And it also contrasts with the conflicts of interests and mystical dangers that characterize marriages and existence in the conjugal household. The *i-orubadari* relationship is superlatively the mark of youth and life in the men's house. As such it stands as the third element in the structure which otherwise includes the natal and conjugal residences—and is unique to itself.

Bororo say that a boy must not be allowed to sleep in his parents' house after he has begun his own sexual life and that therefore he must be initiated and sent to live in the men's house. They can offer no explanation of this necessity, other than it would be "wrong" and possibly damaging to all parties' health. In one myth (M5; in Lévi-Strauss 1969: 59–63) a pubescent boy refuses to be initiated. His "*i-maruga*" (interpreted by informants as the *i-maruga* of birth and name-giving) makes him ill by flatulating into his nostrils every night while he is asleep. (Flatulence is most abhorred by the Bororo, who associate it with the digesting food in the intestinal tract and term its stench "*jerimaga,*" the smell they also perceive in sexual fluids and in corruption generally.) The boy discovers her activities and kills her one night by thrusting a sharpened club up her anus. He then buries her body surreptitiously in the hut, with the help of various species of armadillos, all strongly associated with the *aroe*. He himself is transformed into an anthill, often the dwelling place of certain kinds of *bope*.

This myth reveals not only the *i-maruga*'s obligation to ensure her *i-wagedu*'s compliance with traditional norms, especially as these involve the *aroe*, but her use of the powers of *raka* to punish his failure to comply with these. Further, the lethal effects of the maternal hut's organic products upon the boy who fails to leave their sphere indicates some fundamental opposition between masculine and parental generative powers. This involves much more than a kind of mechanical conflict between their respective *raka*, for there is no indication that the dangers of mutual pollution actually increase after a son's puberty. The Bororo state that the parents are "ashamed" to have their adolescent son in the household, for "he might hear and smell their copulations." Shame (*pagudu*) among the Bororo is inherent in all anomalous human acts but especially characterizes those in which the operations of one's *raka* become either socially or physically visible. The parents of a newborn child are said to have much "shame," for example, and thus attempt to conceal the birth for as long as they can. But since the parents' shame clearly does not extend to their daughter's own experience of sexuality, the reasons for their son's exclusion from their conjugal life must have to do more with the social than the natural character of male sexuality.

I think these reasons involve two elements linked with the different social implications of male and female sexuality. Women are subject to the periodicity of their menses, which associates them with other manifestations of *raka*'s natural rhythms. As the bearers of physical transformations, their powers must be controlled through their physical permanence in one segment of the village circle and with the nontemporal permanence of the *aroe* categories which define the social character of these units. But men, who must directly create symbolic order through their dealings with the *aroe*, must have the freedom to transcend the definitional limits of their physical existence, determined as it is by the mother's own social nature.

Further, the son's sexuality will ultimately produce a creature physically resembling himself but of a social category which stands in opposition to that occupied by himself, his mother, and sister. Moreover, his sexual rights are over those women who share both physical substance (*raka*) and social identity with his father. To enjoy these rights literally under his father's nose amounts to a kind of incest. That is, father and son employ their sexuality in mutually exclusive fields. These must be maintained spatially as well as physically separate. A daughter, on the other hand, is subject to the same rules of exogamy as led the mother to her union with the father. There is nothing contradictory in her obeying those rules in bringing her lovers to her maternal and paternal home.

Finally, the basic reason, I believe, for the intimacy between father and son among the Bororo is the categorical interdiction on their sexual competition. A man gives up his mother and sister to the males of the other moiety in return for free sexual access to their own female relatives. This reciprocal contract is in effect negated if males from opposite moieties exercise their sexual rights within the same domestic unit, associated as it is with continuities of natural and social identity. The right of masculine sexual access to a femininely defined territory must be his "foreignness" to it, and he is hardly an outsider to his own natal household. It is for this reason that the Bororo find something obscenely contradictory in the sexually active male remaining under the parental roof, and why the *aroe,* who concern themselves above all with the intermoiety regulation of sexuality, are involved in the mythic case of a transgression against this rule. Or, in other terms, it is the social terms which define the categorical nature of one's *raka,* or rather its consequences, and not the physical nature of that substance in oneself and the others from whom it derives, that determine masculine exclusion from the parental household.

After initiation, then, a man must live in the men's house. But no such social and ritual expression of female puberty takes place. To be sure, some years before puberty is expected to occur she has her ears pierced by her *i-edaga,* with the same kind of *baragara* (ritual dagger) used to perforate her brother's lower lip. This usually occurs during the final rituals of an initiation, which is to say as part of the terminal funeral ceremonies. After this operation, which permits her to wear the earrings often given by men to their mistresses, she may commence sexual life, but with none of the public spectacle or, apparently, private sentiment which accompanies a male's comparable transition. However she behaves, the Bororo are convinced that her first menses are associated with her sexual activity. They deny that a woman can menstruate except after intercourse, although they likewise find no physical connection between the two kinds of events. Defloration does not bring about menstruation, nor are the monthly courses in any way related to amount or intensity of a woman's sexual activity. "It is a mystery of the *bope,*" say informants. Girls seem to have their first sexual experiences very early, as young as eight or nine. In one village a girl of ten or so was married to a man in his late thirties, with the somewhat reluctant approval of her parents but general public opprobrium. After various affairs most women have their first public marriages around fifteen or sixteen. This first union seldom lasts more than several months or a year, for, informants said, "she has not yet learned to be a wife," meaning her demands upon her husband

Daily life in the men's house

were likely to be very unrealistic and troublesome. After several such attempts the majority of girls appear to enter into a relatively stable union marked by the appearance of children, which may last five years or a decade, or even longer.

The unstable quality of conjugal relations among the Bororo has been mentioned, but neither its causes nor its character have been described. Most domestic quarrels originate in one spouse's alleged failure to fulfill some marital responsibility, especially duties concerning the production and preparation of food. Thus the husband should provide game or fish daily; the wife is supposed to bring in vegetable foods, wild or cultivated, just as often. In practice neither spouse has to work this hard, since they share in the foods gained by other members of the household and in the cooked dishes given by other households. The Bororo eat two main meals a day, with almost continuous snacking throughout the day and night. The morning meal is largely vegetable, featuring gruel made from corn, manioc or rice, and beans (the last three being cultigens introduced by the Brazilians), plus whatever protein might be left over from the preceding day. The evening meal should ideally have a large game animal or fish as its main dish, accompanied by the fruits of palm or the cashew tree, wild tubers, or nuts. But the pattern changes from day to day and from season to season. The Bororo have no fixed concepts about either the symbolic or the esthetic composition of menus, and must be among the worst cooks in the world.[21]

The crucial social element in the spouses' relation to food is their mutual complementarity in its preparation and consumption. That is, it is far more important for the husband to provide any form of wild game, and his wife to get vegetables and to cook the meal carefully, than it is for the meal to contain various categories of food or be abundant. Husbands complain about ill-cleaned and badly cooked food (with considerable reason), about meals being late or eaten in their absence. Wives legitimately demand that their husbands secure more game. Since both getting and cooking food is a household rather than a conjugal affair, complaints usually involve other members of the household, either explicitly or by implication. Thus, a husband's ill humor with his wife's cooking offends his mother-in-law and wife's sister, who do not hesitate to retaliate with long lists of his own shortcomings.

Men seem to be, in fact, more usually incensed over their spouses' failure to distribute cooked dishes properly than angered over their preparation. As mentioned earlier, a man should provide his parents, unmarried sisters, and i-edagas with a certain amount of their nourishment. The distribution of most large game animals is governed by very precise rules concerning the allocation of its various parts to the agnatic, matrilineal, affinal, and ritual relatives of the hunter. Furthermore, a "good" man should see to it that dependent aged people and orphans in the village, no matter their complete lack of relationship with him, receive part of a bounteous kill. The responsibility for such distribution to all relationship categories except ritual kin is entirely the wife's. Most of them view the outpouring of food from their own hearths with ill-concealed resentment. Especially they appear to "forget" presentations to the husband's matrilateral relatives, with whom they are generally on very bad terms. Their attempts to hoard food in the household are, of course, supported by its other female members. The only mitigating element is the attitude of the senior in-married male, the "father" or "wife's father." He supports his daughter's husband's commendable desires to comply with his social duties and usually has enough influence over the younger women in the residence to ensure that they carry out their share in these. There is, in fact, a marked tendency for households run by an older, morally conscientious female head and her husband of many years, and including their own daughters, to function much more smoothly with respect to these presentations than those with more heterogeneous inhabitants.

Wives owe their husbands sexual fidelity, and husbands their wives gifts of both practical and non-utilitarian value (Crocker 1969b). The

Bororo quite explicitly equate this reciprocity, saying that all female sexual favors should be "paid for" (e.g., that one's mistress is entitled to "*mori-xe,*" compensation), and that there should be some rough equivalence between frequency and length of sexual services and their material rewards. One of the most pernicious effects of the Brazilian presence has been to change the character of these gifts and to inflate the amounts demanded by wives. Bororo women, especially younger ones, now consider themselves to have rights to a certain standard of living, defined in terms of a sufficiency of metal pots, kettles, buckets, and other utensils (scissors and machetes), and of textiles such as blankets, dresses, and mosquito nets. At the same time, they are covetous of prestige goods: perfumes, beads, jewelry, sunshades, ribbons, and the like. The only way Bororo men can gain these items is through wage work for Brazilians, which pays very badly indeed, and for the most onerous kind of labor. Even though the manufactured items are not individually very expensive, even the minor ones require a great amount of paid work. A large cooking pot, for example, can only be purchased with over a month of wages. At the same time, men desire to buy guns, cartridges, fishing nets, and fishhooks, which are likewise grossly inflated in relation to income. And, of course, the husband's parents and unmarried sisters are entitled to their share of what little he can purchase. Many conjugal battles arise over the conflicts of interests engendered by these expectations, and divorce is often their only resolution.

Not an infrequent way to end a marriage involves the wife's destruction of her husband's utilitarian property (but never, to my knowledge, his *aroe* ornaments and instruments, which would anger the spirits very much indeed). She is very thorough: his clothing and blankets are cut up and burned; his hunting bows and arrows are broken; nets are slashed to pieces; guns are smashed; machete and ax are thrown into the river. This act is extremely significant in both economic and symbolic terms. The items thus destroyed represent two or three years' labor, and until he can replace them a man is literally helpless. But worse, an adult's property is part of himself, his social personality, even his soul. Through them he acts out his character as it is defined by his obligations and rights to others. They are the tangible equipment whereby his *raka* manifests itself in his ability to kill game and fish, and indeed, become imbued with his own force and the blood of his prey. When the *bope* wish to make a man sick, they sometimes take the spiritual essence of his weapons and throw it through the sky, so rapidly it burns up. (So the Bororo explain the significance of falling stars.) Mortally wounded by this loss of his *raka* and his soul's extensions, the man soon dies. The bitterness produced by a failed marriage could not be better expressed than in the wife's attempt to emulate the work of the *bope*.

# The Spouse as Other:
# The Negation of Self

The exact degree of conjugal discord among the Bororo is difficult to assess. "Divorce" rates particularly are no help, since co-parents are apt to "float" back together after separations of some years. Still, even in the most apparently tranquil unions, private complaints if not strife abound. The basic difficulty appears to be a combination of conflict of material interests and contradictions in the way male and female natures are defined. First, a man makes no economic or political commitment to a particular marriage, nor does his clan derive any particular benefit from it. The payment for his rights over the sexuality of women in the other moiety has been and continues to be made through his subclan's prestations of *aroe* representations and, more generally, by the mass of symbolic reciprocity between the moieties. In effect, all the women of one's own generation in the opposite moiety are categorically "wives" (*i-to-reduje*) prior to and after marriage to any one of them. Only the birth of a child "particularizes" any given union. Even then the role of pater is disassociated from that of husband. Second, while a women derives perhaps more utilitarian and social advantage from marriage than a man does, there is nothing which constrains her to conserve any given union, for reasons analogous to those just given for men. Thirdly, the material interests of a couple are in conflict. The sexual division of labor which renders them necessary to each other also means that each must attempt to divert their common resources (chiefly their integrated labor) into their separate concerns and obligations. The "sexualization" of all productive and symbolic goods means that they own nothing in common. Even the garden which they both care for belongs to the wife. The only thing they share is their child, but even with him their relationships are founded on entirely different principles.

Finally, there is the way contradictions in male and female natures are exacerbated rather than resolved by marriage. Each human being is an amalgamation of that natural force called *raka* and the social identity expressed through the *aroe*. This opposition is resolved on the sociological level by spatially separating the functioning of masculine *raka*, especially in sexuality, from the operations of *raka* in women who share both natural and social identity with these men. This is done institutionally through associating "matriliny," the uterine transmission of categorical social identity, with exogamous moieties and uxorilocal residence. For males their "souls" are in one half of the village, their *raka* in the other. This segregation, plus the inversions of social and natural identity permitted in the *aroe* rituals, resolves many of the contradictions in man's nature. But these do emerge in the similarity of obligations he has toward his sisters and his wife, even though these also derive from the antithetical principles. That is, he owes services and gifts to his wife for the "natural" services she renders him, but the same prestations to his sisters for the sake of their common social identity.

A woman's experience of the paradoxes inherent in her sexual character are far more severe. Her "natural" life is carried out in the same site that expresses her social and spiritual identity, and it threatens to pollute all who live with her. If a man escapes symbolic incest by removing himself from prohibited categories at the beginning of his sexual life, his sister pays the structural penalty by being forced to copulate "with" her parents. The "crime" may be associated with woman's essentially impure and corrupting nature, as reflected in the danger of her menses. The resolution of her paradoxes is gained through the production of a child, which continues both the natural and social existence of her ancestors. But as long as her spatial co-existence with her husband continues, she experiences the contradiction between her "natural" and "spiritual" selves. The simplest way to resolve her dilemma is to get rid of the husband.

Thus, in their lives Bororo experience and attempt to integrate cosmological and physical powers which have human beings at their mercy. Meandering from village to village, from one household to another, they try to find a context of relationships that will help them overcome their dilemmas. As men and women become older, they begin to seek some stability of purposeful activity that will give their lives a continuing meaning, beyond the joys and troubles of physical existence. They try to establish enduring bonds with persons in the other moiety, for these are the only avenues to increments of social status. So it is that with age comes a deepening interest in the *aroe*, for these define permanency and meaning as much for individual existences as for corporate ones. As the Bororo say, "The young are full of *raka*; all they want to do is copulate and eat. But as they grow older they come to know the *aroe*." In fact, the conflicts of youth do center on competition for sexuality and for material resources. As couples age, with children growing up and with increasingly important roles in *aroe* ceremonies, the context of conjugal strife changes, becoming eventually centered on ritual roles and the relationships these engender.

About the time men begin to take seriously the role of *i-edaga* in their maternal clans (which is to say, during the adolescence and young adulthood of their sisters' children), they begin to be increasingly selected as representatives for dead members of the other moiety (as *aroe maiwu*). Most subclan *emijera* actually represent an average of seven defuncts each. This ritual role centers on a very complex relationship with a close female relative (nominally the mother) of the deceased and her husband, a member, of course, of the representative's own moiety, and sometimes of his own clan. The relationship precludes absolutely any conflict between its three members, and it is maintained to the death of all of them. It is suggestive, I think, that nearly all the senior political rivals (members of the same moiety) in most villages are related in this ceremonial way. As remarked earlier, the Bororo utilize the ties of cross-moiety relations to resolve conflicts within each moiety. All the same, the competition between "brothers" for status remains intense. There can be but one chief in any subclan, and Bororo constantly compare the ritual abilities and personal moralities of rivals for these positions. The fact that their incumbency is often temporary and the prestige hierarchy within the moiety ambiguous adds to the intensity of competition: the prize is never completely won. Nor should the covert and subtle ways these conflicts are played out detract from appreciation of their importance for the individual and in the life of the community.

With advancing age the acquisition of the power and moral authority inherent in ritual knowledge and abilities is offset by the devolution of physical capacities of *raka*. These are directly as well as indirectly linked. Not only does a man with multiple cermonial duties have to satisfy his obligations for food prestations, which he and his wife must usually procure themselves, but Bororo ritual roles are often physically arduous. An *emijera* is often required to sing for three to six consecutive hours, and sometimes all night long; some dances go on for as long as two hours. Older men who simply have not the strength to carry out these performances give instruction from the sidelines, but the lack of their physical participation inevitably diminishes their importance. Once again, *raka* (here its lack) is ultimately responsible for the capacity to maintain one's social and natural personality.

Among older women the diminishment of *raka* is manifested in their incapacity to form a child and the cessation of their menses. For them, however, lack of *raka* has somewhat different implications than it has for men. An older woman is "decontaminated," no longer a source of pollution. She can prepare food for the younger adults of the household while they are in states of contamination, and, especially, she makes those dishes sent to the *aroe*. There seems a marked tendency for her to take a more active part in *aroe* ceremonies, partly owing to her obligations as female household head, partly through her complementary roles to her brother and husband, both of whom are likely to be, if not subclan *emijera*, at least encumbered with many ritual duties. She is likely to act as midwife, and thus as *i-maruga,* to most of the births in the household. Many older women pass much of their time in weaving various items from palm fronds, nearly all of which have ritual ends, especially as obligatory gifts to those men in the other moiety who render ceremonial services to the clan. Most importantly, as a woman ages she becomes the ritual "mother" of those men in the other moiety who represent not just her own dead children but many other deceased members of her subclan. She is often referred to and addressed with a special term, "*aroe ao*," "mother of the *aroe*," while her husband is described as "*aroe pao*," "father of the *aroe*."

The Bororo do not seem to associate explicitly the menopause and this much increased ritual activity, which is an accelerating process beginning at different ages for different women. I could not tell from individual life histories if there was marked increase in *aroe* contacts just after the menopause, but certainly most women at least triple their ritual performances and duties between forty and fifty. I am fairly certain that the loss of those feminine characteristics produced by *raka* now allow the woman to be more fully and completely "spirit," *aroe*. In a sense they have become demi-men, able at last to enter into the intimacy of contact with the spirits otherwise and previously exclusive to men. With the falling off and cessation of sexual activity and all it connotes, the old Bororo female appears to overcome finally that basic paradox in her nature, the conflict between its *raka* and its *aroe*. This becomes reflected in the prestige, respect, and authority now accorded her. She at last is no longer the source of conflicts and menaces but a means of integration and synthesis. All of these attributes are reflected in the mediative roles played by the old "*i-maruga*" in Bororo myths (Lévi-Strauss 1969: 56–65). That these also reflect an ambiguity in her powers is to be expected in one who is at once old and "unnatural," in that she no longer has the biological attributes that define female nature. Only toward the end, when she can no longer even hobble around to cook and is too blind to weave her fronds, does a woman attain that ghostly half-life, a virtual retirement from all aspects of society, which seems to afflict men much earlier in their lives.

As men cease to be able to hunt and to participate actively in all productive activities, they gradually fail to carry out the responsibilities which define masculine roles and give males personal status. Simultaneously their ritual activities decline. All of this begins to occur around fifty, sometimes later but often earlier. But women manage to cook, gather, and so on until much later, well into their seventies. The old men manage to retain some degree of influence only as the repositories of Bororo knowledge, often threatening to withhold it altogether from the next generation. As beings who are no longer that synthesis of *raka* and *aroe* which defines the universal conditions of existence but who are rather far more spirit than substance, they are even more ambiguous than an old woman. Her loss of *raka* at least resolves fundamental contradictions in her nature, but men, for whom this contradiction is mediated by Bororo cosmological and social structure, merely cease to be men when they lose *raka*. It is not surprising that nearly all Bororo prescriptions for diet and behavior intend to ward off old age by conserving *raka*. Dependent upon their wives' young relatives and their husbands for all the necessities of life, the old men grumble and complain, trying through invective to maintain some degree of social existence. They often find that their closest ally and confidant is their wife. No longer forced apart by the opposed characters of their *raka*, the couple is finally integrated, their common interests now founded upon their mutual dependency upon the operation of that force in others.

With death the life-long tension between the *raka* and the *aroe* is resolved: the soul leaves the body, whose fleshy substance, the seat of *raka*, now rots away, leaving only the pure bones of form. These are decorated by members of the deceased's father's clan with the same ensemble of red paint, duck down, and feathered cap that they applied to the dead man as an infant, in the name-giving ceremony. As they once created a soul and bound it with *raka*, they now effect the dissolution of that union. One member of the father's clan becomes the living incarnation of the dead person's soul, ensuring its immortality just as the father originally brought the body which once bore it into being. Now ageless, immutable, the soul joins the ancestors and the nominal essences, the "master souls," of all species of life. Free from *raka*, it consumes little, copulates even less, sleeps never, and takes only a vague interest in the living, whose existences are still dominated by organic needs and powers. The ancestors never fight among each other, are never sick; they have no *raka*. Shadows, immaterial, they are only as real as the names for things. They assist their living descendants to maintain the structure of categories and symbolic forms that is the only way for society to integrate the dyads of *aroe* and *bope*, but they cannot bear the least contact with *raka*, that force which brought them organic life and ultimately destroyed them. For just as the *bope* bring about the origin of new life, they, and their agency *raka*, finally end existence. All affliction, all the metonymous sequences between health and illness and back to health, the mystical dangers of childbirth and menstruations, all derive from the *bope*.

# PART II

~~~ 🙟 ~~~

# The *Bope* and Their Relationship with Man

### Design

I found a dimpled spider, fat and white,
On a white heal-all, holding up a moth
Like a white piece of rigid satin cloth—
Assorted characters of death and blight
Mixed ready to begin the morning right,
Like the ingredients of a witches' broth—
A snow-drop spider, a flower like a froth,
And dead wings carried like a paper kite.

What had that flower to do with being white,
The wayside blue and innocent heal-all?
What brought the kindred spider to that height,
Then steered the white moth thither in the night?
What but design of darkness to appall?—
If design govern in a thing so small.

<div align="right">Robert Frost</div>

heron

# 4

## The *Bope* in
## Bororo Epistemology

$B$ororo reality is constituted by the operation of an antithetical dyad, the *bope* and the *aroe*. Each transfuses all dimensions of experience, and, although in some contexts opposed, each operates on its own plane, with reference to different facets of reality. *Bope* and *aroe* are the only categories of supernatural forces known to the Bororo; together they exhaust all of non-empirical reality. Each is manifested in various "pure," undiluted, awful forms, but each is present also in an unstable synthesis within each living creature. Most of Bororo symbolic activity, including that of the shaman, can be seen as devoted to maintaining and re-creating the balance between each element in this synthesis.

I must stress the ubiquity and universalism of both categories because at first glance one is tempted to consider them as collective representations in which *aroe* can be equated with "culture" and *bope* with "nature." This would be a considerable distortion of the subtlety and nuances of Bororo thought. Informants do sometimes say that "everything" is either "a" *bope* or "an" *aroe*. But they mean, usually, that one element or the other predominates in any given entity or class of entity. In a sense, there is one great continuum running through the universe from total "bopeness" at one extreme to pure "aroeness" at the other, with multiple levels of reference and association. Every being is found at some point along this continuum, often not at the same point for each level, with "more" *bope* in it than the things to one side, but "more" *aroe* than things to the other side. Human beings and certain natural species occupy the center of the continuum.

The purpose of this section is to explain why certain species occupy particular points on the continuum and how they serve as points of often dangerous contact with the *bope*. That is, I try to show the way Bororo maintain social and natural order through the symbolic manipulation of various animal metaphors and metonyms. This section sets out the logic and categories of the system, its "semantics," while the next shows its "syntax" in analyzing the shaman of the *bope*. Although I follow Bororo practice in referring to certain species, substances, and organic conditions as *bope* or *aroe*, it must be remembered that such characterizations are never mutually exclusive. As in the social sphere, all things are simultaneously themselves and their antithesis. The entire analysis turns upon this point, which I state here merely as a maxim.

The life-force in all things is *raka,* which with its flow and ebb sustains every species. The class of entities which provide this power is referred to as *bope*. There are numerous subclasses of *bope,* with varying powers and different forms. They are all capable of transforming themselves into nearly anything and seem to pass a great deal of time thus flitting from one material form to another. The very fluidity of the *bope* thus contrasts with the permanency, the nominal constancy, of the *aroe,* which always remain the form whose name they bear. In their essential condition the *bope* are described as homunculi about a meter high, with jet black skin, red eyes, and cloven feet.[1] They are completely covered with long, black, stringy hair. One informant said, "Even their eyes have hair." (The Bororo think hair, especially that of the body, is exceedingly ugly, animal-like; they associate hairiness with anomalous states and the inability to differentiate moral conduct.) The *bope* are characteristically very hot, so much so that one would be burned at a short distance from them. They give off a strong reek (*jerimaga*) of decaying matter, comparable to the smell of a corpse. Each of these attributes has a penumbra of associations analyzed later in the section, which generally convey the *bope*'s metonymous connections with all organic flux, especially with birth and death. Indeed, to see one in all its existential ugliness usually results in almost immediate death, so mechanically lethal are its physical attributes.

As a category, the *bope* are credited with controlling all natural change, whether this is as critical as the formation of a child in the womb or as trivial as a rain squall. Various subclasses of *bope* are said to cause severally rain, thunder, and lightning. Other categories are responsible for tornadoes and windstorms, for earthquakes, for solar and lunar eclipses, and for falling stars. They are responsible for the alternation of seasons between wet and dry; they make all the vegetable world fructify. Directly or indirectly they cause floods and droughts. (But they have no dominion over the fishes, which alone in the natural world are controlled by the *aroe*.) In this dyadic cosmos the heavens and the earth are the domain of the *bope*, but the *aroe* have suzerainty over rivers, lakes, and the underground. This correlates with the intense association between the *bope* and all heat, especially fire. Indeed, the sun and the moon are themselves aspects of the *bope*, who thus control the diurnal cycle of light and heat, darkness and cold. All incidental variations in climate are credited to them, including cold snaps. Since these are sometimes so severe as to kill certain plant species, between their control of climate and their power over rain the *bope* effectively extend their powers of life and destruction over bloodless entities lacking the ironic self-destruction of *raka*.

As noted earlier, women's menses are explicitly associated with the waxing and waning of the moon. The *bope* are said to cause the onset of menstruation as well as its cessation during the menopause. The regularity of the human phenomena is connected with their natural analogs, the rhythms of all organic fertility. The periodic fructification of nature, the seasonal waves of births among wild animals, the regularity of the menstrual cycle, all derive from the *bope*. Hence these things are not merely the agents of transformation but are also the sentient masters of natural time, of biological pattern and event. The whole temporal process for the Bororo has a marked order and determined cycle. While the *bope*'s interventions into the natural world may be manifested in chaotic disruption and anomalous pollutions, they are also responsible for the stability of organic change. All natural transition may transform, but it does so in a predictable and reliable order.

Human beings are burdened with the necessity of integrating the consequences of such changes into the realm of timeless forms dominated by the *aroe*, but the *bope* are not capriciously antagonistic to the principles of nominal order. The social and symbolic difficulties arise when the natural world violates the rules governing its cycles, as in eclipses and sterility. These disasters, however, are always considered consequences of antecedent human failures to maintain their responsibilities in the integration of form and substance, that is, of man's violation of "natural order." This order and the organic rhythms it controls are embedded in the structure of the village circle and the rules controlling the conduct of all relationships founded upon a community of substance. The *bope* may be creatures of anomaly, of corruption and physical transformation, but they sustain the consistent repetitions of birth and renewal.

Sociologically rather than cosmologically, the *bope* are intimately part of every Bororo's individual experience, far more so than the *aroe*. Interest in the topic is literally inexhaustible. Every adult has had his own immediate contacts with these beings, at least in one of the forms through which they manifest themselves to humans. Not only is affliction, with its attendant *bope*-related treatments, almost a daily occurrence in the village, but nearly all transactions with nature are suffused with an awareness of the *bope*'s immediacy and the relevance of the rules governing interaction with them. As early as a child can walk he must toddle over to a shaman when he is possessed by a *bope* and offer the spirit a cigarette. Nearly all Bororo have relatives or affines who are shamans; from them they hear all kinds of private experiences with the *bope* and details of their operations in the organic world.

Far more than the *aroe*, the *bope* provide a set of assumptions which direct attention to certain aspects of the formless world of sensation and which interpret these perceptions so as to guide action in the social as well as natural domains. The operation of this set within the organization of marriage and of the residence has already been demonstrated. But *raka* is only one metaphor whereby powers of the *bope* can be symbolically expressed and their potential danger for humans be controlled. More directly, the ideas and practices concerning them allow the Bororo to organize their transactions with the natural world in such ways as to integrate these with social relationships. This comes about mostly through the prescribed treatment of the natural species called "food of the *bope*," which the latter half of this chapter describes in detail.

But if the *bope* provide a structure for all manner of exchanges between and within the social/natural domains, they are also a context for comparative freedom to speculate, improvise, and discover the mysteries of non-empirical reality. Unlike the immutable and frozen world of the *aroe*, described with almost Talmudic precision, there is much variety of opinion on the *bope*'s attributes and powers, nearly all of which is equally valid since it derives from individual experience, whether direct or intimately secondhand. And consistently, whereas communal rituals featuring the *aroe* are marked with that casualness of formulaic manner noted for religious activities in many other societies (Evans-Pritchard 1965: 44–47), those proceedings in which the *bope* appear are fraught with seriousness and, frequently, emotional intensity. This does not mean that the *aroe* are devoid of sentimental and psychological significance for the individual but rather that by definition their powers and man's relationship to them are ordered according to immutable, *a priori* patterns. The *bope*, as the determinators of all unique, singular events, are much more relevant to any particular Bororo's own appreciation of the historical situation in which he finds himself. A child's birth, a relative's death, one's own perception of his organic being, all these relate only to the *bope*.

Perhaps a reasonable analogy in Western life would be common attitudes toward church life, with its obligatory regularities and esoteric symbolic forms, and astrology, or any other system of divination that promises to relate the idiosyncratic problems of individual existence to preexistent cosmic forces. The difficulty with the analogy is that the *bope* can actively intervene to alter the shape of individual destiny, as well as predict and determine it. From the standpoint of a sociology of knowledge, then, the *bope* provide the means whereby received tradition and contemporary experience can be adjusted to one another. Given the radical pressures upon the modern Bororo, it is not surprising that they find it necessary to employ this cosmological dimension more and more, both for conceptual integration and for symbolic action directed to social harmony.

## Social and Geographic Affiliations of the *Bope*

The material presented here on the attributes of the *bope* and human relationships with them represents a cross section of Bororo opinion on these topics. As mentioned above, there is considerable latitude in belief, with a relatively limited amount of orthodox dogma. Some of the data were obtained from *bari* (shamans of the *bope*) and represent the consensual views of ritual experts rather than "popular" belief. I shall try to indicate the views held by an "ordinary" Bororo and how these direct the actions he customarily takes regarding the *bope*. But it must be stressed that certain *bope*-related practices, primarily those concerning the animals and plants over which the *bope* possess certain rights, are collective representations viewed as universally and absolutely obligatory. Observation of these practices defines identity as a Bororo; the necessity for them and their details are known even to little children. From these collective assumptions fan out a variety of beliefs, approximately equivalent in legitimacy and for the most part seen as noncontradictory. Certain of the social dimensions of these representations are ambiguous, however, and are variously interpreted by different Bororo. The most basic of these involves the paradox that the *bope* are *aroe*.

The Bororo say that Meri, one of the common titles for the preeminent *bope*, created everything in the world. He devised all cultural things, even those of western civilization. Brazilians (*barae*) themselves, along with their artifacts, are inventions of the *bope*, but as nominal forms are among the totemic *aroe* of the Bokodori Exerae clan.[2] All classes of *bope* themselves, on the other hand, "belong to" one or the other "chiefly" subclans of the Bado Jeba clans, specifically to the Bado Jebage (the subclan of Bakorokudu), or to O Exerae Bo Exerae (the subclan of Karia Bokodori) (see Appendix A). That is, the *bope* are included among the clan essences of the Bado Jeba; they are in that sense *aroe*. Each subclan even has ceremonial representations of Meri and his younger brother Ari among their *aroe etawuje* ("totems"), along with other rituals involving the impersonation of various particular *bope*.

Some Bororo seek to explain these contradictions in various ways, but probably most persons merely take them as incomprehensible dogma. Everyone agrees that one of Meri's manifestations or aspects is the sun, *meri*. Similarly Ari reveals one attribute of himself in the moon, *ari*. As the Bororo say, "*Meri aroe etawujedu* ('the representation of the sun's *aroe*') is with Bakorokudu; *ari aroe etawujedu* ('the representation of the moon's *aroe*') is with Karia Bokodori." Now, the total set of clan *aroe* provide an exhaustive system of categories which encompass all reality at the level of the pure forms it manifests (Crocker 1977b). Sun and moon, as well as the other natural phenomena controlled by or manifesting the *bope*, certainly must be included in the universe of pure forms of being, of nominal essences. Some informants seemed to feel that only in this perspective were natural forms to be considered *aroe*. In their more usual aspect of embodying the principles of organic transformation and natural cycles, they were *bope*.

This is a simplification of what I regard as the more profound indigenous interpretation: Within the cosmological structure of the differentiated associations of social units with *all* things in the universe, the *bope* themselves must be credited as having pure nominal form, as well as being the principle of substance and change. Their inclusion in this structure must be consistent with the logic that orders it. The Exerae moiety, led by the Bado Jeba clans, has among its collective *aroe* the essences of beings who live in the skies and upon the earth. But the *aroe* of the Tugarege are fish, water birds, parrots, all things of the *aroe*. These associations are themselves expressions of a structure analyzed later on. Here it should be noted that Bakorokudu and Karia Bokodori are also the possessors of the *aroe* of the two culture heroes Bakororo and Itubore (both Tugavege), who founded Bororo society by devising its relations with all *aroe*. It is consistent that Meri and Ari, who created the world and who, as sun and moon, signify transforming yet cyclic time, are also among the *aroe* who must order the social universe and temporal processes. In short, the *bope* must be *aroe*, at least in certain epistemological contexts, so that the logic of social classification can reach its tautological completion. None of this means that the relationship of the Bado Jeba, or Exerae in general, to the *bope* qua *bope* is in any way altered, no more than any clan has special privileges or duties toward the *aroe* forms which define its social character. Further aspects of the *bope-aroe* paradox are discussed later.

Although the category *bope* designates a conceptual unity of attributes, it may be internally differentiated in particular shamanistic contexts. The Bororo distinguish generally between *maereboe* ("bad" *bope*, also called literally *bope pegareu*) and *bope pemegareu* ("good" *bope*). The contrast has more to do with the spatial and other attributes of each class than with their general morality. The *maereboe* are believed to live in constant association with man, on or near this earth. It is they which assume the form of the black, hairy homunculus described earlier. Many of them live in particular sites well known to the Bororo. Often an unusually large or otherwise peculiar termite hill is said to be the dwelling place of a certain *maereboe*. In my experience every termite hill found in a tree was considered the home of a *maereboe*. Large dead or deformed trees are favored residences. *Maereboe* are inevitably to be found in the vicinity of abandoned villages and in old constructions, Bororo or Brazilian. In the jungle *maereboe* stay around patches of fallen timber, in low places infested with thorn bushes and vines, and generally anywhere the Bororo call *rurureu*, "dirty" in the sense of especially painful to human encounter. *Maereboe* also live in isolated large stones, and whole bands of them may infect groves of trees along small watercourses, the same places where bands of monkeys are found.

The reasons for the association between these aspects of the landscape and the *bope* are consistent with the general attributes of each element, rather than reflecting any particular trend toward animism among the Bororo. The termite hills, which seem to provide the most common *bope* home, are to be sure bizarre and impressive structures, which certainly do not belong in trees in anybody's classificatory system. But termite honey is also one of the preferred foods of the *bope*; as the Bororo say, "It tastes like blood. . . ." Villages or structures are usually abandoned after many, inevitably *bope*-caused deaths occur in them. Large dead trees are favored roosting places for vultures, one of the most preferred *bope* familiars. Unusually dense and impenetrable parts of the jungle are the normal habitats of wild pigs and tapir, two of the *bope*'s favorite food species. Monkeys are frequent animal familiars for *bope*. In short, all these associations derive from the metonymic extension of *bope* characteristics to aspects of the landscape and the natural world. As shall be seen, the entire domain of the *bope* is pervaded by metonymy, just as that of the *aroe* is dominated by metaphor.

The "localization" of the *maereboe* in the environment nearest the Bororo does not mean that these malign beings are in any way confined to these areas.[3] The *bope*'s omnipotence is reflected in their ubiquitous presence among human beings. They are constant invisible visitors to the village, where their passage is betrayed by various signs. The sudden noise caused by the contraction of a roof beam, a rustle in the thatch on a windless day, an object which suddenly falls from the rafters, a "dust devil," all these show that the *bope* are there. All curious, non-species-like behavior in domesticated animals and birds demonstrates they have been entered momentarily by the *bope*. Bororo dogs are pitiful curs, which slink away at a harsh word; thus, if a dog approaches stiff-legged and growling, clearly a *bope* has entered it. Tame parrots and macaws sometimes begin to squawk wildly, for no apparent reason, and thus signal the arrival of the *bope* within themselves.

Dogmatically, the *bope* are said to have no particularly hostile intention in visiting the village. They are simply going about their daily business of observing the Bororo, quite ready to punish any slight neglect in the just prerogatives owed them but not capricious in their menace. When the *bope* wish to attack someone, or to warn them of such an attack, they employ either certain animal and bird omens (described below) or cause a wild animal to act in an unnatural way. Privately, Bororo respond to these manifestations with anxiety and an immediate demand for the shaman. But their public attitude toward the daily signs that the *bope* are among them and toward their known homes is one of attention and wry humor. They say with a certain bravado, "The *bope* will not harm us unless we have offended them." The reason for these contrasts is that the *bope* take offense very easily, and it is difficult to distinguish the signs of their mere presence from those of their particularized hostility. One can never be sure one has not made the *bope* angry. While the Bororo are not terrified of the *bope*, they are certainly uneasy with even the most innocuous signs of their presence, even if their standards of conduct do not permit them to express their feelings.[4]

The foregoing material represents common ideas and sentiments among adult Bororo. I will next present information obtained from shamans and from informed *emijera,* who individually possess only limited bits of this esoteric lore. There are multiple social reasons for these limitations on information about the *bope. Bari* (shaman of the *bope*) are usually reluctant to discuss their specialized knowledge at length, especially with nonshamans. They claim the *bope* do not wish them to divulge their secrets and that these spirits have even slain shamans or others who did not respect the privileged quality of their knowledge. Among other things, these inhibitions ensure against obvious discrepancies between shamans' individual accounts of *bope* attributes. They also make it nearly impossible to employ information about the *bope* to achieve public prestige, since traditional knowledge must be openly displayed and legitimized by expert confirmation to be a valid element in personal authority. Furthermore, the shamans reserve the right to judge the veracity of any particular secular version of the *bope*'s characteristics on the grounds that only they have had contact with these spirits and that their privileged position qualifies them alone to verify either historical or personal interpretations of their nature. But at the same time it is publicly held that individual shamans only know as much as their individual *bope* permit them to know. Since the *bope* realm is marked by the mutual hostility and endless deceit of the spirits occupying it, any one shaman is likely to have been tricked and given purposefully distorted visions of *bope* existence.

However, the Bororo assumption that there is a "truth" underlying all the vagaries of individual experience and knowledge applies to *bope* matters as well as to all others. I was therefore able to utilize information contained in previous ethnographies, especially the Enciclopedia Bororo, to convince shamans that I was sufficiently aware of details of *bope* organization and characteristics to be able to recognize the accuracy of their individual accounts. I also worked with shamans both individually and collectively, cross-checking and citing their personal accounts among them to ensure some kind of consensus on matters relating to the *bope*. The following information cannot thus be considered to represent any particular Bororo's own vision of the *bope,* nor should it be taken as a representative sampling of expert esoterica. I can only justify my procedure on the grounds that I assume that, if underlying all the Bororo existential contacts with that variety of phenomena they call *bope* there is a single structure, this system can be only apprehended through as complete a catalog of these contacts as possible. Following indigenous distinctions, the materials are presented first in the form of the categories recognized in the *bope* pantheon, and next through the variety of contacts individuals have had with members of this pantheon.

## *Meri* and the Pantheon of *Bope*

The *bope* cosmos is divided into three "bands," or levels, each with its own unique color and restricted to certain kinds of *bope*. The *maereboe* live both upon the earth and within the "inner sky," the *baru kigadureu* or "white sky." This forms a large bowl inverted over the earth. It is the heaven usually visible to human beings, the one occupied by most birds, clouds, and the winds. Confined to this sphere are the spirits of dead shamans of the *bope* who were evil during their lifetimes, abusing their power and harming their fellow man. (As soon as a shaman of the *bope* dies, he ceases to have a soul, an *aroe*. This element within him is transformed into a *bope,* so that after death his spiritual part does not go to live with the ancestors, but, as appropriate to its nature, dwells with the *bope* themselves.) The *maereboe,* even those which have a certain home on this earth, tend to flit between here and the white sky.

This "sky" (*baru kigadureu*) is especially known as the dwelling place of the *Butao-doge.* A large group of *bope,* these are described by shamans as having very long hair which stretches down to the earth. As they advance across the skies, their streaming hair turns into rain. Some people say their principal dwelling place is to the west, for most rains in the wet season come out of the west. (Tropical storms can be seen miles away as great moving curtains lit with flashes of lightning.) A few *Butao-doge* live near man, within the *tai* tree (jacaranda, *Machoerium* sp.). This tree constantly drips "water," even after the dry season has well begun. *Butao-doge* also control or manifest themselves through thunder, lightning, and high winds, "winds so strong," said one nonshaman, "they tear up trees and even kill people." Some shamans distinguish between subclasses of *Butao-doge* and their associated meteorological phenomena. Thus, *Boe-yarurugodu* is a huge animal-like monster covered with folds of dry leathery skin; thunder is the sound of his skin brushing against itself as the monster "hunts" through the sky. *Boe-ragudugodu* makes lightning, while another subclass, *Boegabe-doge,* causes high winds and torrential rains. No one seems sure of their precise attributes, other than that they resemble other *Butao-doge.*[5] Rainbows are the only aspect of weather not caused by the *bope.* They are, instead, the *aroe* of the anaconda (*jure*). This *aroe* does not like too much rain and causes it to stop by projecting itself (or one part of itself) through the heavens. This must be true, say the Bororo, because rainbows only appear with the end of rain, and thus *jure aroe* must be able to stop them.[6]

The *Butao-doge* are thought rather innocuous *bope* who may sometimes hurt particular Bororo by lightning or hurricanes on behalf of the *maereboe* but who otherwise leave man alone. It is otherwise with the *bope* of dead shamans who had been evil, cruel men in this life. For unlike the souls of all other Bororo, which death transforms into immortal *aroe,* those of shamans become *bope.* These also live in the white sky and are among the most implacable, nasty *bope* persecuting the Bororo. Such shamans' *bope* are often tied down beneath the trees on which vultures are accustomed to roost. There they are buried in the terrible stench of vulture excrement, the most polluting substance in the universe. The *bope* so punish evil shamans not for revenge against their wicked acts toward the Bororo but because as *bope* they manipulate their powers for their own selfish ends, angering the other *bope* very much. (This is the only instance in which the Bororo associate different postmortum fates with moral behavior.)

The use of the vulture for their punishment is perfectly consistent with other elements in the system. Vultures, the consumers of rotting flesh, black with ugly naked heads, able to soar for hours at the very top of the white sky, have so many *bope* attributes that, as one shaman put it, "the *bope* do not even have to transform themselves to be vultures—they already are!" The two remaining categories of *bope* that live in this "white" zone are interesting just through their relative lack of *bope* attributes and generally benign attitude toward the Bororo.

The *Tupa-doge* do not even appear like other *bope,* but instead resemble Brazilians, wearing clothes and shoes, possessing guns, horses, houses, and extensive gardens. Their father is *Wai-ya,* a *Kie;* their mother is *Wai-ya Rodo* and belongs to the Bokodori Exerae clan, along with all the *aroe* entities associated with the Brazilians. (Both clans are Exerae; their incestuous union is at once characteristic of the *bope* and of the Brazilians, neither of whom are believed to have any sense of sexual morality whatsoever.) They have villages at various points in the white sky and live uniquely upon the rice, beans, sugar cane, and melons they cultivate there. Thus, they do not eat any of the game animals or vegetables strong in *raka* consumed by all other kinds of *bope.* They never cause affliction among the Bororo but can cure some diseases caused by other *bope* and are especially beneficent with sick children. Nearly all Bororo shamans count *Tupa-doge* among their possessing *bope.* Most female shamans have only these spirits as their familiars. They are generally very kindly disposed to the Bororo and cordially detest the *maereboe* and other bad *bope.* Unfortunately, their powers to cure affliction are somewhat limited, as their lack of fondness for *rakare* substances might indicate. This category is a thoroughly anomalous one; it may represent an attempt to incorporate the Bororo's ambiguous experiences with the Western world. There is also the possibility of direct influence from the cult of Catholic saints and the local Brazilian mediumship which utilizes it. In any case, the benign attitudes of the *Tupa-doge* are offset by their relative feebleness. *Uwaikuru-doge* are thoroughly *bope,* and powerful ones at that, but they never cause individual illness or accidents. They are, however, extremely quarrelsome and make fights break out among people. Long ago they precipitated wars between Bororo and other Indians. They live very far away to the west and seldom possess contemporary shamans. For this reason, not much is known of their attributes except that they are as belligerent with other *bope* as with each other; hence, they seek to discomfort these by curing people they had made ill.

Stretching above the white sky are two broad bands of heaven called the *baru kaworureu,* "blue-green sky," and the *baru kujagureu,* "red sky." Some say the first lies below the second, others that they interpenetrate each other rather than form distinct layers. These are the domains of numerous particularized categories of *bope,* and of the *bope pemegareu* ("good *bope*") generically, as well as the *bope* of deceased shamans who discharged their duties well during life. These may often serve as the

familiar *bope* for living shamans, especially if they are related matrilater-
ally. Oscillating between the two bands, but mostly staying in the red
sky, are *Meri-xera* or *Etu-o,* "father of the *bope*" and his wife *Kikorado,* or
*Etu-je,* "mother of the *bope*." Some informants thought that the former
was a Bado Jeba Xebegiwuge, and the latter a Bado Jeba Xobugiwuge,
both of the Exerae moiety, but were uncertain. Their status as "parents of
the *bope*" should not, in my opinion, be taken too literally (*vide* Albisetti
and Venturelli 1962: 773–76). The sense of their titles might be best rendered as "Originators." *Etu-o* is very remote from the Bororo and certainly cannot be regarded as any sort of supreme being. No prayers or
offerings are directed to him specifically, nor is he credited with special
authority over other types of *bope*. He does have a vague function as the
final recipient of the presentations given the *bope* by the Bororo. At most
he might be regarded as a sort of logical capstone for the totality of *bope*.
*Etu-o* is nominally included among the "good" *bope* but is never, although any of the others may be, among a shaman's familiars. *Etu-je* is
described as lacking breasts but possessing a vagina, totally covered with
hair, and very ugly indeed. She has a certain role in the surreal initiation
of a shaman, described in the next chapter, but otherwise has little interest for a contemporary Bororo.

The sorts of *bope* living in the red and blue skies seem limitless, to
judge by the number distinguished by the different shamans interviewed.
However frustrating for the analyst, this devolves from the tenets of Bororo cosmology. The *bope* as generators of all transformation are fluid,
evanescent creatures, forever oozing out of one form and into another.
They can change into one another as instantaneously as they can assume
the shape of a vulture or other being. The more malicious attempt to
trick shamans by "becoming" one of their familiars. All of this amorphousness contrasts with the *aroe,* which are literally the personification
of timeless categories, unaltering forms of name and being. The Bororo
can thus utilize the inexhaustible and individually validated universe of
the *bope* to integrate traditional dogmas with novel experience, as well as
for the conceptual typologizing they excel in. For these reasons, I do not
regard it as necessary to present an exhaustive account of all types of *bope*
described to me. The varieties described below are at once typical and the
most common among different informants.

*Imokuri* seems to be a single entity rather than a class. It is described
by shamans as a huge, pale, oozing mass, a jellylike substance with flashes and sparks dancing about its semi-translucent interior. *Imokuri* is noted
for its capricious, mischievous qualities. It constantly transforms itself
into all manner of things—women, children, dogs, Brazilians—in order
to play spiteful tricks on people. It often makes people sick and then,
denying its responsibility, will cure them, a reversal unique among the
*bope*. Its usual manifestation is through turbulent, crackling "wild fires"

in the savannah. *Imokuri* is extremely dangerous to any shaman who has it as a familiar, since it delights in deceiving him and thus causing him all manner of misfortune. It is also very sexually lustful, even more so than most *bope*.

Iworo-doge are a class of *bope* with such marked powers of transmogrification that not even shamans know anything of their real form. Like *Tupa-doge,* they never eat of the meats relished by other *bope* but do accept cigarettes. They are extremely adept at curing ill people but, sadly, are extremely severe with the shaman they possess, killing him, his wife, or child for the slightest error in ritual or personal morality. They are fond, for unknown reasons, of the acuri (*iworo*) palm and the wine produced from it. They assist the Bororo in hunting by making their shaman unusually acute of hearing so that he can locate game at great distances.

Juko are a *bope* category that in appearance are just like capuchin monkeys (*juko*). They divide their time between visits to earth and the red sky. When they possess a shaman they can only whistle, like monkeys, and scratch themselves vigorously. (*Bope* generally seem to itch excessively, to judge by the constant scratching of a possessed shaman. The previous chapter noted that persons in conditions of ritual danger, when their *raka* was menaced, had to employ artificial means to scratch. The Bororo apparently assume that itching is one of those "natural" urges associated with *raka,* which must be carefully circumscribed by rules it if is not to harm its possessor. The *bope* scratch constantly for the same reason they incessantly copulate: their stocks of *raka* are endless.) The *Juko Bope* prefer to eat the vegetables and fruits which serve as *bope* food, rather than the game. They are not very effective in curing, but neither do they inflict much illness.

Adugo are another type of *bope* in animal form, that of the jaguar (*adugo*). When one of them possesses a shaman, it refuses to touch vegetables but only eats meat, directly from the plate without using its "paws." It likes to smoke, as do all *bope,* and is fairly adept at curing, especially of those afflictions resulting from some infraction of the rules on the hunting of game eaten by the *bope*. These and the preceding are the only two classes of *bope* which have essentially the form of animals, although all other types of *bope* may enter jaguars and monkeys or change into them, as they can all the other species thought to have features in common with the *bope*.

Bureikoibo is another single *bope* entity. It lives in the blue sky, where it maintains large herds of all the animals eaten by the *bope* penned up around his house. Thanks to his captive larder, he is exceedingly fat, very loathsome in appearance. He reeks of the usual *bope* smell of corruption (*jerimaga*) so powerfully that people can scarcely bear it. When he manifests himself in a shaman he is always very cheerful and good-natured, joking with the spectators, breaking wind (with noisome effect), and noisily devouring the food given him. But he prefers to remain in his own dwelling, habitually possesses few shamans, and often does not respond to a request to cure someone.

*Bureikoibo* is as much a character of myth as an active form of *bope*. Anciently this spirit lived deep inside the earth. He had discovered corn and oversaw its wild florescence. In those days there was no need to cultivate gardens since vast amounts of corn could be gathered from the jungle. One day five or six women went out to collect corn. One of them hurt her hand in breaking off a corn stalk and said to it in anger, "*Bi*" ("die"). (The implicit reference is to the *mori-xe* custom described in the preceding chapter, in which any natural agency which hurts a Bororo must be killed.) *Bureikoibo* overheard her, since the *bope* are always aware of human actions, and thought she had cursed him. Angered, he said that from henceforth the Bororo must cultivate corn for themselves; he took himself off to the red sky, where he continues to dwell. His gift of corn is one reason why the first fruits of this crop are offered every year to the *bope*.

But this is not the main reason for the prestation, which is only one of a series of obligatory gifts of different kinds of food the Bororo must make to the *bope*. These transactions are the central relationship between the *bope* and the Bororo. Failures to comply with the rules governing them constitute the source of nearly all affliction. They are the major substantive theme of this book.

## The Myth of *Meri*

It is difficult to regard the formal relationship between man and *bope* as anything less than a contract, even a convenant. The basis for it can be briefly summarized. The *bope* have certain rights over a precisely defined set of animal, fish, bird, and vegetable species, in recognition of which the Bororo must offer members of these species to the *bope* as "their food" (*bope ure*). This is done through the intermediary shaman, who is possessed by one or more *bope*. Through the passive agency of the shaman, the *bope* consume small amounts of the game or plants. The shaman is, in Bororo views, no more than the physical vector for the transaction, more to be pitied than honored for the dangers his tasks incur. In return for these prestations the *bope* are obliged to refrain from harming Bororo capriciously and without reason, to advise them of afflictions they intend to impose, so that humans can take whatever defensive measures possible, and to protect them from wild animals and destructive powers of nature generally. The terms of this contract are given in a myth known to almost all Bororo, of which a synopsis follows. (The

Salesians give a very complete interlinear account of the last episode of this myth; see Albisetti and Venturelli 1962: 241–43. It follows nearly word for word the versions I heard from eleven informants. The following includes earlier episodes of Meri and Ari's adventures.)

Very long ago before Baitogogo and Boroge [i.e., before the origin of human society] the *bope* Meri and his younger brother Ari lived on this earth in the aspect of men. They showed the people many things but were very bad to them too, constantly robbing, fighting, and copulating with other men's wives. They were completely without shame, even fornicating with their own sisters and other members of their maternal clan. Once Meri told Ari to find out which women had large vaginas, since his penis was so long and large the organs of most women could not begin to accommodate it. Ari searched, and reported that only one woman seemed appropriately endowed, their *i-tuie* (elder sister or mother's sister). So Meri and Ari went into her house late at night and copulated with her. She pressed her hand, which was covered with genipapo (a blackish vegetable dye), across their faces. In the morning she could tell who had been with her during the night. Thus, both Ari and Meri have to this day black streaks and blotches on their faces, up in the sky where they are the moon and the sun. Another time Meri asked his younger sister to accompany him hunting. He had her sit on the entrance to the den of a paca (a small species of Agouti, *Cuniculus paca*), so he could kill it as it left from the other entrance. But instead he stuck his penis into the hole, where it wound round and round until he had succeeded in fornicating with his sister. Meri and Ari were also very greedy, constantly eating. They kept to themselves all male deer, tapir, capivara, rhea, seriema, wild pig, genipapo fruit, quince, and so on [that is, all the current food of the *bope*], not letting anyone else eat these foods except as leavings from their meals.

Once Meri arrived in a man's house while he and his wife were out fishing. Now both of them were *o* (soco or herons [Ardeidae]), although they had the appearance of humans. The husband owned the night, which he kept in the form of a black powder within a gourd. Meri wanted the night. He saw the sleeping young son and daughter of the absent couple and ripped their jaws down, all the way down to their stomachs. They died. When the man and his wife returned, they wondered who could have done such a thing. They knew Meri was about, with his nasty tricks, so the *o* took his gourd of night and poured out just a bit of it, just a little bit, so the night was short. Nothing happened. So he poured out some more, and this time heard screams of fear, O O O O O, from Meri, who was very scared of the night and wanted it to end. So the *o* went to Meri and asked him if it was he who had killed the children. Meri said not, he would never think of such a terrible thing. But the *o* doubted him and, going home, poured out a great quantity of powder, so that the night was very long and did not cease. This time Meri howled and howled with fear. So the *o* went to him, and again asked if he had killed the children. Meri again denied he had, since he was always lying, lying, lying. But the *o* said, "If you will cure my children, I will give you *boe xo*, the night." So Meri went along with him back to the house, where he sewed up the great rents in the children with urucu and duck down. When he blew upon them, they returned to life. Yet today the soco has two thin white lines running down from the edge of its mouth all the way to its stomach. Then Meri turned the couple and the children into *o* and said, "You are called *o*; this is your name. You shall live on the banks of rivers and eat nothing but small fish; these will be your food." The *o* gave Meri the night, but made him promise that whenever the *o* did not want the night, he would call *o o o o o o o o* and Meri would end the night.[7]

Then Meri went on. He found a man and a woman cutting open a tree to get honey. They were kinsmen of his, members of the Bado Jebage subclan. They were using a very beautiful stone ax which Meri wanted. He magically formed an ax, but very poorly made, ugly and dull. He went up to them and proposed they trade axes. They refused, but he fought with them and made them trade. They tried to use Meri's ax, but it broke. Then Meri said to them, "You will be no longer people, but will eat honey with your bills. You will be called *nari* or *eregejeje*" (a type of woodpecker considered to have beautiful red and black plumage and a diet exclusively of honey, possibly the golden-collared woodpecker, *Veniliornix cassini*).

Then Meri went on. He found a man fishing with a very beautiful bow called *bakaraia ika,* which belonged (and still does) to the clan of *bope*-inspired things, the Bokodori Exerae. Meri wanted the bow, so he made a thing of rotten wood and vulture feathers but caused it to appear just like the man's bow.[8] He offered to trade one for the other, but the man refused. Meri fought with him and finally was able to make the exchange by sheer force. When the man attempted to shoot a fish with Meri's bow, it broke. So Meri said, "You will be no more a man but will live on fish alone, and will spear them only with your beak. You will eat no more *okoge* (dourado), no more *orari* (pintado), but only *tubore* (small "sunfish" and generically all small fish, minnows, and the like). Your name will be *Kadogare* (ringed kingfisher, *Ceryle torquata.* The dourado and pintado are large "game" fish, averaging 3 or 4 kilos in adult specimens, and often taken with fish arrows and spears. The kingfisher is among the clan *aroe* of the Bokodori Exerae.)

Meri and Ari went hunting and set fire to a large open field in order to drive the game toward them. The fire raged out of control, but Meri saved himself by climbing a tall tree. Ari, though, as usual more stupid than his elder brother, climbed a small sapling and was burned to death. An *okwa* (small wolf) happened along and, smelling roasted meat, ate up all of Ari. Meri heard the wolf howling, "Roasted meat is good. Roasted meat is good." He killed the *okwa,* cut open its stomach, and resuscitated Ari from the half-digested pieces.

There are several other stories demonstrating Ari's ineptness and ignorance, and contrasting these with his elder brother's wisdom. Ari is often the victim of Meri's schemes, though the latter always rescues him in the end. There are also many tales of Meri's deeds of this earth, all with the just-so quality evident in the preceding ones, accounting for how such and such a species was created by Meri and why it has its distinguishing marks and diet. These stores form no set cycle and are recounted independently of one another. The one Meri story known to all Bororo, however, is the following one:

> Then Meri went on. He came to a group of *Iwagudu-doge,* whom he asked for a drink of water. They gave it to him in a beautifully made *pori* (ceramic pot or bowl, among the clan's totemic *aroe* now). After drinking, Meri deliberately smashed the pot. Then he said to them, "You will make no more pots, nor shall you have any mud. You are no longer men but *karawoe*" (or *karao,* water birds also among the *aroe* of the *Iwagudu-doge*). "You must eat the small insects found on the mudbanks of the river."
> So the Bororo became very angry with Meri and all his bad ways, and thought how they might rid mankind of this pest. So they decided to decorate him with great quantities of resin and duck down (i.e., to ornament him as an *aroe,* a gift of great value). They piled on great masses of down, more than had ever been seen before or since. Then two men started fanning him with *bakoreu* (a type of woven rectangular mat suspended by two cords from a short stick, and utilized by the shaman when possessed by the *bope*). More and more men joined in the fanning, until Meri began to rise slowly into the sky. Harder and harder they fanned, rising with Meri (since he had changed them all into birds of one species or another). Once they had ascended him to the red sky, they told him how it would be between *bope* and man. "Your name is Meri, and you are a *bope*. You shall live in the sky and eat only tapir, wild pig, capivara, deer, seriema, rhea, pirarucu, surubin, jau, mangaba, corn, cashew, all the *bope ure* (all the *bope* food species discussed below are cited). These things we will give to you. If any of them escape us wounded, or if a man eats them without giving to you, you will be angry with him; you will kill him immediately. But if he gives them to you, you will not make him sick or cause the wild animals and snakes to attack him. You will make him live a long, long time, and his wife and children also."

An extended analysis of this crucial Bororo myth cannot be attempted here, since it would require the introduction of numerous materials and structures outside the domain of the *bope*. For example, all persons and things encountered by Meri are associated with the Exerae moiety, for complex, unsystematic reasons. But I shall explore one level, that illustrating the contrasts between humans and *bope*. Briefly, it seems evident that Meri's actions are a systematic inversion of proper moral behavior. He effects reciprocity by force, whereas the Bororo insist (and their myths reflect) that no one can even covertly solicit a gift. All prestations must come from the free will of the giver, and the receiver must be properly humble and seek to make an appropriate return. But Meri's "gifts" are mere dross; and he even tries more drastic measures to secure what he covets (as when he kills the children of the *o*). The Bororo assume that the maker/giver of any item takes responsibility for its enduring efficacy and that he is ashamed in the extreme when his gift does not fulfill its function. Finally, Meri concludes his transactions by changing men into birds, whose plumage, habitat, and diet reflect the circumstances and tools they were utilizing when he encountered them. (I think that Bororo ceremony, at least in the *aroe* representations, has precisely the contrary aim, the transformation of animals, or the "idea" of animal species, into men.) At least Meri reveals some sense of symbolic justice (or perhaps the implicit assumptions of mythic thought do so), since all the bird species produced by his mystical powers are intimately associated with the *aroe* in terms of their attributes and diet. Of course, this is consistent with the activities of *bope* even now: by killing men, they change them into *aroe,* ancestral souls.

All of this has striking correspondence to some themes in Lévi-Strauss, those regarding the mythic inversion of natural and cultural differences to produce social differentiation (1963a: *passim;* 1962b: 144–76; 1963b: 15–32). Bororo clans, like Indian castes, are culturally heterogeneous: each controls a unique set of ritual property essential to the performance of ceremonial roles complementary to those controlled by other clans, and necessary to the entire community. Unlike castes, Bororo clans cannot be ranked in any single, encompassing hierarchy (Crocker 1969a and 1979). Nor in any sense are they organically unlike one another. Each clan's relations with its totemic *aroe* are entirely metaphoric and nominative. There are no postulated relations of descent from them; clansmen freely kill and eat their own *aroe,* obeying only those species-specific rules which all Bororo must follow. The Bororo, then, are "naturally" homogeneous and so may intermarry. The paradox here, between cultural specialization and organic identity is neatly resolved by Meri's transformations. He causes men following unique crafts to change into different *natural* species, forever organically specialized for those activities, and thus true "castes."

It is perhaps for this reason that Meri is especially nasty to members of his own clan and, to a lesser extent, of his "own" moiety, the Exerae, defying the normative standards regarding proper conduct with siblings. He and Ari copulate with their own sisters. He wrests away the material possessions of his clan brothers by force, and he even kills his own nephews and nieces (the children of *o*; herons are an *aroe* totem of the

Bado Jeba Xebegiwuge). His relations with Ari, his brother, are marked by deception and betrayal. The Bororo now point out that sun and moon have precisely opposite and opposed paths in the cosmos and conclude, "It is difficult for brothers to stay together." In the final episode, though, Meri is treated just as he has treated others; he is assigned a name, a habitat, and a diet.

But the striking element in the myth, one that reveals some basic aspects of Bororo thinking about the *bope,* is how Meri, through all his anomalous, immoral, disordered conduct, creates natural order, originating species and assigning them a perpetual ecological, symbolic, and categorical status in the universe. It appears that the *bope,* although the animating principle of organic transformation and serial change, are themselves subject to the prescription that things must be themselves, reflect the attributes and roles implicit in their names. They cannot go dashing about the universe, changing things at will and upsetting proper morality. The Bororo, by identifying Meri and defining the terms of their relationship with him, establish the principles whereby the reciprocal transactions between society and the *bope* must be governed.

These principles are summarized in the obligation to render to the *bope* their "foods," the species they prefer to eat, by reason of the great amounts of *raka* such species contain. So "strong" are they, say informants, that the *bope* need not act to punish anyone who consumes them wrongly, for he will sicken and die mechanically from the contaminating powers which inhere in them. Giving such foods to the *bope* before humans eat them is at once a moral prescription and a means whereby their power is reduced to the point where they are safe for most human consumption. The analysis of why these species rather than others symbolize the *bope*-human relation must take account of their dual character as objectively dangerous and as symbolically appropriate gifts for the *bope.*

## Foods of the *Bope:* Ethnographic Particulars

The *bope ure* species are given in Table 4.1. I have indicated the parts considered most potent in *raka* and hence the object of particular shamanistic care in butchering and eating. "Types within species" details which sexes and ages of the species must be given to the *bope.* The division into "cooked" and "raw" indicates which species can be eaten by the *bope* (that is, the shaman) without cooking and which are so powerful that their strength must be reduced by cooking until they are safe for the shaman who, even though protected by the *bope,* still has some human vulnerability to these "poisons." The list is given in the order most utilized

Table 4.1. *Bope Ure* Species

| Bororo | English | Zoological Name | Types Within Species | Species' Crucial Parts and Organs |
|---|---|---|---|---|
| 1. *Ki* | Tapir | *Tapirus terrestris* | Both sexes<br>Young and adult<br>Cooked | Head, vertebral column, hindquarters |
| 2. *Uwai Xoreu* | "Black" alligator | *Caiman* gen. | See below<br>Cooked | Head, tail, and lower stomach |
| 3. *Atubo* | Big horned or swamp deer | *Blastocerus dichotomus* | Adult male only<br>Cooked | Head, upper part of vertebral column |
| 4. *Baxieje* | Pampas deer | *Blastocerus campestris* | Adult males and females<br>Cooked | Head, upper part of vertebral column |
| 5. *Pogobo* | Brocket deer | *Mazama americana* | Adult males and females<br>Cooked | Head, upper part of vertebral column |
| 6. *Orogu* | Small horned deer | *Mazama simplicornis* | Adult male only<br>Cooked | Head, upper part of vertebral column |
| 7. *Pari* | Rhea (South American ostrich) | *Rhea americana* | Both sexes<br>Young and adult<br>All eggs<br>Cooked | Head, neck and area around tail |
| 8. *Beo* | Seriema | *Cariama cristata* | Both sexes<br>Young and adult<br>All eggs<br>Cooked | Head, neck and area around tail |
| 9. *Okiwa* | Capivara | *Hydrochoerus hydrochaeris* | Both sexes<br>Young and adult<br>Raw | Head, vertebral column, paws, wide strip of stomach longitudinal |
| 10. *Jugo* | Queixada, wild pig | *Tayassu pecari* | Both sexes<br>Young and adult<br>Raw | Head, vertebral column, paws, intestines |

(*continued*)

Table 4.1. (Continued)

| Bororo | English | Zoological Name | Types Within Species | Species' Crucial Parts and Organs |
|--------|---------|-----------------|---------------------|-----------------------------------|
| 11. *Jui* | Caitetu, wild pig | *Tayassu tajacu* | Both sexes Young and adult Raw | Head, vertebral column, paws, intestines |
| 12. *Kidokia* | Pirarucu | *Arapaima gigas* | All members of species Cooked | Head, gill fins, tail, stomach, ribs, plates from below head |
| 13. *Orarije* | Surubim | *Pseudoplaty-stoma cor-ruscans* | All members Cooked | Head, tail, stomach |
| 14. *Poru* | Jau (Amazon catfish) | *Paulicea lutkeni* | All members Cooked | Head, tail, stomach |
| 15. *Metugu Kuja-gure* | Red-necked dove, parari | *Zenaidura au-riculata nor-onha* | All members All eggs | Head, neck, area around tail |
| 16. *Bato* | Mangaba | *Hancornia speciosa* | First fruits Raw | Entire |
| 17. *Eko* | Pequi | *Caryocar brasiliensis* | First fruits | Entire |
| 18. *Jatugo* | Caja (hog plum) | | First fruits Raw | Entire |
| 19. *Boko* | Quince | | First fruits Raw | Entire |
| 20. *Kimao* | Fruit of cotton plant | | First fruits Raw | Entire |
| 21. *Oto* | Wild tuber | | First fruits | Entire |
| 22. *Oko* | Morera (like mangaba) | | First fruits | Entire |
| 23. *Oturo* | Wild tuber | | First fruits | Entire |
| 24. *Pagaje* | Wild tuber | | First fruits | Entire |
| 25. *Kido* | Fruit of the almece-gueira (mastic tree) | | First fruits | Entire |

(continued)

Table 4.1. (*Continued*)

| Bororo | English | Zoological Name | Types Within Species | Species' Crucial Parts and Organs |
|--------|---------|-----------------|----------------------|-----------------------------------|
| 26. *Aima-gadu* | Pau-do-ser-rote | | First fruits | Entire |
| 27. *Kuiada* | Maize | | First fruits Raw | Entire |
| 28. *Pu* | Wild tuber | | First fruits | Entire |
| 29. *Pore-dawu* | Wild cipo | | First fruits | Entire |
| 30. *Poruru* | Wild cipo | | First fruits | Entire |
| 31. *Jowe* | Honey of the ta-taira bee | *Melipona ta-taira* | After each discovery Raw | Section from each comb |

by informants, which tends to reflect the relative symbolic importance of each species in the group.

There are many notable features of this list of "ritual foods" which have caught the attention of all ethnographers of the Bororo. The extent and precision of the designation of various natural species as *bope ure* are all the more remarkable since all Bororo have agreed on these details for at least fifty years[9] (Steinen 1942; Albisetti and Venturelli 1962: 241–42[10]; Tonelli 1928; Cruz 1943). The extreme care with which Bororo adhere to the obligation to render up these substances to the *bope,* and the dramatic manner in which the shaman accomplishes this task, impress Brazilians who know them only casually.[11] Individual Bororo, normally casual and relaxed in their intimate contacts with the supernatural world, show anxiety when they must deal with the *bope ure* and worry vocally that they may have inadvertently committed some slight fault. And, as mentioned earlier, nearly all afflictions among contemporary Bororo are attributed to some infraction of the rules surrounding these species. For not only are humans required to offer the *bope ure* to the shaman before they can be safe for general consumption, but the procuring and preparation of these species must be carried out with precision.

The myth states that the *bope* may legitimately be offended if one of "their" animals is wounded and escapes the hunter. Such an event seems considered a kind of lèse majesté, especially if the animal is hurt severely enough so that it later dies, never to be properly delivered up to the *bope.* This idea actively constrains Bororo hunting. I have often seen Bororo refuse to shoot at one of the *bope ure* if there seemed to be any chance they could not wound it mortally or successfully pursue it later. For this reason they practically never seek to kill alligators, which slip away into deep holes in the river when wounded. Again, hunters, when alone or with a single companion, will usually not try to pursue tapirs, whose tough hides protect them from suffering immediately from one or two projectiles. Tapirs, and wild pigs also, are therefore usually hunted by groups of men, which is to say in the context of the collective hunts organized under the aegis of the *aroe*. And, if far from the village and lacking a shaman in their company, hunters will refuse to kill any kind of *bope ure* whatsoever, owing to the difficulties in obtaining the necessary shamanistic intervention. One reason the Bororo lavish so much attention on their bows and arrows and other weapons is explicitly attributed to their concern for the efficacy of these in hunting the *bope* food species. The proliferation of classes of specialized arrows for tapir, pigs, deer, fish, and birds (cf. Albisetti and Venturelli 1962: 932–53) is attributed to the same motives. Several men also justified their preference for firearms on the grounds that these were "better" for the killing of *bope* game.

None of this should be taken to indicate that Bororo fail to pursue these restricted species with any less vigor and skill than they devote to the hunting of other quarry. On the contrary, the meat of the *bope ure* is considered to be the best tasting of all game, as well as vital for the maintenance of the *raka* of the hunters and their relatives. Any Bororo who must go for more than a week without eating them feels himself deprived and malnourished. In short, the *bope ure* are the epitome of things that are dangerous but good to consume. And they are perfectly suited to human diet, if only the rules surrounding them are properly obeyed.

These rules also stipulate the manner in which each species is to be butchered, cooked, and eaten by the *bope* (that is, by the shaman). The first of these tasks is so precise and complex in its traditional regulation that only shamans are considered to possess the requisite knowledge and a certain degree of invulnerability to the dangers involved. This presumption often makes for considerable practical difficulties. If a large *bope* animal is killed far from the village, the successful hunter cannot cut it up into pieces to facilitate transportation. (He can, however, gut the creature to prevent its spoiling.) He must transport it to a shaman, or one must come out to where it was killed. This problem arises especially in the cases of tapir, capivara, alligators, the larger deer, and the fish species (which may weigh up to 20 or more kilos, but which can also be transported by canoe to the village's proximities). Once present, the shaman proceeds according to a strict sequence of skinning and butchering which varies for each species.

In the case of tapir, the vertebral column is first carefully sectioned into pieces, each containing a single bone. Then the head is cut up, first slicing away the sides and then removing the tongue, eyes, and brain. The intestines are next removed, and then two large pieces from the animal's rump, one from each side. The front legs are cut off at the body, and divided into thigh, leg, and hooves. The same procedure is followed for the back legs. Finally the trunk is sectioned, working from the head backward. Each rib is removed separately, and the stomach cut into long strips. Each part of the animal thus dissected out has a specific name, "given it by the *bope*." The butchering techniques for the other quadrupeds follows roughly this order, with priority and special care being given always to the parts listed as crucial. These are considered to be especially potent in *raka*, for, as several informants said, "Without them the animal cannot live." They manifest this quality by tasting very strongly of *jerimaga*, the odor associated with *raka* and the *bope* generally. For this reason, these parts are retained by the shaman, recooked the next day, and again eaten by the *bope*. Only after this can ordinary people consume them safely.

In some animals certain organs are considered so extremely powerful that they cannot be eaten even by the *bope*, and instead can be used only to make "medicine" (*jorubo*). The most potent of these is the bile gland (*eku*) in black alligators and the male alligator's testicles. If the bile gland is accidentally punctured before or during removal, thus ruining the meat, the *bope* are exceedingly angered, and they kill the shaman or the slayer of the alligator within a few days. Once he has safely extracted the bile gland, the shaman blows on it and rubs it into his head. He is thus furnished with a powerful medicine for his encounters with evil *bope* (see following section). The same procedure is followed with the testicles of a male alligator. This reptile and the *kidokia* (pirarucu) are considered the most dangerously imbued with *raka* of all the *bope* food species, and as presenting special perils to the shaman who must butcher and cook them. The pirarucu has no especially deadly organ, but it possesses a curious bony plaque just below the head. This must be "eaten" (sucked) twice, after which two small holes are bored in its edges and it is worn on the forehead of the shaman while about his various duties. It increases his powers and affords him a degree of protection against the dangers met in his contacts with the *bope*. The musk glands found along the inner rear thighs of both sexes of pampas deer and brocket deer, and in the males of the two varieties of horned deer, and the testicles of all male deer, are treated like the alligator's bile. But they are considered less potent, and some shamans do not utilize their magical properties.

After butchering the animal, the shaman and his wife boil the meat completely, or, with species that may be eaten raw, the shaman may proceed directly to calling the *bope*, becoming possessed, and eating the *bope ure*. This process is described in the next section; here it should be mentioned that the order in which the pieces are eaten replicates that in which they were removed from the animal. The Bororo claim that a shaman would not be able to butcher the *bope* species with any safety unless guided and instructed by his familiar *bope*. They also admit that shamans beginning their careers will solicit advice and help from a more experienced shaman in the butchering of the *bope ure*. This is the only context, to my knowledge, in which there is any degree of instruction in the mysteries of shamanism among the Bororo. Of course, there is no prohibition on anyone attending the preparation and subsequent eating of the *bope* food. Experience of such procedures is a weekly, if not daily, element in every Bororo's life from infancy. Spectators must take care not to come into physical contact with the blood, offal, or parts of the animal, lest they be polluted, but other than that the processing goes along in a fairly offhand manner.

All the dangers in the killing and delivery of the *bope* species to the spirits derive from the *bope*'s "jealousy" over the natural entities which are consecrated to them. That is, the *bope* are thought to be aware of human actions in carrying out their obligations with respect to these entities, and to act deliberately in punishing any error, deliberate or accidental, in the accomplishment of the stipulated procedures. But simultaneously the substances involved are credited with autonomous powers so deadly that their consumption without shamanistic intervention is tantamount to suicide. "The *bope* do not have to notice, you just die."

Some years ago there was a severe epidemic of measles at Korugedu Paru, in which most of the children between three and ten died. In trying to treat the illness, the village's shamans were told by their familiar *bope* that the children had eaten *bope ure* that had not been first given to the *bope*. It seemed that most of the children had been attending school at the nearby Indian Service post, as required by Brazilian law. Since the post was too far from the village for the children to return home for the noon meal, considered essential by Brazilians, the children were fed at the post. One lunch contained bits of deer killed by a non-Bororo and consequently not given to the *bope*. The children died.

For this reason the Bororo are reluctant to comply with the requirement to send their children to school. Nor will most normally accept any meals from Brazilian hands. Even if the foods themselves are innocuous, the vessels in which they are prepared and served may well be contaminated through prior contact with *bope* foods not first given to the *bope*. (Younger Bororo adults are noticeably more inclined to eat among Brazilians, just as they are to enter into other kinds of contacts with them. Older people point out that their juniors are constantly dying, afflicted by one disease after another, and generally without *raka*.)

In treating an illness the *bope* speak through the shaman, revealing the circumstances in which the patient had contracted his illness. Most of these "causes" involve some inadvertent contact with the polluting *bope* foods before they have been completely eaten by the *bope*. In one case, the sister of a shaman's wife was alone in the household one afternoon and, discovering a bit of tapir's tongue, happily gobbled up this choice morsel. But the shaman had only eaten it once, then setting it aside for a later recooking and a second offering to the *bope*. The sister became very ill, but since the meat had lost some of its potency in the first eating by the *bope,* the shamans were able to save her.

In another case, a bit of deer meat had not been thoroughly cooked and still had traces of blood around the bone. In his greed for the stuff the hunter's brother, who had been given this piece as part of his proper share of the kill after the shaman had prepared and given it to the *bope*, ate it right down. He sickened and died about half a year later. In a third case, a group of three men had visited some Brazilians and become thoroughly drunk. On their way back to the village they discovered some rhea eggs and decided to take these with them. But, in his befuddlement, one of them dropped the eggs he was carrying and was splattered by their contents. He died a few weeks later.

Most of the *bope*'s "explanations" are similarly very circumstantial accounts of the trivial situations in which someone came to have malign contact with their foods. Many Bororo profess to be unaware of the fault which led to their illness, even after the *bope* related its details. In the majority of cases, these faults are twenty or thirty years old when their committor finally becomes fatally ill. All an individual's history of sicknesses, accidents, and general health problems may then be traced to a single original "mistake." Prior variant explanations by the *bope* are attributed to the fact that the *bope* constantly lie, that a person could well have multiple contacts with "raw" *bope* foods, and that the "power" (*raka*) of these substances takes many curious twists and turns in afflicting an individual before finally, and inevitably, killing him.

Afflictions and deaths officially attributed by the *bope* to deliberate or at least partly volitional offenses against them are much less frequent than ones explained by completely innocent contacts with their unpurified foods. Nearly all the former involved offenses in hunting the *bope* animals. In one case an old man apparently suffered some form of nervous seizure or a heart attack, and fell into the cooking fire. He was not discovered until after he had been badly burned. His death a few days later was attributed by the *bope* to his loss of a wounded deer in his youth. For years he led a remarkably healthful life, since he took great care to avoid the area where he had lost the deer. Finally, little remembering the episode, he entered it again and was soon very seriously ill. In treating him, the *bope* said that the particular *maroeboe* who lived in that area had by no means forgotten the offense against it and that he should never again venture into the place. But finally, when very old, he did, and his seizure and burning were the consequence. One shaman said that in this case the *maroeboe* had enlisted the aid of *Imokuri,* the *bope* especially associated with fire. It wanted to punish the old man severely, to make him suffer before he died. *Imokuri,* who found the whole scheme of using the man's infirmities of age against him very comical, was happy to oblige. (As this indicates, the powers of certain *bope* are thought restricted to the areas they live in. They can afflict and even kill someone who offended them only when he or she enters these areas. However, they can sometimes secure the cooperation of more omnipotent *bope* to work vengeance at any distance.)

The minor number of afflictions attributed to deliberate offenses hold true only on the level of public, *bope*-derived explanations. In private, most cases are said to originate in some completely volitional act characterized by both stupidity and a near-defiance of the *bope.* Often the culprits are drunk, a condition which leads to fights between kinsmen and housemates, and other violations of Bororo moral norms. Or some member of a household in which a shaman resides, typically a wife's sister, is not able to control her (or his) greed for the *bope* foods and eats them before they have been sufficiently offered to the spirits. There are also a number of offenses against the shaman himself or his wife, such as adultery with her, which are considered volitional offenses against the *bope.* There is a marked tendency for the patient's relatives, especially his agnates and affines, to perpetuate the public version of his innocence, and his ill-wishers, among whom figure prominently his matrilateral kin, to spread word of the "real" reason for his affliction. The last are usually obtained, or alleged to come, from shamans who are not themselves treating the case but who can learn its true character from their own *bope* familiars. But in no instance does the specific nature of the fault alter treatment or have any direct social or symbolic consequences. Most Bororo accept that the great majority of afflictions derive from the lethal powers inherent in the *bope* foods themselves, without any deliberate intervention by the *bope.* The precise origin is material only for gossip or for intellectual inquiry in the ways of the *bope.*

Further details of cases, their explanations, and treatments are given in the next section. But enough material has been presented to allow an analysis of why the species designated as "food of the *bope*" should be considered so organically powerful and to explore the complexities of the symbolisms involved in relating affliction to this cause.

capivara

# 5

≈⁓ᵥⱽᵥᵥᴥⱽᵥᵥ⁓

# First Fruits, Sacrifice, and Dangerous Foods

$T$he initial problem is why the *bope* foods should be dangerous in their condition of natural, polluting substances but also consecrated to a class of supernatural forces, who punish all violations of their rights over these substances. Why do the "gods" so jealously demand "dirt"? There are two theoretical aspects to this issue: the conceptual attributes of the *bope* food species that distinguish them from other "meaningful" animals, and the nature of the relationship between men and spirits that the ritual treatment of these species expresses. In terms of traditional anthropological thought this contrast has been expressed in terms of the differences between "first fruits" and sacrifices. The *bope* foods can be regarded as combining attributes of both these institutions. First fruit ceremonials have been most often interpreted in terms of their automatic, cyclical attributes, as being bound up with the social consequences of seasonal variations in local ecology. They have a marked element of what Victor Turner has called *communitas* (1969: 125–45), a sociopsychological condition in which the whole collectivity sets aside its customary hierarchies and unites to celebrate its most fundamental common values. First fruit rites often have a purifying, cleansing character, with the explicit intention of ceremonially removing pollution and thus reestablishing a sacred order which had degenerated or gotten frayed and messy. There is also a marked contractual element in these seasonal rites, which portray society and the supernatural as having mutual duties and rights in regard to one another. Finally, the specific entities regarded as first fruits are dangerously potent, lethal to human consumption until after the spirits have partaken of them. They themselves may symbolize or incarnate deities; thus, to partake of them is to effect a very direct physical union with these powers. Their potency may derive from their medial, anomalous condition in which they combine attributes normally associated with entirely separate domains, such as those of men and of the supernatural.

First fruits are in themselves sacred, rather than deriving their sacrality from the ceremonies which employ them both as means and as ends in themselves. The classic analysis of the theoretical and social significances of first fruits rites is in Durkheim's *Les Formes Elémentaires de la Vie Religieuse*. Even though the ethnographies on which he based his work may have been incorrect and some of his conclusions logically unacceptable (Evans-Pritchard 1965: 57–69), his interpretation of the profound consequences of the periodic eating of totemic creatures has been a major element in the anthropological study of religion. In the Bororo case, his thesis should at least apply to the vegetable species included in *bope* food, for even if these are in no fashion "totemic," their periodic consumption is surrounded with many of the objective features he attributed to the *intichiuma*, "rites of increase."

By contrast, sacrifice seems most often situational and circumstantial, directed first toward such specific events as personal misfortune which do not involve the entire collectivity. Yet, it can also be intended for the removal of categorical pollution, for the reordering of all moral relationships when the whole of the society perceives its integrity threatened. Then, through "scapegoats," sacrifice operates in a much less mechanistic, automatically efficacious fashion than do first fruit rites. It may be necessary to repeat the sacrifice, for instance, or the spirits may signal their refusal of the ritual by allowing the affliction to kill the individual. Ethnographically, the distinction between first fruits and sacrifice is often difficult to make, especially within certain ethnographic areas such as New Guinea where such creatures as pigs seem to be treated as "sacrificial fruits." The use of one or the other perspective probably derives more from various theoretical attitudes of the particular analyst than from any precise conceptual differentiation between the two institutions (Mauss and Hubert 1899).

My assumption is that first fruits always involve some element of sacrifice but that sacrifice by definition lacks the periodicity and collective quality of first fruits. Perhaps the sharpest contrast between the two can be made in terms of the character of the entity given up to the spirits. A sacrificial victim most commonly seems to be an element of ordinary diet, not anomalous in any way and symbolizing those parts of the natural world most closely identified with man, rather than with spirit; that is, the object sacrificed is almost universally domesticated. This suggests that it is a metonymic extension of the self, expressing either that self's best aspect (as in a son or daughter), or worst (as in a scapegoat), or, most usually, some ambiguous mixture of the self's attributes, which neatly appears in a particular domesticated species. Further, the sacrificial ritual itself endows the victim with much of its mediatory capacity, so that the same metonymic logic can be used to substitute one kind of victim for another (Lévi-Strauss 1962b: 296–302). But this flexibility should not be exaggerated. The capacity of lesser victims still to convey the self's identity rapidly vanishes. Although the Nuer may use a cucumber rather than an ox in sacrifice, they seldom do so. And Beidelman has shown just how apposite to the sacrificial context are the ox's symbolic associations with its owner (Beidelman 1966). Also, some individuals within a species have qualities, whether natural (such as color—a black cock), or socially imposed (castration, docking, dehorning), which set them apart as especially appropriate sacrificial victims. In short, the individualization of the victim is appropriate to the singularity of the afflicted person on whose behalf the sacrifice is conducted.

First fruits by definition are not particularized members of their species; most often (and certainly among the Bororo) the particular objects given to the spirits should be exemplars of all the essential attributes of the species. Nor are the Bororo's sacrificial victims "domesticated," except in the case of corn. Further, the rites which employ them as vehicles of communication have the explicit double purpose of bestowing upon the deities their rightful due and of making the designated species safe for human consumption for a circumscribed length of time. The social eating of the "fruits" is the essential terminal act in the ceremony, whereas it may be only a welcomed side benefit in sacrifice.

It seems pointless to generalize further about contrasts between these two ways of using animals and plants to maintain and transform relations between society and non-empirical reality. As with many other anthropological generalities, the contrast between sacrifice and first fruits loses analytical utility in the measure as the terms become increasingly global and must include widely variant indigenous practices. The point here is to apply these concepts to the *bope ure* to see if they illuminate some aspects of the significance of these foods as points of articulation between Bororo and *bope*.

Certainly the species which must be eaten by the *bope* have many aspects of first fruits. First, nearly all the vegetable substances involved are first fruits in a literal sense. Next, the collective contractual obligation rather than the individual petition is the explicit indigenous reason for the transaction. Although the Bororo are careful to let the *bope* know that it is so-and-so who killed the game or gathered the plant, this is certainly not done in order to secure the good offices of the *bope* for any particular case of affliction. Nor does it matter in the least if a man has provided the *bope* with vast quantities of food over the years; they judge his activities as strictly as they do the behavior of one who has given them almost nothing. Indeed, several informants said that to seek deliberately to secure *bope* food so as to win their favor was very foolish, since it merely increased the chances of offending them. Every particular offering of food to the *bope* is presented as one more instance of the entire society's compliance with the rules governing the relation between it and the *bope*, rather than in individual terms.

To be sure, after eating, the *bope* speaks through the shaman promising long life and freedom from hurt for the person who obtained its food and for his or her children and relatives. This is logical enough, for just as individuals are obliged to render up the meals required by the *bope* on behalf of the entire society, so only the individual rather than the community is rewarded for so doing, or punished for infractions against the rules. But these punishments are precisely the *cause* of afflictions, rather than the means of terminating them. If the offerings of the animals, birds, and fish included among the *bope ure* have a sporadic and circumstantial character, this derives uniquely from the fortunes of the hunt and not from alterations in social or personal conditions. In short, the whole idea of sacrifice appears foreign to the Bororo and may well be antithetical to the cosmological assumptions implicit in all shamanistic systems.[12] Rather, the *bope* foods are certainly first fruits at least in their quality as elements in a contract between spirits and men. This is certainly explicit enough in the myth explaining the origin of the institution and is manifest in the *bope*'s guarantee after eating that they will respect their side of the contract in forbearing to hurt mankind.

But there is something more to the substances involved in the transaction than their quality of tithes or payments. The preceding material has shown that the *bope ure* entities are considered dangerous in and of themselves, quite aside from the *bope*'s voluntary participation in human contacts with them. However, this dangerous quality is one of valued potency rather than of "uncleanness." If they are polluted, it is because they are surcharged with the force that endows all living things to procreate, act out their destinies as determined by the organic nature of their species, to be what they are within the world of natural being. The *bope*'s consumption of "their foods" removes the lethal quality so that they can be eaten by humans, though never with complete impunity.

This quality, the potency of *raka*, is as much an inherent quality within the species as, say, their coloring. Its variable degree between the separate species making up the *bope ure* is revealed in the conceptual and practical differences in the ways these are ritually handled, in terms of the subdivision between those which are "strong" and those considered "weak." The former must be cooked before being eaten by the *bope,* lest they kill the shaman. And parts of these creatures considered especially potent in *raka* must be eaten by the *bope* a second time before ordinary people can eat them. Even then, these parts are thought so imbued with *raka* that they continue to be too "strong" for children, invalids, parents just before and after childbirth, and others whose personal *raka* is vulnerable. The "weak" foods, including the wild pigs, capivara, and all fruits, are those which the shaman may eat "raw" and which all individuals regardless of particular condition may partake of after his (the *bope's*) meal. This does not mean that their diminished potency makes the *bope* any less jealous of their rights over them, nor does it detract from their power to kill anyone so foolish as to eat them before the *bope* have. They are still autonomously *raka.*

Cooking, then, merely enables the shaman to eat the especially potent substances; it is simply a way of allowing a human being, even though under the protection of the *bope,* to incorporate their power without harm to his own mortal self. Whether or not their food is cooked makes no difference to the *bope.* The point is that these distinctions emphasize the way the Bororo consider the *bope ure* as organically different from other natural substances and, hence, as requiring technical as well as ritual means to make them safe for humans. Thus, the second theoretical aspect becomes relevant: the conceptual attributes of the *bope* food species considered as elements in Bororo taxonomic classification. This means that all the entities classed as food of the *bope* are perceived as in some fashion unique elements in the domain of nature.

It would seem a reasonable assumption that items classed together and treated in the same ways might be seen as having something in common. But investigation does not entirely support this. In the Bororo case, some foods are dangerous only to certain categories of persons in special conditions, as before and after childbirth. Other items are thought "polluted" for reasons involving indigenous principles of zoological classification. Bats, say the Bororo, are quite inedible because they fly like birds but bear their young live; they hang upside down and are active only during the night: "We do not know what to do with them" (see also below). This confirms Douglas' (1966) general point that all "unclean," polluting entities are anomalous. All dangerous or inedible things are somehow "out of place"; for equivalent if not identical ways, their attributes contradict the principles of classificatory logic employed by the society. But, as Bulmer (1967: 22) says, "Things can be out of place in so many ways, in terms of so many different, even if linked, dimensions." The general difficulty with Douglas's procedure is that it assumes that all criteria used in indigenous taxonomies are mutually exclusive and internally consistent, as indeed they are (or should be) in Western scientific classifications. It is a commonplace that classification can only proceed by neglecting certain aspects of reality and emphasizing others. It does not follow, however, that the neglected elements then disappear from human perception. Things are classed and related in different systems according to the various interests of the people doing the categorizing. They are quite likely to have different interests in one context and in another: cultures have multiple taxonomic systems which cover the same empirical ground in contrasting ways. The same class of thing may be present in several systems but categorized in each according to a different set of criterial attributes. In one system's terms the class might be ambiguous and not fit the principles employed; in another, operating with a different set of criteria, it may be entirely fitting and proper. Consequently, it is logically false to speak of a species as being anomalous, for only certain qualities can be, and then only in terms of a specific system of contrasts.

Furthermore, these various systems are not watertight compartments. Most human beings are not so single-minded that they are unaware of alternative modes of relating any entity to other things like or unlike it, even when they are busily occupied in acting out the principles used in only one of these modes. Therefore, since quite different sets of attributes are combined in the same class, it can provide in certain contexts a means of moving from one categorical system to another. I believe it is this type of mental shifting of cognitive gears that Lévi-Strauss has in mind when he speaks of "transformational systems." He assumes that certain classes of entities, preeminently natural species, possess especially crucial bundles of criterial attributes in that they either defy all logical classifications or unite all the principles employed in a unique synthesis. The first class contains those so anomalous they can articulate both natural and social taxonomies, such as Douglas's pangolin and Bulmer's cassowary (1966, 1967). The second class are those considered as "perfect animals" and ideal for any number of social ends, including consumption. But my thesis here is that, for both groups, human interaction with these entities must be conducted according to strict rules, for both are highly dangerous if for completely different reasons. If the total anomalies are by definition unfit for eating, then the "perfect animals" are the essence of food—but only if prepared and consumed according to rules. The *bope* foods are such "deliciously dangerous" entities just because they are in no way anomalous but are everything animals should be, in terms of Bororo classificatory principles.

Felicitously, during fieldwork I was unaware of any of the preceding arguments. Upon discovering that the Bororo attached great importance to the ritual treatment of an extensive but circumscribed list of animals, birds, fish, and plants, I assumed that all these things ought to have something in common and that this something was likely to be classificatory anomalies. I accordingly set out to explore Bororo ethnozoology and botany, with much frustration since these systems are characterized by a lack of higher-level inclusive lexemes and are said to be covert categories by the ethnozoologists (Berlin, Breedlove, and Raven 1968: 296–97). With informants I tried every imaginable way of relating and distinguishing natural species: taxonomies according to diet and habitat, nocturnal against diurnal, seasonal variations, color and plumage, mode of locomotion, family dwelling against pack animals, anatomical morphology, and on and on. For a few days it seemed that a distinction between animals endowed with external testicles as opposed to those with interior sexual organs was promising, but it did not apply to the fish and bird members of *bope ure,* let alone to the vegetable elements.

After several months of my haranguing them about these matters, the Bororo had become quite sensitive to my demands about "things that were out of place, and not as they should be." One evening at twilight I was lying in the *bororo,* the central dance plaza, among all the men who gather every night to stare at the sky and arrange practical and ritual affairs for the next day. I managed to distinguish a bat flying overhead from all the other evening birds, and I remarked idly that in my country we thought bats were "funny." There was a moment of stunned silence, and then a chorus of assent. "Oh yes," everyone said, "We think too that bats are very strange. It is a warm-blooded thing that flies by night but has no feathers, and it sleeps hanging upside down. It is all black and suckles its young."[15] In response to my questions the men said that those things were just too peculiar to have anything to do with either *bope* or *aroe.* As for eating them, there was no particular interdiction on doing so, but no one had ever thought of doing so, or would.

There was a general sense of relief that at last my obstinate queries had been understood and an appropriate area for their satisfaction been found. Subsequently, it was relatively easy to inquire about things "like bats" that were so anomalous they were not even regarded as possible sources of food. These various species were very useful in revealing the logic of various taxonomies. The river otter (*ipie*) was specifically noted as blurring one of the most critical distinctions in a taxonomy of habitat, that between land, furbearing mammals and scaly water creatures. Within the same classification the river dolphin[14] (*jakoreu*) was said to be like a bat in its bundle of contradictories: "It breathes air and nurses its young, yet it lives always in the water." Opossums and sloths are ambiguous in terms of a taxonomy that contrasts between animals capable of defending themselves and animals that depend on agility to escape predators. Both also live in trees, otherwise inhabited by mammals that epitomize speed and grace for the Bororo, the coati and monkeys. Other species were considered nonfoods because of the domestic intimacy of their association with men. Dogs and the various parrot species raised by the Bororo as pets are not considered as foodstuffs, although chickens and pigs, introduced by Brazilians, and the young of many wild animals are raised, slaughtered, and eaten with relish by their owners. When asked to account for their different treatment of household animals, people said simply, "Dogs and macaws help us; they are like us and do not defecate inside the house." Insects are generally considered nonfoods, but certain species are seen as so peculiar in morphology and habitat as to warrant avoidance of all contact. These include the giant "walkingstick" (*aturua,* Fasmideos suborder) and large kinds of spiders. The Bororo do not believe any specific harm might befall the killer of any of these, but just that such peculiar things are best left alone. This characterizes their general attitude to all the explicitly anomalous species, aside from the domesticated animals.

The Bororo do not prohibit these nonfoods in any specific fashion, nor are there any consequences, mystical or "organic," which they believe might attend their slaying or consumption. Instead, they just are never considered as possible sources of food. Perhaps the most significant aspect of this set of anomalous creatures, at least in terms of comparable elements in the symbolic systems of other societies, is that by no means all of them are imbued with ritual significance. While they may be anomalous, this feature in and of itself does not endow them with mystical importance. The bat, otter, dolphin, and macaw have great symbolic efficacy for the Bororo, but this quality only partly derives from their status as anomalies within the principles of Bororo ethnozoology. Further, creatures such as the various armadillo species, monkeys, anteaters, freshwater stingrays, and lizards are contradictory in terms of the multiple classificatory systems in which they are categorized, and they are also imbued with considerable cosmological significance. Yet this does not prohibit them from being eaten quite regularly and without any particular rules as to preparation and distribution.

The Bororo recognize a class of wild species as being only marginally edible, although the precise composition of the animals and other entities so regarded tends to vary from individual to individual. That is, there is no element of collective representation insofar as the possible consumption of these creatures is involved. Many Bororo refuse to eat snakes on the grounds that, uniquely among earth-dwelling animals, they have no legs. But some persons will consume rattlesnake and anaconda, reasoning that their special attributes render them something more than "snakes."[15] Most people do not eat any of the carnivores, mammalian or avarian: jaguars, large hawks, wolves, and the smaller felines. This is not because these creatures are in any way taxonomically ambiguous, rather the contrary. The specific reason for not eating them is that "they taste bad." A few Bororo are said not to mind their poor flavor, but such persons are usually old or crippled, without close relatives who provide them with frequent gifts of proper meat (i.e., that of the *bope ure*).

The consumption of carnivores seems consequently as much a matter of necessity as peculiar taste in food. The general reluctance to eat them also derives from their position in Bororo cosmology and from their ritual uses which reflect this position. The details of this symbolism are discussed in Chapter 9; they are all based on an analogy which compares human beings with carnivores, so that to eat the latter is tantamount to a kind of metaphorical cannibalism. Other creatures serve in various contexts as metaphors for various aspects of man, and these too are seldom eaten. Such include wild parrots of all kinds, certain herons and flamingoes, and fish hawks.

Again, there is no specific injunction against eating these species, only a vague feeling that it is not appropriate and that their flesh is repugnant. The usual Bororo attitude is similar to that of many Americans toward tripe, brains, stomach, tongue, and other organs, "thinkable" as foodstuffs but inedible in fact. Certainly the Bororo do not imagine that any harm, physical or mystical, attaches to their consumption. At the most, to eat these things is shameful, both because it implies the consumer is so helpless and socially isolated as to have to descend to subsisting upon "offal," and because these entities are identified in various fashions with humankind, specifically with the universal principle of soul, *aroe,* which all men possess. At the other extreme of the cosmological continuum, the species considered to manifest various attributes of the *bope,* such as vultures, certain hawks, and owls, are likewise possible to consider as edible, with no proscription against consumption, but in fact no one does eat them. Informants said that, if one were dying of starvation, such species just might serve as food, but only then. In contrast, the truly anomalous animals within Bororo taxonomy (such as the otter, bat, and opossum) were said to be inedible even *in extremis.*

Bororo dietary practices reflect a range of taxonomies and symbolic systems, in which the perceived attributes of various species are also associated with various principles as categories in their cosmology. These latter associations are at least as important in determining the possible edibility of any particular zoological entity as its position within any of the taxonomies utilized by the society. This is true whether the species are considered as separate classes or whether they are grouped together in more inclusive taxa on the basis of perceived similarity between certain of their attributes and those of the *bope* and the *aroe.* Only a few species can be regarded as total anomalies. These creatures, such as the otter and dolphin, serve as logical pivots in Bororo symbolism, points of articulation of "transformation" between different social and natural classifications.

But the species which are "food of the *bope*," as the Bororo finally succeeded in making clear to me, represent the essence of perfectly good natural categories. Then, if there is nothing ambiguous in their perceived attributes, the problem is to determine why such a heterogeneous assemblage should be considered to share some critical common feature which make them fit vehicles for transactions between *bope* and man and, more crucially, appropriate symbols for certain problematic aspects of social relationships associated with misfortune and disease.

## The Symbolic Meaning of the *Bope* Foods: *Raka* and *Jerimaga*

For a long time during fieldwork I was completely unable to find the element which was common to the jumbled set of animals, birds, fish, and plants that compose the *bope ure*. The traditional Bororo answer turned out to be that all the animals had "cloven hooves" (i.e., that they were ungulates), but this criterion did not apply to the fish and birds, nor was it internally consistent, since the Bororo happily eat beef whenever they can without any mention of the *bope*. Finally my *i-edaga*, a man of extraordinary learning and perception, was bothered enough by my insistent queries to become interested in the problem. He appeared one day with a wide grin and said that he had finally discovered the common attribute. "All the *bope ure*," he said, "have *jerimaga*." This is a particular smell or taste, most often described as musky, rank, decaying, or rotting.

The question of of whether all the *bope ure* do in fact taste of *jerimaga* notably more than do other natural entities is a difficult one. In my own experience, all the *bope* foods I ate were certainly musky, but no more so, and in some cases less so, than such animals as the coati. Subsequently, I asked virtually every adult Bororo I came to know for a list of edible things that were very *jerimaga*. Nearly all gave a list that included most of the *bope ure* but some other species as well, and individual lists overlapped but certainly did not coincide. When I asked bluntly if all the *bope* foods were in fact especially *jerimaga*, most informants responded, after some reflection, that they were, but that they had never thought of the fact before. The most I could determine was that *jerimaga* was characteristic in varying degrees of many substances and certainly not exclusive to the *bope ure*, even if these are perceived as especially laden with this smell. In fact, other things and conditions in the Bororo world are regarded as having a very great degree of *jerimaga*, much more than the *bope* foods.

Bernardo Xiwabore, the
author's *i-edaga* and principal
informant

    *Jerimaga* has already been mentioned as the odor characteristic of all *rakare* substances. Semen, blood, and menstrual fluids are all very *jerimaga*. So is all decaying organic matter, including human corpses. A man and woman after intercourse smell of it strongly, so that they should immediately bathe to avoid passing the pollution on to others. Very sick persons reek of *jerimaga,* as does the shaman when possessed. Finally, certain wild species besides the *bope ure* are considered to be very *jerimaga,* the vulture most of all. As one might suspect, the *bope* themselves are said to have the most *jerimaga* of any thing or condition, which is why the shaman smells so strongly during possession. One possible translation of *jerimaga* is "supernatural B.O."

    *Jerimaga* is inherent in substances which are undergoing the process of transformation from one organic condition to another and which consequently manifest simultaneously destruction and creation—the essential qualities of the *bope. Jerimaga* is the sensory dimension of *raka.* The two terms are aspects of a single conceptual state, or rather movement, for *jerimaga* is characteristic of all things in the process of dynamically losing *raka.* As all substances especially imbued with *raka* are polluting, so too is the stench this force gives off. Cooking, washing, and natural decomposition are consequently the modes whereby society can alter and control the dangers of this power. Things and conditions with much *jerimaga* not only threaten stable conditions of being by proximity, but they are themselves in dangerously fluid movement which, if not controlled by appropriate mechanical and symbolic actions, leads to the complete dissolution of *raka* and the total transformation of the things possessing it.

The presence or absence of *jerimaga* is a sign (rather than a symbol) which guides the Bororo in their conduct toward the powers of *raka*. This emerges clearly during the process of the funeral cycle, which is based on the practice of double interment. Intermittently the grave is opened to check the decomposition of the corpse, but it is only necessary to dig far enough to smell the relative amount of *jerimaga*. When the odor has almost completely disappeared, the bones are said to be "done" (*akedu*), the same term used to describe food when it has been completely cooked. In fact, the cook often smells the boiling food and judges its progress by the gradual disappearance of *jerimaga*. In terms of Lévi-Strauss's culinary triangle, the Bororo usage of *jerimaga* as a definitional element in the processes of organic transformation by cooking and putrefaction amounts to a behavioral validation of his theoretical triad. So too does the Bororo refusal to broil or to roast any of the *rakare* foods, on the grounds that such a technique is insufficient for the removal of *jerimaga*.

It is logical that the *bope* should have a special affinity for species of plants and animals which are especially marked by an abundance of *jerimaga/raka* and that these entities should be regarded as in some fashion preferred by the *bope*. However, there appears to be a contradiction, since the *bope ure* are not only perfectly good food, if handled according to complex rules, but they are also hardly in that condition of organic flux otherwise common to things reeking of *jerimaga*. I thought that it might be possible that this smell could be used in two different modalities by the Bororo: as an index for describing various organic conditions so as to control their transformations, and as a principle of taxonomic classification. I therefore inquired about Bororo views on all types of smell.

It turned out to be a very fruitful area of research. They distinguish eight principal types of smells-tastes and endow them with considerable symbolic importance. There does not seem to be a globally inclusive, explicit taxonomy based on these eight classes, although informants agreed that all substances in the world could, in principle, be assigned to one of them. The difficulty, they added, was that most things were a blend of two or three odors. Some were, of course, more unequivocally a single smell than others. Just as things strong in *jerimaga* are associated with the *bope,* elements clearly giving off the aroma of *rukore* are connected with the *aroe*. *Rukore* is described as a vaguely sweetish, "sticky" smell. It is found in corn, sugar, white mud, and duck feathers, all items intimately involved with the *aroe*. The other six classes of smells form a continuum between the two extremes of *jerimaga* and *rukore,* just as the substances they describe are a fusion of *bope* and *aroe* elements.

The general system is too vague and full of overlaps between the different categories to permit its use as a general plan for conceptual organization and practical action, except at the two extremes. There the importance of smell as a definitional criterion for revealing the true nature of a substance and as a symbolic operator[16] emerges in many planes of Bororo activity, as already noted for funerals and cooking. But smell intrudes constantly in daily life. Flatulence, for example, being strongly *jerimaga,* is much to be avoided. When anyone breaks wind in a public setting, the whole group goes through elaborate hackings, spittings, and coughings to expel the polluting odor from their bodies. It is thought especially shameful for men of dignity who possess ritual titles to flatulate; to guard against this possibility, they daily consume the berries of the urucu plant. These berries are also used to make a red paint which is used in almost every representation of the *aroe* and which is, of course, considered very *rukore*.

I was initially very perplexed at the importance of odor and taste for the Bororo. Roughly similar perceptual orientations were hinted at in ethnography (e.g., Radcliffe-Brown 1964: 311–15), but the Bororo seemed unique in their thorough attention to the symbolic and classificatory properties of smell. At the time I had read only *The Raw and the Cooked* of the *Mythologiques* series, in which significatory odors are mentioned only in passing (1969: 176–80). But with *From Honey to Ashes,* Lévi-Strauss established the symbolic dominion of smell in that area, and the Bororo ceased to be so anomalous. However, the analytical problem of the reeking *bope ure* not only was unresolved by becoming part of a larger culture-area pattern but was even intensified. For what does a particular odor *mean,* aside from its position within a system of contrasting properties? While for the Bororo the connection between *jerimaga* and the universal forces of death and creation appears well established, we are still left with the problem of why the *bope ure* and only they should at once have this smell and yet be regarded as good, if dangerous, to eat.

# The Symbolic Meaning of the *Bope* Foods: Nature, Sexuality, and Food

The philosophical and methodological issue presented by the *bope* foods is this: Do the fundamental categories guiding Bororo conduct toward the things they kill and eat reflect preexisting conditions of natural reality, or do they derive from the logic of Bororo social classifications and their experience of the rules which direct social order? Are the *bope* foods perceived as especially imbued with *jerimaga* just because they are normatively the mediators between man and *bope* and logically must participate in the perceptual characteristics of the spirits who consume them? Or are they appropriate mediators owing to a range of symbolic associations and positions within a variety of taxonomic systems? In the last case, their quality of common supernatural reek would be merely one more reason for their suitability as agents for the contract between society and spirits, rather than the perceptual cause of their special status.

Various aspects of Bororo animal symbolism suggest the second set of hypotheses as more nearly correct. First, there are creatures such as vultures and skunks which are viewed as having much more *jerimaga* than the *bope ure,* but just for that reason, the Bororo say, not even the *bope* would consume them. Second, their ritual use of such species as carnivores, parrots, and hawks, none of which are characterized by any particular smell, indicates that even though the Bororo may utilize smell in certain contexts as an index to symbolic behavior, this principle does not operate consistently and universally. More theoretically, I now regard any analytical approach which seeks to discover a unitary set of attributes unique and "definitional" to a class of ritually important substances as ethnographically misleading and logically incorrect. Wittgenstein (1953) demonstrated that the notion that something common underlies all the entities which we subsume under a single class term is false. "It is comparable to the idea that properties are ingredients of the things which have the properties, e.g., that beauty is an ingredient of all beautiful things as alcohol is of beer and wine, and that we therefore could have pure beauty, unadulterated by anything that is beautiful" (1953: 17). It can be shown that in a series of items no single property may be common to them all, although they share many elements in common. For example, the series ABCE ABCD ACDE BCDE ABDE is composed of items which have a strong "family resemblance," in Wittgenstein's terminology, yet they have no one common attribute.

This point seems to me so crucial that absence of its incorporation into the anthropological treatment of pollution, dietary rules, and animal symbolism deserves in itself some attention.[17] There seem to me two reasons for this neglect. Anthropologists have considered these topics either in terms of the anomalous position of a single species, such as the hyena or cassowary, in different systems of classification and action (Beidelman 1966, Bulmer 1967). Or they have analyzed the position of a range of species within a single categorical scheme (Leach 1964, Tambiah 1968, Crocker 1977b). The great theoretical problem presented by the *bope* foods comes from the way they are a heterogeneous *class* of entities which must be considered in terms of the totality of the taxonomic and ritual systems utilized by the Bororo.

The issue has now become to seek out the "family resemblances" among the *bope* food species. *Jerimaga* can now be considered a partial synonym for these resemblances, the mark rather than the single cause of their perceptual unity. Later in the section other sets of "families" associated in various symbolic fashions with the *bope* will be described and analyzed in order to round out the full range of Bororo attitudes toward the totality of the *bope* manifestations in the realm of nature. Subsequent chapters will provide comparable data for the *aroe*. For now, the problem is why certain animals and plants are thought to be alike in their simultaneous danger and excellence as foods.

I remained baffled by this problem for some time; finally, I realized that another species belonged implicitly to the *bope ure*—man himself. A variety of indigenous customs and beliefs imply this classification. The distinguishing characteristic of an evil shaman among the Bororo is that he steals the soul substance of others and consumes it, thus causing their immediate death. Such a shaman becomes very fat and reeks of *jerimaga*, as a result of the potent human *raka* he has consumed. The *bope* also attack people in much the same way, taking their souls while asleep and feasting upon them (see Chapter 7). Several shamans related that in their dreams they had witnessed the *bope* settling down to a feast of stolen souls, in which "the *aroe* did not look at all like people, but like real *ki* (tapir), *atubo* (deer), *pari* (rhea), *okiwa* (capivara), *jugo* (queixada), *kidokia* (pirarucu), etc. Several informants stated that decaying corpses smelled of *jerimaga* "just like tapir meat." The Bororo also collectively term themselves "the children of *pogobo*" (brocket deer), since in one origin myth a Bororo man mates with a female deer of this species to repopulate the earth after everyone but him has drowned in a flood caused by the *bope* (Crocker 1969a).

The sexual aspect of the inclusion of human beings among the *bope ure,* at least in terms of the *bope*'s own conduct toward them, is very marked throughout a range of Bororo beliefs and practices. As noted in the preceding chapter, the *bope* are thought to be very full of sexual desire and to recognize no rules in the satisfaction of their lust. Such a satyriasis is appropriate for spirits symbolizing the passions of organic life and the creative powers these bestow. The *bope* much prefer humankind as their sexual objects and incessantly try to copulate with sleeping women. One of the most reiterated elements in a young girl's moral education is the necessity of sleeping on her side, with her legs tightly closed, so as to frustrate the *bope*'s desires. Some informants said that the *bope* could enter the body of a fornicating man so as to participate in his sensual pleasure, but others denied that this was possible.

All Bororo agree, however, that the *bope* can enjoy the shaman's wife through the body of the shaman himself and that the spirits come to regard her as their special sexual object. For this reason, it is extremely ill advised to have sexual relations with a shaman's wife or widow, unless one is a shaman oneself. Furthermore, a consistent element in the stories about evil shamans involves their motivation by implicit cannibalistic hungers as well as by sexual desire (see following chapters). In fornicating with a desirable woman, the shaman's soul (or rather his *bope,* since he no longer possesses an *aroe*) "eats her up."

Outside the context of assumptions about the *bope* and their activities, the Bororo draw the almost universal equation between eating and copulating. A man's penis is sometimes said to be "cooked" in the vagina. Fire is often employed as a metaphor for sexual passion, just as the *bope* themselves are always very hot, as shown in the profuse sweating of a possessed shaman. Bororo women tend to equate sexual potency and a man's ability as a hunter, complaining bitterly if one or the other kind of "meat" is lacking. I never heard any one of them make the explicit comment reported by Siskind (1973: 105) for the Amazonian Tenetehara, among whom a woman's response to the failure of the hunters to bag any game during the day was ". . . there's no meat, let's eat penises." But the sentiment strikes me as typifying Bororo female attitudes. For the masculine part, a man's consumption of a meal sent him by an unmarried woman is the crucial acknowledgment that he accepts her proposal of marriage. Matrimony itself is defined by the husband's responsibility to procure meat, eminently that of the *bope ure,* and by the wife's to cook it properly. As all the material presented in the last section revealed, the residential group is a single organic unity because the biological processes of eating and copulating go on within it. But those data also demonstrated that for the Bororo sexuality is an exceedingly dangerous condition, which destroys human beings unless managed by obedience to rules governing the consequences of *raka.*

All of these associations indicate a myriad of associations between the *bope* food species and sexuality, and specifically that aspect of cosubstantial organic life which most menaces the participants in a marriage and, by extension, those who reside together. The *bope ure* symbolize these dangers and provide a set of metaphoric codes for expressing and manipulating them. But questions remain: Why should this particular set of creatures carry such a crucial set of associations? How can their ritual treatment serve as a code for the maintenance and restoration of the normative order essential to conjugal life?

The basis of the system lies in the analogy that the *bope ure* and sexuality are both dangerous but good, consumable if treated according to rules. That the rules in one case involve shamanistic intervention and the participation of the *bope* and, in the other, moiety exogamy and the proscriptions of menstruation and childbirth, requires separate explanations. The analogy does not directly equate women with the *bope ure.* Women are as menaced by the cosubstantiality of married life as men, and it was seen above that for them there is an equivalence between the *bope* foods and masculine generativity. However, the fact that the *bope* are treated as almost all male and that their assumed sexual relations with the Bororo are necessarily with women suggests that the foods reserved for them might be especially associated with female qualities, especially with the institutionalized opposition between the sexes. How, then, are the *bope ure* "like" women?

These species, with the exception of the alligator, are the ones most often sought and killed in the collective, ritualized hunts undertaken three or four times a month. This is not to say that the Bororo restrict themselves to these species during the hunts or that individual hunters do not often kill them when hunting ordinarily. But the entire set of animals, birds, and fish in the *bope ure,* and only they, are cited repeatedly in the *Koege Paredu,* the song cycle which is sung by most of the hunters in the men's house the evening before the collective hunt. Some informants were of the opinion that tapir, wild pig, capivara, rhea, and the forest deer were most effectively hunted by large groups of men. It is certainly rare for a single hunter or even two together to kill any of the first three species. These ritual hunts are always dedicated to the *aroe.* In them the hunters represent those deceased members of the opposite moiety for whom they are the ritual avengers and replacements (*aroe maiwu*). The hunts, as any action or object intimately associated with the *aroe,* are rigidly prohibited to women. They may not even view from a distance any part of the proceedings. If they should inadvertently come across the hunters, whom the Bororo regard as *"aroe"* during the entire course of the hunt and its ritual aftermath, the *aroe* themselves afflict the women, and the entire hunt is likely to be unsuccessful. The men claim that the women believe it is the souls of the deceased who participate in the hunt and actually kill the game. (The women know quite well the truth of the matter but go along with the men's elaborate pretensions with the usual wry humor they show toward all masculine-dominated ritual activities.)

When the game finally arrives in the village, it is first given to the *bope* through the shaman. Usually the services of two or three shamans are required if the hunt has been even moderately successful. The meat is then given to the ritual "mothers," the close female relatives of the dead persons who are being represented, on behalf of their ritual "sons," the *aroe maiwu.* After cooking or, in the case of the species especially laden with *raka,* recooking, the "mothers" season the food, retain some of it for their own households, and send the rest to their "sons" via their husbands, the ritual "fathers" of the dead and their replacements. Both these men, "sons" and "fathers," are members of the same moiety, opposite that of the "mothers" and the deceased persons. The "mothers" also prepare the vegetable foods appropriate for the *aroe* discussed in the last chapter, and send these dishes to their "sons." (See diagram.)

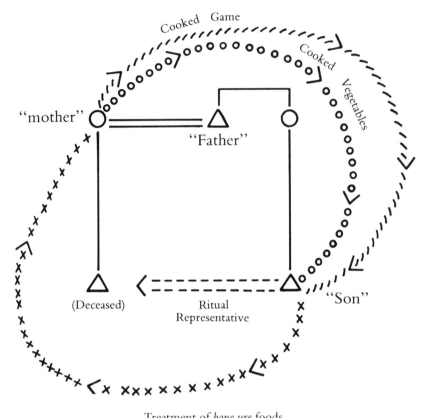

Treatment of *bope ure* foods

In sociological fact the game is killed, delivered, and ultimately consumed by the men of one moiety, with the females of the other moiety preparing both it and various vegetable dishes likewise eaten by the men. In representational terms the meat is killed and cooked by the souls and women of one moiety and eaten by their counterparts in the other division. All of these transactions proceed according to the strict rules surrounding the treatment of *bope ure* foods. They may thus be regarded as an elaborate metaphoric parallel to the exchange of feminine sexuality between the moieties. That is, the *bope* food species are those explicitly hunted by a group of men symbolically opposed to all femininity, with weapons that can be contaminated by the organic processes unique to women, and which are eaten after being purified through the *bope*'s intervention and exchanged across the moieties. Thus, moiety exogamy and dietary rules emerge as parallel methods for safely enjoying the powers of *raka* and sexuality, and therefore manipulating human capacity for creation-destruction. The ceremonial inversion involved in these particular transactions can be for the moment interpreted as another technique for coping with the dangers within all *rakare* things and conditions (cf. Crocker 1977c).

But none of this explains why the species treated as foods of the *bope* should also be considered, in their separate characteristics and as a set, appropriate metaphors for the social control of organic forces. Their prominence within the ceremonial context of representation of dead souls is like the attribution of *jerimaga* to them: It is a *post hoc* consequence of their special classificatory status, not a cause of it. Further, the vegetables prepared by the "mothers" and eaten by their *aroe* children usually preclude any of the plants included among the *bope ure*.[18] The original problem of the factors composing the "family resemblance" among these entities still remains.

However, it would appear that these factors have something to do with sexuality in general and female attributes in particular. There are various associations between the organic rhythms of women and the periodicity of at least some of the things within the *bope ure*. First, the bulk of the fruits, tubers, and other vegetables in this set become ripe at the end of the rainy season. This traditionally was the period spent in the village, for during the dry season groups of extended families would go on trek, just as among most of the Gê-speaking societies (Maybury-Lewis 1967: 53–59). The corn harvest and its attendant ceremonies also came at the end of the rainy season. This period was generally marked by intense ritual activity, focused of course on intermoiety exchanges of ritual services, food, and women. The plant elements in the *bope ure* might thus be regarded as a set of natural markers for the termination of a time of intense sociality and contact with both organic and spiritual forces, attended by all the dangers inherent in such contact. Of course, most plants bear at the end of the rainy season, and besides it would seem more sociologically and symbolically appropriate if the prestation of "their" vegetable foods to the *bope* marked the beginning rather than the end of this period.

One day during a collective hunt, one of the "*aroe*" suggested that it might be wise to visit a grove of hog-plum bushes (cajá, a *bope ure* plant), since both wild pigs and tapir were very fond of these fruits. It developed that the Bororo consider that all the large ungulates and the two bird species among the *bope ure* prefer to eat the fruits and tubers also found in that set. One informant even inferred that the *jerimaga* common to the animals derived from this diet! The Bororo are apparently sure that at least the plant elements within the *bope ure* are notable for their strong, musky flavor. But this only complicates the problem, for the status of *jerimaga* as symptom rather than cause of the special status of *bope ure* has already been demonstrated. I tried to determine if at least the mammalian members of this set were noted for the periodicity of their sexual activities. Again, the Bororo said that they all tended to bear young at the end of the rainy season, but then so did most animals, as well as birds. While the element of periodic fecundity was common to human females and the *bope ure,* and thus one factor in the "family resemblance," it certainly cannot be considered basic to this commonality of attributes.

More promising was the discovery that the Bororo considered the ungulates and two bird species to be "flock" or herd animals. They contrast this social life with the solitary habits of felines, birds of prey, and such creatures as the armadillo and anteater. Since the Bororo define human identity in terms of the necessity to live within one ordered society, the *bope* food species represent the extension into the natural world of this mutual dependency, and serve as models of its importance. Since human social organization is based on the fixed spatial and categorical order represented through and transmitted by women, here is an additional reason to identify at least some of the *bope ure* as "like" women. But while this helps to explain the inclusion of the ungulates and birds in the set, it hardly extends to the presence of the alligator and fish. The last do not spawn or "flock" in the manner of other fish species, such as the dourado and pintado. These last two are in some contexts used as aquatic metaphors for humankind, precisely because of the marked periodicity of their activities and their sociability. But the fish and alligator do share one characteristic with the other *bope ure:* they are the largest "game" found in the São Lourenço. The pirarucu, surubin, and jáu are kinds of catfish and may attain enormous sizes, up to 50 kilos or more. The alligator likewise provides a great deal of meat, even if it is tough and very "*jerimaga,*" almost too much so to be appreciated as food by most Bororo. Tapir, deer, capivara, rhea, and seriema are probably the largest and most "meaty" animals and birds hunted by the Bororo.

If size and economic importance are the crucial determinants of a species' inclusion in the *bope ure,* one of the oldest and simplest anthropological interpretations of the "ritual regard" accorded to certain natural entities must be resuscitated. Radcliffe-Brown (1964: 279–315) so explained the symbolic status and ritual importance given various species by the Andamanese. But his utilitarian pragmatism has been devastatingly criticized by generations of anthropologists (Lévi-Strauss 1962a, Beidelman 1966, Lowie 1942, Leach 1962), even though his position has not lacked various supporters (Harris 1968, Rappoport 1968). The crux of the issue turns on the ethnographic point that not all ecologically crucial species receive symbolic importance, while natural entities which either are not eaten or have a minimal place in the society's diet are among its crucial symbols. It is certain that for the Bororo the edibility and relative ecological importance of different species have very little to do with their general symbolic character. Eagles and jaguars, which are cere-monially utilized as basic symbolic operators (see Part IV), are seldom eaten, whereas such creatures as monkeys, armadillos, and ducks have great ritual and mythic importance while contributing relatively little to Bororo diet.

On the other hand, it must be said that all the animals, fish, and birds among the *bope ure,* and most of the plants, provide the most protein per member killed or collected. This is a matter of quantification, not of qualification. The arrival of a tapir or surubim in the village is a relatively rare event. Deer, capivara, and the two bird species are rather more fre-quent elements in Bororo diet, but even they appear only about once a week. Although my data are incomplete, they suggest that the *bope ure* species furnish about one-fourth of the natural protein consumed by a community in the course of a year. Fish other than the three *bope* species contribute nearly half of this food. The rest is made up of such animals and birds as armadillo, anteaters, various species of pheasant, wild tur-keys, monkey, coati, and a wide variety of water fowl. It hardly seems convincing that the Bororo would be so attentive to a kind of pound-for-pound comparison between the animals they hunt as to make this the basis of all their elaborate distinctions between those creatures eaten by the *bope* and those whose flesh is uncontaminating, even if sparse on the bone. On inquiring about this point, I did receive the information that the *bope ure* were not only the preferred game of the Bororo but also of carnivores and birds of prey. Perhaps, then, these species are perceived as symbolizing the totality of a kind of balance of nature, of reciprocal sym-biosis between "eaters" and "eaten" in which the Bororo appear as one among many carnivorous species.

This interpretation appeared most promising when I first began to think about it, for it was consistent with other aspects of Bororo sym-bolic treatment of natural species that are analyzed subsequently. The distinction between carnivores and herbivores is a basic one in their sys-tem, and certainly the identification of man with the former class is total and fundamental (see below and Part IV). But the great difficulty remains that man, and especially woman, also seem identified with the *bope ure.* Furthermore, the fish species and alligators did not seem particularly re-garded as the customary prey of felines and hawks. Nor could I under-stand why such animals as monkeys, armadillos, anteaters, and coati, not to mention such delicious smaller rodents as the paca, were excluded from the *bope ure* when they certainly were among the carnivores' diet, including man's.

I remained perplexed at this point in the analysis for some time. A structural pattern seemed to be emerging, but there were too many pieces which did not fit, quite aside from the bothersome difficulty of a lack of ethnographic data supporting the interpretation. Finally, in going through the texts of various song cycles, I was struck by the way in which all mammalian, reptilian, piscian, and avarian species, save those among the *bope ure,* appeared consistently in lists composed of things that either harmed man, or were "harmless," *baxe kudugu,* usually because they rarely if ever contacted humans. On checking further, it became apparent that the Bororo assume that all the *bope ure* animals are the pre-ferred food of carnivores precisely because they lack any natural means to defend themselves or to flee before their hunters.

This conclusion may at first strike those familiar with Brazilian fauna as inaccurate or even zoologically false. However, I can only repeat Lévi-Strauss's dictum that, if the primitive "science of the concrete" is amazingly attentive to a myriad of objective natural facts, the symbolic interpretation remains based in sets of conceptual structures deriving as much from social experience as from empirical reality (1962b). When the specific characteristics of each *bope* food species are considered from the perspective of their vulnerability (or "easy to eat"), Bororo attitudes may not be as unlikely as they initially appear.

The tapir, the very quintessence of *bope* food, is apparently sluggish and dull-witted (Ihering 1963: 52–53) and can defend itself only with its hooves. Its usual mode of defense is to flee ponderously to the nearest large body of water, at which point it attempts to escape by swimming. As far as the Bororo are concerned, the only practical danger involved in hunting tapirs is that, owing to their size and tough hide, they are hard to kill, requiring multiple arrows, clubbing, and throat cutting. They can be grievously wounded and still escape a single hunter or even a small group, resulting in the *bope*'s wrath that one of "their" foods was allowed to get away. For this reason, the Bororo prefer to hunt tapir collectively, as noted above.

All the deer species have only their fleetness to save them from preda-tors. The Bororo say the only trouble jaguars have in killing deer is find-ing them in the first place. As far as man is concerned, the only risk implied by deer is the same as that for tapir, that the wounded creature might escape. Capivara have much the same qualities as tapir, save that they are even more vulnerable to all carnivores, man included. The rhea is noted for its speed, but, since it always attempts to flee across the sa-vannah, it can be run down by any of the larger felines. Older informants claimed that in their youth, when they carefully observed all the rules for the protection of *raka,* they too were able to kill rhea by chasing them either singly or in groups. As for the seriema, a kind of half-sized rhea (and termed *pari o-medu,* "rhea's younger brother"), it is absurdly easy to track and kill. Its very characteristic cry, which it utters at frequent inter-vals, facilitates locating it. Then its habit of dashing along for a hundred meters and flopping into the top of shrubs or saplings makes it the game of the old and crippled or very young among all carnivores. (A very indifferent hunter, I killed so many seriema that the shaman to whom I usually gave them finally told me in disgust to stop massacring the birds, that both he and his *bope* were sick of eating them. Their flesh is, indeed, so rank that the Bororo little appreciate them as food, singularly among the *bope ure,* and this is probably the only factor which has saved the species from local extermination.)

The two species of wild pig are commonly regarded by Europeans and Brazilians as dangerous quarry, owing to the male's tusks and his willingness to defend himself with them, and to their tendency to run in packs, especially marked among peccary (*quexada*). But I never saw the slightest indication that the Bororo considered these animals in any way menacing. They claimed that nearly always the pigs tried to flee and only rarely did one or two turn on the pursuers, which made it all the easier to spear them. Furthermore, on the three occasions when I participated in pig hunts, the animals went to earth in the boles of dead trees or in small caves. They were driven out one by one and killed easily as they exited. The only dangers the Bororo associate with the wild pigs are, first, the chance that a wounded one might escape and, second, the physical discomforts often imposed by the marshy and thorny habitat preferred by wild pigs. The places said to be the customary area of wild pigs are inevitably the sort of tangled, low-lying, half-swamps called by the Bororo "dirty" (*rurureu*) and associated with the *bope,* as well as with venomous snakes, large poisonous spiders, and other horrors. Most hunters avoid entering such areas either singly or in pairs, not through desire to avoid any supernatural menace but because the opportunity of killing a single pig is simply not worth the scratches, insect bites, and general discomforts, not to mention the risk of more serious injuries. For the same reason, informants said, jaguars and other felines usually stalked wild pigs outside their usual habitats. But in themselves, the pigs are not seen as physically threatening to any carnivore, man included.[19]

The status of the *bope ure* as "vulnerable and defenseless" is enhanced when the fish included in the set are considered. As mentioned earlier, all three species (pirarucu, surubim, and jáu) are together the largest forms of catfish encountered in the riverine systems exploited by the Bororo. The Bororo find them noteworthy for three reasons other than their size. First, they lack scales, which in other fish are regarded as their "shield" or "hide." Second, they are slow-moving and sluggish, usually found in deep pools and still water. For this reason, according to several myths and songs, they could be easily caught and eaten by alligators, otters, and other fish-eating animals. And finally, they have no teeth. The Bororo utilize dentition as the basis of their fundamental classification of the animal world into carnivores and noncarnivores (see below). All other fish species have some kind of teeth, and the Bororo draw the obvious inference that they use these to eat other fish, as well as to defend themselves. In fact, the dentition in dourado, piranha, pacu, pintado, and other common "game" fish is spectacular.

It is odd indeed that fish as large as the pirarucu and surubim lack any way to consume, defend, or attack. I have no precise record of the point, but I believe some Bororo think that these fish are the usual prey of their toothed brethen, and not only of reptiles and animals. Their perceived vulnerability in the natural world does not, in this case, make them especially easy quarry for human beings. Owing to their usual habits and habitats, they are not often trapped in nets or weirs. The depths at which they live make them almost impossible to take by spear or fish spear. (I use here the ethnographic present, for now the São Lourenço is so dirty as to preclude any kind of fish shooting. But informants alleged that in former days the water was very clear, at least during the dry season, and arrows and spears were the most common ways of fishing. Nowadays manufactured hooks are used.)

During nearly two years among the Bororo I saw only one pirarucu and two surubim brought into their villages, although others may have been caught and sold to Brazilians. One of the surubim, a small one of 5 or 6 kilos, was taken during a collective hunt in which the waters of a small pond (left by the receding São Lourenço during the dry season) were treated with timbo, fish poison. Such a fishing method is not without its physical discomforts, at least as the Bororo practice it. The timbo has the effect of driving the fish to the surface of the water by slowly impairing the capacity of their gills to absorb oxygen. But it hardly renders them limp and helpless; as they rise, they must be shot with arrows, speared, or netted, or most usually grabbed by hand. Bites and punctures from teeth and fins are not infrequent, although these are very minor injuries.

But the point here is that the Bororo only employ timbo during collective hunts dedicated to the *aroe*. It may well be that traditionally the three *bope ure* fish were most often caught on these expeditions, in which they would have been not only the largest, but also the most evidently defenseless of all the fish taken.[20] The Bororo now only rarely employ fish poison during collective hunts, on the grounds that to be effective its use requires more participants than any one contemporary village can now provide. In any case, the vulnerability of the three *bope ure* fish seems well established in terms of their three perceived "natural" attributes, if not through their characteristics as prey sought by the Bororo during ritual hunts.

There remains among the *bope ure* animals the black alligator. Now, this creature is certainly not considered "harmless" or lacking in physical

The "souls" on a collective fishing expedition

capacity to defend itself. The Bororo do not regard it as actively menacing mankind, as jaguars and harpy eagles do, and dismiss as nonsense
Brazilian tales of its treacherous and unprovoked attacks on individuals.
But they say that only a very able hunter, or group of them, will attempt
to kill an alligator, both because it fights back both with teeth and tail,
and because the likelihood of its escaping after being wounded is very
great. Although this beast does not in any way qualify as vulnerable, at
least its presence among the *bope ure* is itself peculiar.

First, along with the seriema but even more than with that bird, the
flesh of alligator is thought tough, rank, and completely without fat.

Some informants said that alligators were "the vultures of the river," eating any decayed stuff that came their way, as well as living fish and birds; for this reason, they tasted very foul. Most people profess not to like alligator meat very much and will refuse to eat it if any other kind of meat is available. These attitudes contrast with those toward the flesh of other *bope ure,* which is considered, although *jerimaga,* very good to eat indeed, the epitome of "meat." Second, alone among the *bope ure* there is an internal distinction among members of the *Caiman* species as to which must be offered up to the *bope.* Only those which are *xoreu* ("black") must be so treated. It was impossible to obtain detailed information as to what perceptual attributes the Bororo utilized to arrive at the categorization of any given alligator as "black." According to several descriptions, *uwai xoreu* ("black alligator") is very large, nearly always male, and "old." I have not been able to determine if, in fact, there is a noticeable "blackening" of the skin with increasing age among alligators. Nor could I discover whether *jerimaga* actually or in indigenous theory markedly increased with aging in individual members of the species. Of the four alligators killed and eaten by the Bororo while I was with them, none were said to be black; all four were obviously youngsters, one-third to one meter long.

All of this is curious, since the black alligator is considered to be among the most dangerously potent in terms of inherent *raka* of all the *bope ure.* Its bile provides a symbolically important "medicine" for the shaman, and its butchering demands very great precision if the shaman is not to risk his own or the killer's health. I can offer only a very partial and unsatisfying explanation of this species's inclusion among the *bope* foods.

First, it is a carnivore and is thus logically associated with all the nuances of meaning the Bororo accord this class (see below). But it is a very peculiar carnivore, preying both on living and dead matter, a kind of vulture. As the eaters of carrion are considered to manifest a certain dimension of the *bope,* so carnivores bear witness to another dimension: for the first, the *bope*'s character as the power behind all systemic transformations of organic nature is relevant; in the second, these spirits' essentially conjoined power to give and take life is operative. The alligator, like the *bope,* is alone in the universe of natural beings in combining these attributes.

Second, it is only the *black* alligator which is singled out for special ritual treatment. Blackness is again one of the basic perceptual qualities of the *bope,* and its monochromatic presence in the appearance of any thing or being is enough to warrant its association with that class of powers.

It appears that alligators generally, and black ones especially, present something of a conceptual riddle for the Bororo. They are a taxonomic mess, being creatures which dwell both on river banks and in the water,

Mother and son

kill their own food, and eat carrion. But, on the other hand, they do have scales and legs, they eat meat, and otherwise they are as any creature combining mammalian and reptilian characteristics should intellectually be. They are not nearly so peculiar as otters, dolphins, and bats. These fly in the face of all logic: fur-bearing mammals that live in the water, creatures that breathe air and suckle their young yet look like fish, things that act like birds but have no avian attributes whatsoever.

Thus: Alligators are classificatorily possible, but only just, and so their flesh is marginally edible. But when their empirical resemblance to the *bope* becomes especially marked in individual members of the species, the conceptual problem becomes serious. The Bororo, I suggest, resolve it by switching cognitive gears, in effect saying, "These kinds of things have been peculiar all along, but, in the case of this particular one, the peculiarity is just too marked; it demands symbolic treatment before we can consume it."

I return to the case of the anomalous alligator later in the book, after discussing the characteristics of those species which the Bororo term, for reason of their embodiment of attributes defining the *bope*, "Themselves *bope*." All that remains to be said here is that the alligator does not appear in any other symbolic system employed by the Bororo, other than that of the *bope ure*. It is, I think, just bizarre enough that its only classificatory position can be as a marginal and peculiar element in an otherwise consistently defined group. It is thus got rid of, intellectually if not pragmatically.

The plants among the *bope ure* present another set of problems. Unfortunately, at the time of fieldwork I was a very poor botanist, and so my data relating to Bororo classifications and symbolic attitudes toward the flora that surrounds them are extremely limited. Principally there is a metonymic association on three planes between these plants and the *bope* food species. First, the last are thought to eat the former in preference to others. Second, the plants tend to be especially associated with the periodic fructification of nature, and with the women who seek them out and whose natural rhythms their florescence and decay mirror. Third, as far as I could determine, all the plant elements in the *bope ure* actually do reek of *jerimaga*. Hogplums, quince, pequi, mulberries, and *kure* (the wild honey) are very rank, so much so that many Bororo as well as Brazilians are not especially eager to consume them. I could not determine if the tubers and cipo were very "strong." Certainly corn, to Bororo nostrils, at least after cooking, is very little imbued with *raka*. But all three of these substances, fruits, vegetables, and grains, are thought to be the preferred diet of all the ungulates, who root out the tubers and whose depredations, especially those of the capivara, in the cornfields constitute a great difficulty for all Brazilian agriculturalists (Ihering 1963: 29). As far as my material goes, there is nothing otherwise taxonomically peculiar nor especially feminine among the plants within the *bope ure*.

All that I can finally say is that these vegetables have the appearance of logical additions to the *bope ure,* consistent with the most marked perceptual attributes which distinguish these from other elements of the natural world, even if not, clearly, marked by their shared quality of vulnerability to carnivores. In fact, the plant substances most associated with femininity, in myths and ritual behavior, include only corn among all the *bope ure* species. In any case, the vegetable aspects of the *bope ure* constitute neither an important quantitative element in the transactions between man and *bope* nor a symbolic consideration in the causes and cures of affliction.

# The *Bope* as Natural Forms: Vehicles, Signs, and Icons

If, then, nearly all the *bope* foods are considered to embody vulnerability and defenselessness against the harsh usage of their flesh for the sustenance of other modes of being, what does this signify for the understanding of the entire system whereby the Bororo interact and solicit the *bope*?

First, it implies that women, or at least their sexuality and organic processes, are "like" the *bope ure* in that their only natural protection dwells in the powers intrinsic in their organic substances. Women are so very easily accessible, "ready game." And they are so "good" to possess. But, like the *bope ure,* their vulnerable excellence conceals powers of corruption inherent in their flesh and natural processes. Unless handled according to a mass of rules, these powers destroy men, ruining that very *raka* that enables them to enjoy sexuality and to procure the foods they eat. Woman's status as sexual object for both man and *bope* is a metaphoric parallel to the foods that both human and spirit prefer to consume. But the *bope,* with their inexhaustible and immortal supply of *raka,* their fluid lack of categorical form, need obey no rules in their contacts with substances brimming over with polluting forces that simultaneously create and destroy. The autonomy of the contaminating *raka* and *jerimaga* in the *bope ure* can therefore be explained by the nonvolitional, intrinsic character of these powers in all living things, most of all women. Man must learn to subject his own organic impulses to symbolic injunctions if his own share of these powers is not to be destroyed. As the Bororo say, "To sleep with a woman of one's own 'half' is the same as copulating with a menstruating woman; neither the *aroe* nor the *bope* have to notice it" (i.e., the culprit has brought about his own doom by failing to respect the categories which order relationships between antithetical modes of being). By respecting the *bope*'s rights over a set of things symbolizing all that is at once good, facile, and dangerous, the Bororo establish a mode of transacting with nature that parallels the mode governing human relationships, that of the moieties.

Second, if the *bope ure* are "like" the sexuality of women, they also represent that of men. As seen earlier, Bororo women equate masculine virility and their provision of *bope ure.* Men, too, are "easy game," and women need no more than to be themselves to attract them, just as a tapir must only exist to draw the eager attention of the jaguar. But women are not animals; they need in their turn to respect the conventions established to protect humankind from its own organic powers. A husband and wife cannot retire alone to the jungle, to feast on rich meats and acknowledge no restraints in their enjoyment of one another's bodies. They must have society, whether as the provider of social categories and rules or as represented in the person of the shaman, to mediate their relationship. Men's vulnerability to women's natural attraction endangers both of them, and women too must learn to check their physical appetites.

The symbolic power of the metaphoric system constituted by *bope* foods and its ramifications within shamanistic practices is the subject of Part III of this book. In the next chapter I show how further aspects of the *bope* are represented in other sets of natural species, and how the logic of this iconography confirms and extends the analysis of the "family resemblance" among the *bope ure*. Here some negative proofs of the validity of this analysis should be considered. As mentioned earlier, I had long been puzzled as to why such relatively large, and certainly frequent, constituents of Bororo diet as the anteater, armadillo, coati, and porcupine did not figure among the *bope ure*. The answer is, of course, that the Bororo consider these species as well able to defend themselves, and even as dangerous to man and other carnivores.

All the armadillo species in the Mato Grosso (the first four described by Ihering 1963: 14–16) are respected for their large, sharp claws. Further, the armadillo's capacity for rolling itself into an armor-plated ball as a final measure of defense impresses the Bororo. An anecdote which borders on a folk tale, frequently repeated among men, tells of how a Bororo saw a jaguar attempt to kill an armadillo thus protected. "The jaguar batted it with his paws, tried to bite it, waited for it to open. Then he walked away, very, very angry." The anteater similarly is noted for the sharpness of its claws and strength of its arms. The Bororo are convinced that it can disembowel a man and claim that jaguars leave them strictly alone.

Porcupines, of course, are safe from all predators save man. Coati, monkeys, and other arboreal mammals are noted for their agility and speed. "Their bones are never found," said an informant, meaning that they were seldom among the prey of carnivores. The opossum might well qualify as a *bope* food, except that it is regarded as a nonfood along with otters and bats, due to its anomalous features. Such creatures as the freshwater ray and turtles are well equipped for attack or defense. As for all the bird species commonly eaten, the Bororo say simply, "They all fly," whereas the rhea and seriema, alone among birds, do not.

Unfortunately my data on Bororo ethnobotany are simply too sparse to discover if there might be any kind of parallel contrast to "vulnerability" among the plants included in the *bope* foods. However, I think that at least the basic outlines of this interpretation have been demonstrated for the animal world. It now remains to explore other facets of the *bope*'s manifestations in the domain of existential significance, nature.

# 6

⟨〜⟩

# A *Bope* Bestiary

The Bororo recognize two classes of natural species especially associated with the *bope*. One they term "Themselves *bope*" (*bope remawu*), and the other they cite as frequently utilized by the *bope* as omens, to communicate with human beings. There is some overlap between the two sets, and some disagreement as to the animals constituting each class, especially the second. They cannot therefore be regarded as "collective representations" with the same degree of universality, boundlessness, and explicitness that characterizes the *bope ure*. No particular behavior is enjoined toward members of any species in either class, although contacts with them may well result in various kinds of social action. The lists below cite the species in each set in rough order of the prominence given them in anecdotes and individuals' own opinions.

These classes raise a variety of theoretical and ethnographic points. First, for the theoretical reasons already explained in the chapter on the *bope ure*, it seems both fruitless and logically invalid to seek any common attribute among the species which compose each list. Morever, given the relative lack of consensus on the composition of each class, one might suspect that even degrees of family resemblance within them might be much less marked than was true for the *bope ure*. Second, there are parallel classes of entities which manifest the category of spirit opposing the *bope*, the *aroe*, which are discussed in later chapters. Since the dyadic character of Bororo symbolic structure should now be apparent, the full range of the associations between each species, the separate classes, and the two categories of spirit cannot be established until the entire system has been laid out. My intentions in this part are then by necessity circumscribed and limited. The Themselves *bope* creatures and those which serve as omens for those spirits will be examined for what they might reveal about Bororo assumptions concerning the attributes of the *bope*, their presence in the natural world, and how these notions affect both social relationships with the *bope* and serve as metaphors for certain aspects of human transactions.

The Bororo opinion that certain natural species "are" *bope*, and that other species "are" *aroe* is a subtle and complex epistemological position. As noted earlier, *bope* and *aroe* are cosmological principles on the order of the classical Chinese concepts of *yin* and *yang*. As such they are manifested in all aspects of reality, since all things have a double aspect, being at once process (*bope*) and form (*aroe*), But at certain points in the natural world the boundary between perceptual and transcendent realities becomes weak or semi-permeable. At these points, whether living beings or physical processes, the antithetical modalities break through to manifest some of the attributes which define their powers.

The Themselves *bope* creatures are so tangibly filled with appearances and habits otherwise thought unique to the *bope* that a clear distinction cannot be drawn between them and the suprareal principle. These species, just like rain, thunder, the sun and moon, are sensate evidence of the *bope*'s control of organic transformation. They are metonyms for the *bope*, revealing the spirits through mirroring (though in attenuated ways) their appearance and by being in physical conjunction with the serial changes of birth, death, and decay. Therefore, they contrast with the *bope ure*, things that metaphorically represent the human condition as an indivisible union of form and process, but especially as the organic vitality essential in the latter. The *bope ure* are hardly Themselves *bope:* what condition of being consumes itself, save man?

The Bororo do not think that any particular vulture or small hawk or any other natural "sort" of *bope* incarnates these spirits, no more than they flee all contact with rain as itself a *bope*. They deny that the *bope* transform themselves into the species which manifest the essential characteristics of their own nature: there would be no point in simply becoming oneself, and in an attenuated form at that. Rather, all Bororo are sure that when the *bope* wish to participate actively in the world of physical forms they either metamorphose into or take possession of either the body of a man or that of a jaguar, a puma, or a rattlesnake. Their motive for doing so is simple: in those forms they may either enjoy sexuality or kill and eat their favorite foods, those otherwise obtained only through the intervention of man.

As the felines, the *bope* may slay and feast upon the ungulates and the birds among the *bope ure*. In the form of a rattlesnake they lie along the paths used by the animals until one comes along that can be bitten. "The *bope* are lazy," said one shaman, "and they find it easier to kill a tapir with venom than with claws." After dispatching the animal, the *bope* becomes a jaguar or a puma in order to eat it. Some informants said that the *bope* were also accustomed to metamorphose into *uwai xoreu*, "black alligators," so that they could catch and devour the fishes pirarucu, surubim, and jáu, those among the *bope ure*.

Therefore, if the creatures called Themselves *bope* (Table 6.1) are a kind of window in the cosmological wall between spirit and reality, the animals which the *bope* utilize to accomplish their gourmand desires are in a sense doors between these separate dimensions of being. The fact that *bope* are most often supposed to take the form of jaguars for their interventions into this world is especially important, for later material will show that this species is itself a crucial synthesis of *bope* and *aroe* attributes, and as such the basic zoological metaphor for human beings. It should be remembered that *bope* also pass directly into human bodies to enjoy food or sex.

The different species considered to show forth the *bope*'s basic characteristics in the domain of nature are clearly a very mixed bag. The vultures' inclusion among the Themselves *bope* is a foregone conclusion, given the metonymic conjunction of these horrible things with decay, the stench of *jerimaga*, their unrelieved black plumage, their habit of soaring high "at the ends of the *baru kigadureu* ('white sky') next to the sun" and in proximity to all the categories of *bope* that dwell there. The punishment of the *bope* of dead evil shamans, chained beneath the roosting places of vultures, to be there covered with their stinking *jerimaga* excrement, is consistent both with the status of these birds as embodiments of *bope* attributes and with the spirits' use of the appropriate natural forms to relate to various aspects of human conduct.

The two kinds of small caracara hawks are again a consistent identification of the extension of *bope* characteristics into the world of forms. Both appear emaciated, contrasting with the plump bodies of other birds of prey. As do vultures, they tend to hop about awkwardly on the ground. The Bororo claim their diet consists exclusively of the parasitic insects they discover on the bodies of dead and dying animals. They also say the *kaga* and *pia* are found exclusively in the company of vultures, which are otherwise shunned by all forms of being.[21] The caracaras are thus "guilty by association," and their habits and appearance only confirm their suspicious intimacy with death and decay.

The inclusion of four of the *bope ure* species (alligator, rhea, seriema, and surubim) among the Themselves *bope* validates an earlier point, that species may participate in multiple classifications on the basis of different

## Table 6.1. *Bope Remawu* ("Themselves *Bope*")

| Bororo | Familiar English | Scientific | Explicit *Bope* Attributes |
|---|---|---|---|
| *Xiwaje* | Turkey vulture | *Cathartes aura* | Black, carrion-eater, high flying |
| *Bai* | King vulture | *Sacoramphus papa* | Black, carrion-eater, high flying |
| *Pobureu* | Black vulture (?) | *Coragyps atratus* | Black, carrion-eater, high flying |
| *Kaga* | Small falcon, or caracara | *Milvago chimachima* | Thin, black and white, found near dead animals, eats parasitic ticks |
| *Pia* | Caracara, probably black | *Paptrius ater* | Thin, black, red-headed, associate of vulture, eats parasitic ticks on dead animals |
| *Uwai* | Alligator | *Caiman* gen. | Black, carrion-eater |
| *Pari* | Rhea | *Rhea americana* | Thin, largely black, call |
| *Beo* | Seriema | *Cariama cristata* | Thin, black, call |
| *Orarije* | Surubim | *Pseudoplatystoma corruscans* | Plate in neck, smell |
| *Pogodo* | Boa constrictor | *Constrictor constrictor* | Mottled skin, constrictive powers |
| *Bakorororeu* | Coral snake | *Micrurus* gen. | Red and black, small and thin, highly poisonous |
| *Pagedobo** | Blind-headed snake | Ceciliideos Fam. | Red and black, "two heads," "worm snake" |
| *Boreu* | Beetles generically | — | Black, full of "points" and possessing "jaws" |

*I am not sure if this is the blind-headed or two-headed "snake," which are often confused for one another owing to their common worm-like lack of longitudinal asymmetry. But, since the blind-headed snake shares with the coral snake definite contrasting rings around the body's circumference, I think it is this family which the Bororo categorize as a sort of "lesser" coral snake.

criteria salient to the principles being utilized in the particular taxonomy. Here it is the alligator's amphibian and carnivorous nature which is relevant. As noted earlier, it is regarded as a kind of riverine vulture. But again the alligator is ambiguous, for alone among the Themselves *bope,* it participates in a third class of *bope*-related species. It is possessed by or otherwise used as a vehicle for the *bope*'s volitional intervention into this world.

However, the two flightless birds (rhea and seriema) are considered manifestations of the *bope* owing to characteristics entirely different from those which lead to their inclusion among the *bope ure.* First, their calls are thought eerie, almost mocking imitations of human speech, a kind of "screeching laughter" in which proper words are almost but not quite distinguishable or in which they seem unbearably strident (Ihering 1968: 634). Second, their thin bodies and nearly black plumage make them a sort of terrestrial vulture, living on the rotting fruits and broken nuts which abound in the savannah. That the *bope* should both witness themselves through the attributes of these species and prefer them as food is not contradictory, since two different sets of criteria are relevant to their separate categorizations as *bope ure* and as *bope remawu.* I am not too sure as to why the surubim alone among the *bope* food fish should be considered to be a metonym for the *bope.* The peculiarity of the plate found in this species' neck, its strongly *jerimaga* taste, and its habits as a river scavenger doubtless all contribute to its incarnation of essentially *bope* qualities.

, The three kinds of snakes, though, present thoroughly consistent breakthroughs of the *bope*'s attributes into the reptilian world. The coral snakes are, first, curious in that they alone in nature combine exclusively red and black.[22] These colors, together with white, are basic to Bororo ritual ornamentation and color symbolism; their combination is, however, unique to the *aroe* Bakororo, one of the two preeminent chiefs of the underworld and the personification of the forces of classificatory form. Red (*kujagureu*) is the color of *raka* and signifies its life-giving potency. Black (*xoreu*) is equally a form of *raka,* but in its aspect of power to destroy and to transform through decay. The combination of the two shades, without the stability of the enduring principle of categorical *aroe* form codified in the color of white, is itself a testimony to the eminence of the *bope*'s powers unchecked by the opposing principles.

That the only creatures in the world to be naturally colored only red and black should also be so very deadly for their minute size strikes the Bororo as more than sufficient reason to identify them as *bope.* Once bitten by a *bakorororeu* (coral snake), even jaguars and tapirs, let alone man, "do not wait to die." So, too, the *bope* possess total "black" power to destroy instantly any living thing, just as from them proceeds the redness of its *élan vital.* The boa constrictor is also recognized for its size, ability to squeeze its prey into a gelatinous mass, thus killing without teeth or claws, and for the clarity of its markings. But these last, a series of interlinked, regular blotches, are contrasted with the separate black ovals of the sucuri's (anaconda's) skin, which are compared to the jaguar's spots. This difference, and the constrictor's preference for the dry sertão over the sucuri's riverine habitat, appear to explain the former's categorization as itself a *bope,* and the latter's status as an *aroe.*

The general point revealed by the snakes' categorization as Themselves *bope* is that their perceived attributes have only a few elements in common with those seen to be possessed by the birds, reptile, and fish also among the Themselves *bope.* These spirits cannot be defined through one bundle of criteria, any more than can their relevance to human beings be summarized in any single rule of thought or action. But consistently, those points at which the spirits break through to manifest their attributes in the world of natural species are all characterized by metonymy, by associations based on contiguity and sensual proximity to the elements emanating from the *bope.* The *bope* foods in contrast must be metaphors, for they provide the language in which man communicates with the spirits rather than passively witnesses the signs of their natural presences.

Beetles are Themselves *bope* only to a limited and debatable extent. The usual justification for including them among the *bope remawu* was that the *bope* employ them in preference to other things for attacking human beings and making them ill. When the shaman sucks out the pathogenic agent from a patient, it most usually is a kind of beetle (see following section). Beetles are considered appropriate agents for the *bope's* afflictions because they, uniquely among insects, possess a hard shell with numerous sharp points, are totally black, and have organs the Bororo interpret as "jaws." I was told by one shaman that, since beetles live by killing and eating insects, they are a kind of jaguar. Other informants said this was a fanciful and inaccurate explanation of their special symbolic status, since certain kinds of ants were well known as carnivores, not to mention spiders. Beetles are not anomalous in terms of Bororo insect taxonomy, as far as I could determine, nor do they otherwise have the general liminal importance of such things as giant walkingsticks and certain types of spiders (see above and Crocker 1977b). Their marginal inclusion in the list of Themselves *bope* by most informants seems to reflect the incompleteness with which they embody the definitional criteria of the *bope.* Even their use of the spirits as pathogenic agents seems to derive from another set of attributes, discussed in the next chapter.

## *Bope* Omens and Human Action

The creatures employed by the *bope* as omens (Table 6.2) relate to a new dimension of these spirits' innate character and to another mode of their

Table 6.2. Omens of the *Bope*

| Bororo | Vernacular | Scientific | Behavior of *Bope* Omen |
|---|---|---|---|
| *Rie* | Guara (maned wolf) | *Chrysocyon brachyurus* | Approaches and/or stares at hunter |
| *Okwa* | Savannah fox | *Cerdocyon thous* | Barks, approaches hunter |
| *Kugu* | Large owls generically | *Estrigiformes ord* | Hoot near hut |
| *Tagogo* | Field owl | *Lophostrix cristata cristata* | Hoot near hut, seen in daytime |
| *Makao* | Macaua | *Herpethotheres cachinnans gueribundus* | Calls near person(s) |
| *Koxaga* | Seracura (small tern) | *Aramides saracura* | Calls very clearly, at dawn or twilight |
| *Bakorororeu* | Coral snake | *Micrurus* gen. | Appears unexpectedly, does not flee |
| *Pogodo* | Boa constrictor | *Constrictor constrictor* | Appears unexpectedly, does not flee |
| *Bika* | Anu-branco | *Guira guira* | Favorable omen; cry "bika," means "No death" |
| *Bi* | Burrowing owl | *Speotyto cunicularia* | Cry "bi," means "death" |
| *Jiwijiwi* | Finch | ? | ? |
| *Reoreo* | Finch | ? | Cry means "the Fighter" |
| *Tirotorogo* | ? | ? | ? |
| *Baxaxiji* | Type of heron | ? | Calls very clearly |

interaction with man. The Bororo prescribe no particular conduct with regard to the things called Themselves *bope*. Nor do the behaviors of these animals signify anything other than the imminence of the *bope* in natural forms, insofar as their status as *bope* is concerned. To be sure, except for the four species included in the *bope* foods, all of them are totally inedible, and people usually avoid their presence and would never attempt to kill them. They are, after all, full of contaminating *raka* which would corrupt any weapon that touched them. Besides, as one of my usual hunting companions said, "What is the point of shooting at them? They cannot be eaten, and the *bope* do not care." Even though they recognize the "*bope*" snakes as dangerous, the Bororo nonetheless do not kill them, although they do not hesitate to kill other non-edible reptiles (except for the anaconda, which is considered a manifestation of the *aroe* and hence, in its turn, to be let alone). The coral snake and boa constrictor are only lethal to man when the *bope* voluntarily will them so. Since the spirits' powers are infinite, it hardly avails to deprive them of the almost numberless agencies they may employ to work their will on man.

But all these attitudes change when the *bope* omens are considered. In the specific mythic contract with Meri, the Bororo said, "You must advise us when you are about to harm us for some reason (e.g., some human dereliction in the duties toward the spirits). Send to us a *rie*, a *kugu*, a *koxaga*, so that we may know of our danger" (see above). When any one of the omen animals thus appears to a Bororo, he is warned that the *bope* intend some maleficence toward him and his, and he should take appropriate action. Inevitably this involves procuring the services of a shaman of the *bope*, who in audience with his familiars can determine the cause of the *bope*'s wrath and perhaps circumvent it, at least for a time. The problem here is that the *bope* are obliged to warn only one person of their planned hostility, either to him or to any of those associated with him by residence, matrilateral descent, or agnatic ties. Further, the spirits may delay for some time in carrying out their threat. Consequently, no one can be sure just who or how the *bope* menace, save that their omnipresent vigilance over the respect of Bororo for "their" rights has finally been changed into a specific vengeance.

Informants said that the species which serve as *bope* omens were not in any wise embodiments of the spirits, nor did their status necessitate any particular reaction to them as long as they behaved "normally." But when they behaved atypically, departed from usual patterns of their species, then one could be sure the *bope* were communicating with man. If a guara or fox does not flee before the hunter but stands watching him come closer, or even approaches, then they are certainly omens portending some kind of affliction sent by the *bope* to the viewer's near relatives or to himself. But if the guara yelp or howl near the village at night, the *bope* are saying that some Bororo will soon kill a jaguar or puma.[23] When, though, the *okwa* (savannah fox) yelps near the village, on a path or trail, it means that someone in the village will die soon.

All three owl species also warn of imminent death within the village and are considered among the most potent omens. However, informants made very precise distinctions in the significance of the species' different calls. When the *kugu* (large owl) calls over and over near the village, "kuuuuu kuuuuu kuuuuu" (i.e., the hoots that typify owls in English), or calls in a sustained note, "ouuuuuuuuuuuu," it means someone in the village will soon die. But, when the *kugu* calls out "ku ku ku ku ku ku" (short mounting and descending notes), it means that no harm of any kind will come to the village, at least not for a time. The *tagogo* (field owl) warns only of death, but then just when it sings "wao wao wao wao" very near a house. The *bi*'s (burrowing owl's) usual cry of "pissss pissss pissss" means nothing at all. This species is unlike other owls in being diurnal. Whenever, then, a Bororo hears it change its cry to "biii biii biii," he may be sure that someone will die in the next few days. Some informants regarded this owl as the most frequent omen utilized by the *bope*.[24] *Bi*, it may be remembered, means "death" in the Bororo language.

The *makao* is another important omen. When it calls near human dwelling places it warns especially that the *bope* intend to cause a poisonous snake to bite someone, or a jaguar to claw and bite a hunter, or the *barae* (Brazilians) to harm a Bororo, or that an epidemic of bad colds, measles, or other contagious disease will soon strike the entire village. This bird is the macaua (or "acaua"), identified by informants as a species of medium-sized hawk that feeds exclusively on snakes and "somehow" is invulnerable to their poison, alone among the animals and birds. When the shaman treats a case of snakebite, he utilizes his familiar *bope* to be possessed by the *bope makao,* which alone can cure this affliction. This species is symbolically important in a variety of other contexts, including that of the "revenge" animals discussed in Part IV.

The *koxaga* is one of the birds the Bororo find full of associations with both dimensions of the cosmological dyad, *bope* and *aroe*. This is the seracura, a small tern, with a black chest, coffee-colored sides and rusty wings, and a long blue-green bill. It has a notable complex and melodic call that the Bororo (and at least some Westerners, myself included) find uniquely beautiful and mysterious in all the world of natural sound. It normally frequents rivers and large streams, where it eats small minnows. If it should visit the village, though, and sing its strange melody throughout the day, the *bope* are saying that not just one person is going to die but many, and all kinds of affliction are about to overtake the Bororo in that community.

The *reoreo*, a variety of finch, is described as being very small with a yellow body and drab olive wings and tail. When it calls out 'sh sh sh sh sh sheo sheo shreo shreo," which the Bororo interpret as signifying "reo," "fight" (Albisetti and Venturelli 1962: 900), it warns there will be serious fights between people, perhaps even murders. But if it sings close to anyone "ti ti ti ti ti ti," it foretells happiness; there is much good food coming, or a dear relative absent for a long time will soon visit, or the hearer will receive a valuable *akiro* (gift).

The *tiwotorogo* also warns of fights, but never of any pleasant events. This bird is about the size of a robin, completely black except for a red beak, and usually found only in flocks of half a dozen or so. Its call is described as "xeru xeru xeru xeru xeru," repeated rapidly and for interminable periods.

The *jiwijiwi* is another kind of finch, very like the *reoreo* but slightly larger. It has a dirty white breast with olive drab sides, wings and tail. Its song "jiwi jiwi jiwi jiwi ka ka ka ka" warns that hurt and trouble are imminent. Someone has died in another village, or someone here will soon die; a snake or jaguar is about to bite a Bororo; a man is going to hurt himself severely with an ax or machete; a swarm of wasps is about to sting a group of Bororo.

None of these three species is said to be an omen of sickness, but only of "mechanical" violence or subsequent injury. The Bororo attitude toward the *bope*'s involvement in such natural afflictions is complex. On the one hand, the spirits can certainly utilize any "harming" species to punish the Bororo, and they can even cause a man to hurt himself or to be wounded in fights with others. On the other hand, said informants, these griefs often just occur, such being the nature of social and physical reality, and in portending them the *bope* are simply communicating to man the immediacy of suffering. I think it generally accurate to say that injuries are usually regarded as possible but not necessary results of *bope* volition, while sicknesses nearly always are the deliberate will of the *bope*. The internal contrast between omens that warn exclusively of the former kind of affliction as against those which predict grievous disease and death is at least very clear.

The *bika,* "alma do gato," a kind of catbird, has a red back, wings, and tail while its chest and stomach are white. The unusualness of its plumage makes it a kind of natural synthesis between *bope* and *aroe* characteristics, save that, unlike other "white" birds, its habitat is not riverine but exclusively dry land. When this bird chatters once or twice "bika bika," "no death," it harbingers all kinds of pleasant things, such as successful hunts or fishing expeditions. But when it chatters on and on without stopping, the *bope* are telling man to expect serious afflictions that yet will not, if properly shamanistically treated, terminate in death. The *baxaxiji,* perhaps the whitling heron (*Syrigma sibilatrix*), is thought by the Bororo very ugly, with a tuft of feathers on its head that sticks out in every direction. This bird, and the *kugu,* a large owl, are said to have songs which the *bope* "like" and which only occasionally warn of disasters and accidents. Indeed some informants insisted they were never omens but merely "companions" of the *bope*.

I have saved description of the two kinds of snakes thought to be omens for the last because these are the only species which are among both the Themselves *bope* and the *bope* omens. Merely to see either of these snakes is a warning that an intimate relative of the viewer (a uterine sibling, a real father or mother, or one of the wife's uterine siblings) will soon die, at least if the *bope* can carry out their intentions. "These snakes mean the same as the guara, the *kugu* (large owl), the *bi* (small owl), macaua or seracura," said informants, "The *Roya Kurireu* (the central song of the funeral cycle) will soon be sung in the village." But the *bope* also send the yellow lacatilio, or two-headed snake, to indicate that the next child born in the village will be exceptionally beautiful and full of *raka*. The Bororo say that any snake which has any exclusive combination of red, black, and blue-green (*kigadureu*) must be Themselves *bope* and can also serve as messengers of the spirits. But any reptile with yellow in its markings must be associated with the *aroe*, who love this color along with white and who love all beautiful things generally.

Omens present difficulties of analysis and integration into otherwise consistent symbolic systems based on zoological elements. The problem derives from the way an almost limitless number of associations may trigger off metonymous connections with one or another class of suprareal forces. Although, as has been clear, something of this difficulty is present with the species said to be Themselves *bope*, at least the range of *bope* attributes directly replicated in these creatures is at once limited and tends to combine in any particular species. There are multiple and reinforcing reasons why the Bororo should consider vultures and alligators to incarnate the idea of *bope*.

With the omens the indigenous logic is much more heterogeneous; the connection between an omen species and the *bope* is usually vague and often inconsistent from one informant's explanation and the next's. This is as we might suspect: the omens have generally sufficient "natural resemblances" with the *bope* to signify their coming interventions into human affairs, to act as their agents. At the same time, their mirroring of the *bope*'s essential physical forms and characteristic powers is sufficiently distorted to make them less windows than semi-opaque openings between empirical form and transcendent process. In the continuum running between the manifestations of *bope* and *aroe* in the sensate world (Table 6.3), the omen animals, capable of signifying good as well as bad, occupy a sort of ill-defined, shifting position on the way to the domain of the *aroe*, although still well on the *bope*'s side.

The metonymic associations which direct the categorization of things as Themselves *bope* continue to operate with the species considered omens. But now the connections are random and nonconsistent within the class. It is now a matter, one might say, of individual poetics rather than collectivized myths. Whereas the social attitude toward the *bope* animals is relatively standardized, individuals seem to vary markedly both in their responses to omens and their particular understandings of why or what the *bope* communicate through them. A comparison might be made with our own responses to advertising which seeks to identify

Table 6.3. The *Bope-Aroe* Continuum

| | Them-selves *Bope* | Omens | Agents of *Bope* | Agents of *Aroe* | Them-selves *Aroe* | |
|---|---|---|---|---|---|---|
| **BOPE** | Seriema | Guara | Puma | Harpy eagle | Harpy eagle | **AROE** |
| | Rhea | Owls | Jaguar | Tapir | Ducks | |
| | Boa con-stric-tor | Macaua | Rattle-snake | Armadil-lo | Flamin-goes | |
| | Coral snakes | Seracura | Alligator | Jaguar | Herons | |
| | Vultures | Coral snakes | | Otter | Macaws | |
| | Alli-gators | Boa con-stric-tor | | | Cormo-rants | |
| | Parasitic hawks | Fox | | | *Tamigi* | |
| | | Finches | | | Anacon-da | |
| | | Small hawks | | | | |

NOTE: This table is misleading in that it excludes the two classes most crucially medial, those of the *bope ure* and the *marege mori-xe*. But since the details of the last classification are not examined until the next chapter, the significance of both classes, which must be understood as structural complements of one another, cannot be investigated here. The table only aims to set out diagramatically one of the major themes of this chapter, the serial, discrete continuum of Bororo natural symbolism, to add one more demonstration of its quality as thoroughly noniconographic.

the desirable consequences of owning proximity to various things in much the same metonymous way that "nature," for the Bororo, broadcasts the meaning of natural species. Some products, antiperspirants and mouthwashes, entail such a series of happy consequences that any right-thinking person must seek them out; what Bororo would frequent vultures willingly? But who can say what complex chain of private associations cause one individual to choose a brand of cigarette or a kind of car on the basis of its physical contiguity to certain "good things" as pictured in the billboards? Some Bororo consider foxes to be things which in their habitat, appearance, and diet are all too proximate to the *bope* for cognitive comfort, and when these creatures physically come near man, it can only mean dire things. Some Westerners, however, will quite happily buy a car called a "Fox," though they may be unable to identify with certainty the implications of agility and cunning implicit in "Fox" as opposed to "Dog."

In terms of Bororo classifications of the natural world, the striking element in the omens is the relative frequency of carnivores and the absence of all species thought Themselves *bope* (aside from the snakes), including birds of prey. Indeed, these owls and canines alone announce grave affliction and death, along with the snakes which can kill. The finches and noncarnivorous hawks, who only portend mechanical injuries, are specifically included among the omens only owing to the meanings the Bororo discover in their characteristic songs. Although my informants did not always agree with those of Albisetti and Venturelli (e.g., 1962: 371–72) in the identification of each song with specific versions of Bororo phrases, they did say the calls were "strange," unlike those of other birds.

Again, individual imagination and poetics must be considered. It is quite likely that some Bororo persons find an uncanny resemblance between certain bird songs and some parts of human speech. While other members of the society may respect this sensitivity, it furnishes no grounds for collective thought. But such relativity is much less true for the carnivorous omens, the owls, wild "dogs," snake-hawk, and tern. These are universally declared to be omens of the *bope* and to signify very grievous forthcoming events.

The Bororo accord to another set of animals and birds the same symbolic importance extended the *bope* foods and call these the *marege morixe*, "animals of revenge." Since their ritual significance is an element of the domain of the *aroe*, I present the ethnographic details of this class in the chapter concerning these spirits and the principles of human interaction with them. But all these "revenge animals," which serve also as mediators between society, nature, and the universe of spiritual powers, are carnivorous. The species which are both omens and revenge animals represent rather minor elements in the last class, in contrast with their importance among the omens. However, their ability to replicate the *bope*'s capacity to destroy and consume organic being, which serves as the basis for their categorization as revenge animals, is only marginally relevant to their status as omens. The maned wolf and fox, say the Bororo, are rather uncomfortably like the domestic dog. Some informants said that Bororo in the recent past had been able to raise the young of both species and to domesticate them; it was generally considered that domestic dogs could mate with either of their wild counterparts. The wolf especially seems interested in humans: it will sometimes accompany a hunter through the forest, though always at a distance, "to see what he will do."

But this is not the main reason for their divinatory status. One of the basic requirements for Bororo social life is the social discipline of noise. In the village, children are not allowed to scream, nor should adults raise their voices except when singing. A dog which incessantly barks must be destroyed, along with any other domesticated animal which makes random and uncontrollable din. The howls of the wolf and fox are considered to be very much like those of domestic dogs. When, then, these creatures profane the quiet of the village night, their taxonomic ambiguity is given an aural dimension with a human significance, whether for good or bad. Only the *bope* otherwise shout, whoop, and make chaotic noise in the village precincts. Thus, if creatures very like those man controls approach the village to bark and howl, it must mean that the *bope* intend some similar disorderly incursions into human life.

The owls, macaua, and seracura which count as omens are so regarded, I think, for very different associational reasons. The first were explicitly noted by the Bororo as birds of the night, with the exception of the curious *bi,* the diurnal burrowing owl. Their silent flight and carnivorous diet make them appropriate agents for the *bope,* who likewise are nocturnal, nontangible, and exclusively flesh-eaters. But the feature of "night noise" is also operative with the owls, for they and the "wild dogs" are the only species which (the Bororo say) call late in the night. The macaua, or snake hawk, is very close indeed to the *bope.* One shaman said that *bope* might well enter it, "except they don't like to eat snakes either." The invulnerability of this bird to snakebite, at least in Bororo eyes, also signifies that it must be under the special aegis of the *bope.* At the same time, its diet implies a certain proximity to the forces of the *aroe.* Consistently enough, its call warns that Bororo shall be injured in their contacts with the most lethal and dangerous elements of the natural world, the jaguars, non-Bororo human beings, and snakes.

As for the seracura, it can only be said that the haunting peculiarity of its song must make it one of those rare species which enjoys a special symbolic position not through any association with the tangible qualities of spirit, nor through its taxonomic peculiarities, but sheerly on the basis of one circumstantial but dominant attribute. These different birds, along with the two mammalian carnivores, are unique among all the *bope* omens in that they can be eaten. The only justification for this, informants said very clearly, is that they were *merege mori-xe,* carnivores, and "also a great deal *aroe.*" Since they share the elements which otherwise differentiate the two fundamental aspects of existence, the full analysis of their symbolism must be reserved for a later chapter, when all varieties of prophetic activity are discussed.

# The Autonomy of the *Bope*

The *bope* are the agents and masters of organic change, and thus of serial time. Through one set of natural entities they can signal human beings of future events; through another, they show their omnipresence and certain range of their powers; and through still a third, they receive from human beings the nourishment they never need but only desire. The ways the Bororo make contact with them and interpret their character and intentions are complex and involve aspects of the society's conceptual system which have only been outlined. But one thing should be clear: whatever functional relevance to the stresses and sociological dilemmas in Bororo social relationships can eventually be teased out of these various "natural" codes and behaviors, there must be a certain material that can be understood only as thought, or as the agencies for a certain kind of thinking in which the world of natural forms is comprehended rather than interacted with or metamorphosed for social purposes. The *bope,* that is, exist over and above whatever hidden purposes we might discover for them. They are not reducible to one or another kind of "language" to talk about the more mundane aspects of human life. Only if this autonomy is respected can the topic of the next chapter, the shaman and his powers, be addressed.

# PART III

❧

# *Bari:* Shamans of the *Bope*

O, when degree is shak'd
Which is the ladder of all high designs,
The enterprise is sick. How could communities,
Degrees in schools, and brotherhoods in cities,
Peaceful commerce from dividable shores,
The primogenity and due of birth,
Prerogative of age, crowns, sceptres, laurels,
But by degree away, stand in authentic place?
Take but degree away, untune that string,
And hark what discord follows. Each thing meets
In mere oppugnancy: the bounded waters
Should lift their bosoms higher than the shores,
And make a sop of all this solid globe;
Strength should be lord of imbecility,
And the rude son should strike his father dead;
Force should be right; or rather, right and wrong—
Between whose endless jar justice resides—
Should lose their names, and so should justice too.
Then everything includes itself in power,
Power into will, will into appetite;
And appetite, an universal wolf,
So doubly seconded with will and power,
Must make perforce an universal prey,
And last eat up himself.

William Shakespeare, *Troilus and Cressida,* I.3.101

monkey

# 7

## Becoming and Being
## a Shaman

In many ways this section departs
from the ethnographic themes and conceptual tenor of this book. It describes the individual character of Bororo shamans: their personal experiences with the *bope*, from the initiatory contacts through the trials of
apprenticeship, to the idiosyncratic transformations of identity that the
role must inflict. It departs from my generally sociological perspective;
its data little fit the depersonalized systems of metaphoric pollution, vital
excess, and opportunistic attack that have been described as ordering Bororo relationships with the *bope*. But I try to show how the shaman reiter-
ates these systems in his private experiences and in the powers attributed
to him, in ways subtly transformed from the earlier details of their manifestation. At the same time certain qualities of the shaman appear to lie
outside Bororo society and cosmology, and even to contradict the principles of their structures.

Partly this is so because the *bari*, the shaman of the *bope*, is but one-
half the total shamanistic system of the Bororo. The other ritual specialist, the shaman of the *aroe*, no longer exists among contemporary
Bororo. We must deal, then, with a truncated system greatly affected by
recent historical processes and in the throes of transformation. The next
section attempts a reconstruction of the traditional system; this one describes its modern jumble of old and new elements. At least this material
demonstrates that the old thesis of the shaman's psychological abnor-

mality as central to the efficacy of his treatment of affliction simply does not apply to the Bororo. Indeed, the theoretical issue here is why and how the shaman's most intimate, unwilled experiences are regarded as sociologically determined and fundamental to the maintenance of a community's well-being.

For the Bororo, a *bari,* a shaman of the *bope,* is as much cursed as he is blessed. Although the role embodies a variable but definite element of power, it also entails a multitude of liabilities which are collectively thought much to outweigh the benefits. And the premises of Bororo shamanism preclude any element of individual volition or even of consciousness within the role. The *bope* alone choose their representative, on grounds obscure even to shamans. The individual is free to reject the spirits, but he risks seriously angering them by so refusing their "call." The *bope* do have two general criteria for shamanistic recruitment: The *bari* ought to be a member of the Tugarege moiety and should be consanguineally related to a dead shaman. Empirically, the few exceptions to the first criterion are justified by the second.

The first criterion is structurally crucial. It will be remembered that the *bope* are categorically associated with the Exerae moiety, whose four clans and especially the two Bado Jeba units have particular *bope* among their totemic *aroe.* One of the most consistent principles in Bororo social relationships with all types of transcendent forces is that the individual can intimately contact only those forces categorically associated with the *opposite* moiety. Only members of that moiety can represent, or "become" in the Bororo view, the *aroe* which provide the nominal and iconographic identity of clans and persons in the other moiety. To be sure, one may assume bits and pieces of his clan's *aroe:* a proper name reflecting some small differentiated element of their being, a body painting reproducing one aspect of their appearance, an ornament derived from one of their attributes. But he can never costume himself with the totality of icons by which their essential forms can be given material presence in the bodies of men. This transcendent privilege is taken by members of the other moiety.

The structure of Bororo ceremony is such that men symbolically "become" their fathers rather than their mothers' brothers (Crocker 1977c). At death a man's social personality is assumed by a member of the other moiety, the *aroe maiwu,* with the result that during various ceremonies the Tugarege "are" the Exerae (as representatives of dead Exerae) and the Exerae "are" the Tugarege. The mythic explanations of how *aroe* forms came originally to be associated with a particular clan and name group often parallel this inverted structure. A man sees something unique to social experience, and by naming it, claims that form of being for his clan. But his father disputes with him, saying, "I shall 'have' that *aroe*, then you can 'be' it"; i.e., the father's clan shall include this form among its *aroe*, and the son and his clan can ceremonially represent it. The Bororo think of this as a supreme prestation the father bestows on his son, because it shows that one can only be what one is not or possess only what one has given away.

The Tugarege should provide shamans of the *bope*, say the Bororo, because only they call the *bope* "*i-ogwa*," "my father." In classificatory usage this term applies to all men in the senior generation in the other moiety, and to all the *aroe* forms associated with the four clans of that division. Since the *bope* are among the *aroe* of the Exerae moiety, it is structurally appropriate that the Tugarege should "become" *bope*, either as a collectivity in the *aroe* representations, or as individual shamans. Symmetrically, the Exerae should be "shamans of the *aroe*," for the *aroe* are particularly associated with the Tugarege moiety.

All the implications of these inversions cannot be examined until both types of shamans have been described. But I can say now that they are consistent with the symbolic differentiation between the moieties. The Exerae bear the responsibility for ordering all collective rituals and the village itself, through the paramount ceremonial positions of Bako-rokudu and Karia Bokodori. These *pagimejera* ("chiefs of the village") impersonate the *aroe* of the two culture heroes Bakororo and Itubore. But these last are among the clan *aroe* of the Tugarege, who must "command" the two Exerae chiefs to represent these principles of transcendent order, and so to implement the men's council's decisions.

The very title Tugarege means "the possessors of arrows," and the clans of this moiety have myriad connections with instruments of violence and with hunting and warfare. They provide the two chiefs Baitogogo and Borogei, respectively of the Arore and Apiborege, who in addition to their considerable ritual duties, at one time were the obligatory *pagimejera* in warfare. The majority of the *bope ure* species count as *aroe* totems of the Exerae; the Tugarege might be said to have analogic relations with the principal animals they kill for food and with the women with whom they prescriptively copulate. Exerae men tend to portray themselves as masters of esoteric knowledge, bowed down by their simultaneously moral and technical obligations; their Tugarege counterparts seem to accept responsibilities of action more readily and even with relish. But there are too many exceptions, personal and categorical, to these patterns for them to be more than suggestive implications.

Empirically there is a high correlation between the structural prescriptions and the social affiliations of shamans. Among twenty-six *bari* encountered or recorded in genealogies, eighteen were Tugarege. All but one of the seven shamans of the *aroe* in my data were Exerae. Informants regarded this correlation as evidence at once of the prescriptions' symbolic truth, and of the tendency for both types of shamanism to run in consanguineal lines. "When a shaman dies, his *bope* likes to go into his younger brother." This does not mean any sort of automatic inheritance: "It is only partly," said shamans, "a matter of *raka*." The deceased shaman's *bope* attempts to possess someone whom "it knows well," and this knowledge is assumed to exist pragmatically rather more than inherently among consanguines. Such acquired familiarity is alleged to facilitate the new shaman's initiation and mystical training. Given the dangers intrinsic in the role, such benign motives might well be questioned. The legacy of shamanistic powers is an inheritance of most ambiguous value—just about what, among the Bororo, one might expect from an older brother.

But whatever its implications, it is a common pattern. Of twelve living *bari* I encountered among the Bororo (eight of whom were Tugarege), four included the *bope* of a deceased uterine shaman brother among their familiars. I was able to obtain information on this point from only nine of the twelve, however, and feel the proportion of "brother-*bope*" might well be higher. In two more of the nine, though, the shamans had the *bope* of their dead shaman-fathers, and one of those with "brother-*bope*" familiars had again his father's *bope,* which had originally possessed the elder brother. All three shamans with father-familiars were Exerae; their fathers, that is, had been Tugarege, as the normative pattern holds shamans should be. The fourth Exerae shaman was a woman who very seldom performed in that role, and her familiars were not publicly known. All the Exerae *baire* deviated in various bizarre ways from the normal range of shamanistic characteristics.

These patterns of shamanistic recruitment reflect the themes of earlier chapters. The Bororo integration of the structure of social categories with personalistic relations through the idiom of *raka* applies to the selection of shamans, but as a predisposing rather than a determining factor. Since moral, intellectual, and psychological aspects of personality are transmitted through *raka,* there exists a certain "family resemblance" between consanguineous shamans. A categorical status as a Tugaregedu "son" to the Exerae *bope* "fathers" relates the shaman's social identity to the logic of Bororo dyadic classification but, once again, as a sufficient but not necessary condition of shamanistic recruitment. The two kinds of criteria run parallel to one another, and the first even explains apparent exceptions to the latter.

So, the only circumstance in which *baire* are not Tugarege occurs when one of the possessing *bope* is that of a deceased father-shaman, who was himself, of course, a Tugaregedu. The force of personalistic *raka* may override categorical prescription, but it does so in a logically consistent way: the *bope* are always the *i-ogwa,* "my father," of the *bari,* either classificatorially or consanguineally.

Finally, the Bororo were amused when I protested that since the souls of dead Tugarege shamans were *bope,* these spirits could not all be elements of the Exerae. True enough, they said, but had I forgotten that the ritual replacements of these dead Tugarege were all Exerae (and themselves shamans), who therefore "had" or "were" these *bope?* This sort of looking-glass reasoning pervades the organization of Bororo cosmology; the same sort of inverted doubling goes on in the relationships between the *aroe* and social categories, as the next section will show.

Formal criteria may limit the social field from which *baire* may be recruited; they cannot account even in an *ad hoc* manner for why only a few of those theoretically eligible actually become shamans. The Bororo usually try to explain this mystery as due to the trials of shamanistic initiation, in which mystical tests select those fully qualified for the role from the ones just categorically entitled to it. This process dramatically reveals some of the basic elements in the relationship between the shaman and the *bope.*

## The Shaman's Mystic Initiation

The first indication that one is to be a *bari,* that the *bope* have some special interest in oneself, always comes in dreams. Although the Bororo have no systematic theory of dreams, they are greatly intrigued by them. Some claim that a dream reflects the soul's actual experiences during sleep, although in a mysteriously disguised fashion. A few believe dreams are simply the soul's "thinking" about past events and present circumstances, "Just like stories or movies," said one well-traveled man. The universally accepted dogma that a parent's dream during childbirth always foretells the future has much less to do with the nature of dreaming than the mystically surcharged process of parturition. By its challenge to the existing order of things, birth can itself cause more peripheral events if allowed to proceed unchecked by moral constraints, symbolized by the rule, "Remain Awake!" In normal circumstances Bororo regard dreams as they do the omens described in the last chapter, in a largely empirical mode. If they unambiguously portray in detail things which quickly come to pass, one may well be sought by the *bope.*

The first and recurring shamanistic dream is one of soaring very high above the earth, "like a vulture," accompanied by the soul of some living relative who is often, but not always, a shaman. From his remote perspective, the dreamer perceives a curiously altered but perceptually vivid world, in which "things are very little and close to one another." (One nonshaman said he had been terrified by his first airplane flight: "It was just like the *bari*'s dream.") Suddenly he sees a large cloud of smoke rolling across the savannah emitting flashes of light "as sparks flying from a fire."[1] This is the way certain kinds of *erubo,* "medicine," an epidemic or other misfortune attacking the village, always appear in mystical experience. The smoke sweeps down on certain persons well known to the dreamer but, after engulfing them, eddies away. Soon afterwards an illness does fall upon the village; it especially afflicts those individuals singled out in the dream, but they recover. Then the novice shaman, in a vivid dream, sees someone kill a jaguar or sees the "souls" during a collective hunt encounter a vast number of wild pigs which they succeed in killing. Again, these events come to pass, with all the specific vividness of the dream. The person begins to think about the *bope.*

Next, while awake and alone in the jungle, he sees a stone or anthill or stump suddenly move. (These are the homes of *maereboe,* as described earlier.) He notices that when he steps down hard, or sits, he utters an involuntary grunt, "Woh!." (Nearly all varieties of *bope* are given to grunting and making other "animal" noises, but then so are the *aroe.*) "All these things are signs that the *bope* make to him, cautiously so they do not scare him. If he says anything about these strange things to other people, the *bope* immediately anger and cease to like him, and may even kill him." A knowledgeable person who understands the significance of these events may deliberately talk about them just so as to avoid being a shaman, but he incurs a certain risk in doing so. Two Bororo said they had escaped being the servants of the *bope* in this fashion, but neither knew at the time the true meaning of their bizarre experiences, or so they claimed.

Otherwise, the next sign manifested to the apprentice shaman is voices he hears when out alone in the jungle or savannah. These seem to ask, "*Kaiba akodo mode?*" ("Where are you going?") This is the proper form of polite address when one meets an unknown Bororo, or any non-relative. Although no one can be seen, the man should reply, "I am hunting," and, lighting a cigarette, blow the smoke to all four directions of the compass. This is the prescribed action whenever any Bororo is confronted with some manifestation of either *bope* or *aroe.* Blowing the smoke to all sides causes the spirits to partake of it. Tobacco is almost the only thing both classes of spirit enjoy, just as smoking is the only mechanical agency employed by either type of shaman to enter into trance. Anyone seeking either the *bope*'s or *aroe*'s goodwill must give a cigarette to the spirits through their respective shamans. Such a prestation is usually the only payment for the spirits' activities on behalf of men (and for the shaman's).

Shortly after this transaction the future shaman discovers small game, such as a paca or wild turkey, never any of the species constituting *bope* food but usually something considered almost as delicious. On later occasions he notices that the various small finches, owls, and hawks used by *bope* as their omens or thought to embody *bope* attributes (*bope re-mawu*) follow him as he moves through the forest and seem to speak to him. Next he is surprised when a monkey (nearly always a *pai,* a howler monkey) asks him where he is going and demands he smoke a cigarette. Occasionally a coral snake or jiboia, the two snakes considered Themselves *bope,* show themselves to him and, some say, even talk. Finally one day the *bope* itself appears, in its essential form as a small black homunculus, and demands very peremptorily that it be given a cigarette.

While smoking it, the *bope* asks in a rude way what the man thinks he is doing, what kind of game he would like to kill, what kind of arrows he has (since usually a hunter carries three or four different varieties, each appropriate for a certain class of game). Finishing the cigarette and going off a little way, the *bope* suddenly disappears. Very soon afterwards the shaman-to-be finds a large game animal, a tapir or wild pig or deer (invariably one of the *bope ure*) and easily kills it.

As the last chapter showed, the odd or curious behavior of any one of the species regarded as Themselves *bope* or as omens portends nothing but evil if manifested to an ordinary Bororo. Above all, the sight of a *bope* in its normal form, or even in that slightly altered condition which resembles a howler monkey, means the imminent death of the viewer or one of his near kinsmen. The inversion of the meaning in these experiences, from negative to positive, is the way in which the *bope* first show their special favor to the one they have chosen as their *bari.*

The powers of the *bope* now have a different import for him: he can come into contact with the spirits and not be harmed, unlike all other people. The way in which the *bope* successively reward the future shaman with game, concluding finally with species among the *bope ure,* indicates one of the basic elements in the relationship: in exchange for his services the shaman himself shall have ample supplies of fresh meat and to this end will himself have good fortune in hunting. There can be no doubt that the *bope* are regarded as providing the game and hence that they directly control the destructive aspects of the shaman's relation with natural being. Some shamans are thought to transform themselves through the *bope*'s powers into jaguars and alligators so as to feed on *bope ure.* Likewise, the *bope* enable an evil shaman to "eat up" innocent people.

Following his successful hunt, which establishes the model of his relation with the *bope,* the future shaman returns to the village where he is quickly overcome by sleep. The *bope* enter him for the first time. He suddenly leaps up, babbling and screaming incoherently, and dashes madly around the house and out into the village. Those present grab him and hold him down, while someone goes for the nearest shaman. The *bope* begin speaking through him, although in a very confused way, and he continues to struggle violently. The experienced shaman offers him a cigarette and talks (in a nonpossessed condition himself) with the *bope*. As soon as the novice becomes calm enough to smoke, the *bope* depart with wild whoops, leaving him trembling and sweating. The shaman may at this time explain to him the meaning of what has happened and usually treats him with a general prophylactic technique (e.g., blowing and massage).

These episodes of possession during sleep continue for some time, for several months in most accounts, during which the new *bari* eats very little but smokes cigarettes constantly. The *bope* are always near him and constantly tutoring their new agent while he is asleep. This is the crucial period during the apprenticeship, and some people do not survive it. For during sleep the *bope* undertake various tests of the new *bari*'s suitability for the role. The public possession is the first overt sign that the *bope* have chosen a new shaman, and every informant recounted in considerable detail his own witness of such events. No known shaman had failed to begin his career without such a sudden possession during sleep.

During these initial trances the new shaman is never violent or aggressive to others. The danger is that in struggling against the *bope* he may do some harm to himself. Informants said he seems to try to run off into the forest, where in his irrational condition he could easily be hurt. Hence, he must be forcibly restrained. All Bororo, including shamans, agree that the initial possessions always occur in the village, and during sleep. Whatever his relations might be with nature, the shaman does not derive his special powers in antisocial, "wild" contexts, or as someone who is ranged against all social order. Indeed, to be a successful mediator he must exhibit a large degree of self-control and obedience to those rules which define Bororo social morality.

In the tests during the initiatory dreams, the *bope* subject the soul of the new shaman to a variety of experiences in which he must discipline his own "natural," *raka*-based desires and fears. The test regarded as the most important comes when the *bope* take the shaman's soul with them to the dwelling of Etu-o, the father of the *bope,* up in the *baru kujagureu,* the furthermost heaven. It seems, according to shamans, just like an ordinary Bororo hut. The *bope* command the soul to go alone inside the house. There he meets Etu-o, who greets him and presents a very beautiful woman, naked at the loins but otherwise wearing splendid ornaments. Etu-o soon leaves the apprentice shaman's soul alone with the girl. She motions to him to come closer and attempts in a variety of ways to seduce him. But a wise man does not show the slightest physical response but talks simply "without stirring," until he can politely take his leave.

All the *bope* gathered outside the house, the Etu-o, look inside, but the girl shakes her head, saying, *Boe bokwa,* "nothing." Then Etu-o addresses the new *bari* formally: "You want to live a long time, you are wise. Nothing bad will harm your kinsmen or your wife's kinsmen. If a sickness comes you will be able to cure it. You will live a very very long time, until you are very old and do not wish life any more, then you will die." The woman, now appearing in her true character as Etu-je, the "mother" of the *bope*, repeats the words. (These amount to a formula uttered in slightly variant forms by the *bope* through the shaman, following their consumption of *bope ure* or at the end of a collective prophylactic treatment of the shaman.)

If the new *bari*, however, has copulated with the woman, or even had an erection, Etu-o announces, "you are very stupid and do not wish to live; very soon you will die." Failure to restrain natural responses, informants were very sure, has led to the death of many potential shamans soon after the wild raving which first announced that the *bope* had selected them as their agents.

Even if the crucial trial is successfully passed, further dangers await the new *bari*. For only the one or two *bope* who originally selected the man as "their" shaman have any particular reason to guard his survival. The *bope* are intensely jealous and hostile toward one another. It is in large part thanks to this that man has any hope at all of prevailing for a time against these spirits, for they are willing to frustrate one another's hostile intentions toward mortals for sheer vindictive nastiness. During a *bari* recruitment the other *bope* are especially angry that one or two of them have such a fine new possession. They constantly attack the new shaman by ruse and force.

When, for example, his soul is being led about by his familiar *bope* during the night, crowds of hostile *bope* gather around and throw various lethal objects, such as beetles, that are otherwise utilized as the pathogenic agents in human illness. The shaman's familiars fight off these attacks, often with the assistance of the Tupadoge and other classes of *bope* generally well disposed to the Bororo. This kind of pitched battle among the spirits is very frequent and constitutes one of the most important arenas for the shaman's nonwaking activities, as shall be seen.

The hostile *bope* sometimes cause a great ball of fire to appear in front of the new *bari*. With the encouragement of his familiar, the shaman's soul must pass through it even though he feels himself in great agony. Or, still during his dreams, the shaman finds himself confronted by a huge, extremely ugly toad, its body covered with festering sores and warts. He must bring himself to touch it, or his abilities to treat disease will be much diminished. During his waking moments the new shaman often finds that the food he is about to eat is swarming with maggots (*atoe*), a sign that the food has not been cooked but is rotting. He must eat it all the same, mastering his natural disgust. Then he will be able to cure a variety of illnesses.

During this initiatory period the *bari* must refrain from all sexual activity until his familiar *bope* advise him that he may resume. This injunction is said to derive from the general weakness of his *raka* during this time and to the greatly increased danger that hostile *bope* may enter him during copulation. At the same time, his familiars instruct him how to enjoy sex in his new condition without being harmed by it. In dreams they lead him around to the various huts of the village so that he can watch the *bope* fornicating with the sleeping women. His soul may itself be commanded to copulate with women of the Bado Jeba clans, since they are the "younger sisters of the *bope*." As usual, the spirits take pleasure in actions which deny the principles of social morality, and especially they enjoy incest. But since according to structural assumptions the *bari* himself is a Tugarege, he breaks no exogamous rule even in his dreams.[2]

This might represent all the ways in which the *bari*, in spite of his contacts with the transcendant and a-social powers of the *bope*, must himself especially respect social constraints on all human behavior. He may be the *bope*'s agent, but he is no less a Bororo, subject to all the responsibilities his ritual titles and his kinship statuses impose upon him even when consciousless.

The phenomenological character of these experiences, and their personal significance for the apprentice shaman, are very ambigious. Their details and sequence are standardized almost to the point of collective representations, known by most adult nonshamans. Yet the three shamans I knew best spoke of them with vivid sincerity, adding variations and personal reactions at once idiosyncratic and consistent with the general pattern. Various problems hindered my inquiry. First, shamans are not supposed to discuss their experiences with the *bope*, even after they have been *baire* for years. This stricture does not apply so strongly to the typology and attributes of *bope* classes presented in the last chapter, since this knowledge forms a part of Bororo cosmology and can be publicly verified in dialogues with possessing *bope*. Nonetheless, some aspects of the initiatory process have entered into the public domain through the years, "leaked" by shamans to intimate friends and relatives. Further, a very great shaman of the middle São Lourenço, Cadete, had considered himself so powerful as to reveal his experiences with the *bope* with impunity. Therefore, the accounts of shamanistic recruitment I received undoubtedly dwelled on its socialized aspects, which does not reduce their personal validity or theoretical significance.

Second, the majority of living shamans I encountered were Tugarege, as doctrine holds they should be, and several were members of my wife's adopted clan, whereas I was considered an Exerae. Talk of sexual matters across moiety lines is generally interdicted and is especially forbidden to brothers-in-law. The Bororo generally took my feeble efforts to participate in their culture very seriously, especially when it suited some ulterior purpose. I was effectively blocked from detailed inquiry into the salubrious side of *bope*-inspired experiences, and especially could not get particulars about the critical initiatory test, the encounter with the seductive Etu-je. But my clan elder brother, Kadegare, one of those Ex-erae shamans who had been possessed by the *bope* of his shaman father, did tell me privately of this and some of his other early encounters with the *bope*.

Kadegare was married to a woman of our own moiety, and this breach of structural etiquette was generally taken, not without reason, to reveal Kadegare's general lack of sexual discretion. He told me that the encounter with Etu-je had been terrifying, so much so that his fear more than his self-control had saved him. "She was very very beautiful indeed and did everything that a woman does with a man." Kadegare liked to hint broadly that he was no longer so inhibited in the *bope*-conducted nocturnal tours of the village, offering sly comments on the relative carnal merits of various women, without respect of moiety lines. He did roam about at night, and I suspect that at least some of Kadegare's exploits were anything but dreamed.

Ordinary Bororo are quite sure that the shaman's mystical experiences are entirely "real," that no clear distinction can be made between them and ordinary sensate knowing. This does not mean they suspend all judgment and abandon their usual skepticism. There is a continual process of social verification of shamanistic accounts, all the livelier for being partially covert. The *bope* do not provide utterly new modalities of experience; Bororo epistemology does not admit of this possibility.

Shamanistic power does not rest upon access to an exclusive realm of knowledge, but only, to the extent that it sociologically exists, upon the *bari*'s status as a vehicle for the *bope*'s interactions with society. A certain amount of specialized knowledge and the adroitness of experience may facilitate action as such an agency, but they are not its basis. A person's whole nonvolitional character, his inherited *raka* and categorical status, lead to his selection by the *bope*. The *bari* is far more an actor than a knower; the last quality, in contrast, pervades the nature of the complementary ritual specialist, the shaman of the souls. These points, and the issue of the true character of shamanistic experience, can only be further investigated through examining the shaman's activities after his initiation into the domain of the *bope*.

## The *Bope*'s Relation with Their Shaman

Gradually, as through his familiars the new shaman increases his mastery of the ways of the *bope,* he ceases to tremble constantly and begins to resume his normal activities. He is finally able to invoke the *bope* deliberately and to be possessed by them while he is awake. People gradually begin to bring him *bope* food for him "to give" to the spirits. After a time, he is asked to attempt cures. On the thoroughly empirical basis of his successes and failures in the treatment of affliction, he establishes a particular reputation as a shaman. The Bororo differentiate very closely among various shamans, on the grounds of their proven abilities (or lack of them), and the particular set of *bope* familiars each one has.

These last determine the types of shamanistic power. The two most general categories are *bari boejamedu boe,* "the shaman of the game," and *bari du kurodurebwe,* "the shaman of the plants." The former eats, while possessed, all the *bope* foods, but the latter only consumes the plants in that group. Both kinds engage in all other shamanistic functions: treatment of the ill, mass prophylactic cures, prediction of the future, and so on. None of my informants knew of any woman shaman among those of the first type, although the second includes both men and women. The reason for the difference between the two types is that the "shaman of the plants" has only Tupa-doge among his familiars. Alone among the *bope,* this type of spirit disdains meat and is generally favorably disposed toward the Bororo (who are themselves the ultimate *bope ure*). Unfortunately, they are not generally so powerful as other sorts of *bope* and seldom prevail over any concentration of these.

*Bari* are further distinguished by the particular *bope* they have as familiars, some of which are regarded as especially good in curing specific illnesses. The Tupa-doge, for example, are often effective with children's intestinal disorders, while the *bope* of the snake hawk (macaua) is the only spirit capable of curing cases of snakebite. But the almost complete lack of Bororo interest in classifying and diagnosing disease is paralleled in their assumption that the *bope,* and the shamans they possess, are generally a nonspecialized mass. "What one *bope* has caused, another could cure," said one shaman with great confidence. The merits of any particular *bari* finally derive as much from the kind of rapport he has with the familiars as from the specific identity of these. And this rapport reflects his moral conduct toward his fellows and the whole animate world.

The familiar *bope,* those who originally recruited the shaman, are considered to be intensely "jealous" and very demanding in their relations with him, no matter what the usual characteristics of their type might be. They regard not only his person, but his belongings and even his spouse, as their own exclusive property. They view him and his as they do the species in the *bope ure.* Therefore, the Bororo reason, the shaman and all that is in intimate contact with him are as physically polluting as the raw substances of these species. The *bari*'s cut hair should be thrown into the river, and his nail parings buried, so that others do not come into inadvertent contact with them. He maintains his possessions in a secure place where none but he and his wife have access to them. If these are stolen, broken, or idly handled, the *bope* become exceedingly angry not only with the offender but also with the shaman for having taken so little care of "their" belongings.

Clearly, these things are intrinsically contaminated. A *bari* may not dispose of his old worn-out clothing unless his *bope* explicitly allow him to do so, and then they are burned, just as the possessions of a dead man are burned instead of being casually tossed out of the house like all other Bororo refuse. The shaman must take great care not to damage or lose the most inconsequential of his belongings, and he guards zealously those items most involved with his professional tasks. The *bope* soon kill or make very ill a shaman who breaks his knife, since it comes into frequent contact with the flesh of *bope* animals during butchering and is indispensable to the offering of "their" food to the *bope*. Likewise no nonshaman should touch the knife, other than the *bari*'s wife, for it is defiled.

Sometimes persons give the *bope,* through their shaman, a pot, or skewer (*joto*), or special kind of fan, in gratitude for a cure. All such items are among the equipment used by the *bari* in the preparation of *bope* food: the pot for cooking and storage, the *joto* to stir and pick out pieces of boiling meat when cooked, the fan to renew the fire and cool the possessed *bari*. If any of these things break, the *bope* inflict an illness on the original maker, and often on the shaman as well. So they are constantly remade by the giver or one of his affines. The utilitarian character of these cooking instruments is much superseded by their symbolic importance, at least for the skewer and fan. The shaman uses them in his mystical battles with the hosts of evil *bope* who attack the village at night, and their form is determined by this function rather than the more mundane one. The *joto* is 1 meter or more long, made from the same tough heartwood used for bows, and sharpened to a long, fine point. It is an awkward skewer but an admirable short spear. The special fan, *bakureu,* is even less empirically instrumental. It is made from the twisted fibers of the buriti palm, woven together into a small mat by longitudinal strands of the same fiber, and hung from a palm spine by two cords at either end. The construction involves much time and expertise, as does that of the *joto*. In fanning, the *bakureu* is whirled around the stick until the ends of the cords are reached, when direction is reversed. Its action is cumbersome and dissipates air in a circle; the Bororo nearly always use an old palm-leaf tray or fan when a fire needs urging. But the *bakureu* can be worn around the neck, with the "fan" itself hanging across the chest, where it protects the shaman from the missiles thrown by the *maereboe* (cf. Albisetti and Venturelli 1962: 212–14, for illustrations and descriptions of various types of *bakureu,* which are elements of clan property).

Shamans themselves usually attribute their own illnesses to the *bope*'s excessively jealous regard for things they considered their property, no matter how trivial. One *bari* said his recent severe sickness had come about because, when his canoe overturned some months ago, he had lost the belt to his pants. (Other Bororo, though, were appalled at the transparency of this fabrication. They alleged this particular shaman, Manukuje, whose case is discussed below, had erred in his preparation and consumption of *bope* foods on innumerable occasions.) In another case, a shaman (Kadegare, mentioned earlier and also discussed below) was temporarily blinded when his shotgun backfired into his face. He claimed that the *bope* were punishing an incident of several days earlier. His wife's sister's daughter's husband, resident in his household, had returned home very late and quite drunk. Stumbling around the dark hut, the son-in-law accidentally tipped over the pot which contained those particular bits of swamp deer which must be "eaten" twice by the *bope*. They had been initially consumed that afternoon, and were to be re-eaten the next day; unfortunately, the scurvy pack of half-starved dogs living in the household fell upon the pieces and managed to make off with several chunks from the vertebral column before the befuddled son-in-law could drive them off. The *bope* were very offended and arranged an appropriate revenge. Others said that, while this version was possible, it was more likely that Kadegare himself was drunk and tipped over the pot.

Of all the *bari*'s possessions jealously regarded as their own by the *bope*, none is so infused with pollution and danger as his wife, the *aredu bari* (literally "shaman's girl"). There are various reasons for this. During his trances the *bari*'s wife serves as the spokesman for society, responding to the *bope*'s questions put through the body of the shaman: "Who has killed this animal?," "What is wrong with this sick person?," and so on. The shaman's wife actually does most of the cooking of the *bope* foods and accompanies her husband in butchering them. The *bope* enjoy her sexually through their agent, her spouse. All the shared organic *raka* between the couple, including the foods they eat, mean that the wife is more thoroughly imbued with all the dangerous powers resident in the body of her husband than any other of his possessions. Only another *bari*, say the Bororo, should marry the widow of a shaman, for only he, through the good offices of his familiar *bope*, can withstand the contagion inherent forever in this woman. Adultery with the shaman's wife is tantamount to eating *bope* meat before it has been given to the spirits: "The *bope* do not wait for him to realize his mistake [i.e., to seek shamanistic aid] but kill him then."

One of my informants was most impressed by a case remembered from his childhood. A man had used his fingers to seduce the *bari*'s wife, perhaps in the belief that this would deceive or at any rate not anger the *bope*. But the three fingers he used turned black, shriveled up and eventually dropped off. The man died while still young, in a somewhat mysterious drowning.[3] The informant concluded vigorously, "one must not even touch the *aredu bari*."

Some women allege that it is dangerous to quarrel with shamans' wives, many of whom seem to hold themselves somewhat aloof from the usual female bands that work and gossip together. But I would not say they enjoy any particular prestige, no more than do their husbands, sheerly through their intimate association with the *bope*. This connection is, again, purely mechanical, a matter of physical contagion and contiguous association. The shaman and his wife are to be avoided, except when their services are needed. The only aspects of their existences which draw them back into community life and furnish some status are those deriving from the ritual positions they may occupy within their respective clans and through the complex set of relationships involving the representation of the dead. Even in that context, however, the shaman occupies a place set apart, for only a *bari* can be the representative of a deceased shaman in the other moiety. "After all," say the Bororo, "the dead *bari* has no *aroe* but is a *bope* itself, and only another *bari/bope* can represent it." For a nonshaman to be the representative would have much the same disastrous consequences as marrying a *bari*'s widow. (This alone justifies Exerae shamans, according to some informants.)

The moral ambiguity of shamans is perhaps most intensely mirrored in the ambiguity surrounding the status of their personal *aroe*, their "souls." In terms of categorical dogma, as outlined in Chapter 4, all *bope* have an *aroe* in that, despite all their amorphousness and inclination to metamorphoses, each in its typological variety does have a nominal form and so an *aroe*, complete with social affiliation. Such is also true of the living shaman, who obviously possesses a distinctive fleshly envelope, a name (the essence of human *aroe*-ness), and a social persona expressed in the formal obligations and rights of the clan *aroe* system. He is anything but that near total manifestation of bopeness in the world that a vulture represents, not even that partial refraction which is an omen. The one shaman whom I could persuade to discuss the issue declared that he "was" a *bope*, as a *bope* "was" a jaguar, implying his *aroe* only temporarily became a *bope*. (A nonshaman, hearing this, said with contempt, "an alligator maybe.") This appears a typical Bororo sophistry, resting on the argument that if *bope* can have *aroe*, why could not a particular *aroe* become a *bope?*

Yet the central tenets of Bororo cosmology do possess the absolute antitheses of *bope* and *aroe*. Moreover, the shaman's central test during the mystical passages of initiation require his "unconscious essence," his dream-soul, to act as a *bope*. Some of his most crucial shamanistic duties (detailed below) require him to sleep or enter trance so that his "other" self can join his *bope* familiars in battle against hostile *bope*. It seemed obvious to most informants that that self *had* to be *bope*. With the *bari*'s "soul" the Bororo confront the central paradox of their cosmological system, that humans are at once *bope* and *aroe*. Most nonshamans appeared to think most if not all *bari* "lost" their *aroe* in the initiatory process; others accepted the metamorphosis argument. This ambiguity pervades all that follows. I have tried to express it through a neologism: the shaman's "*bope*-soul." I will use this term to characterize those moments when the shaman's "other self" is at once intensely human and antihuman.

The contradiction is laid to rest when the shaman dies, often young, at least in social perception. One common attitude about shamans is summarized in the commonplace, "There are no old *bari*." Actually, according to genealogies and always subject to the hazy Bororo recall of individuals' absolute ages, shaman's mortality rates seem no different from those of other Bororo. But the funerals of shamans are notably different from all others, for reasons that illuminate certain aspects of their relations with society, and which stress the peculiar nature of shamanistic mortality. The reason for treating a defunct shaman in special ways comes from the belief just mentioned, that his soul, instead of going off to be an *aroe* among the ancestors, becomes (or already before death has been) a *bope* itself. The shaman's *bope* has all the qualities attributed to the *bope* generally: whatever the shaman's personal characteristics in life, they are all utterly transformed at death.

Stories are told of how even "good," respected shamans instruct their relatives to leave the village immediately after their death, and most persons act upon this advice. In Bororo cosmology all souls are reluctant to leave the company of the living and must be persuaded and comforted along their journey to the transcendent *aroe* villages by the shades of predeceased relatives. But, as the *bope*'s domain is eminently of this world, the souls of dead shamans may continue to dwell among their kinsmen. Jealous of the living, they seek to turn their relatives into shamans or to work harm upon them.

The *bope*-souls of shamans who were wicked during life become even more evil at death: they change into *maereboe*, that category of *bope* which lives upon the earth and which is the most maleficent to human beings. Confined beneath the roosts of vultures and covered with their *jerimaga* dung, they are occasionally released by their old familiars to do havoc among the Bororo. Therefore, the bones of shamans considered guilty of witchcraft (*erubo epa,* see below) are buried far separate from one another, instead of being cleaned, decorated, and deposited in a lake or cave. This somehow diminishes (the Bororo are not sure why) the *bope*-

soul's power. But such action is very rare. It is considered very "ugly," not just by the deceased's relatives but by the general public. No matter how suspicious may have been a shaman's conduct in life, or threatening his metamorphoses into inhuman spirit, his demise confirms his humanity and calls for that reintegration of society and nature accomplished by the Bororo funeral.

This is not to say that the shaman's moral ambiguity is not otherwise recognized at his death. In most cases the defunct's immediate relatives (children, spouse, members of his former residential group, and more occasionally consanguines and their spouses) do leave the village where the death occurred, usually only for a season but sometimes permanently. The more powerful and/or witchlike the shaman in life, the more likely such departures are, and the more apprehensive the entire community. If it then appears that diseases and accidents increase markedly after the shaman's funeral, the Bororo conclude his *bope*-soul is powerfully malicious, and they forthwith change the village site and seek the collective intervention of the community's remaining shamans. Such actions appear to follow, roughly, the death of about every third shaman, but even then ambiguities remain.

The decision to change a village's location involves many idiosyncratic factors.[4] Villages tend to be moved 100 to 500 meters about every dozen years. In that time the houses become so decrepit and the whole place so thoroughly filthy as to be irreparable. The Bororo say the village has become too "full of death" to be habitable; they may claim that a virulent *bope,* perhaps that of a certain defunct shaman, has taken up residence near it. But this is almost a self-conscious justification: the *bope*'s proximity is a succinct way of conveying the weight of morbid associations with that particular site, its whole worn-out decrepitude. The tendency for the members of a dead shaman's household to move away is both more common and less ambiguous.

But all of these displacements indicate again the primary metonymic fashion in which all aspects of the *bope* affect the Bororo. The bonds of potential affliction follow those ties the shaman established during his lifetime: first they touch the persons who lived with him, then those who had some element of common *raka* with him, such as his consanguines and agnates, and then, in a much diminished way, they affect the physical body of the community itself. The dead shaman's power to afflict his housemates is so immediate as to justify a rapid physical dissociation from the place they shared with him, a direct and obvious sundering of empirical contiguity. But these powers have markedly diminishing capacities to affect those physically and socially distant from the shaman's lifetime spheres of consubstantiality. Hence, the pragmatic attitude toward dead shamans: although their potential capacities to harm are great, they

A shaman's widow (in mourning)

are not without boundaries, and it would be foolish to credit them with more respect than they prove to deserve. If subsequent events show that the shaman's *bope*-soul is more maleficent and powerful than had been anticipated, the combination of moving the village and utilizing the collective powers of the shamans there resident is usually enough to defeat him.

None of these measures prevail for those who had shared the shaman's physical existence, most especially his wife. They continue to be threatened for the rest of their lives, by at least the contagion they carry in their physical persons, and perhaps by a more personalistic and conscious malignancy. The metonymic powers of the *bope*, therefore, rest not just on spatial contiguity and literal resemblance but also include a kind of metaphorization of these physical associations. The sharing of *raka*, whether by birth or through conjugality, creates a proximate "likeness" which can never be diminished by time or space. Further, the logic prevailing here is at once that which characterizes vultures and coral snakes as Themselves *bope* and yet which designates remote and innocent deer as "food of the *bope*." A dead shaman's wife is doubly dangerous: not only did she physically participate in his being, she was also "his." This doubling of autonomous pollution and classifying intelligence has proved to define the *bope*'s dominion over natural and social categories. It is no less marked in other aspects of the shaman.

# Invisible Wars:
# Shamans and the *Aroe Butu*

The duties of the *bari* include some less visible than those of conveying *bope* food to the spirits and curing the ill. Most of all, he is obliged to protect the general welfare of all village residents during the night, when the hostile *maereboe* and other types of *bope* seek to work malicious harm on all Bororo. The spirits come to "eat the *aroe*" of sleeping persons and to fornicate with women, actions which are nearly homologous. Usually the *bope* familiars of the village's shamans, with the help of the shamans' *bope*-souls, manage to defend the village and repulse the invading *bope*. Most of these pitched battles occur at night, but sometimes the *bope* steal into the village during the day; for many Bororo are accustomed to sleep at odd hours, shamans among them. Since the shaman's *bope*-soul is absent from his body while he is asleep, either defending the village or voyaging into the past or future, no one must awaken him abruptly—lest his soul be prevented from returning to his body or hindered from defending the community's residents. The person who wakes the shaman is himself in grave danger, since the *bope* little appreciate having their servant's soul snatched from among them in the midst of some crucial activity.

During his various mystical battles against the hostile *bope,* the shaman uses the gifts he has received on behalf of the *bope* from those people the spirits have cured. These include prominently the *joto,* a slender wood skewer about a meter long, used to stir the cooking *bope* meat and to transfer it to palm-leaf plates; the *batureu,* the "suspended fan" described earlier, used to fan the cooking fire and to cool the cooked meat, or the shaman when possessed; various spoons and open-work "dips" used to stir and serve *bope* foods; the knife used to butcher the game; and the pottery bowls, or more recently, the metal pots and pans in which the *bope* foods are boiled. The importance of these items is more mystical than utilitarian, as explained earlier, owing entirely to their uses in the mystical fights with the *bope.* The *joto* is the most important offensive instrument, the shaman's *bope*-soul using it as a kind of spear to attack the hostile *bope.* The knife is similarly employed.

The *batureu* is worn around the neck so that it hangs down over the chest, as a kind of chest-plate; though made only of twisted palm fibers, it is infused with the power of the shaman's familiar so that it deflects the missiles thrown by the malign *bope.* With the spoons, dips, and plates the shaman can also deflect the same missiles. It is indicative of the shaman's thoroughly passive status as a mere agency of the *bope* that in these battles he cannot use his own bow and arrows or shotgun, if he owns one, or clubs or spears. "Only the things which are truly the *bope*'s can be used by the shaman's *bope* in the fights," for only these have sufficient inherent power to prevail against the lethal forces of the hostile *bope.*[5]

Usually each of the village's shamans acts as separately and independently during these mystical fights as he does in his other *bope* activities. But on one occasion all the shamans of the community must fight together. This occurs during the *aroe butu,* literally "the fall of a soul," the actions after a falling star is thought to have hit the earth. Since the details of this ceremony, almost the only collective one in all human dealings with the *bope,* reveal much concerning man–*bope* relations, I give an extended account here which draws on material published by earlier ethnographers (Cruz 1945; Albisetti and Venturelli 1962: 168–70), as confirmed and amended by my own informants. This ritual is referred to in the earlier sources as *aroe kodu,* "the trajectory of a soul," which Albisetti and Venturelli also translate as "meteorite." As they note (1962: 170) and I confirmed, the ritual as described below only occurs if the meteorite is heard to fall to earth. A shooting star, if unusually brilliant, might warrant a truncated and semi-private version of the ritual, performed by a single shaman. For this reason, my informants referred to the complete ceremony as *aroe butu.*

Occasionally the *maereboe,* including the evil *bope* of deceased shamans, succeed in entering the huts and stealing various property. This usually happens, according to shamans themselves, when the *maereboe* attack in numbers so great that the village's defenders, humans and spirits alike, are outflanked. (Nonshamans blame the shamans' lack of vigilance or sheer impotence.) The *maereboe* take something intimately associated with its owner, usually a man's bow and arrow, a woman's woven palm basket, or a child's toy.[6] While no one is sure just how, it seems that the object itself is taken while its "shadow" or, some said, its *aroe* was left behind (inanimate objects are not considered to possess souls, so this usage is purely figurative). The soul of the sleeping owner invariably is drawn after the stolen object, almost as by a magnet. After a dozen or more objects together with their owners' souls have been stolen, the *maereboe* withdraw from the village, fighting off the defenders as they go. They bundle up the stolen objects in a single package, which is set on fire. The *maereboe* then fly through the sky with their blazing trophy, finally throwing it to earth where it strikes with a resounding crash. The *maereboe* then descend to earth and prepare to eat the stolen souls.

Bororo men spend each twilight with several hours of following dark lying on their mats in the dance plaza, gazing up at the night sky. They discuss the correlations between shifts in the constellations, and the slow transition from one season to another. The flash of an occasional comet excites only random comment, but an intense and apparently near one may elicit a request to a shaman to explore its significance. But if the thing is heard to fall to earth, the men react with considerable alarm. Such a noise, which seems to be liberally interpreted, signifies that the *bope* have actually succeeded in carrying off their prey from this village. Soundless meteorites, according to several informants, only mean that the spirits have succeeded in robbing property-souls from some distant population, Bororo, Brazilian, or, if far to the north, even American.

The men immediately delegate one of their number to convey a cigarette to a shaman, so that he can discover from his *bope* which village members have been robbed of their possessions and souls. Shouts spread the word across the village. Everyone, women and children down to young toddlers, sets off a chaotic uproar. People scream urgently, fire off guns, beat on pots, pans, and logs, crash rolled-up mats against the ground. All of this is meant to frighten the *bope* away from the stolen souls. In the single *aroe butu* I witnessed the din was impressive, and nearly everyone was acutely anxious, on the verge of panic. Even the *emijera,* the titled subclan chiefs, always self-possessed and calmly dignified, were obviously very worried and led the noise-making, which struck me as having the quality of a cathartic outbreak. The women rushed to gather in a few houses within each moiety, while the children screamed with fear.

In the midst of all this confusion and random sound, each *bari* in the village was given a cigarette, and each retired immediately to his own house. Traditionally they each went to sleep in the midst of all their *bope* paraphernalia (*joto,* knives, *batureu,* and so forth), well apart from their wives and children. In the case I saw, two shamans went into trance and remained possessed for several hours, with the *bope* babbling through them, incoherently, of the struggle to regain the stolen souls. A third was possessed but soon fell over backward unconscious; he did not wake until late the next afternoon. Two more shamans went to sleep after smoking part of their cigarettes.

As soon as all the shamans are asleep or possessed, their familiars lead their *bope*-souls to where the thieving *bope* have gathered around a long line of what appear to be dead tapir, deer, pig, capivara, and so forth, almost all the species among the *bope ure.* All the spirits are shouting, "Come! Let us eat deer, tapir, rhea, *bope ure* this." The *baire* and their familiars immediately attack, throwing their *jotos* and knives at the thieves. These reply with showers of beetles and the other pathogenic agents they are accustomed to use in causing afflictions. But the shamans have been given chest shields made from flint and from the bark of the jatuba tree (*bariga*), better protectors even than the *bakureu* fans they are already wearing. Helped by their familiars, the shamans are able to fight their way up to the animal bodies, and with supernatural aid identify which are the stolen souls, transformed by the *maereboe* into one kind or other of *bope ure.* Each shaman picks up two or three carcasses and flees, protected by his familiars and sometimes by the Tupa-doge, who intervene with their guns if the fight seems to be going against the side of the shamans.

The souls are then taken to a safe spot far from the village where they are removed from the animal (or "transformed" back into themselves) and washed thoroughly, first with *pobo bekurureu,* "blue water," and then with ordinary water. These washings remove the "stench of death," or *jerimaga,* which of course is common to the *bope ure.* Unless washed away, this smell would make the soul's owner very weak, without *raka;* he would be polluted just as if he had come into contact with the animal's blood or excrement. After passing some *erubo* (plant medicine) over the soul so that it will be strong and healthy, the shamans return it and all the other stolen souls to their sleeping owners, who have been unaware of their danger. If the shamans do not arrive until after the soul has been eaten, or fail to recover it, its owner sickens and dies in a very short time.

Each aspect of the *aroe butu* may occur independently of the others. That is, a soul may be stolen through the robbery of one of its owner's possessions and may be subsequently recovered by a *bari* before eaten in the form of a *bope ure.* The battles occur, on various scales, almost constantly, and do sometimes go against the shamans. The village's shamans also collaborate in active, nondreamed cures of the entire community, when an epidemic is threatened.

But the significant elements in all of these events are most clearly evident in their serial appearance in the *aroe butu,* which in effect summarizes nearly all of the nonconscious dimensions of man's relations with the *bope.* There is first the identification of humans with the *bope ure,* a critical element in understanding this system of prestations, as the last chapter showed. Then the individual is virtually equated with at least some of his property, a point which has considerable significance for the analysis of social personality and ritual conduct among the Bororo (see Chapter 2 and Crocker 1977c).

Next, there is a quality of randomness to the collection of stolen souls that reflects one of the most essential qualities of the *bope* attacks against mankind: their unpredictability. The shamans say that all the persons whose souls are stolen have offended the *bope* in one way or another, or that one of their parents have. By no means have the victims committed the worst or the most recent offenses among the village's residents. Their selection is as much determined by the *bope*'s ability to gain access to dwellings and personal property as it is by particular infractions of the *bope*'s rights. The *bope* seek especially to steal the souls of young, beautiful girls, so as to copulate with them before eating them. Unless married themselves to a shaman, these girls, along with children, have the least contact of any Bororo with the *bope ure.* They may be symbolically analogous to these substances, but they are apt to be innocent of any but the most minor disobedience to the rules surrounding them. For that matter, children's souls are stolen too, for they can be transformed into the young of wild pigs, very delicious indeed, according to the Bororo, and much esteemed by the *bope.* The justification for harming them, of course, must lie in a parent's faults, but these were not grave infractions in the cases I heard.

When the shamans reveal the identities of the souls they have recovered,[7] all the village is very surprised at the odd heterogeneity of the collection the *bope* managed to gather. Perfectly healthy persons as well as those suffering from various ailments are included with the very old, the young, and the adolescent. "None of it makes any sense," said one informant, not a shaman, "but the *bope* are like that." The *aroe butu* shows just how helpless mankind, and shamans too, would be against the *bope* were it not for the internal conflicts among them. The shamans succeed in winning back the souls only through the help of their familiars. These are not all-powerful, however, and sometimes the human-familiar / *bope* contingent loses the battle. The surreal violence of these struggles stands in marked contrast to the most important norms of Bororo society, which interdict all physical aggression between Bororo, and most especially forbid organized civil war. The *bope*'s rivalries and violent hostilities establish them as an antisociety, marked by anarchic disorder and natural anomaly.

But most importantly, the *aroe butu* reveals the importance attributed to the shaman's dream activities. There can be no question that the Bororo feel their society acutely threatened by the noise of a "falling star." That the most effective action against this menace is for the shamans to go to sleep testifies not just to social confidence in their nonconscious powers but also to the validity of the beliefs concerning their dream activities generally, outside the context of *aroe butu*. The shaman's ability to defend the entire community from imperceptible attacks is a matter of collective representation, not some hallucination put forward by a neurotic individual. At the same time the shaman's "actions," his presumably volitional behavior during the mystical battles, occur when the agency of all activity, the body, is in the most absolute state of quiescence—asleep.

This merely affirms the pattern: the shaman is the passive vector of the *bope*'s transactions with society, whose person and property are dangerous only for the infused contagion within them, and who, in order to effect lasting changes in the *bope*'s intervention into human lives, must surrender all consciousness and personal will. When awake, the shaman is no more than another man, save for the latent pollution resulting from the *bope*'s use of his body. When he is, according to his own desire, possessed by the *bope*, he may cure illness and foresee the future. But when he is totally asleep, then he "acts," and accomplishes in his dreams far more than what other men can do when awake. This inverted continuum is no mere structuralist's invention, for all Bororo assumptions about the epistemology of will center on the necessity of a conscious, *knowing* actor, who can impose his volition upon the animate world only insofar as he is aware of the principles of its ordering and his own capacities as a physical being. The Bororo collectivized repugnance toward aging derives in large part from their perception of old age as interdicting the facility of corporeal action. The shaman is a kind of antiman, insofar as his capacities to affect both natural and transcendent reality are concerned. This condition is manifest in his functions.

# Possession and the Offering of Food

Most of the shaman's daily activities are as those of any other Bororo, according to his household's varying needs and his social duties as clansman and relative. But intermittently, daily or biweekly or once a month, depending on his status in the community, he is asked to manifest publicly his unique relation to the *bope*. Most often he must render the spirits their meats; more occasionally he treats the ill. Whatever the circumstances and no matter the individual shaman, the stages of his possession by the *bope* occur in nearly identical ways. I next describe the shaman's behavior in *bope* food offerings simply because this is the most common occasion for this process.

When a hunter has killed one of the *bope ure,* he asks one of the village's shamans to offer this food up to the *bope*. He does so through an intermediary, one of his own immature children, a wife, or young sibling, for to go himself would be the sort of self-assertive bragging detested by the Bororo. Almost always the shaman butchers, cooks, and consecrates the game in or just outside the hunter's conjugal hut. Only if the animal is unusually large and potent in *raka,* or one of the very lethal species such as tapir or alligator, does he conduct these operations in the already polluted precincts of his wife's hut. Always the shaman's wife superintends the actual cooking, sometimes aided from time to time by her husband employing his special instruments, a *joto* (skewer) or *bakureu* (suspended fan). Often a mature hunter or knowledgeable relative butchers less powerful types of *bope* food. Then the shaman does not arrive upon the scene until the food is ready for the *bope*. The cooked meat is already arranged on several layers of fresh palm leaves, usually those of the acuri or babacu palm, and his wife has ladled out some of the broth in a freshwater clam shell. The shaman removes whatever clothing and ornaments he may be wearing, as these things are "of the *aroe*" and hinder the *bope*'s speedy arrival. The man who has killed the game has prepared a cigarette, which he gives to the *bari,* who lights it with a fire brand.

Closing his eyes, the shaman begins to inhale the smoke in great rapid draughts. As he exhales the smoke, he chants rapidly, calling his familiar *bope,* starting on a high, almost falsetto note and running down the scale toward the end of the phrase. Rocking his body back and forth and starting to sweat, the shaman accelerates the tempo of his smoking and calling. He begins during the last to strike the edge of his right hand against his mouth, very rapidly. His chanted words become run together and partially incomprehensible. He also begins to employ certain terms by which only the *bope* name the species belonging to them (Albisetti and Venturelli 1962: 979–83). Constantly the *bari* calls out the name of his familiar *bope,* telling it that it should come to eat tapir or deer or wild pig, that the meat is good and ready to be eaten.

The process of possession may last from ten minutes to over an hour, but generally takes about half an hour. During this time, and especially toward the end, all manner of *bope* begin to swarm around the shaman: the *maereboe,* who are very near and smelled the meat even while it was being cooked, along with various other kinds of *bope,* including the *bope-*

souls of dead shamans, and a random assortment of the named varieties. They wish to eat the meat and try to deceive the *bari* into accepting them as the familiar. The scene, as described by shamans, struck me like something from Hieronymus Bosch: swarms of things, some like small alligators, others like vultures, still others resembling monkeys, and more with no natural counterpart, all swarming and writhing and flitting around the house.

This is a dangerous moment, for if the shaman is possessed by the *bope* which is not among his familiars, it will have little mercy upon him. Simply using his person as an instrument, a kind of "knife and fork," as a somewhat acculturated informant put it, this spirit eats up the meat and upon its departure simply takes the shaman's *bope*-soul with it, resulting in a grave illness or even death. Shamans describe these later moments of the initial possession as a time when they feel "confused," "upside down," overwhelmed by sensory disorder. Many shamans do become possessed by *bope* other than their familiars and suffer from it, at least in their own telling. Only a wise and experienced shaman can distinguish neatly among all the horde of *bope* that come crowding in, drawn by the odor of tobacco and cooked food, and tell which among them is really his familiar.

When this one does arrive and is recognized by the shaman, he allows it to enter his body, which it does with a great "whoop." The shaman's chanting has been heard all over the village, and this tremendous shout announcing the *bope*'s possession of its agency resounds from the encircling trees. People speculate why the *bope* have been called, and they comment upon the nature of their coming into the body of the shaman.[8] The change in the shaman himself is dramatic: suddenly, after his feverish cries and violent rocking, he now sits quietly, running his right hand over his mouth and over his closed eyes. He vigorously scratches his hair and his chest, less often his limbs. The shaman's possessed body is languorous, heavy, sleepy. (These actions and sensations are threatening to persons in conditions of ritual danger, as related in Chapter 1.)

Shamans say possession is much like a dream. They are "conscious" but passive spectators of a distorted world filled with bizarre activity. The atmosphere seems to be red or blue, as are the two upper skies inhabited by the good *bope*. The people around are grotesque: some have enormous stomachs, others have only heads or feet, some are entirely white while others are all black. The *bari* feels extremely hot, as well as very itchy and sleepy. When he regards the piled-up meat of the *bope ure* animal, he may see great masses of horrible larvae, *marugodu jokureu* (identified by Albisetti and Venturelli [1962: 786] as "jungle larva with round spots over the skin, little encountered"), crawling all over the meat and even over himself. If the *bari* tries to pick these off the meat, he will not be able to cure anyone. The larvae are made to appear by the good *bope,* his familiars. Alternately, the meat appears full of *ate* (or *atoe*), the long white grubs that infest rotting meat. Again, the shaman must ignore these.

Many Bororo say that while the *bari* is possessed he is completely insensible to his *bope* actions. They cite as proof his questions after the trance as to what the *bope* did and said. Several shamans confirmed this, comparing their usual experience of possession to a feverish dream or a consciousless sleep. Only occasionally are they aware of that distorted world just described.

The *bope,* speaking through the shaman, addresses questions to the shaman's wife, speaking in a rapid, brusque, grunting monotone quite different from the usual cadences of Bororo speech. It asks who has killed the animal, for what reason, to whom it will be given (i.e., in the prestations within the ritual representation of the dead, the *aroe maiwu* system), the circumstances of the hunt, the kill, who carried the game back to the village,[9] and so forth. It continues to smoke heavily but sporadically. The shaman's wife replies to all the questions in a monotone. If the *bope* is especially powerful, it employs so many terms unique to the *bope* that the auditors claim to understand little of the dialogue.

The shaman then lays aside his cigarette and begins to eat the *bope ure.* If the piece is large, he (or it, the possessing *bope*) is careful to take bites from every section, from both ends and the middle in the case of long leg bones and ribs, or from front, back, middle, and sides with such pieces as the loins. The *bope* eats with much loud smacking, uttering pleased little grunts; the Bororo otherwise are fastidious, even dainty, in their eating. (It seems to the shaman that the *bope* is eating up all the meat, leaving only the bones, but when he comes out of the trance he sees that actually only a few bites from each piece have been taken.) Finally, the familiar *bope* departs in much the way he arrived, after saying, "I am going now, to take this food to *paxe* and *pao*" ("our mother and our father", i.e., Etu-je and Etu-o, up in the red sky). Usually only one of the shaman's two to six familiar *bope* possesses him during any particular eating of a *bope ure,* but sometimes one may depart halfway through the meal and another take its place. This is particularly common when members of large species, such as the tapir or swamp deer, are being consumed. No shaman can ever be possessed by more than one *bope* familiar at a time.

After all the major pieces have been eaten, the shaman, still possessed, may call the bad *bope,* the *maereboe,* to come eat up the scraps and drink of the broth. They appear as the various carrion birds, vultures and hawks, in whose forms they initially attempted to enter the *bari* and eat the meat. Shamans said that, although these *bope* do not actually possess the shaman, they can still consume the food through his body. When every piece of meat, no matter how small has been at least mouthed, and the broth sipped, the shaman relights his cigarette and begins again the rapid muttering and heavy rhythmic smoking with which he began the trance. He asks all the *bope*, "Do not let anything happen to our people here. Hide the snakes under the earth. Keep bad *erubo* ("medicine," usually here in the sense of epidemics) away from our village. Do not let jaguars and harpy eagles attack us. Keep us safe from all the harming things, the stingrays, the anteaters, the alligators, the wasps, the piranhas, the sucuris, the coatis, all poisonous plants. Cure those Bororo that are sick. Do not let anyone die." The specifics of this formula vary slightly from occasion to occasion and between different shamans, as noted earlier, but generally the *bope* are asked to fulfill their side of the contract which humans have just respected in the prestation of the *bope ure*. The shaman's muttering becomes more rapid and loud until with a loud whoop the *bope* departs.

The aftermath is very prosaic. The shaman quickly regains his normal composure and, with his wife, sets about gathering those pieces especially strong in *raka,* which must be offered again the next day. These will then be eaten by himself and members of his residential group. The hunter, or the person to whom he gave the animal, usually picks out two or three of the lesser pieces with no fixed social destination, such as the lower ribs, and gives these to the shaman. These meats, and the cigarette, are the only recompense the shaman receives for his services. The total "income" of food gained from a shaman's ritual activities constitutes a relatively feeble proportion of all the animal protein consumed by his domestic group.

In the case of Celilo, the shaman who did most of the *bope ure* offerings at Korugedu Paru, his share of *bope* foods accounted for about 30 percent of all meats eaten in his household during one month in the dry season. But Celilo was a most conservative man, and very assiduous in discharging his ritual and social responsibilities of food prestations; an able hunter, he gave away over half the game he killed. Otherwise the proportion of *bope ure* eaten in his house would have been even less.

Manukuje, another eminent shaman, was ill a great deal of the time, and an indifferent hunter even when well. During some periods his share of *bope ure* was the sole protein eaten by his family. However, even in his case, gifts of food from other households constituted most of his group's subsistence over extended periods. Whatever material or social benefits might accrue to the shaman through the performance of his ritual role, an enhanced diet is not markedly among them.

During the night following the offering of the *bope ure,* the shaman's familiar comes to him during his sleep and causes his *bope*-soul to mount upon its back, just as one rides upon a horse, or when someone is carried piggyback.[10] First they fly around the village several times, clockwise if the shaman is Tugarege, counterclockwise if he is Exerae. (These are the usual circuits made by the shaman's soul during his nocturnal wanderings in the village's defense. The customary ritual direction is counterclockwise, from east to north to west to south and back to east. This is the course followed by all dancers in ceremonies involving the *aroe*. The reversal of the circuit by a Tugarege shaman indicates that this affair involves only the *bope*. The Bororo explanation is that each shaman visits his own moiety first, beginning in the east.)

Next, the shaman on his curious mount rises into the white sky. All the *maereboe* flock around, either in their natural condition or as vultures and hawks, crying out, "Give the food to me. Give it to me. It is I. It is I. I want the food. Give it now!" For the *bari* is carrying the entire beast offered earlier in the day, not just those small bits he ate then, but the whole animal. Just how he can do this, while yet the meat remains on earth, is a "mystery of the *bope*," not understood even by shamans. The *maereboe* and the *bope* of dead shamans urgently desire this prize and try to induce the shaman to give it to them by threats and cajolery. (One of the first rules of Bororo etiquette is that one must never ask for something outright, least of all food. But the *bope* recognize no social rules, and, after all, it is "their" food the shaman is carrying.)

The *bari* resists all of these efforts and, avoiding the *maereboe* and bad *bari*, continues to ascend through the blue sky until he arrives at the red sky, where he goes to *uxe* and *uo*, the mother and father of all shamans and all *bope*. He gives the *bope ure* to them and, before they eat, repeats the formula used earlier at the offering's conclusion, asking the *bope* to give health and long life to the community, to control dangerous animals, and so forth.

After eating with Etu-o and Etu-je and all the other *bope pemegareu* ("good *bope*"), the shaman's *bope*-soul rides his familar back down to earth and the soul returns to the shaman's body. The several shamans I discussed the topic with said they seldom could remember upon waking all details of this dream-experience, but they were sure something like it occurred after every possessed eating of a *bope ure*. Riding upon the familiar's back is the shaman's usual means of transport during his voyages into the sky and over the earth, and all shamans can recount details of these experiences. Once again, the shaman's waking activities are complemented and extended by his unconscious dream-actions. The offering would not be complete without the conveyance of the *bope* game up to the red sky, and indeed, shamans regard the possessed consumption on this earth as merely a kind of shadowy prelude to this, the real prestation.

# Bororo Afflictions and
# Shamanistic Cures

The identical techniques appear in the other "deliberate" activity of the shaman, the treatment of illness: the mode of possession, the dialogue, and the dreamed reduplication of the day's events are just as they are in the prestation of *bope ure*. But unlike the categorical necessity of the shaman's participation in this transaction, the decision to seek his intervention in affliction is a lengthy, complicated one. As I mentioned earlier, the Bororo have few systematic classifications of illness and have limited notions about "usual" or "morbid" stages in their development. They do possess an extensive vegetable pharmacologia, which associates specific plant medicines with certain afflictions and which includes fairly effective modes of coping with physical injuries. (This knowledge is described by the Salesians, and especially by Hartmann [1967] in an excellent monograph, and is therefore not treated here.) Most adults are familiar with this system, although a few individuals in every community, including one or two shamans, are known for their sophistication and dexterity in "medicines." Therefore, when a person begins to feel unwell, he, or some more knowledgeable relative, collects, prepares, and applies these vegetable remedies. Accidental wounds unusual in character, pain, or blood are immediately referred to an expert.

Just when the shaman's aid is requested depends on the progress of the affliction, the patient's age, status, medical history, and ritual condition, general contextual factors affecting the patient's household or entire community, and much else. Generally any illness or wound which lingers unchanged for a week justifies a request for the shaman. So does the appearance of such symptoms as persistent vomiting, prolonged diarrhea (especially in an infant), stupor, high fever, "extreme" physical weakness, or unusual internal pain. The Bororo recognize that persons vary markedly in their willingness to admit a need for the shaman. Some are considered hypochondriacs, others stoical to the point of self-destruction. Contextual elements are most important. If a meteorite has recently fallen or if the community is suffering some epidemic, many demand shamanistic treatment for any passing malaise. Persons living in households discharging critical ritual duties, such as those of an *aroe maiwu* or his ritual parents, are notably more attentive to minor aches and injuries. And the matter is further complicated by the way responsibility for treatment is socially distributed.

Adults may independently decide when they need the shaman's help (or rather the *bope*'s), but nearly always they extensively consult relatives and friends, and often several shamans. Often they give the impression of avoiding a decision until one is strongly recommended by a moral/jural superior. Parents are obliged to secure all medical treatments for their immature children, while the couple deemed the household's heads are similarly responsible for their elderly housemates. Failure to obtain timely and appropriate care for a sick dependent or subordinate is abstractly a grave fault, harshly judged by public opinion. But the vagueness of Bororo ideas about illness and particularly their lack of criteria for prognosis make such opinions hard to justify. Further, there is no active risk in the *bari*'s treatment. Neither the *bope* nor the shaman can employ this contact to harm further the patient. Nonetheless, the shaman's highly public intervention does amount to a social declaration of the affliction's gravity. Many Bororo, whether acting on behalf of someone else or themselves, much prefer to deny such implications of future tragedy.

These descriptive vagaries must not overshadow the general quality of Bororo responses to affliction. They treat all suffering persons with sympathetic concern, growing in public measure as the patient worsens. Illness, whatever its supposed nature or cause, is never an occasion of embarrassment or moral consternation. The character of the *bope* and their contract with man preclude such response. (Afflictions caused by the *aroe,* the topic of the next chapter, are differently interpreted in the abstract. But the *aroe* are never blamed for the morbidities of contemporary Bororo.) The whole course of sickness, even in its early stages, is marked by the visits of relatives, coclansmen, affines, agnates, neighbors, and simple friends. Shamans call in any of these capacities and render initial opinions and secular advice. These visitors often bring special dishes, a succulent cut of meat, any plant medicines they think suitable.[11] The whole atmosphere in the patient's household is redolent of that on public wards in American hospitals, but without that quality of mechanical packaging of human woe which suffuses those institutions. This Bororo response to affliction is marked by a vague, diffuse concern, no less real for its lack of intellectual organization. Medically, there is a very experimental attitude. First one remedy then another is tried. The patient strives against his physical helplessness and proclaims hopes for his quick recovery. Ultimately, the shaman is called for. There are few expectations about any of these measures, little rationalizing about their mechanics or diagnostic implications. The *bope* have final dominion over any human life, and social measures to counteract their powers can be only stopgaps.

This lack of either intellectual or pragmatic order is surprising in a domain so physically and demandingly immediate. But it suits the mechanical, a-personal character of *bope*-caused affliction. Although these spirits follow principles of regularity and order as far as their life-giving powers are concerned, they are not so constrained in their meting out of injury, disease, and death. It is useless, Bororo attitudes imply, to search for reason and regularity in illness. It can only be understood *post facto,* and even then the cause, nearly always some minor error toward the *bope ure,* is disproportionate to the gravity and nature of the consequence. Perhaps these collective sentiments result most of all from recent historical experience. Two hundred years ago the Bororo may have numbered 50,000; today their population is 1 percent of that (Crocker 1967). These losses were sustained in the most chaotic ways: through inexplicable epidemics, war with enemies armed with mysterious weapons, strange new diseases that carried off the healthiest of the young. All of this will be examined in more detail in the next chapter. Modern Bororo are sure of one thing: the shaman is their last recourse against the actions of the *bope*—but only because *some* of them work positively through him.

The shaman, usually accompanied by his wife, arrives at the patient's house at twilight or later, for most of his public duties are performed at night, the time when the *bope* prefer to be abroad among humans. The patient, who has already made a cigarette, gives it to the *bari*. If he or she is unable to do this, a father, spouse, or sibling must make the cigarette, but the patient must hand it to the shaman. The shaman begins to smoke in his usual deep, rapid, gasping way, muttering the name of one of his familiar *bope* and urging it to visit him, just as in the offering of *bope* meats. The loud cries as he strikes his hand against his mouth can be heard all over the village, and people comment on who is sick, the putative cause, and gossip about the "real reason" for the sickness. The arrival of the *bope* is announced with a prolonged, quavering whoop or yell, whereupon everyone relaxes and goes about his business.

According to shamans, none of the *maereboe* seek to enter them as they do during the initial moments of the *bope ure* offering, but otherwise the whole experience of possession is exactly the same as that described above, with the distortions of color, perception, and the like. Sometimes, even, the patient's body seems to be swarming with the same larvae or grubs that appeared on the *bope* meat. The *bope* begins the treatment by blowing tobacco smoke gently all over the patient's body and massaging it, finally concentrating these attentions on the part of the body especially afflicted. Large amounts of tobacco smoke are exhaled and rubbed into this area. Finally, the *bope* begins sucking, between rubbings of tobacco smoke, and finally the pathogenic agent is extracted.

Usually this is a beetle, generically *boreu,* which the Bororo term collectively *erubo bope,* the "medicine of the *bope*." Various species are commonly employed by the *bope* to afflict mankind. Among these are *jerigigareu,* the stag beetle, perhaps the most mystically lethal (cf. Albisetti and Venturelli 1962: 248–49, for illustration and description), and *ekure,* a class of small beetles similar to domestic insects. *Boreu* also covers all types of cockroaches. The Bororo think these insects extremely ugly, noting they are full of painful projections, black, and often smell bad when crushed—of *jerimaga,* of course. The *bope* may also inject a *betaga,* a type of praying mantis (*Scolopendra gigas*), a *boporira,* a small sharp piece of flint; or *joradu,* charcoal; or *pio,* boiled beeswax from the arapuas bee (*Trigona ruficus*). All these have various associations with the *bope:* the charcoal with the fire used to cook their food and with their usual heat; the beeswax because the honey is among the *bope ure;* the mantis because it is known to eat other insects.

The *bope,* acting through the shaman, must also remove *bekuru,* any viscous substance (such as mucus), identified as the product of the beetle's operation in the person's body, and *atudu,* pus, with a similar origin. Usually the inanimate items are found in the patient's joints and muscles, whereas the beetles and other insects occupy the internal organs, especially the heart and the head. All these items, and again particularly the beetles, are used as missiles by the *bope* in their wars with the shamans' *bope*-souls and their familiars.

When the pathogenic item is finally sucked out, the shaman spits it into his hand but never shows it to the sick person, else it might immediately enter him again. It may, though, be glimpsed by the spectators. The *bope* rubs it into the shaman's head, so that he in turn might have it as ammunition in his fights with the *maereboe.* Most Bororo are skeptical of this removal, saying that many shamans conceal the beetle or other thing in their mouths and only pretend to suck it out. But they also insist that truly good *bari* do not have to resort to this sort of subterfuge and will allow their mouths to be examined just before the extraction. These kinds of shaman are credited with very great curative powers, but according to nonshaman informants, they are now very rare. Several informants volunteered the opinion that even if the *bari* had the pathogenic agent concealed all along, it seemed the disease passed into it during the treatment with tobacco and smoke and sucking. The shaman concludes with more applications of tobacco smoke and massage. The *bope* assures the patient and his relatives that he will be sick for a time but will eventually recover; then, it leaves the shaman.

The *bope* usually introduce several pathogens into a sick person's body. Shamans say it is best to remove them one at a time, in different sessions, so as not to weaken the patient. Often, too, once a person is ill other maleficent *bope* join the original sender of illness and successively introduce their own lethal objects, even after the shaman has extracted those sent in the initial attack. An essential part of the cure involves the familiar *bope*'s identification of the particular *bope* causing the malady, and the reasons for its persecution of the sick person. The more hostile *bope* join in the affliction for similar or diverse reasons, the more difficult it is accurately to identify the causes and agencies of the illness, and the more

likely a fatal outcome. Shamans thus explain why most ultimately terminal illnesses stretch over a long period and present many diverse symptoms in their course.

Often the agent and cause of death are only identified when the
corpse is disinterred during the final phase of the funeral cycle, and some
foreign element, beetle or other, is found somewhere in the nearly de-
composed corpse. This item is taken to the shaman who did most of the
premortem treatment, and his familiar *bope* can finally determine its original sender and the reasons why this *bope* determined to kill the defunct.
Once again, these procedures stress the futility of attempting to discover,
let alone anticipate, the motives and procedures of the *bope* when they
decide to attack any human person. It is only because the shaman's familiars intervene and try, for their own selfish reasons, to frustrate the intentions of the other *bope* that there is any hope that the patient may be
cured, and then only for a time. But even this intervention is purely
mechanical, addressed to symptomatic relief. Diagnosis is critical to
treatment only in terms of discovering the identity of the afflicting *bope*
and the cause for his anger with the patient. The shaman's capabilities, as
bestowed through his familiar, extend only to this symptomatic treatment and diagnosis. In short, intellectual knowledge has little to do with
shamanistic skill.

The general attitude of the shaman toward affliction is summarized in
the concluding statement of the shaman/*bope* that the patient will recover;
he manifests sympathy, confidence in his treatment, assurance in his familiar's powers, and yet a certain personal disassociation from the whole
process. It is all a matter of the *bope* and does not involve his individual
capacities. In my experience shamans are reluctant to give a pessimistic
diagnosis until it becomes evident to everyone that the person is, in fact,
dying. The Salesians state that *baire* sometimes predict the exact time of
death; if it appears the patient will survive this moment, they proceed to
suffocate him (Albisetti and Venturelli 1962: 249). This allegation was
indignantly denied by my informants, shamans and laymen alike. I never
heard a *bari* accused of murder directly. Nonshaman Bororo sometimes
complained in private that treatment was not as extensive or as thorough
as it might be. In past times, according to these people, the *bari* "did not
rest" in his ministrations to the afflicted but treated his patients three to
five times a night. But then there also existed wicked shamans, who
killed mystically but never mechanically. Nowadays, it is said, shamans
are much less powerful and are negligent of their duties, for which reasons the Bororo are rapidly dying. Such a judgment must not be taken
too literally, for the same informants also attributed the high mortality to
the laxity of youth in following all the prescribed methods for ensuring
good health, and particularly to their sexual intemperance. But evil

shamans were never cited as a cause of high morbidity: one cannot distrust the last hope.

In grave and prolonged cases nearly all available shamans minister to the patient, including those living in adjacent villages or merely passing through the area. It is not rare for several shamans to treat the same person in the course of a single evening. In these circumstances no particular *bari* can be directly blamed for the death of a patient: shamanistic treatment is not individuated either on the side of the curer or on that of the afflicted human being. It is, however, true that in the past some shamans achieved a great regional and even tribal recognition for their skills (Albisetti and Venturelli 1962: 243–49). Contemporary Bororo do compare shamans' relative abilities, citing their successes and failures in treatments, their predictions and other powers.

But such evaluations are also socially recognized as influenced by relationship to the shaman in question through kinship, affinal, agnatic, and ritual ties. Since every *bari* is obliged to treat any patient who asks for his services, determination of relative skills is impossible; any one of three or four shamans may be credited with a cure or indirectly blamed for failure. But in the latter case, the public can cite ample cause for prejudice in any person's negative judgment in terms of his or her preexisting relationships with that particular shaman. Finally, modern Bororo seem to feel that no social end can be served by playing off shamans against one another. That tactic is appropriate to the *bope,* not to the humans who are their helpless and endangered pawns. This may not have been so in the past, before the sharp loss of population and when there were shamans renowned for their extraordinary powers. This question is pursued below and in the next chapter.

Shamans are keenly interested in all possible techniques of curing, including those imported by Westerners, but I cannot say they are a class markedly distinguishable from their nonshaman peers either in this concern or in the extent of their traditional knowledge of *materia medica.* Certain nonshamans are acknowledged as experts in the setting of broken bones, or in their mastery of *erubo,* plant medicines. They are consulted before and after the shaman is called, and a certain amount of credit, increasing with each successive cure, is accorded them when any of their patients improve. In brief, no single individual, shaman or layman, can ever be socially recognized as the sole agent of anyone's return to health, nor is any particular treatment, pragmatic or mystical, singled out as particularly efficacious. Again, the *bope* are recognized as the nearly independent cause of all curing, just as they are regarded as the source of all affliction. This certainly does not prohibit various shamans from becoming expert in the application of plant medicines (*erubol*) or from acquiring and using more mechanistic skills, such as bone-setting and what we would regard as first-aid techniques, including the staunching of blood and the cleansing of flesh wounds. But they employ these skills largely separately from their shamanistic abilities, since the only unique powers their association with the *bope* provide is the extraction of pathogenic agents and diagnosis of the immediate sources of affliction. To be sure, it is impossible to differentiate clearly among the abilities credited to any given shaman, and certainly many are expert pharmacologists and technicians, who treat their patients to the best of their myriad talents. There is a certain degree of "halo effect" in the reputation of any shaman, in which his more pragmatic skills are included in the perception of his ritual capacities. Still, the theoretical distinction is clear to the Bororo: shamans cure through their *bope* familiars, and only thus.

## Collective Cures

Shamanistic cures are not confined to individuals. When the community seems menaced by some common misfortune, such as an epidemic, one shaman in the village may be asked by the men's council to undertake a mass cure in the *bororo,* the dance plaza. This happened, for example, after most of the men at Korugedu Paru went to Cuiabá at the request of the Indian Protection Service (now F.N.A.I.) to participate in a touristic "Indian festival" and returned to the village with very bad colds. These spread rapidly throughout the village, until most adults were completely incapacitated. One of the main causes of this "epidemic" was the Bororo habit of cooling a fever with a bath in the river, so that many persons were in the early stages of pneumonia. The community's capacity to feed itself was severely impaired within a few days, and the men's council quickly asked Celilo, the village's foremost *bari,* to undertake a mass cure. In another instance, a collective cure was requested when several *bari* had seen in their dreams masses of *erubo,* the clouds of black smoke signifying an epidemic, advancing toward the village. In this case Kadegare was asked to perform the cure, since his familiar had been the first to reveal the menace.

The mass cure, which is as much prophylactic as specific to any illness, always takes place in the *bororo,* the dance plaza, late at night. All the men, women, and children in the village who are able to walk make their way to this place when they hear the usual loud muttering announcing the imminent arrival of a *bope* in its shaman. Each person presents the *bari,* or his wife if he is already too far submerged in trance to take notice, with a carefully made cigarette. There is considerable stress upon each person's establishment through this gift of personal contact with the *bope.* People comment favorably when a baby scarcely old enough to toddle manages to hand over the cigarette made by its father or mother's brother to the shaman. Old persons hobble forward to proffer their cigarettes, and even adolescents manage to restrain the giggling and boisterousness which otherwise mark their presence in any public gathering. The general atmosphere is that of absolute seriousness and attention, very different from the casualness of ceremonies or the pragmatic nonchalance characteristic of *bope* cures and the offering of *bope ure*.

All persons, of whatever age, say when they give over their cigarette, "*Xe, i-edage*" or "*Xe, i-ogwa*," "Take, mother's brother" or "Take, father," depending on whether they are, respectively, Exerae or Tugarege, following their moieties' categorical relationship with the *bope*. Some persons, mostly adult senior men or chiefs, may mention their names and subclans and may add a solicitation that the *bope* not harm the Bororo. The *bari* smokes a bit from each cigarette and then adds it to the bundle accumulating in his left hand. When all have delivered cigarettes, the *bope* begins to ask questions in its usual rude fashion; all present respond nearly simultaneously. The dialogue follows the usual pattern: the *bope* asks why it has been called among men; the people reply that many are ill, that they are afraid of dying and need help.

After a few minutes, the leading chiefs of the village (or *pagimejera*) address the *bope* in formal, elegant fashion, the same mode that they use in the evening orations to the village at large. They successively tell the *bope* that many are sick, suffering from a variety of afflictions, that many Bororo have already died, and that this new epidemic must not be allowed to kill them all. The possessing *bope* replies in its usual reassuring fashion. After these dialogues, in which the nature of the contagion afflicting or threatening the village is detailed by its spokesmen, the *bope* again address the general assembly, asking them if they wish to die or shall they continue to respect the contract between men and *bope*. They all reply vehemently, as the questions warrant. Then all present are "treated" by the *bope*, first the children, although few of them may now be ill. "The children go first," said informants, "because they need more care than adults."

Usually, when very young children up to the age of seven or eight are involved, the mother brings the child up to the *bari* and holds him or her while the *bope* blows smoke on the child's face and then upon the shaman's hands, which are rubbed gently over the chest, concentrating on the heart. If the child has a specific ailment, a rash or burn or infected wound, the *bope* repeatedly blows smoke on the affected part.

Following the children, all the women who have given cigarettes and then the men are treated by the *bope* in rough order of their cigarette donations. The treatment is standardized for everyone. The patient sits cross-legged before the shaman, who places his right hand on the person's head. First he blows gently on the face and then upon the sternum; next he blows upon his own left hand, which he then rubs over the patient's sternum. Finally, the shaman concludes by blowing a series of diminishing puffs over the patient's chest and lower face. None of these actions occur in the curing of individual disease which focuses upon the sucking extraction of some pathogenic agent and not upon the general "blowing" over the patient's body. The shaman acts identically toward everyone presenting a cigarette, and the whole ritual is clearly a "warding off" of potential danger rather than a curing of present sickness.

After the shaman finishes treating everyone, he begins the rhythmic smoking and rapid chanting which initiates and concludes possession. As the *bope* departs in a series of long, quivering shouts, everyone present joins in the shouts. This direct public participation in the shaman's acts occurs only after a mass prophylaxis but is inevitable in rituals involving the *aroe,* a significant point. The participants retire to their usual evening places, and the officiating shaman goes to all of the village's shamans in turn, giving them each several cigarettes from the number donated earlier. In every delivery, the two shamans both hold the cigarette with their right hands and chant softly "ho ho ho ho ho." Then the receiving shaman rises and blows over the chest and face of the shaman who did the mass treatment, and the latter reciprocates in kind.

Just before going to sleep, each *bari* will smoke the cigarette. Then in a dream his *bope*-soul will go around the village with its familiar, treating each person who gave a cigarette earlier to the *bope*. This treatment involves simply blowing cigarette smoke all over the person's body, but, owing to their enhanced powers, the shaman and his companion cause the smoke to penetrate throughout the patient's body, fortifying if not actually enhancing his *raka* and hence his resistance to all manner of disease. The village council in theory rotates the performance of mass cures among all the village's shamans, overtly so that the burden of "defending the village" falls on them all equally, covertly (but acknowledged readily in private) so that the shamans will not be jealous of one another.

This ritual "cure," actually prophylaxis, seems to be an innovation within the last two generations. Exactly the same cure was traditionally performed by the *aroe etawa-are,* the shaman of the *aroe*. This specialist performs numerous rituals in which he is possessed by an *aroe,* either the ancestors or the divine monsters, and in which he seeks the benefit of the entire community (see following chapter). Nearly all his activities are carried out in the dance plaza, before the entire community, whereas aside from the mass cure and "the falling star" (*aroe butu*), the shaman of the *bope* only becomes possessed inside private dwellings and on behalf of a single individual. To be sure, the *bari* must mystically defend the collectivity of the village, but he accomplishes this obligation "passively," in his dreams.

The problem is that no *aroe* shamans exist among the Bororo today. Since certain important rituals demand the participation of this specialist, the Bororo are confronted with a dilemma which they usually resolve through one of their typically convoluted but internally logical bits of reasoning. Some shamans have as familiars the *bope* of their dead brothers, who had as *their* familiar a *bope* which possessed a more remote relative who was at once a *bari* and an *aroe* shaman. These shamans can fulfill at least some of the more critical roles of the *aroe* shaman, by communicating through the brother's *bope* to his familiar, and thence to the *bope*-soul of the former shaman of the souls. It is significant, I think, that among the shamans at Korugedu Paru only Celilo, an Exerae, had such a chain of spiritual relationships. He was the one, overt and covert policies not withstanding, who was usually called upon to perform the mass cures, as well as to do the other tasks of an *aroe* shaman. All the dimensions of this issue cannot be presented until I have described the attributes of the "other" shaman. However, this collective cure seems to be the only recent modification of the *bari*'s role. Neither the massed action of the community's shamans in dreams nor their mutual obligation as defenders of the village is anything less than completely traditional.

deer

# 8

## The Shaman and
## Moral Order

Shamans are everywhere ambiguous, suspicious personages. They traffic with unknowable, nonperceptible powers; they mysteriously cure the most painful and horrifying diseases; they may be, as individuals, peculiar and strange, not at all like other men. Yet in their almost categorical lack of political authority they cannot be understood in terms of the theories advanced for the analysis of power (Balandier 1970; Swartz, Turner, and Tuden 1966; Bailey 1969). They cannot be considered either priests or prophets; thus, none of the insights into the symbolism of these figures can be utilized (Beidelman 1966; Pouillon 1964; Clastres 1974). Instead, as I said in the first chapter, they seem analytically closest to witches, but, unlike witches, they are socially approved if fundamentally distrusted. Among the Bororo, the only person capable of being a witch, in the most usual definition of the term,[12] is a *bari*. The discrimination between good shamans, who cure and protect men, and bad ones, who eat up the souls of others and cause them all kinds of hurt, is often difficult to make. Categorically, the Bororo hold that *erubo epaw*, "evil medicines" or bad shamans, are never members of their own village but come from distant Bororo communities. Their *bope*-souls accompany the *maereboe* when they attempt to eat souls or to rob them in the "falling star." Or they send, through a combination of pragmatic and mystical techniques, a contagion against the whole village.

The association between witchcraft and social distance is the only direct, institutionalized manifestation of intervillage hostility I found; it should not, in my view, be taken too literally. The declaration amounts to a public affirmation of trust in "our" shamans and, at the same time, to a recognition that they are capable of deliberate misuse of their powers. Further, most informants were aware that members of other villages were inclined to view "our" shamans with great suspicion, quite possibly with reason. Several informants strongly hinted that any shamans with a modicum of good sense would confine any evil-doing to other communities, where their crimes would be difficult to prove and, certainly, to avenge. But I was told of three separate cases in which a village's shaman was so strongly suspected of witchcraft that he was killed by the young men (*i-pare*), acting on the orders of the men's council. However, all three of these cases occurred when my informants' grandparents were young, which is to say fifty or more years ago.

I suspect that whatever social tensions the behavior toward a shaman-witch traditionally expressed, resolved, or exacerbated, they have surely been affected by the demographic and political changes of the past three decades. Almost all adults are very conscious of the need to maintain collective solidarity against the Brazilian society that encompasses them and of their total political incapacity in regard to that society. Local Brazilians themselves firmly believe in witches and are convinced that any "Indian" may have occult powers. Most Bororo seemed to reason that public accusations of witchcraft within the community would merely provide a pretext for further detested incursions of Brazilian authority within their society. My suspicion originated during the last period of fieldwork in the summer of 1967, when I witnessed the only public process involving suspected witchcraft in almost two years with the Bororo. This case occurred at a time when the Indian Protection Service was internally disorganized and had left the community of Korugedu Paru almost completely to itself. There was a rebirth of social confidence in the society's capacity to direct itself and, simultaneously, the public emergence of various political rivalries. There were also greatly increased numbers of "social dramas," in V. Turner's sense (1957). One of these involved allegations of malpractice against a shaman; not only was it the most serious case during this period, but people hinted in not very veiled terms that witchcraft was probably involved.

The problem began when one Dita, a divorced Bokodori Exeraedu in her late twenties and a vivid, dynamic personality, took her small daughter, about two, to Kadegare, the Exerae shaman mentioned several times earlier. Kadegare was nominally her *in-odowu,* sister's husband, because he was married to her older clan sister, a case of moiety incest. As such his relationship with her should have been characterized by marked respect and willingness to render her whatever services he could. Dita subsequently alleged that Kadegare refused to treat the little girl, saying his *bope* had told him the child would die and that nothing could be done for it. Greatly troubled, she took the child to Manukuje, a Tugarege shaman with no personal ties with Dita. His *bope* not only treated the child but gave the usual assurance of its eventual total recovery. Dita then began gossiping about Kadegare's general failures as a shaman and as a relative, and she implied his refusal of treatment stemmed from her earlier rejection of his sexual advances.

Most people thought that Dita had fabricated the entire story after misunderstanding Kadegare, who had badly injured his foot playing soccer with some Brazilians. An afflicted *bari* should not be asked to cure someone; by doing so, he would come into contact with his familiars who are already displeased with him, as witness his illness. Dita, then, had no right to ask Kadegare to treat her daughter. Some people pointed out at considerable length that Kadegare was obviously in bad rapport with his *bope* and could hardly be regarded as a competent shaman even after he recovered from his latest accident. Dita's own motives were maligned: she was angry with Kadegare since he had refused to give her some piglets that she thought he owed her. And finally a few people darkly suggested that Kadegare had tried to "eat up" Dita, and, failing in this, he was consuming as a *bope* her baby daughter. He had further reason to be jealous of her children, the only youngsters except for a baby among the Bokodori Exerae, because his wife had suffered several miscarriages and their only living child was very sickly, in contrast to the usual rude health of Dita's children. This fact alone gave her a certain social prominence, and senior men of the clan were already beginning to take an interest in her son, a lively five-year old who almost by default would some day be the chief of his clan. Kadegare desperately wanted a son, and it may well be that his advances toward Dita were of an experimental variety, to determine if moiety incest always resulted in feeble progeny. (Further aspects of Kadegare as shaman and person are given below.) In any case, the mixture of sexual, political, and economic elements in alleged witchcraft seems typical of Bororo practices.

Gossip and argument about the details of the case grew so pernicious that the men's council determined to resolve the matter. They requested that Dita and the other women most active in spreading the gossip attend them in the dance plaza and relate their versions of the issue publicly. After stern lectures by the assembled clan chiefs as to the canons of traditional morality and the seriousness of allegations about shamans, Dita was called as the first and principal witness. She proceeded to deny her previous story categorically, to the tremendous disgust of various informants who had anticipated at least the discomfiture of one or the other parties to the dispute and at most a fine dramatic conclusion.[13] Dita affirmed her appreciation of both Kadegare and Manukuje as shamans, said she had realized all along that Kadegare would not be able to treat her daughter, and otherwise retracted her earlier, private position. The two shamans spoke at length of their dedication to the community's welfare, the clan chiefs indulged in further panegyrics about Bororo morality, and the whole affair concluded with much bonhomie, as vigorous as it was hypocritical. None of my informants thought subsequently that Kadegare had been in the least exonerated and affirmed that his actions would be closely watched by everyone.

I gathered several accounts of shamans' misuse of their powers, including some defined as *erubo ewaw,* witchcraft, claimed to have been witnessed by informants or by their close relatives. A generation ago, for example, in a village some distance up the São Lourenço, a shaman began to covet his brother's wife, a very lovely young girl. She refused all his advances, and so at night he stole her soul and, with his *bope,* ate it all. For some time he had been suspected of such practices, since he had become very fat and fatness in a shaman almost always results from such a diet of souls. The brother's wife became very ill and soon died. But during her funeral cycle the shaman in turn suddenly fell sick and vomited up various feathers and plaited circlets of palm. These had been the girl's decorations, eaten up along with her soul. He died, as the Bororo say to characterize any rapid punishment, "before her bones were out of the ground" (i.e., before the secondary interment of her funeral, or within about six months of her death). It was not known whether his familiar *bope* or another had killed him. This particular case was widely known and was regarded as the last definite case of witchcraft in the Bororo villages of the lower São Lourenço.

In another case, occurring about two generations ago, a shaman had a younger unmarried brother who was much esteemed by the village. His public conduct was always very "fine," and the clan chiefs often asked him to act out the duties of the titled chief of his clan. But the shaman was a selfish and ignorant man, quick to anger. His aggressive conduct finally led to a sharp reprimand by the younger brother, in the men's house and thus in public. Such reprimands are commonly reserved for the most serious breaches of social rules, or for someone who consistently defies moral norms; normally they should be given by the elder brother.

The fact that the younger brother in this case was morally superior to his senior, and acted upon this publicly, gave great shame to the shaman. He determined to have his revenge. Through his dreams, and with the aid of his familiar, he first injected a beetle in the younger brother; when this was extracted by another shaman, he caused a rattlesnake to bite the young man, who died in a few days. My informant thought that the shaman might have transformed himself into a rattlesnake to accomplish this. Not long afterward the shaman's canoe was found floating upside down by the banks of the river. He was never seen again. No one can be quite sure what happened, but it is suspected that the *aroe,* who punish severe derelictions of social rules and who are intimately associated with rivers, acted to avenge the younger brother.

A fourth case was unusual in involving cross-moiety conflict. A shaman and a young bachelor were both interested in the same girl, a men's house associate and therefore normatively inaccessible to the shaman, since he was already married, although unhappily. There was a further complication in that both girl and boy belonged to the Arore clan, of the Tugarege moiety, while the shaman was a Bado Jeba Xebegiwuge, of the Exerae moiety. The bachelor became angered when the shaman succeeded in seducing the girl, since she would be dangerous henceforth not only to himself but to all the other *i-pare* (young men); she had become "a thing of the *bope*'s." The Bororo who knew the story found the young man to blame, for his desires were incestuous, whereas the shaman was harming no one and would have married the girl. Further, he was an excellent shaman and had cured both the girl and the bachelor of serious afflictions. But the boy was so jealous that he put vegetable poison (*erubo ewaw,* see below) on one of the private paths of the shaman's household. The shaman soon died, for not even *baire* can resist poison. It may have been, too, that his *bope* were angry with him: "He talked a lot and was not calm." As he was dying, the shaman swore vengeance upon his murderer, saying that as soon as he discovered who it was he would kill him.

After several years, the bachelor (who never succeeded with the girl after all) went out fishing by himself. He did not return, and the men of the village went out looking for him. They found his tracks going across a small beach and disappearing into a shallow pool, but nothing more. After several days, his body was found floating in the river. This case is significant not just for the cross-moiety element, almost unique in Bororo social conflicts, but for the mixture of utilitarian revenge and mystical sorcery. Although informants said the dead shaman's *bope*-soul "ate up" the bachelor, causing him to drown, and hence could be considered a witch, at the same time they considered his action justified.

These were the only extended and internally consistent cases of witchcraft I could obtain. Deaths by "misadventure," such as snakebite, lightning, drowning, or the attack of wild animals, are sometimes attributed to the maleficence of shaman-witches in other villages, but in such a vague and random way that no one considers acting on such suspicions. The whole issue of the shaman-witch is complicated by the inability, or reluctance, of ordinary shamans to discuss the matter. First, too specific knowledge of witchcraft implies, as it does in other cultures, some degree of possible culpability. Shamans did not even want to talk about details of *erubo,* the plant medicines which include poisons anyone may use to harm or kill, let alone describe how the shaman-witch accomplished his desires.

The major issue in determining a shaman's personal responsibility for witchcraft involves the decision whether he, of his individual human volition, has "eaten up" or otherwise attacked human souls, or whether his *bope*-familiar, or anothe *bope,* has been at work. Since all the vectors of affliction possibly accessible to a shaman-witch are also used by the *bope,* the only way to determine human guilt is for another shaman to witness, during his dreams, a shaman engaging in witchcraft. Traditionally, informants said, the shamans of a community had to agree on the identity of a witch, whether a member of the village or not, before the men's council would make a formal decision to punish the malefactor. Such agreements, everyone agreed, were very rare indeed.

More often, the suspected witch was killed with vegetable poison by a nonshaman, who thus either protected himself or avenged the death of a kinsman. The only conclusive proof of a shaman's witchcraft comes after he is dead, when his relatives begin to sicken and die one after the other. The familiars of the shamans called to treat them reveal that it is the dead shaman's *bope* which is responsible. There are, of course, practically no social repercussions to this discovery, since those most obliged to defend a kinsman's reputation are those most endangered by the witch. The Bororo admit, too, that just because a shaman attacks humans after he is dead does not mean he did so when alive. As noted earlier, all dead shamans cease to have any component of human personality save for their kin relationships, and these are anything but protective against their maleficence.[14] In any case, none of my informants had ever heard one shaman publicly accuse another of witchcraft. Shamans maintain a certain solidarity toward the public and never even hint of another's "professional misconduct," except perhaps when drunk or with their most intimate friends.

At the same time, at least in contemporary villages, shamans are punctilious with one another, rather ostentatiously stressing whatever particular kinship, affinal, or ritual bonds that exist between them rather than their common, mystical status. There is not the least hint of a guild or fellowship. Competition among shamans, as noted earlier, is covert but intense. At some time in the past this competition might have involved allegations of witchcraft, but I doubt it. The position of shaman is ambiguous enough without fostering public recognition of their negative powers. Generally, then, the shaman-witch among the Bororo is a vague hypothetical possibility, a matter for speculation and historical anecdote rather than a vital element in the living system. The lack of importance of witchcraft in this society poses an important negative question in the comparative study of shamanism in lowland South America, and as such will be raised again in Part IV.

## The Shaman as Master of Time and Form

Shamans of the *bope* have two kinds of mystical abilities which arouse collective interest far more than their association with witchcraft: their power to change themselves into certain animals, and their capacity to predict the future, including success in hunting and fishing. Though all of the shamans I talked to, including the four resident at Korugedu Paru, categorically denied that they ever metamorphosed into animals, other Bororo smiled knowingly at such denials. In popular belief, every mature shaman can, through the good offices of his familiar, change himself into a jaguar, alligator, or rattlesnake whenever he chooses, both in dreams and while in trance. Witch-shamans often employ such natural agencies to strike down their victims, which is one reason why my shaman-informants were so vehement in their public denials of this power.

These transformations, however, are considered to be an integral part of the shaman's role, just as much as his dream-activities. The explicit aim in metamorphosing into a jaguar is to kill a *bope-ure*, preferably a large tapir. In this form the shaman can also kill many wild pigs and several deer. As a rattlesnake he lies in wait beside game trails and bites a tapir, pig, capivara, or deer when it passes. As soon as the game is slain, he changes back into his usual human form and carefully removes all claw marks, signs of bites, and so forth from the body, usually by stabbing it with an arrow or knife. If a nonshaman were to see these marks, the *bope* would be angered, and cause him to fall ill or even die. However, the shaman's wife may observe them, "for she is almost like a shaman herself." Once the *bope ure* is killed, it is taken back to the village and offered to the *bope* in the usual way. It is simply because the *bope* wish to eat their foods that they cause, or allow, the shaman these transformations. The shaman may also assume these forms in dreams in order to protect the village, especially against bad shamans, and to travel to other villages where he may help the *bope*-souls of local shamans to cure sick people there. Some say that it is as these animals, especially the jaguar, that the shaman travels into the future. Others believe that the shaman of the *bope* sometimes changes himself into an alligator, or a jaguar, in order to drive fish and game to the hunters. Of course, all *bope* are capable of such transformations, although most informants were uncertain about whether these actually metamorphosed or simply entered an existing animal.

Shamans of the *bope* can assist the village's hunters in other ways. The most common is simply to ask the shaman's familiar where game will be found. The shaman is given a cigarette, goes into a trance, and his *bope* speaks to the hunters. "In such and such a place there is a tapir. Surround him well, on all sides. He will run in this direction, or in that, or perhaps double back on his tracks. If you do not kill this one, you will not kill any others during this hunt." The *bope* then "strengthen" the hunters' *raka,* so they will be better able to see and hear the animal and to kill it easily. The *bope*'s powers thus to affect hunting are limited to the *bope ure,* and then usually to tapir and wild pig. The *bope* have no control whatsoever over fish, not even the three fish species among the *bope ure.* And sometimes the spirits have pity upon "their" animals and say, when asked to assist the hunters, "No, today you will not kill tapir or pig, but you will kill a jaguar or a puma" ("revenge animals," and so of the *aroe* as much as of the *bope*).

The most usual context of these requests is during an unsuccessful collective hunt. Contemporary shamans are considered rather feeble in these powers. The Bororo estimate that even the best of them are accurate only about half the time, and consequently they are only infrequently asked to help in hunts. But informants also realistically said that game had become increasingly scarce in recent years: "Not even the *bope* can discover animals where none exist." The *bope* can also reveal the locality of various *bope ure* during the shaman's dreams, but upon waking he acts upon this knowledge himself, going to the area and killing the game. Of all the shamans at Korugedu Paru, only Celilo was noted as a successful hunter, and this was credited to the powers of his *bope* familiars. The other three shamans resident there were usually afflicted in some fashion or other and seldom went hunting at all. As the Bororo say, "The *bope* take away more than they give."

Formerly it sometimes happened that a second *bari* upon learning of another's predictions would send his familiar to the area and have it chase away the game, sheerly to disgrace the first shaman. This caused people to say that the second "was more than the first," for even though neither shaman mentions it, the hunters find signs that the game had been in the area very recently, and they divine what has happened. If the first *bari*'s *bope* was strong, it kept the game in the predicted area. None of this is used to explain contemporary shamans' lack of success in this area, though, for they cannot even discover where game is, let alone drive it away. (Even when his predictions were accurate, the historical shaman received no additional pieces of the game over and above those normally reserved for the *bope,* nor did the hunters compensate him in any other way for his services.)

The shaman's predictions of the future derive again mostly from his dream experiences, although he may be asked to divine various inconsequential matters in trance. These last are much like the predictions of game: the *bope* are asked where lost property can be found, or if a promised visit from relatives in another village will soon occur, but their replies are skeptically received. Any shaman's vision of future events in dreams is taken only as seriously as the accuracy of his earlier revelations warrant.

The power of revelation is inherent in the *bope*'s attributes. They are able to voyage as easily into the future as they are to travel between this earth and the farthest reaches of the heavens. They control all the "natural" markers of time, the cyclical waxing and waning of the moon, the passage of the rainy and dry seasons. No more do they recognize social time, transgressing freely the boundaries of age and generation, copulating with their categorical "mothers," "sisters," and "nieces," the women of the Bado Jeba clans. The *aroe* transcend time, but the *bope* are at once its principle and its antithesis. Therefore, when in their travels they take along the sleeping *bari*'s *bope*-soul, it may witness future events. Usually these are afflictions, especially the attack of a jaguar or rattlesnake, befalling a particular Bororo. As soon as he awakes, a shaman tells others of his dream, especially the one he saw hurt, so that he or she can avoid the locality where the accident would take place.

If especially competent, a *bari* and his familiar will act during the dream itself to prevent the thing from ever occurring. Prevention is especially attempted for epidemics, which appear in the dream in their usual guise of dark clouds of smoke rolling across the savannah. They may be the responsibility of the *maereboe,* or the malign *erubo* of someone in a distant village. The shaman's soul and his familiar attack this cloud with fans, breaking up its force so that the village either escapes completely or only suffers mildly. Shamans themselves say that their dreams are often very confused, just like those of ordinary people, and that they must often try to "go back" in a subsequent dream to determine just what the dream meant. Or they call the Tupa-doge to discover the truth, which these spirits only sometimes reveal. Then too, it seems that the *maereboe* may cause a shaman's dream experiences to be false, confused.

On the whole, then, shamanistic dreams are considered only marginally more accurately predictive than those of nonshamans, and much inferior to the dreams of a woman and her husband during childbirth. The dreams of great shamans in past times were almost as accurate as these last, but such shamans have not been among the Bororo for decades.[15]

I have described so far the collective aspects of Bororo shamanism. The next sections attempt to personalize this account by examining the biographies and characters of several shamans, as well as the details of some of their treatments of the sick. This material helps determine the relationships between the shaman's attributes and procedures, the details of particular afflictions, and offenses against the *bope ure,* the theoretical foundation of the entire system. I will use these data to sharpen the connections among these elements, between them and the theory of *raka,* and show how they illuminate Bororo social dilemmas.

## Three Shamans, Three Therapies

Our first public encounter with the Bororo took place at Tugo Paru, a Bororo village in close proximity to a small Brazilian settlement. After reading sundry ethnographies and travelogues, my wife and I had come to the conclusion that all indigenous people had a perpetually voracious appetite for salt; accordingly, we decided to present the entire community with a munificent gift of this substance. It later developed that the Bororo care extremely little for salt, but they received our gesture in good spirits. As the *pagimejera* (village chief) was painstakingly distributing the salt, we noticed a thin, delicate-featured man wandering about the edges of the crowd. His bearing and attitude were so markedly peculiar, so different from the other Bororo, that I immediately took him for a shaman. This was our first introduction to Manukuje, indeed one of the better known shamans in the middle São Lourenço, but thoroughly unlike all other shamans I subsequently encountered.

Manukuje was about forty when we met him. His marked "oddness" is difficult to describe. He was at once more brusque and prone to lose his temper than nearly all other mature men, but also cringing, vainglorious, and ingratiating. He was a poor hunter and an even worse gardener, but he excused these faults on the grounds of his constant illnesses. He was, in fact, nearly always sick with a variety of unusual problems, and he died in 1968, according to an unverified report, of tertiary syphilis compounded by what appeared to be cancer of the stomach. He belonged to the Iwagudu-doge clan and hence was, appropriately for a shaman of the *bope,* of the Tugarege moiety. His own clansmen and affines disliked him for his indolence and constant requests for food and goods, and he was practically never asked to play any of the titled roles associated with the Iwagudu-doge.

Manukuje was married to Juanita, of the Bado Jebage subclan of the Bado Jeba Xebegiwuge, a younger uterine sister of the *pagimejera* (village chief) at Tugo Paru. She was unusual among Bororo women in having

A young girl (Manukuje's
daughter)

three surviving children, the youngest of whom, a boy about four, was
her and Manukuje's offspring. She was also caring for the orphaned
daughter of her elder sister. Various other young relatives, her consanguines or classificatory clan members, floated in and out of the household. Thanks to these visitors, Juanita's industry, and especially to the
young men who successively cohabited with Agwa, her eldest daughter,
the household managed to exist despite Manukuje's nonproductivity.
Manukuje was socially well placed to be a major personage, but his affines disliked him cordially, and without their support he could take little
advantage of his structural position.

Manukuje began to have the initiatory shamanistic experiences much
younger than most *bari*, not long after he was initiated, apparently when
he was about sixteen or seventeen. He was initially contacted by the *bope*
of his father, also a shaman but inappropriately an Exerae, who had died
when Manukuje was a "boy," between, I think, six and ten years of age.
He was soon entered by his father's familiar, Emokuri, the *"bope* of the
fire,"  who is an amorphous trickster. Subsequently, he acquired a Tupa

familiar, and the *bope* Aroe Momogodu. By his own account he usually called on and was possessed by Emokuri, especially when he was treating illnesses. His father's *bope,* in common with the *bope* of many dead shamans, was especially fond of "pinga," the local rum, and would insist when possessing Manukuje upon being given three or four stiff drinks. In fact, Manukuje would have been an alcoholic, except that he could not afford it. The Bororo were quite aware that he profited from his ritual status to gain alcohol, and they even joked about it with him.

But, in spite of the nearly universal public scorn for his character, Manukuje had a considerable transvillage reputation as a shaman. He was called to treat most afflictions at Tugo Paru, where there were two other shamans, and when he later moved to Korugedu Paru he was almost as active as Celilo. Even though he was nearly always in trouble with his familiars, as manifested by his constant sicknesses, people agreed he was very adroit at curing. His predictions, too, were regarded as usually accurate, if sometimes partly distorted, and he certainly uttered many more than any other shaman I knew. The contradiction between his social infamy and his perceived shamanistic abilities can be variously explained.

First, Manukuje was an inveterate gossip. He spent most days lounging around the village, visiting his drinking cronies and talking with the women, themselves usually more prone to spreading information of varying accuracy than men. (Bororo women themselves admit this.) Consequently, he was very well informed on all aspects of village life: domestic quarrels, political rivalries, suspicions of theft and adultery, the minor details of household relationships. While Manukuje could not use this knowledge directly in his shamanistic intervention into affliction, he was able to employ it in his predictions and accounts of his *bope*-soul's activities during dreams. Just how he utilized it indirectly in treatment will be seen in the later analysis of one of his cases.

Second, Manukuje's very peculiarities accorded well with the collective representations of a shaman's personal attributes. One of his stranger habits was wandering about at night, when everyone else was either asleep or sitting quietly in their huts. He encouraged the belief that he went off into the jungle during these nocturnal expeditions. Ordinary Bororo do not even consider getting more than a few meters from the village at night, for the jungle's usual risks are infinitely compounded by darkness and the nocturnal habits of all carnivores (including the *bope*). People assumed, of course, that Manukuje could survive these trips only because he changed himself into a jaguar or rattlesnake. I was told that when he was younger the village would often wake in the morning to see a fine deer or wild pig in front of his house. Manukuje was the only shaman in my experience to give such direct confirmation of the belief in the shaman's capacities to metamorphose himself.

Nor did he fail to carry out the shaman's night patrols of the village. Consistently people told me of waking during the night to find him inside their huts, or even standing over them. He would not say a word but after a time would go out silently. (He so visited our house twice, to my knowledge. It is most upsetting to wake up with that horrifying feeling that something has entered the room while you were asleep, to find a peçuliar Indian staring fixedly at you from a meter's distance.) Manukuje slept a good deal during the day, as might be expected, and this too was consistent with public expectations of shamanistic behavior.

Finally, Manukuje's generally eccentric social behavior, his demands and self-justifications were all so counter to the norms for adult males that he could be understood only as a shaman. To be sure, his kinsmen and affines said his ritual position did not excuse his ill conduct, pointing out that other shamans were not at all "like that." However, even they admitted that Manukuje's shamanism was probably as much cause as consequence of his oddities. In brief, he confirms the traditional hypothesis that the role of shaman provides a psychological "out" for abnormal personalities. But he alone among Bororo shamans that I encountered was thus markedly sociopathic. Nor was his reputation as a healer any more considerable than that of several others, while several men nearly as "strange" as Manukuje, in Bororo terms, were not shamans at all. This does not disconfirm the possibility that various aspects of Manukuje's personality were instrumental in his treatments. In order to examine this issue I will explore details of one of these.

One of the notables at Tugo Paru was a man in his later forties, Joaquin, another Iwagudu-doge. He maintained a large household, thanks in large part to his salary as an employee of the Indian Protection Service. But his was neither a stable nor a peaceful residence. His wife was a nagging shrew, his stepdaughter and other female dependents had a certain propensity to marry lazy alcoholics, and his own relatives, including Manukuje, were unrelenting in their demands upon his resources. He himself was an arrogant, ambitious man who wanted to achieve prestige among both Brazilians and Bororo, and especially to be village chief. But his esoteric knowledge was limited, and his ill-concealed ambition was antithetical to the model of an *emijera*. Moreover, the constant bickering in his household, which sometimes evolved into physical violence during a drinking party, was equally counter to the traditional image of a chief's serenity and dignity. Finally Joaquin became very ill with what appeared to be pneumonia. He called for Manukuje, with whom he was intimate between the frequent quarrels that marked their relationship.

In his trance Manukuje's *bope* revealed that Joaquin was ill because several months previously he had eaten a piece of sorubim, one of the *bope ure,* prepared by a Brazilian and not previously offered to the *bope.*

(Joaquin protested later he had not recognized the meat as sorubim.) But then matters were aggravated, the *bope* went on, when Joaquin's wife and elder stepdaughter found a bottle of rum that Joaquin was keeping to give, "a little at a time," to Manukuje's own *bope* and between them drank nearly all of it. The *bope* was especially angry with Joaquin for not concealing the bottle more efficiently. It ominously added that "some people had better watch out," meaning that it would soon take vengeance on the wife and daughter. Manukuje treated Joaquin five times over a period of about two weeks, three times extracting beetles and twice massaging with tobacco smoke as Joaquin grew better. In the sessions following the initial one, the *bope* added nothing to the original diagnosis, other than the usual formulaic assurances that Joaquin would recover his health. During this time neither Joaquin nor any member of his household killed and offered any *bope ure*.

The "*bope's*" diagnosis was a master-stroke. The ambiguity and potential lethality of Joaquin's far too intimate relations with Brazilians were summarized in a single telling episode. The chaotic state of his household, as well as rum's importance to its dynamics, were symbolized in the illegitimately consumed spirits. The fact that neither Joaquin nor his spouse had originally intended the entire bottle for Manukuje's *bope* but had merely given it a drink when it demanded one in an earlier trance was in a sense being offered as further evidence for their disrespect for the *bope,* and also for their failure to run their establishment in proper fashion. One element in traditional domestic organization is a studious regard for the sanctity of personal property, as well as each member's voluntary contribution of some of his possessions for the common good. If anything characterized Joaquin's household it was the complete lack of such regard and cooperation, especially between Joaquin and his various female dependents.

When, subsequently, his wife fell ill with a lingering fever and vomiting, Manukuje's *bope* gave the obvious diagnosis of her affliction's cause. She had drunk its rum. This case was unusually clear in the relation between the *bope*'s explanation and a social condition; other cases described below are much more oblique. Already it can be seen that the Bororo shaman does not accomplish his healing through the kind of functional resolution of social difficulties that is found, for example, in African witchcraft, at least in its anthropological rendering. Nor does the "cause" he or his *bope* hypothesizes have any particular relevance to the specific character of the affliction. Instead, the shaman merely "describes," in veiled terms, a state of disharmony that subtly justifies the patient's disorder without linking it directly to human relationships.

If Manukuje was notably deviant from Bororo norms, then Celilo, the leading shaman at Korugedu Paru, exemplified traditional ways. He was, to begin with, a member of the Jerigi Otojiwu name-group of the Bado Jeba Xobugiwuge, which owns various important ceremonies and the great ritual title of Karia Bokodori. Celilo was often asked to play this role, an indication that he had the esteem of his clan members and of his affines. His wife was the senior active Paiwoedu in the community, which meant she was the ritual "mother of the *aroe*" for a considerable number of deceased Paiwoe. Celilo was consequently the ritual *aroe* "father" of many men in his own moiety. Both he and his wife were extremely conscientious in their prestations of various types of food to their ritual, affinal, and matrilateral relatives. They provided a substantial part of the vegetables and meats consumed by his own clan's household, which adjoined their own in the village circle and was unusual in the number of aged dependent clanswomen and spouses it contained. Invariably they welcomed visiting Paiwoe to their hut, even when, as happened in the summer of 1967, the number, lack of industry, and protracted stay of these made severe demands upon their own resources. Celilo, as I have mentioned several times, was more often called to cure illness, offer up *bope ure,* and conduct collective prophylactic cures in the dance plaza than any other *bari* at Korugedu Paru. Celilo also delighted me by his habit of decking himself out in full ornamental finery, including elaborate body and facial painting. Most modern Bororo usually slop around in the rags their cheap Brazilian clothes soon become and rarely appear in traditional regalia outside of ceremonies. Indeed, so conservative was Celilo in his appearance and conduct that this in itself made him a bit different from other mature males.

In spite of his efforts, Celilo was regarded with prejudice by most adult Bororo at Korugedu Paru. One of the principal reasons for this distrust was the fact that Celilo was, alone among nearly all Bororo, fat. He was not spectacularly nor unhealthily so, but he was obviously fat. Plumpness in a shaman is usually attributed to his diet of human souls. At one point the women's gossip about his suspicious appearance reached such a degree that Celilo found it necessary to address the village during one of the evening discourses, when usually only men considered chiefs of the village (*pagimejera*) are asked to speak. He told the community that he and his familiars had defended it for many years, that they had cured many sick persons, and that if he continued to be defamed he would cease his mystical efforts. No one took him entirely seriously, for no shaman can "retire" but must continue to be possessed whenever people, and his *bope,* so desire it. However, the gossip did decrease.

Another reason for his diminished status was that Celilo, although generally very healthy, did not have any living children, nor did his wife. It is almost impossible for any mature male to have much social esteem unless he has children, for reasons described in Chapter 2 (see also

Crocker 1969b). Some informants attributed his generosity to clansmen, ritual sons, and especially affines as an effort to build up a personal network of ties approximating those possessed by fathers. Finally, Celilo was politically eclipsed by his clan brother Ugo, who presided over the other Paiwoe household in the village. This included Ugo's son-in-law Kano, the clan chief (*emijera*) of the Bokodori Exerae and usually the village's chief (*pagimejera*). Ugo himself was the clan chief of the Bado Jeba Xobugiwuge, and thus Celilo's nominal elder brother. Moreover, his ritual knowledge was considered far superior to Celilo's, and, finally, he had an adult son, three daughters, and several grandchildren. For all Celilo's dressing up and generosity, he could never be anything but outside the kin system which dominated politics in Korugedu Paru. My own feeling is that all this led him to protest a bit too much.[16]

As a young man Celilo was noted for his bellicosity and aggression, and some of this reputation colored his current status. He told me he first began to have peculiar dreams and to see strange things in the jungle when he was about thirty, after he had been married for a time and had ended his wild escapades. He was first possessed in a unique way. Celilo was hunting upriver when he saw a small *uwai* (alligator) sunning itself on a sand spit. For no good reason he decided to catch it alive, and actually had it in his hands when it slipped away and into a large hole under a stone at the edge of the river. Celilo returned to the village in a daze, saying all sorts of incomprehensible things, trembling, stumbling, and "burning up." Perhaps, Celilo said, the *bope* who had been trying to possess him had become angry and was trying to kill him immediately. (Ugo strongly endorsed this interpretation; he had an elder brother's usual tendency to put the worst possible interpretation on any event befalling a younger sibling.) That night the *bope* entered him and he jumped up, ran shrieking around the village, and had to be held down by several men. Later on his wife spoke to the *bope* in Celilo and persuaded it to eat something, some pieces of wild pig already given to the *bope* by a shaman. The *bope*, mollified, did not immediately kill Celilo.

The next day he persuaded an old, knowledgeable shaman to return with him upriver to the rock. There the old *bari* called his own *bope* and asked it what to do. The *bope* replied that they should wait until midday when the alligator would leave its hole, and then close up the hole with a large piece of wood. At midday two alligators came out, including the one Celilo had nearly caught the day before, and their hole was promptly sealed. When the alligators shortly returned, Celilo killed them both. Celilo himself said of this episode, "I was not to be a *bari,* but to be dead." After this his initiation followed the usual course, with the original *bope* becoming his first familiar. In 1967 he had five familiars, including the first: Koiwo, a *bope pegareu* ("bad *bope*") that lives always in termite nests and eats only the *bope* food plants; his elder brother's *bope,* and through it Bureikoibo, the *bope* which has all the *bope* food species penned up around his home in the "red sky," and which also possessed Cadete, the powerful village chief who was simultaneously a *bari* and shaman of the *aroe;* another "bad *bope*" which once killed a man called Torikogudu and now calls itself by this name; and finally a Tupa-doge.

The following case of Celilo's is typical of most "unsuccessful" shamanistic cures. Not long after we arrived in Korugedu Paru, a middle-aged Bado Jeba man died after a long illness. Several years earlier he had offended the *bope* by letting a wounded tapir escape. He became sick, but Celilo's *bope* cured him, warning him never to return to the spot where he had lost the tapir. But after some time he did so. That night, as Celilo's *bope*-soul was going around the village with his familiar, they encountered a *bope* coming along with a broken arrow in its hand. They smoked together, and Celilo asked it what it was doing in the village. The *bope* said it was coming to return an arrow "to that one," indicating the hunter's domicile, "perhaps he forgot it, or lost it." Celilo knew, of course, that it had come to kill the man, and so he told the *bope* to give him the arrow. The *bope* at first refused but then handed over the arrow after Celilo's *bope* was joined by a Tupa-doge (a "good *bope*"). Shortly after this the *bope* managed to steal the arrow back and, when the man returned for a third time to the unlucky place, made him very sick indeed. Celilo attempted to cure him, but the possessing *bope* said to the patient, "You were stupid. You did not do as you were told. Now there is nothing I can do; you are going to die." (It is not uncommon for the *bope* to speak thus when it is clear to everyone, including the patient, that he is in fact dying. The *bari* always attempts one last cure, though, and occasionally there are miraculous recoveries credited to the familiar's powers.)

The deceased, called Manuel, was a mild and self-effacing man who lived in apparent harmony with his wife and the heterogeneous collection of her clan relatives which composed her household. He remained aloof from the village intrigue, acted in few ritual representations, accomplished just enough of his obligatory prestations to his own clan and his affines not to be complained about, and generally had an unremarkable life. No doubt he had had his special troubles, but I could gain no inkling of what these might have been. He was said to have died because when young he allowed a wounded tapir to escape and was so foolish when old as to return to the site twice. There was, again, no direct relationship between the diagnosis of his illness's cause, its treatment, his particular human situation, and the details of his affliction.

Yet the reasons for his death might be construed as a metaphor for his flawed life. Manuel frittered his existence away, neither succeeding nor failing, drifting through the tide of days. He was just the sort to let a wounded animal escape rather than make a sustained effort, and then to neglect a bit of circumspection as just too much trouble. A "falling down" sort of man, irritatingly blameless in his misfortunes and exciting neither pity nor anger but a kind of guilty contempt. To be sure, wounding but not killing a *bope ure* species is a standard element in the lexicon of offenses against the spirits, but in over three dozen shamanistic explanations of specific afflictions I only heard it invoked in the case of Manuel. Surely this case raises in miniature the central problem of this book: just what do the Bororo mean when they credit a man's death to his breaking the rules concerning the *bope ure;* and what functions, if any, does this meaning have in the treatment of affliction? At this point it appears that only the scrap of an anology is involved, that what is being described in terms of the *bope ure* system is not any single, particularized human situation but the general structure of all codes for the maintenance of relationships between human beings and between society and nature. One last case will show that shamanistic therapies need not be quite that undetermined.

Kadegare has been mentioned several times earlier in this work. A member of the Bado Jebage subclan of the Bado Jeba Xebegiwuge, he had been married incestuously (in terms of moiety exogamy) to a woman of the Bokodori Exerae for about five years. The ambiguity of his position, and his own perception of it, was well expressed in the site of his household, which very accurately occupied that part of the compass reserved for the Bokodori Exerae, but a hundred meters out of the village circle. Such a site was completely unique in Bororo tradition, which equates village residence with tribal membership. Kadegare himself said he was forced to live away from the village because of the domestic animals (mainly pigs and chickens) he raised, nearly all of which he sold to Brazilians. This sort of entrepreneurial activity is very un-Bororo, partly just because conditions of village life mean that "commercial" animals cause all manner of social problems. They are either wandering off and being killed by neighbors' dogs or disappearing ("stolen," according to the owner) or getting into other households' food and belongings. Kadegare, in his own view, was merely being "decent" in removing his animals from the village.

However, other persons gave less flattering interpretations of his action. Many said he was insanely jealous of his wife, who had been a well-known "men's house associate" in her youth and, according to several men of her age and the opposite moiety who should have known, her talent in that role was matched by her enthusiasm for it. Moreover, her then unmarried daughter Agwa, a very pretty girl around twenty, was said to be as delectable as her mother had been. While mother-daughter polygyny is not forbidden by the Bororo and indeed is the most common form of plural marriage, intergenerational polygyny does receive a certain mild opprobrium.[17] Kadegare, who could little afford additional reasons for social mistrust, was suspiciously insulated against the public scrutiny (aural as well as visual) of conjugal relationships—so much a part of village life. Although he ostentatiously treated Agwa as a daughter, most smiled at the transparency of his deceit. Still others, like Dita in the case described earlier, hinted that Kadegare's a-sociality was just what might be suspected of a witch, since he could comfortably consume human souls in his isolated home while minimizing the risk of discovery by one of the village's shamans.

In my view, the structural elements in his marriage were predominant in his removal from the village. His affines admitted that while Kadegare did his best to accomplish his duties as in *in-odowu,* "sister's husband," his membership in the same moiety often prohibited him from fulfilling many of them. An *in-odowu,* as noted in the second chapter, should make the elaborate ornaments his wife's clan needs for prestations. Like any normal male Bororo, Kadegare had learned the details of construction of most of the opposite moiety's ornaments but not those of objects belonging to clans in his own moiety. Further, said his brothers-in-law, it was "ugly" for an Exerae to make ornaments on behalf of other Exerae—"this is a service which should go between the 'halves'." Further, in many ceremonial contexts Kadegare had to carry out his duties as a member of the Bado Jebage while simultaneously acting as an affine in his own moiety. Normally, of course, the Tugarege and the Exerae have mutually exclusive rituals, so that such conflicts do not arise.

Finally, and probably most critically, Kadegare could not structurally be the *aroe* father of ritual representatives of dead members of his wife's clan, and thus he was partly excluded from the most important system of economic and political relationships in the village. He could, however, be himself a representative, and was so for several dead Tugarege. As one of his *i-medu* (wife's brothers) said, "we do not know what to call him, and we do not know how to treat him—no one can be both an *in-odowu* (sister's husband) and an *i-mana* (elder brother)." Such are the almost insurmountable difficulties which befall anyone who seeks to contradict the social logic of a thoroughly "elementary system" of marriage. Kadegare's way of responding to all these contradictions was crude but effective: he simply physically withdrew from the village.

Kadegare's own clansmen distrusted him for his arrogance and obvious lust for political status. Others in the village agreed and pointed out the objective proofs of his poor relations with his *bope* familiars. First, his wife had had several stillbirths and miscarriages, even though before her marriage she had borne several healthy children. Her and Kadegare's only living child, a boy around two, was constantly ill and not commonly expected to survive. Some attributed these difficulties to the ancestors' disgust with moiety endogamy, while others said the *bope* were not themselves pleased by such an "unnatural" union.[18] Second, Kadegare himself suffered from a variety of afflictions, usually due to accidents which seemed to me to have very curious circumstances. Kadegare's shotgun misfired and exploded backwards into his face, almost blinding him. Playing soccer with Brazilians, he made a vigorous barefoot kick, entirely missed the ball, and struck the ground instead, so that his big toe was nearly ripped off. He fell from a tree, where he had climbed to gather wild fruit, and badly sprained his leg. All these accidents occurred within about a year. Just earlier, he told me, he had fallen off a truck, overturned his canoe in the rapids, been mauled by a young puma, bitten by a poisonous snake, and deeply gashed himself with his own machete while cutting firewood.

Between these events, which left him usually unable to hunt or garden and therefore incapable of his various obligatory prestations, Kadegare was sick with the usual variety of illnesses that regularly incapacitate most adult Bororo. He was by no means as seriously (and, as it proved, terminally) ill as Manukuje, but he was "accident prone" to an uncanny degree. Because of this evidence of the *bope*'s displeasure with him, he was not often asked to treat afflictions, although he served as mediator in the offerings of *bope* foods nearly as often as Celilo himself. Some generous persons said that Kadegare was a relatively young man (he was in his middle thirties) and ascribed his difficulties with his familiars as well as his social errors to inexperience and lack of knowledge. They thought that by ensuring his familiars a sufficiency of "their" foods, the *bope* might be mollified and Kadegare himself might gain understanding. It was, after all, in the collective interest for the village to have a number of competent shamans. (This mingling of a sense of dependence on the shamans, and a certain distrust of their individual capacities and personalities, is one of the most common social attitudes toward them.)

Kadegare became a shaman about five years before I met him, when he was in his late twenties and after he had been married a number of times. He was first possessed by the *bope* of his dead elder brother, also a shaman, and by an unnamed familiar of that relative. He later acquired Emokuri, the "*bope* of the fire"; the *bope* of another dead *bari*, a Tugarege for whom Kadegare is the *aroe maiwu* or ritual replacement; and the *bope* familiar of that *bari;* and finally a Tupa-doge. Kadegare is different from other shamans in having relatively few and redundant familiars, including a high percentage of dead shamans' *bope*. The first difference is explained by his relative youth as a shaman, and the second by his concern for social prestige. I had the distinct impression that Kadegare was not averse to utilizing his ritual status in furthering his political ambitions, and several informants hinted at similar views. Unlike other shamans, including Celilo and Manukuje, Kadegare took little interest in the *bope* per se, as what might be termed a "domain of discourse." In my private conversations with him he was ignorant of many of the details of *bope* cosmology well known to other older Bororo, including nonshamans. But this lack of concern contrasted with his fascination for details of esoteric lore and his competence within the domain of ritual knowledge, both concerned with the *aroe*.

All of this struck the Bororo as contradictory, since a man who "knows" should also be a model of Bororo ethics, which Kadegare manifestly was not. In short, Kadegare was a puzzle to the Bororo, to me, and, I suspect, to himself as well. But, as far as his performance as a shaman went, his role-playing seemed as little affected by his character as did the actions of other shamans by their own diverse personalities. Kadegare entered into trance, explained the causes of illness, and treated affliction just as other shamans did, and the ratio of his success and failure, despite his reputation as a poor healer, seemed about comparable to those of his fellow specialists.

Once Kadegare was asked to cure Phillippe's seven-year-old son, who had been suffering from diarrhea and a high fever for over a week. Phillippe's situation was in some respects unusual but not rare among contemporary Bororo, and it illuminates certain of the marital dynamics and structural factors which have been the themes of this work. Phillippe was an earnest and hard-working man in his early forties. A member of the Kiedu, one of the high-ranking name-groups among the Kie clan, he lived next to his father and his stepmother, herself a Kiedu and a parallel cousin of his dead mother. Phillippe had been abandoned by his wife, the mother of his son, some three or four years earlier and had never remarried. Phillippe's life centered around the boy, who accompanied him everywhere. Although industrious and a recognized craftsman in wooden trade objects, Phillippe was ignorant of most ritual esoterica, hunted poorly, and seemed to me rather stupid. His wife, an Arore, and by repute a demanding and bitter nag, was said to have left Phillippe after a dramatic confrontation in which he had accused her of numerous affairs, and she countered by a long citation of his inability to provide her with food and material goods. Before leaving him, she broke his bows and arrows, burned his clothes, and generally left him propertyless.

The anomaly of his domestic situation made Phillippe something of a social isolate. As a bachelor, he should have lived in the men's house, but his uninitiated son was not permitted there. He could not live among the Aroroe without a wife and should have resolved his problem by marrying a classificatory wife's sister. Unfortunately, there were no marriageable Arore women at Korugedu Paru or, indeed, in the middle São

Lourenço. He was forced to live next to his father and stepmother and to participate economically and socially in their household, within his matrilineal clan. The Bororo generally disapproved of the situation, largely on the grounds that the son should be raised in his own clan, but empathetically recognized Phillippe's dilemma.

Phillippe sought out Kadegare after the boy's illness seemed to be worsening. The curing ceremony was attended by Phillippe's parents and most of their housemates, for a child's sickness always attracts even more public sympathy than that of an adult. Phillippe prepared the *bope*'s cigarette, as a parent should for a sick child, and gave it to Kadegare, who was soon possesed by the *bope* familiar of one of the dead shamans whose *bope* he also had. The *bope* soon revealed that the boy was ill because the *jota* (skewer) Phillippe had made and given a shaman in another village had broken in a few months. Furthermore, the boy himself had eaten a very small bit of wild pig prepared by Brazilians and not offered to the *bope*. But Kadegare's familiar assured everyone present that the boy would soon recover and extracted a large beetle from his stomach. After a second treatment in which Kadegare removed a bit of charred wood from the boy's hip-joint, the boy did in fact recover.

Here the explanation of an affliction's cause again subtly addresses certain aspects of the patient's social situation. Owing to his odd domestic position, Phillippe engaged in a certain amount of wage labor for Brazilians; he could not maintain his own garden without a wife, and the boy hindered his hunting and fishing. The boy had been waiting for his father to finish work when the employer's wife, pitying the waif, gave him the contaminated pork. Obviously this would not have happened if Phillippe had maintained a traditional household, even one with his matrilineal kin. Further, the *bope* were punishing Phillippe through his son for his inability to "make things properly," the same incapacity which caused his wife to leave him and which she emphatically underscored in her destructive parting.

Again, I cannot show that the *bope*'s oblique references to Phillippe's domestic troubles had any instrumental relation to the effectiveness of the treatment. But they did elegantly express the character-logical genesis of these troubles, and the disasters which must overcome any who escape the more routine dangers of conjugal life. Among the Bororo, one is damned if one marries but equally if not more damned if one does not. Kadegare may have also been obliquely contrasting Phillippe's anomalous situation with his own marriage, which even if it was "wrong," at least showed his acceptance of the necessity of conjugality and of the rules governing behavior between spouses. But though these subtleties of explanation were no doubt lost on Phillippe's suffering little boy, and perhaps even on dull-witted Phillippe himself, they were well understood by the rest of the village.

The relationships between the mechanics of shamanistic therapies and the specifics of individual afflictions have never been clear, for reasons I explored in the introduction. The material just presented suggests that this failure of anthropological acumen may be due to the fact that such relationships do not functionally exist. Instead of relating personal calamity to the moral dynamics of an idiosyncratic personal situation, the Bororo shaman generalizes the particularity of a single case to fit the demands of a global, mechanistic system. This reduces personal responsibility for affliction from guilt to regret, all the more since the offense has most often the quality of an unwilled accident. Perhaps such a sublimation aids the patient in objectifying his or her illness through explaining its mysterious onset, but just how would be difficult to show. Further, many afflictions result from the errors of parents or spouses. Nothing suggests that the etiology of affliction or its therapy relate in any direct way to the dynamics of these relationships. Indeed, the *bope* punish a child rather than its offending parent because they are so strongly identified with one another, owing to the bonds of common *raka* and co-dwelling. But the relations between consanguine or clan brothers, or between sisters, perhaps the most endemically stressful in the Bororo system (Crocker 1969a), are never even obliquely mentioned by the *bope* or their shamans. (It may be that these were under the dominion of the *aroe* in the days when they still possessed men, a topic considered in the following section.)

It should be clear that the victim of the *bope*'s wrath *is* at fault, nearly always for an infraction of the rules governing behavior toward the *bope ure*. The explanatory system is not as mechanistic and random as that of Western medicine. Further, as in the cases of Joaquin and Phillippe, the *bope*'s (or the shaman's) justification of the affliction may obliquely refer to certain general aspects of the patient's domestic situation or, as in Manuel's case, even to his character. Still, these justifications do not symbolically refer to a particular social relationship as disordered or immoral, as witchcraft accusations have been argued to do; shamanism does not function as a "strain gauge."

Offenses against the *bope* are also not entirely comparable to those against such codes of holiness as the laws of Leviticus. It is true that the *bope ure* substances have that quality of autonomous potency characteristic of liminal things imbued with *mana* and/or pollution. But, as I argued in the last chapter, they have this quality not because of any ambiguity in their classificatory positions but in spite of their total lack of anomaly. The Bororo attitude toward them does approximate the general Hebrew notion of holiness, as defined by Douglas (1966:53): "Holiness means keeping distinct the categories of creation. It therefore involves correct definition, discrimination and order." But even this is not quite correct; the *bope ure* have their special position because they are *owed* to the *bope,* who are jealous masters of "their" foods. It is as if the deity required that a bit of each ox or sheep consumed by man be offered up first to him. This obviously expresses a sense of moral discrimination and order in the universe, but not one devoted to issues of right and wrong. Instead the Bororo objectify a code of conduct through correct behavior toward natural species, and they distinguish between "proper" and "improper."

The Bororo assume a consistency in human character: if a person errs in conduct toward human beings, he is very likely to be less than correct in his treatment of the *bope ure.* Theft, for example, is one of the most heinous offenses against Bororo morality, as the "Fallen Star" (*aroe butu*) attests, but there are no public sanctions against human thieves. Practically, there is good reason for this, because theft is extremely difficult to prove and a false accusation is itself a criminal offense. The Bororo, however, are supremely confident that anyone so heedless of the rights of humans will sooner or later neglect those of the *bope.* There is no expectation that he will necessarily "steal" one of the *bope ure,* consume it without shamanistic intervention; the Bororo do not predicate that degree of consistency in human behavior. At most the offense against the *bope* may reflect some general disorder in the patient's social relationships.

Joaquin's household *was* in a perpetual state of chaos, just the sort of place where property rights were casually flouted. The "theft" of the *bope*'s rum by Joaquin and his wife symbolized this disorganization quite neatly. It may be that individuals guilty of the more extreme crimes (murder, rape, or aggravated assault) are shamanistically found to be culpable of equivalent violence against the *bope,* the flagrant denial of the *bope ure* rules. But social sanctions do intervene here, and, furthermore, such immorality is very rare among the Bororo. Far more common is the sort of case represented by Manuel: persons who carry out the letter of their social responsibilities but with indifference and imprecision. They are just the sort to let a wounded *bope ure* escape, or a wife labor all day with only their lackadaisical assistance. Finally there are the threatened afflictions revealed after an *aroe butu,* when the Bororo marvel that even the *bope* would rob a soul for such slight offenses as tossing a dog a piece of gristle from a deer's thigh. But, of course, here the affliction has been averted, and the shaman's revelations are functionally only a warning of the *bope*'s vigilance, never post-factum accounts of the nexus between offense and punishment.

To dwell further on the *bope*'s character as providers of negative sanctions would falsify their nature, as construed by the Bororo, and their contributions to Bororo ethics. It should be manifestly clear now that the pains of disease and accident are not "sanctions" for this society. Their relation to moral delicts is too nebulous, their nature as regrettable but inevitable dimensions of life too firmly imbedded in the doctrine of *raka*. We need to consider their opposite, positive meaning. My analysis in the last section showed that the rules of the *bope ure* were a code summarizing all rules for discipline of the self's desires, and most especially those evoked by entities which lacked all capacity to thwart satisfaction of those wishes. I further argued that these entities implicitly included members of the opposite sex, and the self itself. But the material presented in this chapter clearly precludes any direct functional equation of this code with standards of social morality. The shamans of the *bope* even appear to avoid, in their mystically inspired accounts of affliction's origin, too simple parallels between a specific offense against the *bope* and the particular wrongs done human beings by the patient. However, the covenant between human society and the *bope* does hold the promise that all who scrupulously respect its minute conditions shall receive long and fruitful lives, or, in Bororo terms, their *raka* will accomplish its full destiny. As remorselessly bleak as their recent history has been, the Bororo still find ample human confirmations of this tautology's validity. The aged members of their communities are considered *ipso facto* paragons of social virtue and punctilious regard for the *bope ure*. And, given the waning of social tensions with increasing age inherent in the Bororo life cycle, as described in Chapter 2, the former assumption about virtue is daily confirmed. Given the infirms' lack of frequent contact with the *bope ure*, so is, but less frequently, the latter: it is easy to be punctilious on rare occasions. But the young people, riven by the tensions of conjugality and acculturative pressures, are constantly, mysteriously afflicted, or else their children are. When, from time to time, some apparently blameless person is stricken, at whatever stage of life, the case proves only to confirm the Bororo assumption that no human existence is free from error, including that of one's progenitors, and existence itself is vulnerable to the mechanics of its own operation.

Bororo shamans may include among their numbers all manner of psychological deviants or be a role open to the most cynical self-aggrandizing manipulator of public opinion. Whatever their motivation, their conduct and revelation of the spirits' nature and intentions toward humankind must reflect to their audience's satisfaction the premises of collective representations. These assumptions include that the *aroe*, too, intervene directly in human affairs and manifest themselves through the agency of living personalities. Or so they once did: the thesis of the next chapter is that the shaman of the *bope* cannot be understood without comparison to his inverted counterpart, the shaman of the *aroe*.

# PART IV

## Aroe Etawa-are: Shamans of the Aroe

Written in Butler's Sermons

Affections, Instincts, Principles, and Powers,
Impulse and Reason, Freedom and Control—
So men, unravelling God's harmonious whole,
Rend in a thousand shreds this life of ours.

Vain Labour! Deep and broad, where none may see,
Spring the foundations of that shadowy throne
Where man's one nature, queen-like, sits alone,
Centered in a majestic unity;

And rays her powers, like sister-islands, seen
Linking their coral arms under the sea,
Or cluster'd peaks with plunging gulfs between

Spann'd by aërial arches all of gold,
Whereo'er the chariot wheels of life are roll'd
In cloudy circles to eternity.

Matthew Arnold

harpy eagle

# 9

◦~∾∾~◦

# The Stench of Death

The Indians of South America have been dying for over three centuries, and now the whole tragic process is nearing its end. The survivors realize the societies which formerly gave coherence to their lives are putrifying or defunct. Their remaining choice is to die or to acculturate.[1] In these circumstances we ethnologists are, as a colleague once put it, morticians, and our studies necessarily a kind of embalming. One of our persistent responses is a tendency to cosmetize the corpse, to dwell on an "ethnographic present" constructed from the uncertain memories of old informants and a few shards of exotic custom. Or we examine minutely the structures of myths, which never having lived cannot be moribund. The Bororo, for a variety of historical and ecological reasons,[2] have managed to conserve the greater part of their traditional lives, so that for the most part I have been able to describe a "living" system.

In the one part of Bororo shamanism that is devoted to the *aroe* and is now defunct, the question of historical change ceases to be something which can be ignored or written around; it becomes the central issue. As the last chapter showed, shamanism of the *bope* is now a fragment of a once complete structure. It consequently poses two linked theoretical problems: the system must be reconstituted in such a way as to explain the surviving portion; and this resurrected structure must encompass the reasons for the disappearance of this part and not the other. Still, no entire reconstruction of a vanished society is required here, for the Bororo social system has survived relatively intact. Further, the last *aroe etawa-are* in the middle São Lourenço died only in 1953, and there were rumors that one was active in upstream villages in the early 1960s. The majority of my adult informants had known such specialists and witnessed their functions. All other aspects of the practices and beliefs involving the *aroe* remain very much part of social reality. In native opinion, the only significant change has been the lack of shamans of the *aroe*, and the nearly complete absence of affliction attributable to the souls.

Explaining this historical loss involves one of the basic issues in shamanism: how is it that only certain individuals come to participate in an intimate relationship with the spirits, an engagement in which their volition plays ostensibly little part? More than one Bororo said they wished very much to be a shaman of the *aroe*, but the spirits apparently did not wish it. My working hypothesis is that this "failure" of the *aroe* to manifest themselves in men is due not so much to any withering of the *aroe* practices or of the relationships they symbolize but, paradoxically, to their nonproblematic qualities. It is in the troubled domestic sphere, far more disarranged by acculturative pressures and recently accelerated population loss, where dramatic and irresolvable conflicts have been exacerbated. Accordingly, the *bope* system, through which such troubles are expressed, has acquired practical dominion over Bororo understanding of affliction's causes and remedies. If this hypothesis is correct, the shaman of the *aroe* will again appear if certain demographic and economic trends are reversed so as to change the structural dynamics of households and the intimate economies of domestic politics.

In this chapter, I first describe the general attributes of the *aroe* and their partial reflection in various sets of natural species. One of these is the "animals of revenge," the *marege mori-xe*, which mediate between men and the collectivity of souls in a way analogous to the functions of the *bope ure* in the relationship between human society and the *bope*. In Chapter 11 I discuss the recruitment and the powers of the shaman of the *aroe*, paralleling as much as possible the comparable data on the *bari* presented in the last chapter. This leads to an analysis of the dyadic shamanistic system as it appears to have existed historically and to an exploration of reasons for the current disappearance of the *aroe etawa-are*. Since the complex of ideas and practices dedicated to the *aroe* is the theme of a forthcoming work, I do not go into as much detail about this cosmological category as I have about the *bope*. In particular, the elaborate funeral cycle and masculine initiation, in which the shaman of the souls figured prominently, are only mentioned here. My theme in this work is this shaman's attributes and powers in nonceremonial contexts, and the systematic fashion in which these qualities complete that part-structure already set out for the shaman of the *bope*. In elaborating the system in its entirety the meaning of its multiple zoological codes at last is established, and its relation to Bororo social processes finally becomes clear.

## Attributes and Powers of the *Aroe*

*Aroe etawa-are* means literally "he who knows the ways of the souls," in which *awa* (or *awara*) has also the sense of "roads" or "paths." This stress on knowledge of connection, of relationships between elements, appropriately contrasts this shaman's capacities with those of the *bari*, helpless agent of the placeless, liminal *bope*. The *aroe* so known include not just the shades of the ancestors and the souls of living persons but those fantastic essences of living species and divine monsters which fix the categorical order of Bororo society. The *aroe* can no more be interpreted as one complex metaphor for that society than the *bope* can be seen as an image of "nature." Although the *aroe* do embody the principles of transcendental nominal form, including the "totemic" ones that define the different states of being which are Bororo clans, they also summarize the whole of perceptual and imagined reality, including at one level of abstraction the *bope* themselves. Bororo intellectual and active relationships with the *bope* and with the *aroe* reflect this fundamental difference in the epistemological character of each class of cosmological being.

Men seek to embody the *aroe* through the symbolic processes of costume, dance, and song, but these essences are remote from daily living and difficult to apprehend. Men avoid, if not flee before, the *bope*, which are nonetheless constantly manifest in nature and the organic flux of oneself and other social beings. By contrast, perception and action are possible only through the *aroe*'s classificatory principles, through which all things can be categorized, compared, differentiated, typologized, analogized, named, and personified. Sometimes, just as with the *bope*, these *aroe* principles are found manifested in an intense and summary way in some natural entity or phenomenon. But even these material illuminations of essence are somehow dimmer and more allegorical than the comparable forms which show forth the *bope*. For something equivalent to the *bope*'s sun and moon or vultures, the Bororo must invent a divine bestiary featuring phallic gargoyles, the *aije*. These can be shabbily represented by men, but they are not "real." The transcendent being of categorical principles exists in a dimension far removed from those accessible to human faculties.

The dwellings of the *bope* are concrete and localized, manifested in termite nests, an advancing shower cloud, or, at their most remote, in the sensate blue bowl of heaven. The realm of the *aroe* is otherwise: unimaginable, non-apparent. The Bororo cannot situate it, other than to say it is "somewhere" under the ground, in a sort of alternate universe that mirrors in a shadowy, distorted way the topographical and typological features of this perceptible one. It is cold and damp there, dominated by rivers or perhaps currents, since the whole domain has the translucent, washed quality of a submarine world. These watercourses all run from east to west, in tandem with the sun's course. All forms of being dwelling there have an insubstantial perfection, and there are no organic processes whatsoever, no temporal change, no birth or death. According to the ancient revelations of the *aroe etawa-are*, one village of ancestral souls is located far to the east and is under the direction of the *aroe* Itubore. Another is found at the extreme west, under the leadership of the *aroe* Bakororo.

These *aroe* are the "souls" of the two culture heroes who instituted the moieties and otherwise devised the organization of society. Some say they were never ordinary men but always essences. They are the *aroe* counterparts of Meri and Ari among the *bope*. Bakororo and Itubore are among the clan *aroe* of the Arore in the Tugarege moiety but are ceremonially represented, respectively, by members of the Bado Jeba Xebegiwuge and Bado Jeba Xobugiwuge in the Exerae moiety. These representations are crucial to the most important villagewide rituals, above all to funerals, initiations, and the giving of names. Each village of the ancestors reproduces perfectly the Bororo village plan and has an enormous men's house in the center. There are no gardens, however, and very little hunting, since the *aroe* eat little and then only vegetables and small fish. They detest strong meats, above all those of the *bope ure*, and avoid the reek of *jerimaga*, which is one reason they visit ordinary Bororo villages only during ceremonies.

In between the two polar villages the *aroe* universe is divided into eight symmetrical sections radiating out from a central point. In each of these wedges usually dwell the *aroe* essences which are the totems of the eight Bororo clans (see diagram). The character and form of these essences are not clearly known, and perhaps their transcendent mystery is simply unwordable. According to the shamans of the *aroe*, who alone among living men have seen the *aroe*, each essence is a pair of beings which together exhaust all variation within the species or thing for which they serve as Idea and Name. They are something more than Platonic ideals, for they are also plumed and banded and ornamented in awe-ful ways, far larger than and different from their natural derivatives. When an ordinary mortal first sees one, he cannot recognize it for what it is, until an accompanying *aroe* names it.

### Kie

*AROE*

*Bai* (king vulture)
*Pari* (rhea)
*Ki* (tapir)
*Aigo* (puma)
*Jure* (anaconda)
*Pobogo* (swamp deer)

### Bokodori Exerae

*AROE*

*Okoge* (dourado)
*Bokodori* (armadillo)
*Ruwo* (snail)
*Xiwabo* (japu)
*Ika* (trumpet)
*Barae* (Brazilians)

### Bado Jeba Xebegiwuge

*AROE*

*Baxe* (herons)
*Ewo* (rattlesnakes)
*Kadamo* (kingfisher)
*Rea* (armadillo)
*Meri* (sun/*bope*)
*Kaibori* (pestle)

### Bado Jeba Xobugiwue

*AROE*

*Adugo* (jaguar)
*Okwaru* (armadillo)
*Buiogwa* (piranha)
*O Xoreu* (bittern)
*Iworo* (palm)
*Pana* (resonator)

**Village of Bakororo**        WEST                    EAST        **Village of Itubore**

### Iwagudu-doge

*AROE*

*Nabure* (macaw)
*Tamigi* (screamer)
*Jugo* (peccary)
*Ipie* (otter)
*Aije*
*Bakorororeu* (coral snake)

### Paiwoe

*AROE*

*Kugu* (owl)
*Korao* (parrot)
*Pai* (monkey)
*Buke* (anteater)
*Rie* (wolf)
*Orarije* (surubim)

### Arore

*AROE*

*Iwagudu* (crow)
*Kido* (parakeet)
*Akiwa* (capivara)
*Kuje* (mutum)
*Marido* (buriti)
*Buke* (net)

### Apiborege

*AROE*

*Aroe Exeba* (eagle)
*Bakure* (monkey)
*Aipobureu* (ocelot)
*Irui* (lizard)
*Tubore* (minnows)
*Baku* (fan)

The spatial order of the *aroe* forms
(only a sampling of each clan's *aroe* is given)

The idea of nomination is much more central to these *aroe* forms than any concept of physical resemblance. Bororo refer to their clan's *aroe* as *i-edaga aroe*, *i-imaruga aroe*, terms which cannot be easily glossed but refer to the relationships established during the name-giving ceremony. The clan acquired its original association with an *aroe* when one of its ancestors first named a form of being unique to Bororo experience. Bororo proper names, ritual titles, and the terms for clan property, all derive in specifying ways from these *aroe*, without diminishing their nominal capacities. These essences provide the categories on which social differentiation and identity is based; they also are the terms which order all perception. Everything in the world, say the Bororo, has an *aroe* (that is, a name) and, since names are spatially organized, a cosmological place.

Relations among a clan's *aroe*, between those essences dwelling in one of the eight other-worldly segments, are not themselves organized. There is no implied logic to their association, which is represented as purely spatial. This reflects the lack of any organic relationship among the units composing the clan. The only order among the *aroe* essences is the physical one which divides them in a nearly random fashion among the eight segments.[3] Such an arbitrary scheme is consistent with other aspects of Bororo classification. They generally lack abstract hierarchical typologies, as was seen in an earlier chapter. They are certainly capable of associating species on morphological, dietary, and other grounds, and they sometimes speak of similar animals as "brothers." But the Bororo seem most aware of the existential fact of speciation, of the unique character of each type of natural form. They comment on how every individual being, no matter how mutilated or aged or idiosyncratic, is still obviously a member of a species, and how this manifest resemblance is duplicated through the generations. I still recall the tone of wonder in my name-giver's query; "Why is it that the eggs of *nabure* (the "red" macaw) always produce *nabure* that grow up to look just like their parents?" With such an attitude, it is no surprise that the Bororo excel at metaphor and homology and display little interest in developing abstract typologies. The central importance of the village plan in both indigenous sociology and cosmology is also explained by such an orientation, for the plan provides the only mode of ordering a universe of unique nominal forms.

The *aroe* seldom venture into this world. The only connections between their domain and man's are waterways and caves, long and unpleasant avenues of access. Occasionally the *aroe* might cause one of their number to manifest itself to a Bororo, as an omen of his immediate death or that of some near relative. Even the souls of dead Bororo soon cease to have any interest in the affairs of the living. Their presence during ceremonials must be invoked, coaxed by offerings of their favorite substances (sweetened water, tobacco, honeyed gruels), and then they drift quickly back to their own realm. The *aroe* of such mythical creatures as the Aije, Para-bara, and Iworo seem more inclined to visit among men. The status of these creatures in Bororo belief is hard to describe, especially that of the *aije*. Most Bororo, including women and older children who are supposed to think that these beasts actually come to the village during ceremonies, know perfectly well that the initiated males anoint themselves in white mud and whirl bullroarers to produce the *aije*'s moaning growls. But nearly every man I talked to was entirely sure that the things actually existed. They described them in detail: huge water creatures, their skins a gray-brown and covered with warts and deep fissures, with small heads and limbs but a long, broad tail. Most persons have relatives who have actually seen the *aije*, with lethal consequences for themselves or their near kinsmen, and several described mysterious happenings in the river, distant splashings by large grayish shapes or glimpses of pale forms deep in the water, which they were convinced were the *aije*.

The Salesians recount how Bororo over the years have independently identified hippopotamuses as *aije* (Albisetti and Venturelli 1962: 18), which was my informants' response to pictures of those animals, and also to those of manatees. The *aije* traditionally served as agents of the *aroe*'s collective anger with men's failures to accomplish their duties toward the souls. The Salesians' characterization of them as "a mysterious being, terrible, powerful and awesome, an extraordinary feline capable of causing the greatest harm to the Bororo" (1962: 18) summarizes contemporary attitudes succinctly if somewhat dramatically. The culminating moment of Bororo initiation occurs when the "*aije*" (the "masked" actors) attack the boys, menacing them with castration and other horrors, before revealing their true identities by speaking the name of the *aije* they incarnate. If the initiates show the least fear, their lives will be blighted and miserable. In the single initiation I witnessed, the boys gave every indication of controlled terror. The human representation of these beings itself involves considerable mystical risk and is undertaken with great care. The men, at least, are convinced that if a woman or uninitiated boy were to see any aspect of this ritual, and especially the bullroarers themselves, the consequences would be autonomously lethal. The *aije*, then, are the equivalents within the *aroe*'s realm of the *bope*'s poisonous snakes and alligators, and no less tangibly real menaces for being imagined.

The epistemological character of other *aroe* beings similar to the *aije* in their lack of correspondence to any manifest species is yet less specific and more subject to individual interpretation. These entities do not compose any coherent pantheon, at least not since the last *aroe etawa-are*, and Bororo descriptions of them struck me at times as being Ideas, uncongealed fragments of poetic thought. For example, one variety called Iworo are said to be huge mounds of leaves with no discernible permanent shape, agitated from within as if by an internal whirlwind, rustling away across the savannah to unknown ends. The Parabara are two thin unimaginably long "things" stretching up to the furthermost stars and producing a sort of dry, sharp clacking.[4] On hearing various groping attempts to describe them, I always had the image of Length. But any inventory of the commonly known *aroe* does not produce a catalogue of philosophical abstractions. Certain mountains in the upper São Lourenço have their *aroe*, as do such utilitarian implements as bowls and children's toys. Although the Bororo do not carry their totemic urge as far as do the Australians, collectivizing such phenomena as human mucus and sand (Worsley 1967), they are unsystematic and imaginative enough to challenge any analyst. Further, here far more than with other reaches of Bororo mind, I began to suspect that the more prominent "totemic" *aroe* had been devised not for intellectual reasons but for social ones. They seemed to be constructed for ease of representation and for the sake of gamelike ceremonials that could be played with them.

It is a matter of Bororo dogma that for each *aroe* there is some ceremony which can represent it, complete with songs detailing its attributes, costumes reproducing its essential features, movements imitating its own actions. The element of mimicry in these "representations" (a precise translation of the Bororo term for such ceremonies, *aroe etawuje*) should not be taken too literally. The actors in the *Aroe Adugo Etawujedu* ("Representation of the Jaguar's Soul") neither resemble nor imitate actual jaguars. *Aroe* ceremonies often personify such non-existent entities as the Aije and Parabara, which by their nature cannot be realistically portrayed. Further, these symbolic activities are finely discriminated according to their relative value in terms that refer ostensibly to their aesthetic qualities, more subtly to the status of the social units that bestow and perform them, but never to their utilitarian or symbolical significance outside the narrow context of *aroe* representations.

For example, the *aije* are associated with the Arore clan, and their various subforms with other clans of the Tugarege moiety. By costuming various actors belonging to the Exerae moiety, furnishing them with diverse bullroarers, and otherwise enabling them to personify the *aije*, the Arore and the rest of the Tugarege bestow a prestation upon the Exerae which allows them to marry any woman of the latter moiety. It is true that the Exerae actors "represent" the *aije* and take the risk of so incarnating them. But this danger is much less than the honor of becoming such a transcendent spirit. To such a prestation, the Exerae can only respond in metaphoric kind, enabling the Tugarege to "be" the Exerae's most glorious and preciously decorated *aroe*, those of the anteater or armadillo or jaguar. The beauty of the material adornments which re-create their nominal being lends them prestational significance equivalent to that of "being" a lethal *aije*.

An *aroe etawuje* ("representation of the souls")

The lack of literal portrayal expresses the assumption that the actors "become" *aroe*, nominal essences, never those less than perfect entities which are "real" members of that species. The playful aspects of the ceremonies, as well as their self-conscious aesthetic qualities, also involve just this assumption. The act of twirling a bullroarer more than a meter in length at the end of a long pole is itself perceived as much as an athletic feat as a sacred act. Many rituals have rules, such as never allowing the *Marido* (a huge cylinder of vegetable fibers that is the Bororo equivalent of the Ĝe racing logs) to touch the ground, which relate more to games than to religion. If the *aroe* provide transcendent categories, they also are the means whereby men interact for the sheer pleasures of sociality.

Whatever the uses the Bororo make of the *aroe*, these are dictated by tradition and never open to innovation and speculation. The utility of the *aroe* as principles of classification and modes of reciprocity would be destroyed by such freedom. For all of its mystery and esotericism, the realm of the *aroe* is finally knowable, determinate, unchanging. In this lies its power, opposed to the *bope*'s unpredictable flux. Bororo concepts of the sort of existence men have after death, when they themselves become essences, express this calm appeal of reason. The soul of the deceased is first conducted to one or the other of the two human villages in the underworld. He may freely choose which he wishes to settle eventually, but initially ancestral souls move frequently between the two. As the funeral cycle progresses, one or more of each clan's *aroe* are successively represented. The new soul is correspondingly conducted upon a long counterclockwise tour of the *aroe* universe, visiting in turn the domain of each clan's *aroe* forms. There is no precise correlation between this series of encounters and the ceremonies occurring in the deceased's funeral, only a rough parallelism that lacks any mystical efficacy. Most souls choose to visit longer with their own clan's *aroe* and with those of their father's clans. Or they may be simply interested in other sets of *aroe*; in any case, their journey is impossible to predict.

According to the *aroe etawara*, this tour is one of transcendent beauty, so marvelous that it nearly compensates for the loss of organic life. None of the *aroe*, including the ancestors' essences, have much of a physical existence: by definition they have no *raka*. They neither eat (or very little), nor copulate (or seldom), nor engage in those sex-linked actions of hunting and cooking. All is very quiet in the villages of the souls, with no quarrels or gossip or envy. Nothing ever changes there, and the essences pass their time brilliantly ornamented and costumed. This frozen peace seems to fascinate men the older they become but bores the young who are caught up in the exercise of their *raka*. The *aroe* are in every way the antithesis of the *bope* while yet complementing their powers. Timeless embodiments of categorical order, the *aroe* are the grounds of nominal definition. Human relationships with them derive as systematically from this character as do social transactions with the *bope* from their control of organic process.

## The *Aroe* as Natural Forms: Vehicles and Metamorphoses

The symmetry of the dyadic system opposing *bope* and *aroe* permeates all aspects of Bororo conceptual order and symbolic behavior. There are in nature certain creatures which embody aspects of each category's range of attributes: entities said to be Themselves *bope* and Themselves *aroe*. For those things which act as the messengers for the *bope* there is a comparable set similarly used by the *aroe*. If the *bope* move directly in this world in the guise of snakes and jaguars, the *aroe* can enter it in the form of harpy eagles, otters, and pumas, if not through the more potent *aije*. And just as the *bope ure* provide animate means for men to deal with the *bope*, a bounded group of heterogeneous creatures furnishes ways for society to relate to the *aroe*. Finally, since the *bope* are identified with such elemental processes as rain, fire, the heavens, and time, then the *aroe* ought to be associated with comparable natural principles.

The *bope* fructify all animate nature, except one portion: fish and other things that live under the water. These are under the control of the *aroe*. These, as the last section implied, seem given over to a marine environment, perhaps because rivers and other bodies of water are at the furthest remove from the celestial domain of the *bope*. Further, the Bororo appear to find that water creatures exist in ways alien to those dictating the existence of other forms of life. Birds and plants, in spite of their lack of external sexual glands, at least respond to seasonal rhythms, whereas fish reproduce themselves in ways and in measures nonperceptible to man. The *aroe*, then, are found to be intimately conjoined to rivers and lakes, and also to mountains, rocks, and pillars, which are not subject to temporal change. Cold and damp are therefore the *aroe*'s climatic mode, and some believe they cause cool weather. Rocks of whatever size are "of the *aroe*"; there is even an *aroe* representation called *Buturori-doge Aroe*, "The *Aroe* of the Falling Rocks" (Albisetti and Venturelli 1962: 146), a sort of Platonic counter to the *bope*'s *Aroe Kudu*. Finally, given the stress on the physical arrangement of the *aroe* discussed in the last section, it is apparent that they are the masters of spatial order. The principal rivers in Bororoland, especially the São Lourenço itself, tend to flow in an east–west direction, and *Meri*, the sun, the other indicator of "natural" direction, is among the *aroe* of the Bado Jeba Xebegiwuge, for all its manifestation of the *bope*.

Creatures that intimately participate with the *aroe*'s primordial elements are found to reflect various attributes of essence, in relative degrees and diverse manners. The animals which "show forth" *aroe* qualities to such a degree they are said to be Themselves *aroe* are generally but not always water birds, usually with an exclusive diet of small fish, beloved by the *aroe* as food, and often completely white, just as much the predominant color of the *aroe* as black is of the *bope* (Table 9.2). (Bororo folklore holds that faraway to the west there are very high mountains covered with a white substance, very cold indeed; this is clearly "a thing of the *aroe*.") However, birds and to some extent mammals which combine several colors, especially those of red, yellow, and blue, are also associated for this chromatic range with the *aroe*. Beauty, especially in pied forms, is very much a basic quality of the souls, just as the *bope* are the quintessence of ugliness. Variegated birds, especially macaws, provide the feathers decorating nearly all the objects with which the Bororo represent the *aroe*.

Table 9.1 shows that by no means all aquatic birds are thought to personify *aroe* principles. Many waterfowl have no connection with the *aroe*, such as ducks and various water chickens (*Porphyrula* and *Gallinula* sp.). Others, such as the herons, egrets, ibises, flamingos, and darters (biguá), are said to be "companions of the *aroe*"; they are diminished, less intensely significant, versions of the water birds considered *aroe remawu*. Clearly only some kind of intersection of combinatory attributes justifies the classification of a bird as an *aroe*. As with prior sets, only a family resemblance connects these birds, and so there are various kinds and degrees of such intersections. Terns, plovers, and especially the pied lap-

Table 9.1. *Aroe Remawu*: Animals "Themselves *Aroe*"

| Bororo | Portuguese/English | Scientific | Specific Associations with the *Aroe* |
|---|---|---|---|
| 1. *Tawie* | Gaviota, terns | *Larideos Larus* sp. | Habitat and marked black-white plumage |
| 2. *Raproepore* | Mexeriqueira, pied lapwing | *Hoploxypterus cayanum* | Habitat and black-white plumage |
| 3. *Tamigi* | Anhuma, horned screamer | *Anhima cornuta* | Habitat, black-white plumage, "walks" on water, "horns," call |
| 4. *Tagae* | Tachã, southern screamer | *Chauna torquata* | Habitat, black-white plumage, a "little *tamigi*" |
| 5. *Baxekoguio* | Tuiuiu, wood-stork | *Mycteria americana* | Habitat, form, and white plumage |
| 6. *Baxe Kigadureu* | Jabiru (?) | *Jabiru mycteria* | Habitat, form, and white plumage |
| 7. *Kugarure* | Batuira, plovers | Charadiidae fam. | Habitat and plumage, flight |
| 8. *Monoko* | Harceja, giant snipe (?) | *Gallinàgo undulata* | Habitat and black-white plumage |
| 9. *Nabure* | Ararapiranga, red-and-green macaw | *Ara chloroptera* | Variegated plumage, diet, nests in rocky pillars, cry |
| 10. *Kuido* | Arara, blue-and-yellow macaw | *Ara ararauna* | As 9, except for nests |
| 11. *Baxe Otoboareu* | Colhereiro, rose-ate spoonbill | *Ajaia ajaja* | Pink, white, and red plumage, habitat |
| 12. *Baxe Mikoreu* | Garca, white necked heron | *Ardea cocoi* | Habitat, white-black plumage* |
| 13. *Kerekere* | Ararinha, red-bellied macaw | *Ara manilata* | Plumage, changes into seductive girl |
| 14. *Kiakorogo* | Araca, chestnut-fronted macaw | *Ara severa* | Plumage, swamp-forest habitat |

*Some informants did not consider this heron to be fully an *aroe remawu* but rather one of their "companions." Contemporary Bororo also eat members of this species but not any of the others in this class.

wing are distinguished by the absolute clarity and sharp contrast of their black-white markings, comparable only to the plumage of birds of rapine. But the Charadriidae are preeminently birds of river and lake banks, at least those in this family counted as *aroe*.

The screamers are distinguished by their clear black-white feather patterns and by their uncanny ability to "walk" on water, owing to their very large feet and the matted aquatic vegetation they frequent. The Bororo also find their clarion hoots to resemble the cries uttered by the *aroe* when celebrating their arrival or departure, and imitated by the *ika*, a trumpetlike instrument played at correspondingly appropriate ritual moments. I was for some time confused by informants' descriptions of the anhuma's "horns," actually long quills issuing from the bird's head and the leading junction of each wing. These adornments are not credited with any function by the Bororo, nor are they put to ceremonial ends; they simply contribute to the bird's generally extraordinary character.

The two kinds of storks, on the other hand, are so self-evidently *aroe* in all their being that the Bororo gave no specific set of attributes: "They just are *aroe*." Their large, ungainly white bodies, heavy black bills, curiously folded necks, exceedingly long legs, bare heads, the patch of red at the base of the jabiru's neck; these are clearly birds marked with extraordinary significance. I am less sure why the *monoko*, which I believe to be the giant snipe, is considered an *aroe*. It is something like the plovers in the clarity of its markings and its habitat, and this species is much larger than other members of the family. Informants were quite specific on the *aroe* features of the roseate spoonbill. Its magnificent pink, white, and red plumage, as well as its curious bill, make it definitely "of the souls."

Macaws have multiple associations with the *aroe* (Crocker 1977b) and appear in many different contexts to express various aspects of the souls. The characteristics underlying their classification as *aroe remawu* are first their diet of fruits and nuts, preferred foods of the *aroe*, and second, as mentioned earlier, their mottled plumage which decorates all ornaments representing the *aroe*. One species, the *nabure* or red-green macaw, is also noted for its habit of nesting in the rocky niches and caves that the Bororo perceive as openings into the underworld of the *aroe*. The Bororo also domesticate macaws, along with parrots and parakeets, for two reasons: first, as living, self-replenishing banks of feathers, a sort of money for the Bororo; and, second, because the *aroe* of dead relatives are thought to shelter occasionally in these pets when visiting the community. The two motives reinforce one another, for the parents or immediate consanguines of a just dead Bororo have ritual need of macaw feathers for all the decorations involved in the funeral cycle, and the recently deceased are thought to visit their survivors often. While in this form they may enjoy the carefully prepared vegetable food given to the pet macaws and accomplish other ends (see below). So, as the Bororo say, "The 'mothers of the *aroe'* have macaws instead of children," which neatly summarizes both the sociological and cosmological status of these birds.

The *aroe remawu* birds are treated with respect by the Bororo. The storks and screamers in particular seem to arouse a certain unease not unlike that occasioned by vultures and other avian incarnations of the *bope*. While not avoiding them, the Bororo do not go out of their way to encounter them either. Nor again, like the *bope remawu*, are the Themselves *aroe* ever eaten. "Macaw eater" is usually a mild insult, but in certain contexts (a recent death in the family) it is regarded as a serious offense, hinting at symbolic cannibalism. But unlike the *bope remawu*, certain of the *aroe* birds may be killed, in order to gain their feathers. Most Bororo appear to do this with considerable reluctance. No supernatural sanctions follow such a killing but, as several informants said, it seems pointless to hunt such beautiful things. However, faced with urgent ceremonial need, a man may be forced to do so in order to gain the materials necessary for carrying out his social and ritual obligations.

This points up the critical difference between these birds and the beings incarnating *bope* attributes, which itself reflects the asymmetrical social relationships to the *aroe* and to the *bope*. Macaw feathers and waterbird down are essential elements for social interaction and for the ceremonies establishing collective identity. Life cannot go on without pursuit of the definitions and reciprocal modes provided by the *aroe*, and, although it could not exist at all without the *bope*, the only things of theirs consciously sought are their "foods." Or, as one shaman expressed it, "The *bope* are inside, and the *aroe* outside."

There is a crucial implication in the preceding: the Bororo utilize the categories and things provided by the *aroe* to act toward each other, rather than toward the *aroe* themselves. Another set of animals involved with the *aroe* provides at least a conceptual way for society to represent a human soul's relation to the totality of *aroe*. This set involves one of the most widely known pieces of Bororo dogma, having been used by Levy-Bruhl in his analysis of the "primitive" attitude toward death (1910). It is still a central tenet of Bororo cosmology, set aside by mystery and the "obligatoriness" which characterizes collective belief.

During the initial acts of the funeral cycle, the deceased's soul is told to gain vengeance upon the forces which slew its human envelope. To accomplish *mori-xe* (revenge) the soul is instructed to enter serially a jaguar, a macaw, an otter, a hawk or harpy eagle, and an ocelot. In these forms the soul may eat all the *bope ure* with complete impunity. As a jaguar and ocelot, it may consume tapir, wild pigs, capivara, and deer; as an eagle, the rhea and seriema; as a macaw, all the fruits and tubers among the *bope ure*; and as an otter, the three kinds of fish. The ritual instructions to the new soul make it very clear that now the *bope* can no longer harm the soul. It can ignore all the rules formerly constraining its human possessor in its actions toward the food of the *bope*, and whose transgression ultimately led to its human death. The irony of this revenge is not lost on the Bororo, any more than its quality of circularity, of closure of a logical form. The dogmatic formula is so appealing in itself that no ritual action accompanies these injunctions, nor do the Bororo seek to find any empirical confirmation that the soul has accomplished its revenge. At most, if the deceased's household possesses pet macaws it may seek to feed them with corn gruel, stewed fruits from the *bope ure*, and tubers flavored with wild honey. Otherwise the soul's metamorphoses have no social consequences. Partly this is due to the aesthetically perfect "justice" of the formula; partly it comes from the tangible ways the soul's death is avenged by its human replacement, acting on behalf of the collectivity. Informants did not insist upon their belief in every soul's accomplishment of these transformations. Rather, they said, "It *should* be so."

Although the Bororo are usually extremely careful to designate vehicles of symbolic meaning, they are vague in their characterization of the species used for metamorphosed revenge. The creatures named in the ritual instructions are only "examples" said informants. The explicit justification customarily given for the inclusion of animals in this set is that their diet habitually consists of *bope ure*. But many persons admitted that macaws show no particular predilection for the *bope*'s fruits and vegetables. Otters are by no means noted for their depredations among giant catfish. The Bororo are aware that the usual prey of ocelots is small birds and rodents, not deer and wild pigs. If any bird were able to kill the large rhea, it would be the harpy eagle, not the much smaller *kurugugwa* (caracara, *Milvago chimango*) cited in the ritual text. But all these instruments of revenge have other, multiple associations with the *aroe*. *Aroe* of all varieties, and not just the newly dead, enter domesticated and wild macaws both to eat and copulate.[5]

On the other hand, the giant river otter strikes the Bororo as so magnificent that some persons say, "It is almost an *aroe* itself," in the sense of being an ideal essential form, a "totem." They remark on the beauty of its form and pelt; its grace and speed upon land and in water, antithetical domains; its exclusively fish diet, invulnerability to all predators (especially the jaguar and alligator), and humanlike curiosity. The otter appears in myths as a riverine competitor with man. In one myth (Colbacchini and Albisetti 1942: 259–60; Lévi-Strauss 1969: 95–97) the women of a community take otters for their lovers, in exchange for prestations of fish. Learning of this betrayal, men successfully wage war upon the otters but are murdered in turn by their chagrined wives. Representation of *Ipie Aroe*, "The Soul of Otter," is one of the most important *aroe* ceremonials, owned by that preeminent Tugarege clan which also possesses the *aroe* of the *aije*, the Arore. Many of the same associations exist between the jaguar and the collectivity of souls. It is apparent, then, that something more than these creatures' imagined diets makes them suitable for the soul's personalistic revenge. This is their function as society's own instruments of retaliation against the *bope*, the "animals of revenge" (*marege mori-xe*) described next. The doctrine of the soul's transmigrations does not provide instruments through which living men can mediate between the *aroe* and the *bope*. This doctrine is a sort of working out of an aesthetic logic, a kind of poetics, rather than a semantic precept for action.

## "Foods" of the *Aroe*: The *Marege Mori-xe* ("Revenge Animals")

I argued earlier that the *bope ure* stand metaphorically for one dimension of man's nature: his organic being, and the capacities, risks, and disciplines this existence imposes upon him. They represent how and with what consequences human beings are themselves simultaneously *bope*, who kill, cook, and procreate, and the food of the *bope*. But man is also *aroe*, pure form and soul, a name and a categorical place within a larger class, itself part of the eightfold system that orders all reality. This dialectical opposition between transcendent nominal form and organic power to alter physical being is the human paradox: the "vital soul." To confront it, society requires not just human organization and conceptual order but sets of animate beings external to social existence which can serve as instruments through which humanity can transform its own contradictions. Since these are twofold, the *bope ure* provide for relations with one aspect of the paradox, man's destructive creativity, but another is needed for resolving form's involvement in living substance. This is comprised by the set of entities called by the Bororo *marege mori-xe*, literally "animals of revenge."

Upon the death of any Bororo who has received a name, a ceremonial representative must be appointed for him or her from the opposite moiety. Failure to do so is inconceivable; the institution of this representation by the culture heroes Bakororo and Itubore is regarded as *the* constitutive act for Bororo society. It defines the central relationship between the moieties, establishes man's position as the pivot in the dynamic equilibrium between the principles of *bope* and of *aroe*, and asserts society's symbolic power over natural fact. The human agent responsible for all this is called the *aroe maiwu*, the "new soul."[6] This is the man who kills game which his ritual "mother" and "father" distribute as evidence of the deceased's continuing presence in the collectivity. This office is a grave responsibility, and failure to discharge its duties is the most serious moral offense recognized by the Bororo. Obligations of the status include personifying the deceased during its funeral and in later ritual contexts, hunting on its behalf in the ceremonial expeditions described earlier, and carrying out some of the dead person's social responsibilities and privileges. (I must use the neuter gender here because, although the representative is always male—only men can transact with the *aroe*—he impersonates both dead men and dead women. For a multitude of reasons, which should by now be clear, gender does not exist in the realm of the *aroe*.) But the representative's central duty is to slay one of the "animals of revenge." Until he has done this, he is no proper replacement. The *aroe* become angry, the deceased's soul itself, some allege, is not properly incorporated into the afterlife in that it does not become an *aroe* essence, nor are its survivors assuaged of their grief.

The killing of the "animal of revenge" is therefore an opposed inversion to the ritual transmission of the *bope ure*. The first creates symbolic form, the second ensures organic life; the first destroys to no utilitarian end, since the revenge animals are never eaten, the second removes an inherent pollution so that the foods can be safely consumed. The slayer of the revenge animals acts on behalf of society and the deceased; the hunter of *bope* food, for his own and his immediate relatives' private enjoyment. The creatures treated in such coherently different manners should likewise systematically vary in their family resemblances and metamorphical identifications with man's conditions.

The set of animals which are *marege mori-xe* is almost as sharply bounded and as widely known as that group comprising the *bope ure*. Children of five or six are as knowledgeable about one as about the other. Though they may forget a minor species or two, they never confuse the sets. Certainly both receive almost automatic responses from any mature Bororo. That is, when any of the creatures in one or the other classification is sighted, attention is riveted, all other activities immediately cease, and every faculty is devoted to killing the animal. As with the *bope ure*, there is a hierarchy of ritual importance among the revenge animals. Ideally the representative slays one of the first six species given in Table 9.2 and then preferably either of the large felines or the harpy eagle.

He receives in compensation from the deceased's relatives an elaborate body painting, a decorated bow, and up to a dozen ornamented arrows. Such bows, *boeiga o-iagareu*, and arrows, *butuie*, exist almost solely for this prestational use and should be employed by the *aroe maiwu* only during the ceremonial hunts in which he represents the deceased (cf. Albisetti and Venturelli 1962: 483–99 and 932–53 for descriptions and illustrations of these weapons). The representative is also given several

Table 9.2. *Marege Mori-Xe*: "Animals of Revenge"

| Bororo | Vernacular | Scientific | Parts Utilized for Prestations |
|---|---|---|---|
| 1. *adugo* | Jaguar | *Panthera onca* | Skin, teeth, claws |
| 2. *aroe exeba* | Harpy eagle | *Harpia harpyja* | Beak, claws, wing feathers |
| 3. *aigo* | Puma | *Felis concolor* | Skin, teeth, claws |
| 4. *aipobureu* | Jaguartirica, ocelot | *Felis pardalis* | Teeth, claws |
| 5. *awagadari (awogodori)* | "Large" ocelot | *Felis pardalis* | Teeth, claws |
| 6. *rea (rie)* | Guará, maned wolf | *Chrysocyon brachyurus* | Teeth |
| 7. *okwa* | Bush dog | *Speothos venaticus* | Teeth |
| 8. *ratugereu* | Margay | *Felis wiedii* | Teeth, claws |
| 9. *ipoxereu* | Irara, tayra | *Tayra barbara* | Teeth |
| 10. *ieragadu (barakaia)* | Graxaim, South American fox | *Dusicyon brasiliensis* | Teeth |
| 11. *aimeareu* | Gato-mourisco, jaguarundi | *Felis yagouaroundi* | Teeth, claws |
| 12. *bakure* | Night monkey | *Aotes* sp. | Teeth |
| 13. *moribo* | Savannah fox | *Cerdocyon thous* | Teeth |
| 14. *meridabo* | Furaõ, grison | *Grison vitatus* | Teeth |
| 15. *ierarai (xinabe)* | Guaxinim, raccoon | *Procyon cancrivorus* | Teeth |
| 16. *kurugugwa* | Chimango, caracara | *Milvago chimango* | Beak, claws, wing feathers |
| 17. *kugu* | Spectacled owl | *Pulsatrix perspicillata* | Beak, claws |
| 18. *kugu xoreu* | Black banded owl | *Ciccaba virgata* | Beak, claws |
| 19. *bokuruwodu* | Great horned owl | *Budo virginianus* | Beak, claws |
| 20. *tagogo* | Crested owl | *Lophostrix cristata* | Beak, claws |
| 21. *bi* | Burrowing owl | *Speotyto cunicularia* | Beak, claws |
| 22. *kaikai* | Owl (?) | | Beak, claws |
| 23. *makao* | Macauã, snake hawk or laughing falcon | *Herpethotheres cachinnans* | Beak, claws |
| 24. *koxaga* | Saracura, slaty-breasted wood rail | *Aramides saracura* | Beak, claws |

necklaces or headdresses, all these gifts being made in the particular style belonging to the deceased's name-group and subclan. He may use these ornaments and all others owned by that social unit until the end of his own life. This is the *only* way in which corporate property may be alienated; it indicates both the way the representative assumes certain aspects of the defunct's social persona and how he is compensated for such a task and privilege.

The other animals and birds among the "revenge animals" are viewed as partial versions of the jaguars and harpy eagles and are admissable as revenge animals on this ground alone. When they are killed and given to the deceased's clan, they are regarded as only installments on the representative's obligation to kill one of the first six species. For their killing the slayer is rewarded just by a red body painting with some simple facial design, and perhaps an easily made ornament or two. Further, any person in the opposite moiety to the deceased's can kill and give one of these lesser revenge animals to the survivors. It is considered appropriate that both male and female relatives of the *aroe maiwu* should do this, but also highly moral for someone with nothing other than a cross-moiety relation to the defunct. Such prestations are very frequent, and sometimes involve unavenged deaths a generation or more old. Only when one of the large felines or the harpy eagle is finally killed by the *aroe maiwu* is this generalized obligation to compensate the deceased's social unit finally and definitively terminated. Then the representative and the deceased receive new names, referring to some aspect of the jaguar or eagle actually killed. Until this point the latter has been nameless, since it is forbidden to utter a dead person's name. But in this new "name of revenge" the defunct's *aroe* is immortalized, locked into nominal perpetuity among the other *aroe*-names of its clan. Now the long chant *Xibaitowado*, which announces to all the *aroe* that a human death has been avenged, is sung together by all the clan chiefs. The *aroe maiwu*'s special relationship to the deceased's clan and to his ritual parents is by no means terminated but instead continues in a new dimension involving the replication of certain aspects of the defunct's social being. The prestations received by the *aroe maiwu* at this time, the decorated weapons and ornaments, are all called *mori-xe*, "revenge," themselves. They are a complementary reciprocity for the representative's act in killing and giving the "revenge" animal. All of this indicates that what is being given and received is not just simple vengeance but something rather more complicated.

In Chapter 6 I described how one of the central principles ordering Bororo transactions with the natural world, and with the *bope* which provide its animating force, was bound up in the idea of obtaining *mori-xe* for any hurt inflicted upon a Bororo by natural agencies. Such "revenge" always involves the killing of the harming creature, or any member of that species, by a Bororo belonging to the moiety opposite the victim's. *Mori-xe*, as I explained earlier, must be extracted in order to restore the equilibrium between nature and society which the beast's aggression against man has endangered. A human being's death is the ultimate wrong of nature against society and, accordingly, demands more complex symbolic redress for the symmetry of rights to be reestablished. There is a qualitative difference between the simple compensation of killing a being which has injured someone and the slaying of a jaguar to avenge the death of a man, in spite of the common logic behind both series of actions. The point deserves careful elaboration, for since Steinen's initial description in 1894, the Bororo practice of "revenge animals" has figured importantly in theories of the social attitude toward death (Levy-Bruhl 1910, Hertz 1960).

First, every death among contemporary Bororo is ascribed to the *bope*, who are supposed to avenge some offense of the deceased against their rights. It might seem appropriate then for society to kill a *bope*. But the *bope* are immortal and incapable of being harmed in the slightest by human action. Further, their most direct "representatives" among natural forms, vultures and alligators, have no relevance whatsoever to "animal revenge." When I suggested that one might just as well kill either of these creatures as a jaguar, I was met first with incredulity and then with rebukes suggesting that all the time and effort spent on my Bororo education had been a total waste. Two points enter here. The *bope* are no more "part" of the natural world than the *aroe*; both are mystical categories or aspects of being, not "things." Some entities summarize in their perceptible qualities certain dimensions of these conditions, but they are not equivalent to, and hence not substitutable for, either variety of spirit.

Next, the fact that "a Bororo has died" is a state of disorder with different implications from those of "a man has been bitten by a snake," "a bow has been stolen," "a woman has been raped," even though *mori-xe* provides the common mode through which all four conditions are restored to harmonious order. The central principle of *mori-xe* is that through it a prior condition of balanced symmetry is restored by a compensation equivalent to the harm done or debt incurred. The loss occasioned by the permanent destruction of one of society's members must be restituted by some thing comparable to the dead human being. Vultures and alligators are not so comparable. They are too *"bope-like,"* while man for all his aspect of organic being is also nominal form, an *aroe*. The issue becomes similar to that posed for the *bope ure*: in what ways are the *marege mori-xe* comparable to man, and how are these consistent with the Bororo view that their slaying constitutes revenge against the *bope*?

For the first question it is not necessary to work through the same lengthy analysis that *jerimaga* required. When asked why some animals were *marege mori-xe* and not others, the Bororo said quite flatly, "Because of their teeth." Nearly all adult informants went on to associate this anatomical feature with the animals' diet: the teeth and claws, or beaks and talons, of meat-eaters were clearly similar and as a class different from those of noncarnivores. Here an analyst must use an indigenous conceptual principle as explanation for a classification, because there are numerous other social facts supporting the carnivore interpretation. First, the slayer is obliged to prepare a necklace from the revenge animal's teeth and claws, ornament it in the way owned by his social group, and present it to the deceased's ritual "mother" (cf. Albisetti and Venturelli 1962: 360–61, for illustrations). These necklaces are very highly valued by modern Bororo, many of whom will not part with them even though all other traditional property is readily sold to non-Bororo. As for the birds among the *mori-xe*, their beaks and, in the case of the harpy eagle and caracara, their talons are bound to a kind of gourd whistle made by the deceased's ritual "father."

This whistle, decorated in the style owned by the deceased's subclan and name-group, is called the *aroe ekuie powari*, "gourd whistle of the soul's breath" (Albisetti and Venturelli 1962: 47–54). This is a valued symbol of the deceased's continuing existence among the living through his or her ritual representative. It is played by the representative on occasions when he is acting on behalf of the deceased and is always carried by him in the *aroe* contexts, such as the collective hunts. It is otherwise kept by the ritual "mother" in a special basket lined with duck down, and the Bororo believe that the soul itself may occasionally shelter in this basket, especially when it is damp and cold. The feathers and hides of major revenge animals also receive considerable ritual stress: the jaguar skin is painted with designs linked to the deceased's clan *aroe* totems, and it may be worn by the clan chief during rituals. The eagle's and hawk's feathers are distributed according to a precise formula to subclan chiefs among the Exerae moiety (who have these birds among their *aroe* totems) and made into ornaments of great ceremonial importance (Albisetti and Venturelli 1962: 108–11). With the passage of time these perishable items all disappear, but I have seen worn tooth necklaces and blackened gourd whistles given allegedly in recompense generations ago, for the death of a great-grandparent. When eventually the vegetable components decay, they are renewed; these objects constitute the sole traditional inheritance transmitted from mother to daughter.

A second reason for crediting the Bororo's own perception of their classificatory principle is even more convincing. Steinen (1942) reported seeing the Bororo he contacted in the 1880s wearing human lower jaw bones around their necks. My own informants confirmed the traditional correctness of this practice. If a Bororo is killed by another human being, whether in warfare or in murder, the malefactor must be killed as *mori-xe* instead of a jaguar or harpy eagle. In such a case, any one of the enemy would serve as recompense. The Bororo were ending a century's fighting with Brazilians in the 1880s, so that the jaws Steinen saw were probably theirs. In the rare case of intratribal murder, the criminal himself had to be killed, and his lower jaw bone given to the ritual parents of the victim.[7] In both instances the revenge-killing was called *marege mori-xe*. Just as man is implicitly included among the *bope ure*, so too he is a carnivore, and the supreme mode of compensation for a human death.

Next, the indigenous rationale for the inclusion of some species among the *marege mori-xe* and the exclusion of others follows consistently the carnivorous principle, although in terms of Bororo perceptions of reality. In each case, an animal's or bird's appearance in this set is justified on the grounds of the "family resemblance" between its dentition or talons and beak and those of the jaguar and harpy eagle. The list of *marege mori-xe* includes most of the carnivorous mammals common in Bororo territory. When I asked why the night monkey appeared in the list, the response from numerous informants was the same: "Its teeth are like those of the jaguar." The Bororo recognize that nearly all species of monkeys are omnivorous but say they seldom kill warm-blooded animals. However, they insist that, on the basis of its dentition alone, the night-monkey must be largely carnivorous and hence is a revenge animal. On the same grounds coati are excluded from the list, simply because their teeth are perceived as unlike those of meat-eaters. Fish-eaters are not considered carnivorous, for a carnivorous diet consists in Bororo opinion of warm-blooded creatures. Therefore, otters and alligators are excluded regardless of their symbolic importance in other domains.

Here as in previous taxonomies, the particular set of attributes relevant to the classification at hand, the perceptual reasons for the "family resemblance" among the entities categorized in one unit, operate independently of those utilized in other taxonomies. The fact that the owls, the snake hawk, and the wood rail serve as omens of the *bope* is not relevant in the least to their appearance among the *marege mori-xe*. It is true, nonetheless, that the last two birds, and especially the wood rail, seem to be inconsistent with the rest of the class. Snakes are in no way perceived as mammals, nor is the wood rail's diet thought to consist of anything besides small aquatic insects. The latter's bill and claws were recognized by the Bororo as most "unlike" those of the harpy eagle. I can only explain these two anomalies on the grounds that their association with death, and central importance as *bope* omens, as outlined at the conclusion of the seventh chapter, must account for their presence among the *marege mori-xe*. This is a lame explanation, and inconsistent with the analytical principles otherwise used here, which stress the independence of each taxonomy's logic. My only consolation is that the Bororo regard these two species as very minor revenge indeed.

But the two kinds of animals which serve as the definitional source for all the *marege mori-xe* receive additional Bororo attention for their status not just as carnivores, but as the only natural beings capable of destroying man himself. On this ground the jaguar and harpy eagle are featured in myths, ceremonies, and ritual property. Their slaying and the distribution of their bodies is accompanied by elaborate symbolic action and is governed by very precise traditional rules.[8] Killing a jaguar is the culminative act of a hunter's career, and the mediation of both kinds of spirits, *bope* and *aroe*, is sought to ensure the victory of the human over the animal. I do not wish to exaggerate the importance of this deed among the Bororo, least of all to imbue it with a spurious romanticism. But no less should I portray it as less than what it means to this society. Bororo rarely seek out jaguars deliberately, except when they are recent *aroe maiwu*, representatives of the dead. And then they always do so alone. In the contest man and jaguar are regarded as approximately equal, depending on the idiosyncratic condition of each. Slaying a jaguar is final and convincing proof of a man's *raka*, as I suppose the opposite outcome is of the jaguar's. For this reason alone aging men, and those thought prematurely weak in *raka*, are never willingly appointed as a defunct's representative.

Nor are the dangers in this procedure entirely physical. The jaguar is beloved of the *bope*, and they may enable it to extract its own postmortem revenge. Therefore its tongue (and that of an harpy eagle) must be cut out as soon as possible after death, a cigarette smoked over the corpse, and the intervention of both kinds of shamans sought as soon as possible. As for harpy eagles, the Bororo see them as a celestial counterpart of the jaguar. Their Bororo name, *aroe exeba*, means "killer of souls." A myth relates how harpy eagles once slew many Bororo, and even now the Bororo insist that harpy eagles can kill and bear off young children and seriously wound adult men. Informants said, "The beak and talons of the eagle are as the teeth and claws of a jaguar. With them it kills whatever it wishes." Both creatures are regarded as being as beautiful as they are deadly. Once during fieldwork a caracara, which the Bororo say is the "younger brother" of the harpy eagle on account of its diminished reproduction of that bird's appearance, was killed, most fortuitously, because it is extremely rare in Mato Grosso. The men present in the village spent most of an afternoon examining it, correlating its parts to traditional formulas, praising its appearance, and generally giving themselves over to what I can only call an aesthetic experience. As one might guess, jaguars and eagles are almost extinct in the middle São Lourenço. This, however, diminishes neither their symbolic nor their ritual importance.[9]

The centrality of the jaguar and harpy eagle in Bororo thought revolves around the way they serve as natural counterparts to man's capacity to slay his own kind. (The Bororo find that men alone among animals kill other members of their species.) This dual capacity for reproduction and destruction makes them in one perspective *bope* and in another *aroe*, and therefore "human." For like these two creatures, man must destroy the animate world to maintain the transcendent immortality of the nominal categories which he and his dependent society embody. If the *bope ure* stand for that organic capacity of man to perpetuate a new generation and in so doing to waste totally his own ability to survive, then the *marege mori-xe* represent human ability to transform the living world by killing its members but, in so doing, to transmogrify them into immortal principles. The analogy might read *bope ure*: man the destroyer-creator; *marege mori-xe*: man the destroyer-classifier. In a sense, only symbolic reasons compel man to hunt out and kill things like himself; he cannot consume them, as he does the substance of tapir and of "woman," who uses herself up in cooking for him, in producing babies. The Bororo do not say that jaguars and eagles prefer to eat human flesh, only that they attack in self-defense—not a poor way to characterize man's rationale for killing other men, as well as their justification for ensuring the integrity of society (and perhaps their own selves) by the killing of other carnivores.

Furthermore, if the *bope ure* serve as the symbol of man as victim, and hence are much less than embodiments of the *bope*'s characteristic as victimizer, then the *marege mori-xe* are representations of man as actor, and hence much more than incarnations of the *aroe*'s attribute of symbolizer. By no means coincidentally, the Bororo discover that all the *marege mori-xe* are somehow beautiful, albeit in a deadly way that parallels human attractiveness. The jaguar's dappled combination of yellow and black, the eagle's just as mottled black and white, make them a lethal parallel to the macaw's and dourado's innocent iridescence of less dramatic and opposed colors. The grace and elegance of these animals' movements are also remarked and contrasted to the ungainly hopping of vultures, or the stiff awkwardness of herons and flamingos. In their physical being jaguars and eagles mirror forth all the power of luminous form but add to it their capacity for destruction. Only man also approximates this physical paradox, that is, to be at once a perfect synthesis of *aroe* and of *bope*: a vital soul.

Nor are the *bope ure* lacking in attributes of the *aroe*. The tapir recurs constantly in myth and ritual, and within the context of the *aroe* shaman's attributes, as a figure of the vulnerability of form to the forces of destruction and decay, and at the same time of the renewal of form. The *aroe* shaman has the power to transform himself, or send his *aroe*, into many different creatures, but his most usual vehicle is a tapir. In this form he allows "himself," as a tapir, to be hunted and killed by the Bororo during their collective ritual hunts. If he is clever and has the aid of the *aroe*, this death does not harm the shaman's own self, and he can repeat his generosity over and over. And the *aroe shaman* is the embodiment of the *aroe*'s capacity to name and to order the flux of organic process. In one sense, what the Bororo seem to be expressing here is their confidence that as long as the "Aroe" of Tapir is held in men's minds, there will always be tapirs in spite of jaguars and men and other *bope* who must live by killing them. Much the same argument can be made for those lovely and vulnerable creatures, the deer, as well as the rhea and seriema and the Bororo themselves!

The pattern of the central elements in Bororo zoological symbolism, and the way these are employed for transactions with the spirit world, is now complete. (See diagram.) In the continuum of expression that living things give to the *aroe* and *bope*, two sets of creatures occupy a special central position due to their capacity to embody two interdependent paradoxes resulting from the synthesis of these opposed principles in themselves, and in man. Through their actions toward the *bope ure*, the Bororo symbolize the necessity of rules governing the control of organic process, especially that of sexuality. Through the dictates of this process, the world of particular being must be destroyed, but, through its rules, beings reproduce themselves. In the *marege mori-xe* the converse of the same idea is worked out. By killing one of these animals, themselves destroyers of living things, a human death is not just "revenged" but the immortality of his name soul, his nominal form, is assured. It lives on through the gourd whistles embellished with the eagle's beak, the necklace of the jaguar's claws. And the human representative ensures the continuing organic life of the deceased's relatives by killing for them the *bope*

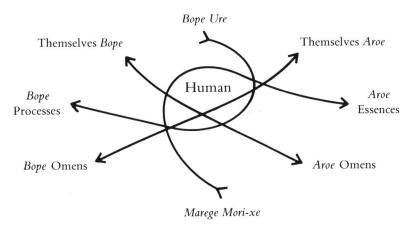

Pattern of the central elements
in Bororo zoological symbolism

*ure*.[10] With this sustenance the ritual "father" and "mother" can go on to breed new life. Killing a jaguar is not some petty "tit for tat" against the *bope*, but the proof that man can master the world of organic form, by a combination of conceptual activity and physical action, which ends a predator's existence for sheerly symbolic motives. I sometimes think that as the most basic implicit *bope* food is man, so the Bororo might long for the past days when a truly suitable *morege mori-xe*, another human being, an *aroe*, might be killed: it makes for better poetics, and for more vital souls.

# 10

⟨≈⟩

# Initiation and Powers
# of the *Aroe* Shaman

If the *marege mori-xe* furnish the
agencies through which man accomplishes his basic structural obligations toward the *aroe*, the shaman of the *aroe* is the mediator who ensures
all other modes of communication between society and this class of spiritual beings. The antithetical complementarity of his attributes and functions to those of the shaman of the *bope* is little short of overwhelming.
But then nothing less might be expected from the dyadic Bororo.

The material given here was obtained from informants who had
known shamans of the *aroe*. Much came from Celilo, the *bari* described in
Chapter 8 who has mystical access to the soul of an *aroe* shaman and who
fulfills some of the ceremonial duties of this specialist. I was able to
gather information on the social affiliations and personal abilities of five
historic *aroe* shamans, but here, as generally with shamans of both kinds,
material tends to be "socialized" and often amounts to a collective
representation.

The first intimation that one is being sought out by the *aroe* occurs
during the chanting of certain songs especially associated with the souls.
Such are the *Oyego*, actually a complex cycle of chants sung all night
before each collective hunt, and the *Aroia Kurireu*, a kind of social anthem
in which figure descriptions of the clans' *aroe*. Suddenly while singing the
potential shaman feels a chill creeping up from the stomach and into the

chest. Other sources indicate that he alternately or simultaneously smells the odor of rotting corpses, and of the urucu paste and resin used to decorate their bones (Albisetti and Venturelli 1962: 119). My informants said that perhaps this was true, but they considered it more likely that such smells would be experienced later in the shaman's initiation into the ways of the *aroe*. Even then, the *jerimaga* ("stench") of corpses is something "of the *bope*," whereas the *kurireu* ("perfume") of urucu and resin is the characteristic aroma of the *aroe*, so that the former cannot be considered any privileged manifestation of these spirits.

The dreams begin soon after this initial contact with the *aroe*. In them the dreamer finds himself accompanied by a small child, around eight or ten (categorically an asexual being), always beautifully decorated with facial paintings, armbands, and necklaces. Together they walk down a wide clean road, toward a large water bird that suddenly changes into a person when they near it. Or the dreamer finds himself and the child floating along just above the bottom of the river, surrounded by fish that change into people, and then back to fish. Sometimes, as with the *bari*, the future shaman of the souls may see in these dreams various things that later actually occur. Nearly always these involve the success of a collective fishing expedition, or the performance of a particular *aroe* representation. Again, the dreamer must not tell anyone of these experiences lest the *aroe* withdraw from him, making him very sick.

After numerous dreams and repeated sensations of cold and "faintness" during *aroe* ceremonies, the shaman finally has a crucial dream experience. He seems to be hunting, accompanied by the "child" (his disguised *aroe* familiar) when down the trail appears a huge *aije*. Normally, in waking life, the sight of one of these monsters is an infallible omen that the viewer or one of his immediate family will soon die, killed by the *aroe*. This one is huge, black, covered with warty cracked skin like a toad's. Voices are calling, "Run away, the *aije* is ugly and horrible, it will eat you up." The child tells the dreamer not to be afraid, to stand his ground and not to flee. Moaning the *aije*'s characteristic "um um um um um," the thing comes right up to the future shaman and then suddenly throws off a kind of cloth-skin and announces its name: it is the *aroe* of someone recently dead. Inevitably the shaman has known this person very well, and always he or she was an Exerae. If the shaman is also an Exerae, as *aroe etawa-are* should be, than the *aroe* is usually a consanguineal mother, sister or brother. If he is Tugarege, the *aroe* is his father or the person for whom he is *aroe maiwu*, the ritual replacement.

The *aroe* must always be an Exerae since it is only members of this moiety who impersonate the *aije* in its social representations. It may be this *aroe* who has desired that the dreamer become a shaman and who will be one of his familiars. But much more commonly it is the *aroe* of a long-dead Tugarege, or even a totemic *aroe* of this moiety, which has decided to make the dreamer a shaman. It enlists the aid of a recently dead Exerae relative of the dreamer in order "not to frighten" him unduly. In categorical principle the *aroe etawa-are* should be Exerae, and their guardian-familiars Tugarege, and in fact every shaman of the *aroe* known to my informants had been Exerae.

This dream–experience duplicates mystically the actual experience of a boy undergoing the Bororo initiation ceremony. In its culminating event, the initiate is led down a path leading from the *bororo* (dance plaza) to a small clearing about 15 or 20 meters directly west of the village, called the *aije muga* (the last term means "place"). Along the path are the Exerae actors impersonating the *aije*, covered with white mud and brandishing bullroarers, who menace the initiate with threats to castrate him and to eat him up. The boy is sustained by his *i-orubadari*, ritual friend, always a member of his father's clan, who murmurs sympathetic words of courage to him. The initiate must not show the slightest fear, although he has been taught since infancy to dread the frightful powers of the suprahuman *aije*. If he does show terror, he will be a weak and inconsequential man, with no hunting ability and likely to die before his time.

After this dream, which parallels the future *bari*'s initial dream confrontation with a *bope*, the apprentice *aroe etawa-are* begins to encounter *aroe* during his waking hours, while he is alone near the river. The souls appear in the forms of the birds called Themselves *aroe*; they either speak to him or behave in extraordinary ways, flocking around him, perching on his shoulder, or lighting on his bow. His response must be that of a novice *bari* confronted with signs of a *bope*: he lights a cigarette and blows its smoke to the four quarters. Finally he actually meets the *aroe* in their "natural" form. They appear as two beautiful children, elaborately decorated, who ask him politely for a cigarette and inquire where he is going. After smoking and talking together for a bit, the children suddenly change into water birds, usually herons or macaws, and fly off. Very soon afterwards the novice shaman finds a monkey, coati, paca, or other small animal, which he easily kills. This is a "gift of the *aroe*" to him.

One informant said that, rather than meeting the two children, sometimes a novice shaman hears the noise of many men fishing. When he meets the men, who appear as quite usual Bororo, he is given *tubore* (very small fish, almost minnows, among the preferred food of the *aroe* and usually taken only during collective fishing trips). After he has finished eating, the men show him how the fish are really *kaku-doge*, small ants. They then change into parakeets and fly off. Other informants had not heard of this and were inclined to interpret it as one of the initial dream experiences. The waking encounter with the *aroe*-children, they said, was the crucial initial meeting of a novice shaman with the actual *aroe*.

After all these things have been going on secretly for several months, one day the apprentice shaman happens to be routinely given the *bapu rogu* ("small rattles") during the course of some *aroe* ceremony or other. These rattles are intimately associated with the *aroe* and are used to accompany songs especially concerned with them. It is both an honor and a test of one's esoteric knowledge "to be given the rattles." Soon after beginning to sing, the new shaman suddenly collapses in a deathlike trance. His companions, some of whom may have suspected his selection by the *aroe* because of his peculiar behavior, treat him like any other dead or dying Bororo. His body is carried to his wife's house, and the funeral ceremony is begun. The clan chief of the Bado Jeba Xebegiwuge is called, and, donning the costume of Bakorokudu, his clan's most important ritual title and one of the ceremonial chiefs of the village,[11] he begins the *Aroeia Kurireu*, the anthem sung constantly during the funeral cycle. The "dead" man's female relatives appear and, with his wife and female affines, begin ritual lamentations.

But those who have suspected his shamanistic potential call both a *bari* and an *aroe etawa-are*. Toward the end of the song the apparently dying man's hands and feet begin to twitch. The two shamans gently blow tobacco smoke all over his body until he begins to mutter, faintly and as if from a long distance, "he he he he he he he." As the song is ending, he utters this noise louder "and closer," until he suddenly sits up. He is immediately given a cigarette and the two shamans quickly ask his name: *a-kiege a-kiege a-kiege*? But he repeats feebly, " e e e e e e." After a little time, he collapses again, "dead."

What is happening here, in Bororo theory, is that the *aroe* actually take away the novice shaman's soul, just as they do when someone dies. Informants insisted that the man is actually dead: not the trace of heartbeat nor breath can be detected. The *aroe* convey the soul to the village of Bakororo (the chief of the *aroe* impersonated by Bakorokudu). On the way many *aije* attempt to terrify the soul, again just as usual after death or during the symbolic "death" of initiation. This time, however, it is the "real *aije*" who appear. The soul is reassured by his guardian *aroe* and by the *aroe* of his recently deceased relatives which accompany him. When the party arrives at the village of the dead, Bakororo comes out to meet them. "Is this a dead person?" he demands. "No," say the guardian *aroe*, "this is a cigarette, this is a sweet water, this is corn mush" (i.e., all the things consumed by the *aroe* shaman on behalf of the spirits).

Bakororo then says he does not want this to happen, that the *aroe* should not take this man for their shaman. He tells them they will have no mercy upon him but will send all sorts of misfortune to him: he will be bitten by snakes, by wasps, by stingrays; he will be badly ill and will be hurt by jaguars and anteaters. The *aroe* will be angry with him and will not help him cure those whom they wish to harm. But the *aroe* assure Bakororo that they will take great care that none of these afflictions shall befall their agent. They say they want to have food and cigarettes, "to have their *aroe etawa-are* there, in the village." Bakororo makes them promise to protect him and sends them hastily back to the village with the man's soul. It is the gradual arrival of this party which is signaled in the "dead" man's hesitant, "he he he he he he," the noise always made by the *aroe*. But even then the *aroe* do not return the man's own *aroe* to his body; instead the familiar enters it. For this reason the shamans eagerly demand its name.

But within a few minutes, "just long enough for the people to see it is a shaman and not a death," the *aroe* again depart with the man's soul. His body falls over "dead" again. This time his *aroe* is taken east, to the village of Itubore. Exactly the same things occur: the menacing by the *aije*; the hesitancy of the chief of the *aroe* to accept the man as a shaman, for his own sake; the promises of the assembled *aroe*. The Bororo believe that almost the same events occur after any death, except that the "hazing" by the *aije* is much more intense for a new shaman, and of course the two *aroe* chiefs welcome the new soul cordially. This event is perceived as a direct parallel to the novice *bari*'s initial violent seizure by the *bope*. Usually, informants said, the *aroe* differed from the *bope* in repeating their initial possession of the shaman's soul over a long period, a month or more. During this time the *aroe* alternately "kill" and resuscitate their new shaman. While he is "dead," they take his soul around to visit the eight sectors where dwell the *aroe* forms of each clan and to the other-worldly rivers where live the true *aije*, so generally instructing him in the ways of the *aroe* world. During all these experiences the new shaman's *aroe* is sustained by the *aroe* of his *i-orubadari*, that is, the ritual friend of initiation, who has died and for whom the *aroe etawa-are* serves as ritual replacement. Without his protection, and that of the initial familiar, the novice shaman would very soon die. (Recall that most *aroe* shamans are elderly when the *aroe* initially contact them; their historic "friends of initiation" are quite likely dead. Furthermore, the Bororo are adept at substituting brothers or patrilateral cousins for an absent or inadequate *i-orobadari*, living or dead.)

In fact, the Bororo ascribe one aspect of the lack of a living *aroe* shaman to the much greater difficulty of his initiatory period, compared with that of a *bari*. The former must actually die and travel into another universe, whereas the latter merely visits places at least physically proximate to this reality, for all the *bope*'s powers. "It is much more difficult to become an *aroe etawa-are* than a *bari*. The *bope* do not kill a man at first. Many [of the former] have died at the beginning, because they did not have the *raka* to stand the *aroe*."

During his "introduction" to the *aroe*, which lasts about a year, the shaman is considered in grave physical peril and must take certain precautions to protect himself. He eats, for example, only corn mush flavored with the meat of small animals, such as doves, quail, paca, small monkeys, "pan fish," foods lacking *raka*. These are all obtained by the *i-pare* (bachelor's age group), acting on the instructions of the men's council. This group is obliged to render services for the collective good, such as repairing the men's house and providing food for the central participants in communal rituals. This means the *aroe etawa-are* himself is considered the responsibility and the benefactor of the entire community, a status which contrasts with the *bari*'s isolation from the collectivity, despite his occasional mystical activities on its behalf.

Toward the end of this period the *aroe* subject the new shaman to a series of trials as they lead his soul about during dreams. He must confront all manner of hideous creatures, often harmless insects of this world (such as the giant walkingstick but never, of course, beetles) that the *aroe* have caused to assume immense proportions. If he shows any signs of fear, the *aroe* will not assist him to cure the ill. If he "conquers," as the Bororo put it, these horrors, the *aroe* next lead him to the real *aije*, for the ones he has thus far met have all been men (or rather their *aroe*) costumed as *aije*. The *aije* asks the shaman to remove a pain it has in the middle of its forehead, covered as the rest of its body by an unimaginably ugly hide, like that of a toad. The *aroe etawa-are* overcomes his loathing and prepares to suck out the pain, but before he actually touches the *aije*'s skin the *erubo* ("pain," pathogenic substance) flies out and strikes against his teeth. "If he could actually touch the *aije*'s skin, he could cure any affliction"; merely coming within a few centimeters is enough to ensure considerable skill at curing. The *aije* instructs the shaman's *aroe* to remove other *erubo* from all the points in the body where he is likely to encounter sickness during his future treatments. Every time the *erubo* flies into his mouth before he actually touches the place. The *aije* assures him of his future powers to treat affliction and of a long life.

However, these are not the critical test. This comes at the end of the initiatory period. Some informants felt it occurred during a dream, others insisted that it "really" happened, during the first solitary hunt the shaman undertakes after his long "illness." The *aroe* appear before him in their usual guise of a beautiful boy and girl. They cause him to change into a harpy eagle or caracara hawk, in which form he kills monkeys, paca, and other small animals. (After his initial encounters with the *aroe* the shaman never eats for the rest of his life any of the *bope ure* species; the *aroe* detest these as too *rakare*.) He proceeds to cook and eat these animals in the forest, together with his guardian *aroe*. As they finish the meal, three *aroe*, in the form of handsomely decorated *i-pare* come through the jungle, bringing with them an extremely beautiful young girl.

As the shaman watches, one or two of the *i-pare* "go to her" (i.e., have intercourse with her). Then his guardian *aroe* tell him to do the same. He is very ashamed and tries at first to evade her. But his guardian *aroe* encourage him, and if he is a good man, already knowledgeable in the way of the *aroe*, he finally copulates with the girl. The *aroe* then wash him with *erubo*, so he will not become ill from the coitus. They tell him, "You will be very good at treating Bororo afflicted by the *aroe*; never will you fail. Those whom you cure and tell, 'You will not die,' your words will not be in vain, they will live a long time. You yourself will go very far, you will live to be *kuridogedu*, very old, always doing this service for the *aroe* and for the people. You will eat corn mush for the *aroe*, drink their sweet water, smoke their cigarettes for a long, long time until you are very tired of living and doing these things. Then you will die."

They then reveal that the girl is actually a *kerekere* (ararinha or red-bellied macaw) or sometimes a *kiakorogo* (araca or chestnut-fronted mac-aw), both types of small macaws, considered very lovely. My informants believed that the *aroe* would not kill the shaman if he were unable to have coitus with this bird-girl, but they would certainly not help him to cure, nor would they often enter him to eat, drink, or smoke. At most, they said, the failed shaman would probably not live very long, being without the *aroe*'s protection and liable to attacks from the *bope*. This test is clearly a parallel to the *bope*'s temptation of a *bari*'s sexuality, with the contrast being of course that the *bari* must refuse seductive sex and the *aroe etawa-are* must succeed in an "unnatural" version of it. (The Bororo, by the way, detest all forms of bestiality. But such acts appear frequently in myths, often connected with the *aroe*, and usually featuring the creation of some new condition of being.) Up until this test the novice shaman of the *aroe* has refrained from sexual relations, for two reasons. First, he has been "ill," in a state of great ritual and physical danger, and intercourse is always interdicted during such times for its loss of *raka* needed to survive the affliction. But more importantly the *aroe* dislike intercourse. Men representing *aroe* ritually must refrain from all sexual acts for at least a week before and after the impersonation. Failure to do this is (or was) the most frequent cause of *aroe*-inflicted illnesses. The *aroe etawa-are* is so often in contact with the souls that he must be almost celibate. Infor-mants commented ruefully and a bit maliciously that, while this shaman did not undergo the same risks as a *bari*, he nonetheless had his trials. But it seems clear that most *aroe etawa-are* became shamans when they were already middle-aged or older, in accordance with the general correlation between *bope* and youth and between *aroe* and age discussed in the second chapter. In any case, after the crucial encounter with the bird-girl, the new shaman assumes his ritual duties.

## Powers and Duties of the "Master of the Souls' Roads"

The mystical powers of the *aroe etawa-are* and his employment of them on behalf of the community are complementary to the functions of the *bari*. The latter defends the village during the nocturnal wanderings of his *bope*-soul and regains the souls of persons stolen during the *aroe butu*, shooting star. His actions are characteristically aggressive, even bellicose. But the shaman of the *aroe* acts supernaturally in altogether another manner and to opposite ends. As mentioned earlier, he is thought to be able to change himself into a tapir, or sometimes into a wild pig or certain kinds of fish. In this form he either drives game to the hunters or allows his animal form to be killed. He does this only during those collective hunts in which men represent deceased Bororo. The *aroe* shaman is generally responsible for these hunts, or that portion of them especially involving ceremony and the *aroe*. These affairs are complex both in their symbolic and sociological details, and a certain amount of background information must be provided in order that the shaman's role be clear.

The hunt, termed quite literally *aroe e-meru* (*e* = "of them," *meru* = "hunt") or *aroe e-kodu* (*kodu* = "run," in the sense of chasing after game), must be proclaimed by Karia Bokodori, the ritual chief of the Bado Jeba Xobugiwuge who impersonates the *aroe Itubore*, one of the two "culture heroes." But, as always in Bororo affairs, it is the assembled ritual chiefs of the Tugarege who decide to call the hunt and who instruct Karia Bokodori to order it. The formal proclamation is made during the early evening, and about eleven o'clock that night the participants and especially the *i-pare*, the bachelor's age group, who should take a very active role in the actual hunt, assemble in the men's house. Depending on the particular type of expedition planned (a hunt, fishing with traps or with timbo, a game drive) one of a set of chants, known generically as the *Oyego*, is sung. At a designated moment during the song cycle the *aroe* shaman is possessed. He informs the *aroe* of the planned hunt, the game sought (always *bope ure*, and during a funeral also "revenge animals"), the particular dead persons being represented, and the community's need for spiritual assistance in this enterprise. The song cycle lasts until dawn, but during it the shaman sleeps and in his dream the *aroe* instruct him on how and where they will change him into an animal, where the game will be found, and other details of the next day's hunt.

Before dawn the next morning the hunters assemble a kilometer or two from the village in a clearing known as the *ipa* and used only during the collective hunts. The ritual "fathers" have brought along the *aroe ekuie powari*, the gourd whistles whose noise imitates the soul's cries, and they hand these over to all the *aroe maiwu*, the ritual representatives, associated with those particular whistles. [12] After playing these briefly, the men settle down according to their clans' position in the village circle, while the shaman of the souls goes to the center and becomes possessed. He again asks the *aroe* where to search for game; he requests their aid during the hunt and also their protection of the hunters against all the "harming things," wasps, stingrays, snakes, and so on, that might hurt them during the expedition. (In the middle São Lourenço at least, these dawn assemblages in the ceremonial clearing have been abandoned owing to the lack of proper *aroe* shamans. The hunters simply pause en route to their chosen hunting ground and distribute the gourd whistles.) The *aroe* assure the hunters they will suffer no hurt but will kill the game they seek. During his trance, informants said, the shaman foresees the entire hunt, including his own transformed being as a tapir or pig.

The hunters leave after the shaman instructs them (or rather the *aroe* do so), but he himself returns to the village where he sleeps. His familiar *aroe* cause his soul to be changed into, or to enter, a tapir (or wild pig or dourado or surubim, depending on the hunt's circumstances), and to run with the transformed shaman through the forest to where the hunters are. Other *aroe* cluster along the route, and shout, "No, do not go, they will kill you, remember your children." The shaman-tapir runs first toward the person who gave him the pretrance cigarette that morning, and that hunter, if able, shoots the easy target. But it often happens that the hunters notice that this tapir is not like others: it has traces of decorations—body paintings, dance belts, and so forth—worn by the *aroe etawa-are*. They have pity on it and do not shoot. Finally, though, one hits it with an arrow or club, and it runs off into a grove or into a stream where the hunters do not follow for a time. The *aroe* remove the shaman's soul from the tapir's body and treat the shaman's very real wound caused by the arrow. Then they take the soul back to the sleeping body in the village.

Meanwhile the hunters finally discover the dead tapir, now quite ordinary, and take it to the village, where the meat is given to a *bope* shaman in the usual way. The *aroe* shaman is given the usual small animals and honey, also gathered by the hunters. Informants said that the shaman of the *aroe* did not by any means transform himself in this way during *every aroe e-meru* but only occasionally. Some were skeptical that the shaman actually metamorphosed into a tapir or that his soul actually entered one. They did not doubt his capacity to do so, only his human volition. "It is very frightening in the dream; it is not easy to approach the hunters. Their arrows seem like snakes which are going to bite the shaman." But all were confident that through the *aroe* the shaman could predict the location of the game and "guide" it toward the hunters. Just how he accomplished this no one was sure: it was "a mystery of the *aroe*." Many older Bororo recalled with marveling delight the enormously successful collective hunts during the times of the *aroe* shamans. *Bope* shamans, they said, "could go a little way into the hunts," but the ability in this area of even the best *bari* was very limited compared with the powers of a true *aroe* shaman.

In much the same way the shaman of the *aroe* is able to transform the feathers of large water birds (the various storks, herons, plovers, screamers, all the Themselves *aroe*) or the leaves of the caete palm (used to make a curious cylinder used in one of the most important *aroe* representations), into such fish as dourado, pacu, pintado, and other large "game" fish usually sought during collective fishing expeditions. (Note that the three varieties of "catfish" that are the *bope ure* are *not* among those "created" by the shaman.) The *aroe* shaman is then transformed into a very tiny fish, who leads the large ones into the fisher's nets and traps. The shaman's fish form is so small that it easily slips through the holes in the nets and traps. However, the nets appear to him very beautiful, all colored red, blue, yellow, white, striped and dappled. Each net seems to make a curious chugging or moaning sound, which is seductive but also terrifying. If the shaman-fish becomes afraid and flees, all the magical fish flee with him. The last are extremely timid anyway, so that the shaman has already told the fishermen, during the morning seance in the *ipa*, that they must be extremely quiet in their operations. The shaman of the *aroe* can also magically create wild pigs, or *jugo*. In his dream the shaman receives from the *aroe* a particular large broad leaf called *atuboreu aru* (I think a type of marsh fern) which he changes into a small pig. This runs about him in a circle and is gradually joined by more and larger pigs. The next day, after telling the hunters where to go to find the pigs, the shaman goes in his dream to join the pigs, where he takes the form of a very small piglet. He "plays and jokes" with the pigs, so that they do not hear the approach of the hunters; then he leads the pack straight to them. Being so small, he easily slips through the line of hunters, while all the other pigs are killed.

The shaman's explicit powers over game are limited to tapir, the three fish species (and especially the dourado), and wild pigs. However, when the men decide to hunt as *aroe* in groups of two or three or singly, the shaman sometimes is able to drive any kind of *bope ure* toward each hunter. His soul provides game for each one in turn, always beginning with the Tugarege and finishing with the Exerae. This sequence follows from the shaman himself being an Exerae; social etiquette demands that his "fathers and sons" receive bounty before his "mother's brothers and nephews." (Inversely, the *bari* in his evening ministrations always selfishly begins with his own moiety whether he is Tugarege or Exerae.) In all collective hunts, even when the *aroe* shaman has not provided game in some fashion, his soul accompanies the hunters while his body sleeps in the village. As soon as the hunt is successful, he wakes up possessed. After he or the *aroe* in him is given sweet water and a cigarette, he tells the audience that the "*aroe*" have killed thus and such kind of animals and that it is time to prepare their foods as they are on their way back to the village.

During the rainy season and for the first month or so of the dry season, the ritual hunts are more commonly fishing expeditions than actual hunts. The labor of building fish traps or preparing and using timbo, fish poison, is said to be possible only with a large group of men. Everything proceeds just as it does in the hunt, with the fish obtained being distributed along the ritual relationships of "son," "mother," and "father." Whatever the game, as soon as the hunters and fishers return to the village, the ritual "mothers" immediately send them bowls of corn or other vegetables, boiled up into a kind of flavorless mush, and bowls of water sweetened traditionally with a type of mud, and now with sugar. When the hunters consume these things, it is believed the *aroe* they represent, and others as well, "eat" through them. While this mystical meal is going on, the *aroe etawa-are* again becomes possessed and the *aroe* smoke and drink sweet water through him. They are thanked for the success of the hunt, and in turn they give assurances of their assistance in future expeditions and of their general benevolence toward all Bororo. When everyone has finished eating, the *aroe* leave the body of the shaman with a large whoop. The men also yell and pound their rolled up sleeping mats on the ground "to help the *aroe* go back." This noise is a signal for the women and children to come out of their huts, for they are not allowed to see any part of the *aroe*'s communal repast.

All aspects of the ritual hunts are rigidly forbidden to women and uninitiated boys. For a woman to witness any part of these proceedings, especially the "*aroe*" in the act of hunting or fishing, is almost as grave as offense against the *aroe* as seeing the actors impersonating the *aije*. "The *aroe* do not wait to kill her." The explicit reason for this interdiction is the women's supposed belief that the defuncts' *aroe* actually return and accompany the men, who themselves are transformed into spirits. Structurally, the interdiction expresses in effect the opposition between the "profane" feminine domain of the village periphery, where the organic processes of eating, sexual intercourse, childbearing, and death go on, and the "sacred" masculine village center, consecrated to the representation of the transcendent and immortal *aroe* forms. The powers in each domain do not so much conflict as contradict one another, and their rigid segregation is the only mode of resolving them and ensuring their harmony. The two kinds of shaman mirror and extend this opposition: the *aroe etawa-are*, who always functions in the men's house or dance plaza, is credited with mystically providing the community with the flesh of polluted animals that sustains not men's souls but their bodies. The *bari*, in contrast, always working in the village periphery, protects the souls of the community. Each shaman summarizes the unique paradoxical combination of *bope* and *aroe* that distinguish the sexes, but in antithetical ways.

The *aroe etawa-are*'s other mystical powers are similar to those of the *bari*. He can predict the future, which the *aroe* reveal to him in dreams, but generally he is thought to be less effective in this area than his colleague. "The *aroe* have to be sent into the future, but the *bope* are there already." As has been shown, the *bope* are the sentient masters of all organic time, while the *aroe* transcend space. The shaman of the *aroe* is thought to travel mystically everywhere in this earth, but in space rather than through time. When the shaman goes off fishing by himself, the *aroe* meet him at the edge of the river carrying a curious sort of hide or bark cloth that my informants could not describe very clearly. This is "the skin of the *aije*." The shaman seats himself in the middle of this, the *aije* wrap him up, and he travels through the river to other villages. He listens to the conversations of Bororo fishermen and may visit their communities. Alternately, the *aroe* may use the skin of a *jure*, the sucuri or anaconda associated with the rainbow, and wrap the shaman up in this to travel about. During these trips the shaman merely informs himself of events in other communities. He does not cure any sickness; nor does he interfere, as does a *bari*, if he encounters any evil, an epidemic of *erubo* or *maereboe* seeking to harm a particular man. Even after he treats someone, his *aroe* does not visit that individual at night and mystically repeat the treatment, in contrast to a *bari*. As the Bororo put it, "The *aroe* have to be asked to help us: they do not do it for themselves." Occasionally their shaman predicts a case of snakebite, or some other minor injury from an animal, or some illness he has seen in his dreams. But all these events are attributed to the *bope*, and the shaman of the *aroe* has neither the power nor the will to interfere with the *bope*. Informants insisted that he never combated the *bope* actively and that his curative efforts both actual and mystical were restricted to afflictions caused by the *aroe*. He never joins in the dream-wars waged by the *bari*'s *bope*-soul, nor does he assist the latter on those occasions, such as the *aroe butu*, when the entire village is menaced by the *bope*. In short, "The *bope* cannot do anything with the *aroe*, nor can the *aroe* go in the way of the *bope*." Each type of shaman is restricted to dealing with his own variety of spirit beings, and his attributes as well as his visible functions derive from the characteristics of each of these classes, including those inversions just mentioned.

## Offenses Against the *Aroe*, And Their Shamans' Therapies

The tangible activities of the *aroe etawa-are* are confined to treatment of afflictions imposed by the *aroe* and to precise roles in various rituals, notably the funeral cycle. Informants disagreed slightly about the details of offenses against the *aroe* and the character of the resulting illness, although all concurred on certain basic elements. The gravest offense against the *aroe* is intercourse before, during, and after participation in ceremonies devoted to the *aroe*. There seems to be some correlation between the importance of the ceremonial role, the duration of the interdiction, and the severity of punishment against its offense. The *aroe* are said to kill a ritual representative if he copulates anytime during the funeral cycle, to send a mild illness to the performer of important *aroe* role (e.g., that of Meri, Bakororo, or Adugo) who has intercourse several days after his performance, but they may not harm at all a man who copulates a day or two after being one of the many dancers in a minor representation, such as that of Mano or Iwodo.

Intercourse offends the *aroe* in both sociological and cosmological ways. It first means a man's withdrawal from the public domain of the men's house, dedicated to matters of the *aroe*, and from participation in his own clan, into the most narrowly intimate of private concerns. No *aroe* representation has any reference whatsoever to particular marriages; individuals participate in them on the basis of membership in their natal clans. While the *aroe maiwu* should belong to the defunct's father's clan, he must not reside conjugally in the same household as his ritual "father" and "mother," which means that it is highly unlikely that he will be married to any female consanguine of the deceased. Second, intercourse manifests the principle of *raka* antithetical to all the categorical powers of the *aroe*. It contributes to organic creativity, whereas the *aroe* generate symbolic renewal. The representative is the most dramatic ceremonial production of such "new life" but to lesser extent every re-creation of *aroe* essences accomplishes the same thing. The fusion of *aroe* and *bope* in man can be maintained in equilibrium only insofar as the most intense expression of each force is separated temporally and spatially from the other.

The most usual form of *aroe* illness, however variable its cause, is called *ake*. The Bororo describe this as a general lassitude and weakness, an inability to hunt or to work properly, and a susceptibility to all kinds of other illness resulting in an early death. Since precisely these same symptoms characterize *rakakare* ("weak vitality"), it seems that the *aroe* are mystically able to reduce the life-force or *raka*. This is logical: the *bope* attack individual's souls, which the *aroe* are hardly likely to do. Empirically, I think the Bororo tend to diagnose tuberculosis as *ake*, although almost any state of feeling vaguely "unwell" also receives this designation. The actual pathogenic substances utilized by the *aroe* to cause affliction are, again logically, things intimately and metonymically associated with the souls. They include *kuje bo* (down generically), *kidguru* (resin, used to apply feathers to skin), *nonogo* (here the berries and leaves of the urucu plant), *mea paru* (cigarette stubs), *nabure orea kudawu* (down of the red macaw), *koido orea kudawu* (down of yellow macaw), *mano oka* (flower of the caete plant from which the *mano* or dance cyclinder is made), and *keo kora* (bits of the long reed used to construct the *marido*, a huge "wheel" carried in one of the most elaborate *aroe* representations).

For very grave offenses, such as the copulation of the *aroe maiwu* (deceased's representative), the *aroe* cause *koido oyaga* or *nabure oyaga* to appear along the offender's backbone. These are the long tail feathers of the two large macaw species, used in bunches of three or four as valued hair ornaments. They cause almost immediate death when so employed by the *aroe*, whose shaman can do nothing to reduce their lethality. But even the nonfatal objects, in respect of their usual function to portray the *aroe* themselves, are eminently just as much cultural items, "man-made" symbols imbued with a range of associations always understood as the material means whereby transcendent beauty can be imitated. There could not be a sharper contrast with the disgusting agents employed by the *bope*: beetles and charcoal and pus. The cultural objects are removed from the patient's body by the shaman of the *aroe* through sucking and massage with tobacco smoke, just as the *bari* removes the items sent by the *bope*, but the difference in the pathogenic agents suitably conveys the difference in the causes and natures of the afflictions conveyed by the two spirit classes.

Aside from "wrong" intercourse, the *aroe* afflict those who have failed to carry out their ritual duties toward the *aroe*, such as the provision of proper food and drink. They so punish ritual "mothers" of representatives who fail to have corn mush, sweet water, or other *aroe* food prepared by the ceremonially necessary moment, or who allow even inadvertently such foods to be consumed by anyone other than the "*aroe*" themselves (that is, the hunters). Three relatively minor afflictions of older women during fieldwork were attributed to such a fault. In one case, the wife of one of my best informants had risen very early to work in the gardens. An Iwagudu-dogedu, she was the ritual "mother" of many representatives and in addition was the female head of the clan. About midmorning an Exerae hunter came home with a small owl he had killed earlier, which, as a ritual representative of a dead Iwagudu-dogedu, he gave to that clan's chief as an installment on his obligation to kill a jaguar. Now, the actual ritual "mother" of this representative was absent from the village, off visiting relatives in another village. Nominally she was obliged to prepare some "*aroe* food" for the successful hunter, for him to consume while the appropriate chants were sung over the owl's body by the clan chief in recognition of this *mori-xe*. In the absence of the actual "mother" the female clan head, herself a sort of generalized "mother of the *aroe*" (and thus often addressed in formal contexts, as noted in Chapter 2) should have prepared the meal. Through a complex series of misunderstandings, at least according to my informant, she had no idea of what was expected of her when she finally returned to the village late in the day. Her affliction amounted to a cold, which passed away in a week and was not treated by a shaman.

In another case, an *aroe* "mother" had prepared a large bowl of stewed manioc flavored with bits of small fish for the participants in a hunt. This, aside from its appropriateness to the meals of the *aroe*, is a normal Bororo dish. Her son-in-law, who as a wage-laborer for some local Brazilians was not a participant in the collective hunt, returned home late in the day, found the household empty and ate a bit of the dish. (The *aroe*-hunters had been delayed in their return to the village by an unusually successful catch of fish and had asked that as many people as possible come to aid them in carrying the game home.) The *aroe* "mother" developed a festering sore that refused to heal and was eventually treated by Celilo, who utilized his chain of *bope-aroe* connections to become possessed by one who had been simultaneously *bari* and *aroe etawa-are*. This sort of cooperation between the spirits is by no means a modern innovation. The *bope* have always been pleased to seize upon a malfeasance of a Bororo to justify afflicting him. But I suspect that post-factum "evidence" of this collaboration has become more frequent since the disappearance of the *aroe etawa-are*.

Some Bororo say that the *aroe* dislike those who quarrel violently over trivial matters with their near relatives and affines. Most doubt this, but do agree that the *aroe* are offended when the relationship between an *aroe maiwu* and his ritual parents is troubled by anger, malice, lust, or any other impropriety. The souls' displeasure may turn to vengeance if such conflicts happen in conjunction with the parties' involvement in any *aroe* ceremonial. Such "ugliness" among humans "spoils the representation." But no informant could remember any affliction linked to such a cause by an *aroe etawa-are*. Behavior between ritual parents and their "sons" is in any case exceedingly proper, at least in all instances I observed, and such relatives appear to be especially conciliatory during major rituals.

But participation in these ceremonials does risk another way of offending the *aroe*. The souls may punish those who fail to remove completely all signs of decoration after playing a ceremonial role secret from women and the uninitiated. Such failure is held to betray the masculine pretense that the *aroe* themselves perform in these rituals. Again there is a hierarchy of importance to such secrets. The *aroe maiwu* must take great care to remove his decorations, and the men who personify the *aije* are only slightly less fastidious. The costumes of other *aroe* roles, though nominally secret, are discarded haphazardly. The *aroe*'s concern in this matter is a diminished reflection of their rage if the actual performance of one of their rites be seen by the uninitiated. Then, all informants were sure, their retribution would be immediate.

If a woman sees one of the actors personifying the *aije*, or the bull-roarer itself, the *aroe* cause her stomach "to swell up and up until she dies." If the *aroe maiwu* is seen, he himself is apt to die as quickly as if he had sexual intercourse, while the woman soon expires with *ake*. There is, fortuitously, a plant medicine which the council can direct the *i-pare* (bachelor society) to prepare and give to the woman if she is considered innocent of all volition in her offense. This medicine had proved efficacious in the few cases of this transgression personally known to my informants, but they had heard of others in which refusal to administer the medicine resulted in the predicted death. Certainly the men took great care to ensure that the uninitiated should not see any aspect of the *aije* or *aroe maiwu*, and otherwise credited the *aroe* with full powers over these rites. The women's attitude was more difficult to assess. They were well aware of the true character of the representations and treated the men's precautions with an amused tolerance.[13] Yet they were careful not to witness the ceremonies themselves. These beliefs and actions are therefore crucial for any exploration of the relationships between Bororo morality and the collectivity of *aroe*.

The *aroe* define and provide the means of proper, cross-moiety transactions, including alliance. Some claim the souls afflict those guilty of moiety incest, but most Bororo felt that such sexual transgressions had autonomous malign consequences, inherent in contact with *raka* "like one's own." Further, they said, the *bope* also found such actions "ugly" and punished offenders. Kadegare's marriage with a woman of his own moiety and the constant illnesses and miscarriages that plagued their union were almost always cited as evidence for this belief. Yet his situation was obviously colored by his status as a *bari*. The three other cases of marriages within the moiety that occurred during fieldwork had not endured long enough for any afflictions befalling the couples to be attributed to their categorical wrongdoing. Nor is it sure that any ever would. Infractions of the rules surrounding the *bope ure* are too ubiquitous, and, as the Bororo themselves observe, persons who ignore the fundamental social prescription of their culture (moiety exogamy) are hardly likely to heed the niceties of those rules.

The *aroe*'s concern with cross-moiety relations is not expressed functionally, then, but symbolically. Women who see the *aije* are not guilty of any sexual impropriety but offend the principles that order all categorical relationships in a more fundamental way. The *bope*, it should be clear, have only a derived concern with these principles. In spite of their powers over reproduction, they have little regard for the categorical modalities through which these powers are expressed. Their agent the *bari* is prohibited from attending pregnant women, and especially one in childbirth: she can only be treated by an *aroe* shaman. For the *raka*-less are vested with powers over the forms through which generation is accomplished, because these determine the classificatory status of the new entity produced. Moiety endogamy is wrong from the *aroe* point of view basically because the infant can receive no *aroe*/name except through a genitor/pater of the opposite moiety. The *aije* are the instruments which express the *aroe*'s power to control the transformation of birth and death through nomination. When a woman sees them, she intrudes her unordered *raka* into the very principle that must control such wild creativity. When the *aroe* destroy such a woman they do so in a way appropriate to her crime: they cause her own reproductive capacity to kill her. The violation and its consequences are variations on those of copulating when representing the *aroe*, or of a boy's failure to segregate his own sexual life from that of his parents, or of not heeding the rules attendant on menstruation, pregnancy, and childbirth. All of these actions are cases of incest in that they commingle persons and substances which, being so very like in various ways, must be kept distinct in others.

The more violent and direct a violation is of Bororo morality, the less the *aroe* take notice of it. Theft, which in the Bororo view includes adultery of either spouse, is an outrageous assault upon the integrity of the owner's personality, which is bound up in his material possessions that permit him to be what he is. Yet the *aroe* would never intervene even if a ritual representative's bow was stolen, if such a heinous crime could be committed by a Bororo. Physical injury from assault, unless involving either kind of shaman or things otherwise directly connected with the *bope* or *aroe*, incurs no mystical sanctions whatsoever. Murder itself must be revenged by men with no spiritual aid, unless it involves operation of vegetable medicines, and in these cases the crime and its punishment can only be alleged. Such lesser sins as greed, slanderous envy, lack of generosity, sloth, and the like can never be subject to the *aroe*'s hypothesized justice, in this life or the next, no matter how much they disturb the tenor of human relationships. No more are the virtuous rewarded by the *aroe* except perhaps in the vague sense of that highest Bororo good, "living a long, long time." The *aroe* are indifferent to men's affairs, except when they fail to prepare the souls' sweet water or to remove a bit of heron down from their bodies. Only then do they afflict men, and only in these cases can the shaman of the souls utilize his powers to heal the suffering.

The *aroe etawa-are* is almost totally segregated from the processes of social morality. He does not appear at all, even as curer, in the most direct of the violations against the souls, that of a woman's intrusion into the *aije* domain. He probably did not treat representatives afflicted after they had intercourse during the funeral cycle. Even on the ritually positive side, he has little direct connection with the redressive measure taken by society to re-establish the *bope-aroe* equilibrium through the "revenge animals" (*marege mori-xe.*) He possesses no sanctions, no mystical curse, no judicial power, to wield against wrongdoers or collective impropriety. But the shaman of the *aroe* is (or was) the embodiment of Bororo moral order.

The most important public duties of the *aroe* shaman involve the performance of various chants within four complex series of ceremonies: the initial and concluding phases of the funeral cycle, initiation, and the "Hunt of the Souls." He also has secondary but crucial roles in name-giving rites and the investitures of chiefs. Drink, food, and tobacco are offered to the souls through the shaman in all these ceremonies, as in most *aroe* representations, but informants considered his chanting of the special *aroe* songs to be just as important as this mediation. These songs include the *Roia Kurireu*, the "Long Anthem," a group of chants known collectively as *Kiege Barege*, "Birds and Mammals," the *Aije Paru*, "Appearance of the Aije," *Xibae Etawadu*, "The Home of the Macaws," and many others. These figurative and often archaic texts describe the *aroe* forms, the exploits of culture heroes (Bakororo, Itubore, and others), and the fusion of natural and social systems through the clans and such institutions as the "deceased's representative," the *aroe maiwu* (Albisetti and Venturelli 1969). They are so long as to require two to six or seven hours to render: phrases, strophes, and sometimes whole sections bewilderingly recur within and among chants. Although most are sung by a male chorus, with occasional solo passages, one man is always recognized as song leader for a given performance. Most adult men know various sections of two or three songs, but few have been able to commit any one to memory, let alone six or eight. Designated leadership of a chant is therefore at once a man's opportunity to demonstrate his esoteric knowledge and a chance for others to correct his rendition. Among contemporary

Bororo, every song is marked by constant shouted revisions from the performers and audience. The enormous prestige resulting from mastery of the songs is reflected in the diversity and quantity of vegetable medicines (*erubo*) supposed to convey a fine singing voice and an excellent memory (Albisetti and Venturelli 1962: 574–75).

To be an *aroe* shaman, I was told, one had to be able to sing all the above chants "without one mistake." If the shaman erred in even a single phrase, the *aroe* would be exceedingly angry and "he would die before the bones were out of the ground" (before the conclusion of the funeral). My informants implied that such total mastery being impossible, the shaman's incredible feats of accuracy were sustained by the *aroe*'s inspiration. Further, something more than mere guided recall animated these performances. Most esoteric knowledge among the Bororo, that of myths and the clans' ornamental property, is transmitted privately as a privileged secret, in (usually) matrilateral lines. Before he can receive this information, the recipient must show that he is morally worthy of it. The *aroe* not only provide the categories through which things are identified but also dictate the ways and means whereby their interrelationships should be ordered. The Bororo assume that to possess this knowledge is to be at once powerful and moral, since one must be worthy of its instruction and yet its mastery implies a command of the principles of effective action.

So when the *aroe etawa-are* chants the intricacies of the *aroe*'s domain, "without one mistake," he divinely guides his listeners through the moral charter of the universe. In this act he expresses the liturgical functions of a priest. But his sacerdotal capacities end here, in knowledge, for this shaman can not directly mediate between the souls and society so as to redeem and re-establish a covenant. This is done by his colleague the *bari*, who acts, however, with regard to the *bope*. Bororo society, then, has no covenant with the *aroe* but rather exists by reason of the nominal and relational principles they represent. The *aroe etawa-are*'s knowledge guarantees this existence but achieves it only when men learn from him.

The Bororo assumption that esoteric learning is an axiomatic correlate of morality is a self-fulfilling prophecy that is validated through other systems of reference, preeminently that of ceremonial property. Every Bororo has the right to employ the ornaments, body paintings, and other items owned by his name-group and subclan. Such egalitarian privileges cannot be used, obviously, to establish individual prestige. But through various prestations of *mori-xe*, ranging from the quick killing of a wasp to the ultimate slaying of a jaguar, persons gain the right to make and wear ornaments belonging to social groups whose members they have so avenged. The relative value of each decoration is correlated roughly with the importance of the particular *mori-xe* it compensates. Killing a snake that has bitten someone earns a simple bracelet or necklace while a slain jaguar or harpy eagle gains the right to a magnificent *pariko*, a large diadem made of macaw and eagle feathers, in addition to the decorated bow and arrows. Traditionally, during *aroe* representations persons not involved in the ceremony itself would outfit themselves with all this achieved regalia (cf. illustrations in Lévi-Strauss 1975: 224ff. ). At this time too, each clan selected one or more of its *aroe maiwu* to represent its totemic *aroe*, which are personified through just these ornaments and body paintings. Therefore the "new souls" are representative twice over, of a particular deceased and of an *aroe* essence. The Bororo are being literal rather than mystical when they say, "The *aroe*, all of them, appear in the village during the *etawuje* ('representations')." At these moments corporate and individual prestige is blazoned forth, reciprocally and across moieties.

Any adult, male or female, may and should offer all kinds of *mori-xe* to those of the other moiety who suffer pain from nature's hostility. Women so acquire on their own behalf a stock of prestigious jewelry which they proudly display. Men also permit their wives and most especially their children to wear upon occasion ornaments they have won. But truly valuable items are gained only by *aroe maiwu* who slay a principal "revenge animal," a jaguar or eagle. Men are chosen for this role only secondarily for their hunting ability: the major criteria are ethical conduct, prompt discharge of their responsibilities, and skillful mastery of esoteric lore. Axiomatically, men of great prestige are *aroe maiwu* for twelve or fifteen deceaseds of the other moiety. They have great bundles of ornamental paraphernalia, which means that they tend to be the only ones sufficiently equipped to undertake major ceremonial roles, which in turn adds to their status. This system of ritual capitalism turns on public estimation of individual morality. Its assumptions are constantly verified because the property it generates serves only to confirm its judgments.

While my data on the social characters of particular shamans of the *aroe* are very incomplete, they do agree on one point: every one of them had been an *aroe maiwu* many times over before becoming a shaman. Cadete, the great *aroe etawa-are* of the middle São Lourenço, had been the representative of "fifty" deceased Tugarege and had a separate dwelling to store all his possessions. Even allowing for hyperbole, there can be no doubt that he and his fellow specialists were men of immense symbolic wealth and great learning. (Cadete was also a *bari*, but this dual role was unique to him, as far as I can discover.) Only persons so endowed could carry out the *aroe etawa-are*'s duties, which require a large inventory of ornaments and instruments to be "well" performed. One episode from Bororo history illustrates the significance of these shamans' possessions in their mediation between society and the domain of transcendental form.

During the first sustained contact with the Brazilians, shortly before the beginning of this century, the Bororo were inundated with new sorts of material things, all of which had to be somehow incorporated into the system. Apparently the shamans of the *aroe* assumed the responsibility (or were assigned it) of discovering the "names" of these novel entities and fixing their relationships to existing *aroe* forms. Largely, as we have seen, Brazilians and most of their possessions were associated with the *bope* and distributed among the various Exerae clans, the moiety of the *bope*. But as Exerae the *aroe* shamans claimed for themselves, and for the moiety of the *aroe*, the Tugarege, multicolored cloth. Only they, shamans and their wives, could use it in any form, and even its possession was forbidden to other Bororo. This abrogation was not as arbitrary as it might appear. Indigenously the Bororo dyed and wove wild cotton into decorative bands of many colors, and the substance and its products are among the *aroe* of the Bokodori Exerae clan. The anaconda's connection with the rainbow is enough to make it an *aroe*, and the general association of dappled or pied colors with the *aroe* has already been described. But even more, one of the most celebrated metaphors in Bororo compares the experience of chanting a long song to passing along a wide multihued band which constantly unrolls before one as the song progresses. It is not, then, as though the *aroe* had any kind of eminent domain over calicos and plaids, comparable to the *bope*'s rights over tapirs and deer, but rather that such fabrics were essential to the *aroe*'s representation.

The Bororo are endlessly fascinated by the myriad details of clan property and jealously guard their own rights in the system, whether ascribed or acquired. In former times anyone's illegitimate use of an ornament would bring about violent recriminations and even fighting. The entire system of *aroe* possessions is so extensive, and so finely differentiated, that honest confusions are bound to arise. The actual use of these ornaments in representations and the clans' participation in the more intricate rituals are again such complex matters that debate about them is almost constant. The men's council can be preoccupied for a full evening with questions about which clan's titled actor should precede which other clan's just as prestigious personification, wearing what bit of feathercraft, at some particular moment in a ceremony lasting five hours.

Nor are any of these matters subject to manipulation for advancing claims or validating changing political status, at least not in principle. They are, in Bororo theory, fixed and immutable: there is a single, right, and knowable way. No one now has any final authority in these disputes, but I think the material presented suggests that such arbitration was one of the most important functions of the *aroe etawa-are*. He alone had the knowledge of both the *aroe*'s property and their correct ritual employment, and he could contact the *aroe* to determine further any obscure point. No doubt he operated very much behind the scenes to render his judgments, but this would not lessen his importance in maintaining social order. More than this, he alone could determine where radically new things would fit into this system.

The power of the *aroe etawa-are* derive then from his authority over symbolic substances and processes, and his ability to incorporate new phenomena into the immutable domain of the *aroe*. Only he can alter the frozen corpus of esoteric learning, or arbitrate between circumstance and norm. He assures that the principles of moral order are maintained through the congruence of ritual practice with traditional precept. For the Bororo this assurance is far more important to social ethics than any retribution for its infraction: rather than correcting wrongs it prevents their occurrence. In this society the serious challenges to public order come not with violent crimes and gross breaches of normative rules but in the petty derelictions of obligation and minor infractions of ritual privilege. All their moral concern is for etiquette, and failure to observe the intricacies of proper form, whether in a ceremony or casual prestations of food, is quite properly cause for affliction from the *aroe*. The disappearance of their agent implies not that his powers are inadequate to the troubles now confronted by the Bororo, but that they are irrelevant to them.

# 11

ᑭᐧᐧᑐ

# The Two Shamans—Dyadic
# Inversions

The *bari* and the *aroe etawa-are* stand
as inverted complements of one another, rather than in symmetrical opposition. They form a sort of "maximal pair," their attributes defining
the polar extremes of Bororo existence. The great difficulty in analyzing
their relationships comes in the way that the social processes relevant to
the *aroe etawa-are* have become moribund. We are left with a congealed
formal structure like the syntax of a dead language, an artifact of mind, a
code for the expression of meaning without content. The problem is all
the more acute because neither type of shaman functionally intervened in
social life in any direct way. Yet the structure itself indicates something of
the subtle dynamics which it once expressed.

One of the characteristics of Amerindian shamanism is the surreal
movement between "high" and "low" domains that contain antithetical
cosmological principles. The idiosyncrasy of the Bororo consists in dividing capacity for this mediation between two agents. The reason for
this does not lie in the ways these dichotomous powers oppose one another, so that to treat with one set renders a shaman incapable of relating
to the other group, but in their complementarity. The *bope* and the *aroe*
are so unlike that each requires a non-overlapping specialization of their
human intermediaries. This asymmetrical duality is institutionalized
through the moieties and again at the level of the clans, and it permeates
natural classifications. "Everything," said one shaman, "is on one side or

the other; nothing is between." Mediation in this sort of structure requires not so much the fluid power of the limens, but the strength of inversion. Being so surely on the side of the *aroe*, a Tugaregedu becomes a *bari*. Being someone whose very name derives from the *bope*, an Exeraedu can assume the shadow transcendance of a "Knower of the Souls' Ways." In a dyadic society less given over to organic differentiation and reversal, it would be reasonable for a shaman to mediate between opposed forces and to accomplish in himself movements from the celestial to the subterranean pole, abodes of equivalent forces. But such a society would not be like the Bororo.

This culture posits its intellectual and social organization on the assumption that everything exists by reason of an internal dialectic. In every possible abstract mode it is itself and its own antithesis. But each thing, or class of things, achieves its identity through the unique way it accomplishes its mediation between the irreducible principles of being that the Bororo conceptualize as "*aroe*" and "*bope*." At one level of abstraction these constitute poles between which entities may be situated on the basis of expression, more or less, of one or the other. But from another perspective each of these obeys the posited logic by becoming its antithesis. We have seen that the beings and phenomena that lie closest to the *bope* pole are nonetheless *aroe*. Even the *bope* themselves, contradict their own nature. Each one or type has its unique name, and therefore an *aroe*. Collectively, in all their transformations, they can only cause what already was.

At the other extreme, the *aroe* are themselves *bope*. Not only do they directly control the renewal of fishes and other aquatic creatures, they alone have the capacity to bring new nominal forms into being. If nothing can exist without a "name" and, in being so classified, be related to other entities like and different from it, then the *aroe* control the final powers of generation. If novel and strange things break in upon the Bororo, their ultimate source can only be the *aroe*. For these reasons the *aroe* can utilize the reproductive capacity of human bodies to kill their owners when they confound form and process. The monstrous *aije* with their phallic "tails" which accomplish a boy's initiation into sexuality are far better incarnations of the *bope* than any vulture or rattlesnake. There is a general monstrousness running through the *aroe* essences that makes them far more awful than the *bope's* putrid little monkeys. If these extremes of Bororo dyadism are related so much through an internal dialectic, the shamans who treat with them must also possess similar paradoxes.

We have seen that the *bope ure* and the *marege mori-xe* represent contrasting modes of synthesizing the contradiction of being simultaneously *bope* and *aroe*. The shamans stand as human equivalents of these, but in a reversed rather than a direct way. That is, an analogy would run: *bope ure*:

*marege mori-xe*: *aroe etawa-are*: *bari*. Each shaman becomes in his most essential metamorphoses a tapir and a jaguar, respectively; the *aroe* shaman becomes that basic "food of the *bope*," a tapir, while the *bope* shaman becomes the quintessential revenge animal, a jaguar. Further, each mystically sustains the other's specialty. The shaman of the *aroe* provides the meat so beloved of the Bororo and of the *bope*, which animates that *raka* otherwise treated by the *bari*. And he, the shaman of the *bope*, nightly preserves and saves the souls, so contained in their material possessions, which together are the province of the *aroe etawa-are*. Consistently, when a *bari* becomes evil he consumes souls, and as sign of this vomits the ornamental feathers used to express the *aroe* and extracted as pathogenic agents by the *aroe etawa-are*.

While the *bope* themselves are cannibalistic eaters of souls, the *aroe* destroy men by taking all their *raka* from them, or by causing their reproductive capacity to kill them. If ever the Bororo need a shaman to treat sterility or to attend a difficult birth, it must be an *aroe etawa-are* whom they seek out. Since he no longer exists, many babies and mothers suffer and die, an ironic tautology indeed. His most important ritual duties, aside from collective hunts, occurred in funerals, initiations, and name-givings, all "life crises" rites involving fundamental transformation in individual identity in its most physical sense. The shaman of the *aroe* is therefore identified with foods of the *bope*, those apparently defenseless creatures which express the rules whereby human beings can prevent their *raka* and that of other entities from destroying their souls. The *bari*, in contrast, is associated with the *marege mori-xe*, because through him and these agencies men can permanently master the flux of time and endure as *aroe*, principles of transcendent order.

In Table 11.1, a summary of each shaman's characteristics shows that this complementarity pervades all aspects of these specialists. It also shows that the inversions are confined to certain intersecting plans, but in others the shamans directly express aspects of their severally possessing forces. The lustful, hot, stinking *bari* is very much a thing of the *bope*'s, while the nearly celibate, cool shaman of the souls metonymically expresses the *aroe*. The former contacts directly the pollution of *raka*, which the latter must avoid completely—but he becomes a tapir. The site, ends, and modes of the *bari*'s curing are diametrically opposed to those of the *aroe etawa-are*'s treatments, and these contrasts are almost equivalent to a general concentric dualism expressing a nature-culture antithesis. But the mystical corollaries of these activities amount to an inversion of their contextual symbolism, with the *bari* redeeming souls (or attacking them) and his counterpart becoming a part of nature to provide for *raka* (or to extinguish it). The *bari* is poor in material possessions, with his shabby and utilitarian "cooking utensils," but yet these things, as well as the cast-

Table 11.1. Characteristics of Shaman Types

| *Bari* | *Aroe Etawa-are* |
| --- | --- |
| Initiation | |
| Smells rotting corpse | Smells "sweetness," urucu and resin |
| Denies "cultural" sexuality | Accepts "unnatural" sexuality |
| Masters fear of fire | Masters repugnance of ugliness |
| Becomes insensibly possessed | Dies and is reborn |
| Tricked and deceived | Threatened and menaced |
| Duties | |
| Eats dangerous food, makes it safe for others | Refuses dangerous food, provides it for others |
| Works at night, for individuals, in periphery | Works at day, for community, in center |
| Goes above, to heavens | Goes below, to water |
| Extracts pathogenic natural objects | Extracts pathogenic cultural objects |
| Transforms into jaguar, snake, puma | Transforms into tapir, hawk, otter, macaw |
| Actively battles with *bope* | Passively request *aroe* |
| Saves *aroe* | Saves *raka* |
| Familiars jealous and demanding | Familiars indifferent and instructive |
| Attributes | |
| Sexually active | Sexually passive inactive |
| Property and self dangerous to others | Property and self endangered by others |
| Master of Time | Master of Space |
| "Hot" | "Cold" |
| Poor | Rich |
| Powerful | Knowledgeable |
| Capable of becoming soul-eating "witch" | Capable of becoming false prophet |

off products of his body, are extremely dangerous to others. The *aroe etawa-are* is wealthy in the most extreme symbolic ways known to the Bororo, but he and his are vulnerable to the most innocuous contacts with the mundane world.

These qualities are material indexes to the absolutely different sorts of power and status that set aside these shamans from ordinary men. The *bari* is an unwitting and pitied agent for the *bope*, whose specialized techniques extend only to butchering procedures known at least in outline by most men. He must strive to follow moral canons yet is frequently criticized for minor derelictions that pass unnoticed in others. The Bororo seem to assume on *prima facie* grounds that a *bari* is constitutionally unable to be "good"; he is just too near the conscientiously amoral *bope*. The *aroe etawa-are* derives all his authority from esoteric knowledge which in itself is a guarantee of his ethical conduct. His slightest error in the ceremonial techniques is severely punished by his guardian souls, whose attitude to him is predominantly critical when not indifferent. All these contrasts and even some of the inversions emerge in the different processes of recruitment for each shaman.

While the initial signs of the *aroe*'s or the *bope*'s favor all involve naturalistic experience, these contrast in almost every other respect. The future *bari*'s dreams involve flying; the new *aroe etawa-are*'s involve walking or "swimming." The "wide clean road" down which the latter walks is a transcendent extension of the *aije rea*, "path of the *aije*," a broad and well-trimmed path that leads due west from the village circle to a small circular clearing used for secret preparations during various *aroe* representations. Just after death the soul also finds itself strolling such a road, accompanied by a decorated child; several nonshamans had similar visions during the course of serious illnesses.

The *bari* finds that places and beings in nature especially associated with the *bope* manifest curious signs of life: anthills and rocks "move," creatures Themselves *bope* follow him and even speak to him. So too in direct parallel a new *aroe etawa-are* encounters things Themselves *aroe*, but the initial meetings with these mystical forces are very different. The *bope*'s first appearance is innocuous, perhaps friendly and even somewhat comical. Its consequences, when soon after the shaman discovers and kills some *bope* food species, are unsubtly rewarding. But the *aroe* first appear as a huge, threatening *aije*, and the encounter, even if the shaman is able to master his terror and not flee, brings no material benefits. Even subsequently, when the *aroe* provide some small game or fish, the new shaman receives little utilitarian profit. Furthermore, the *aroe* present themselves in their "natural" form as two beautiful children only after they cause a newly deceased soul to appear as a menacing *aije*, whereas the *bope* employ no such subterfuges. Yet the contrast between the dark monkeys and the ornamented children is starkly simple. The children are human equivalents of *aroe* essences, in their beauty, doubleness, implicit lack of sexuality, transcendent youth, and polite regard for social forms. As messengers for the *aroe* and instructors into their mysteries, they are better regarded as "guardians" of the shaman than as possessive familiars.

The first public manifestations of each type of shamanism set forth the different ways each relates to his forces. The *bari* is violently, even demonically possessed. Society must quickly intervene to restrain him lest he do some harm to himself. These initial attacks always occur, significantly, in the village; the new shaman does not acquire his powers estranged from the community. In every way the *bope* seize their human agent, wresting him away from his mundane status and infusing him with aggressive life. But the *aroe* proceed to carry off their intermediary, leaving his body cold and lifeless. The intervention of ritual specialists and esoteric chanting is necessary to restore his being, while the newly possessed *bari* need only be given a cigarette to smoke.

There can be no doubting the Bororo sincerity that the *aroe etawa-are* actually "dies" on these mystical occasions. At the conclusion of fieldwork the four-year-old son of Kano Jo, the clan chief usually accorded senior status at Korugedu Paru, was stricken one afternoon with what appeared to be a grand mal epileptic seizure. The social response was dramatic. People rushed about preparing to begin funeral rites, and lamentations rose from the "deceased's" home. But a few decried the fuss, confident that a new *aroe etawa-are* had appeared. They cited the suddenness of the attack, the boy's profound coma and clammy body, his status as a Tugaregedu and member of the Arore, the clan of the *aije* and the culture hero Bakororo, his father and grandfather's positions as ritual leaders; I was largely convinced myself. But one of the wisest men doubted that this was possible, since the *aroe* could never take away a young child to serve as their shaman. It would be absurd for him to conduct chants, metamorphose into tapirs, and drink sweet water on behalf of the souls. However, he added, it was possible that the *aroe* had taken this extraordinary measure to announce their interest in the child. So the boy would be carefully watched and intensively tutored in matters relevant to the *aroe*.

Perhaps the most analytically significant contrast between the recruitment of the two shamans has to do with the mystical "tests" of their sexuality. The new *bari* must restrain all natural response to an attempted seduction by the woman who, as "Mother of the *Bope*" might stand for feminine carnality in all its most tempting modes. But the *aroe etawa-are* must join the souls in a doubly unnatural intercourse: unnatural first because the souls otherwise oppose all sexuality, and second because not a girl but a bird is the partner.[14] Here the inversion is marked: each shaman must be able to act volitionally in a manner opposite that definitional of the supernatural class he is to embody. In other words, the *bari* must be "*aroe*-like" in refusing sex, and the *aroe etawa-are* "*bope*-like" in accepting it. Yet once they have passed this test each shaman "reverts to type," the *bari* able to copulate with sleeping women during his dreams, and the *aroe etawa-are* maintaining sexual purity during the long ceremonial cycles. Each one's accomplishment of these things depends upon his mastery of sexuality: through self-restraint, the *bari* earns licentiousness; through ability to respond, the *aroe etawa-are* establishes control over his *raka*-generated desires. The other tests during the initiatory period continue this logic, in a diminished way and in other contexts. The *aroe etawa-are*, associate of the immortally beautiful *aroe*, must symbolically embrace the most potently ugly things in the world. The *bari* surrenders himself to fire, a metonymic associate of the *bope* but, unlike them, nearly always a positive force of organic transformation. Later, in the accomplishment of their duties, the shaman of the *aroe* will be able to see the lethality of beautiful feathers which make people ill, and the *bari* can eat rotten, grub-infested meat or suck out hideously ugly beetles. Each shaman, then, masters his destiny through controlling its antithesis.

Remaining attributes and functions of the shamans continue themes presented above and in earlier chapters. The *bari* travels through time because the *bope* control all temporal processes; the *aroe etawa-are* voyages through space since the *aroe* define all locality and direction. The animal vehicles they severally employ are what might be expected from their associations with the animals of revenge and the *bope* foods, except for the shaman of the *aroe*'s use of hawks and otters. Although among the "revenge animals," these creatures are also those into which the soul of the deceased is instructed to pass in its revengeful defiance of the *bope*'s rules over "their" food. This latter association accounts for the *aroe etawa-are*'s metamorphoses into hawks and otters, as well as into macaws. Once again, this shaman is a convert, a disguised sort of *bope*, who must resort to mystical transformations or consume the food denied him in his mortal form. In contrast, his colleague the *bari*'s transformations into the great felines and rattlesnakes mark the latter's subtle association with the *aroe*. Jaguars' expression of *aroe* attributes has been shown, but the rattlesnake also intimately participates with the souls. The handles of both types of dance rattles (*bapu* and *bapu rogu*), as well as the tube section of the *ika* (the trumpetlike instrument used by representatives of Bakororo "the chief of the *aroe*") are covered with various mottled designs all said to derive from the rattlesnake's markings. These instruments are used to accompany all chants describing the *aroe* in their various forms and powers; the *bapu rogu* themselves are always used by the shaman of the *aroe* to sing himself into trance. And the Bororo say that the *ewo*, rattlesnake, is "almost a *marege mori-xe*."

The malign capacities of a *bari* are a systematic transformation of his benign ones: a witch who mystically consumes souls instead of saving them, who is driven by the lust and envy and destructiveness which are the negative concomitants of the *bope*'s fertilizing drive. But what of the *aroe etawa-are*? In all accounts, by Bororo or Westerners, he appears as only a positive figure, literally incapable of working harm. Still, threaded among informant's descriptions of his skills was a quality of dubiety, a certain skepticism not of his demonstrated and hypothesized powers, but of novel claims to new knowledge he sometimes advanced. This note was sounded most often in recollections of Cadete, whose authority sometimes bordered on the illegitimate. Cadete was simultaneously a *bari* and *aroe etawa-are*, and it was impossible to discover which role was mistrusted. Yet I think it was the latter. In relating details of the *aroe*, informants were always careful to distinguish Cadete's revelations from traditional lore. While accepting his "discoveries" as insights from an *aroe etawa-are*, they also treated them as subject to rational discussion and modification. This attitude was in marked contrast to that in regard to *bari*, whose claims and boasts were simply credited as axiomatically true. It may be impossible to discover whether the Bororo have ever had any historical experience with "false prophets," but if so, they were surely *aroe etawa-are*. For much the same reason I doubt whether the Bororo will ever be susceptible to millenial movements. If ever they do generate one, its leader will be a true Exeraedu *aroe etawa-are*. In fact, there exists within the Bororo epistemological structure many more checks on new knowledge of the *aroe* than of the *bope*. The esoteric knowledge which is the shaman of the *aroe*'s source of social authority is constantly subject to public validation, as he chants alone or directs ceremonies. Such a shaman may gain enormous prestige by his revelations, but he runs the concomitant risk of being utterly discredited.

## *Aroe, Bope,* and the Bororo: A Triadic Paradox

It is now possible to relate the dyadic structure of Bororo shamanism to the social and philosophical paradoxes that society poses for itself. Not all of these by any means are expressed within this structure, and the ones the most relevant to it have been more severely affected by historical pressures than others. For example, one of the most fundamental contradictions in the Bororo system involves the establishment of hierarchy among equals and reciprocal symmetry between entities completely unlike (Crocker 1969a), yet this has very little to do with the shamans. Or again, the complex transmutations of individual identity accomplished through ritual are foreign to them. Now, it must first be shown that the conflicts mediated by the two types of specialists are at once independent and yet mirrored reversals of one another. Next we must understand how one set of problems, or dimension of a single confoundment, has endured and perhaps increased in intensity, while its twin has, apparently, disappeared. Throughout all this the whole issue of the relationship between shamanistic processes and these human dilemmas must be finally resolved.

The object of the second chapter of this book was to show how the self's maximizing potency of *raka* leads that self to become inexorably entangled with the inimical *raka* of radically different entities, leading to its ironic self-destruction. The *bope ure*, it was then argued in the next chapter, provide a metaphoric code for rules whereby this process might at least be regulated, and the vicissitudes of the individual's transformation through aging and affliction be encompassed. But shamanistic treatment itself, the fourth chapter posited, had little direct reference to the particularistic relational trap in which the sufferer found himself; instead this treatment assigned some distant and half-forgotten slight of the *bope*'s foods as cause of the most diverse afflictions. At the conclusion of the chapter I doubted whether such a diagnosis or the purely mechanistic treatment which accompanied it could be interpreted as having any directly functional therapeutic effect. They express the Bororo's profound conviction that "life is a terminal illness." In more indigenous terms, the integration of *aroe* and *bope* in humankind is always precarious, at once doomed by the blind force of *raka* but redeemed by the soul's transcendence.

The *aroe* counterpose the *bope*'s force of destructive renewal through representing immutable forms and relationships. But while through them men can rise above all organic change and even death, the *aroe* also provide the terms in which social personalities can compete for prestige and status. If the *bope* represent irreconcilable conflict between husbands and wives and within the household, the *aroe* express the struggle between domestic groups, among brothers and sisters. The external trappings of soul, the ornaments and paintings and songs, remain iridescently intact while the body decays, but they divide and hierarchize those who share organic being. Here the *bope* intervene as men stress the human necessity of recognizing "their foods" and express their common physical identity as over against women's. In the collective hunts men go off as souls to kill lethally delicious foods: they join together with the *bope*. But the women, sources of all social differentiation, remain closed in their huts as "the mothers of the *aroe*." Through this kind of systematic inversion each force, *aroe* and *bope*, checks the excesses of the other, producing that asymmetrical equilibrium manifested in more dramatic terms through the *bope ure* and *marege mori-xe*.

The shamans' connections with these processes is an extension of their logic and modalities rather than any sort of direct functional intervention. Even the *aroe etawa-are*'s arbitration of prestige disputes involving the *aroe* were accomplished outside the legitimate functions of his office, and he certainly never directly intervened in open social conflict. As I have argued repeatedly, the Bororo ascription of affliction is highly metaphoric: the shamans' intervention is correspondingly generalized and mechanistic. Nor can I escape the feeling that for the Bororo, the *bari*'s consumption of the *bope* food and mystical protection of the village are far more important than his ability at curing the sick. The first two are prophylactic and tautologically efficacious; the last is a symptomatic palliative that can slow affliction's progress but never heal it. The *aroe etawa-are*'s treatments of the ill were similarly short-term, and just as minor within his overall functions on behalf of the community. But now the issue must be confronted: Why are these last functions no longer accomplished?

## Brazilian/Bororo: History of an Elementary Structure

The Bororo have been intimately associated with Brazilian society for almost a century and have had contact with it for at least twice as long. The demographic catastrophe that has overtaken them is just the most recent of the severe threats to their cultural integrity this confrontation has provoked. In the early years the conceptual system had to deal with myriad new forms of plants, animals, and material items, as well as the beings which possessed them. All these had somehow to be encompassed within the classifications that order things in regard to one another and to society. The Bororo emphasis on material property as definition and condition of corporate identity made the intellectual task all the more difficult. With the arrival of these entities, so closely associated as to be axiomatically part of them, came death, and in such new forms and overwhelming frequency as to be almost a novel phenomenon. There were metal knives, guns, cannons, and strange maladies that killed men almost as rapidly. Moreover, these new men brought with them animals strangely like peccary and overgrown deer, which lived with them and which they raised only to kill and eat. With their boats and horses they had marvelous powers of locomotion and seemed, with their shoes and clothes, to be impervious to all the stings, bites, and other hurts nature casually inflicted on other men. Bororo classification boggled at these peculiar beings and their possessions: Were they *bope* or *aroe*?

I doubt if any society could have resisted such a massive challenge to its integrity had it come suddenly, within the experience of a single generation. Owing to the political-economic characteristics of Brazilian penetration into Mato Grosso,[15] however, the confrontation between the two cultures gradually took place over two hundred years. Over this period the material threat to the *aroe*'s encompassing system could be handled a piece at a time, slowly and coherently, all the more because the novel items rarely entered Bororo possession. The epidemiological losses appear to have been relatively light and episodic until the 1880s, and, at least by contemporary Brazilian accounts, the Bororo were so militarily successful in their self-defense and reprisals that they considered attacking the state capital of Cuiaba (Montenegro 1958). But shortly before the turn of the century the problems of contact dramatically intensified.

The following account of the past half-century of Bororo history is taken from my informants' testimonies, a few surveys based on sketchy official records, travelers' reports, and the Salesians' own history of their efforts among the Bororo. It is intended as an outline of the processes leading to the disappearance of all shamans of the *aroe*. As such it is partly hypothetical and narrowly focused. My main concern will be with the ways the historical changes perturbed the delicate social balance of those forces the Bororo call *raka* and *aroe*, and in ways that proved irrelevant to the *aroe etawa-are*'s expertise.

My oldest informants, born around 1900, said that their first memories were of a wandering, fugitive existence in the jungle. "There were no villages; all had fled because of the Brazilians." Military and paramilitary expeditions against the Bororo had reached a climax in the last decades of the nineteenth century, and "pacification" began in 1887, with an official visitation recorded by one of the participants, the German ethnographer Karl von den Steinen (1942). By 1902, when the Salesians established their permanent mission at Sangradouro, the Bororo had ceased organized resistance against the Brazilians. Reservations under various civil, military, and religious administrations were created here and there in Bororo territory even before the foundation of the Indian Protection Service in 1910. The first director of that Service, General Candido da Silva Rondon, himself half-Bororo, was exceedingly generous in his efforts to assist his mother's people. Informants remembered this period as suddenly one of munificent plenty and harmonious relations with non-Bororo.

But it appears that the tribe, heaped with merchandise, at once cajoled, flattered, and closely administered, soon perceived its status as wards of the state. They compensated for their loss of sovereignty by becoming collective mendicants, demanding ever more "gifts" and refusing to become the productive rural laborers envisioned by their governors. At the same time epidemics of smallpox, measles, and the common cold (soon developing into pneumonia) ravaged both reservation communities and the remaining independent villages. And the discovery of diamonds in 1914, near the Bororo settlement of Poxoreu on the upper Rio Vermelho, brought a boom economy to the region, attracting merchants, settlers, and scofflaws, few of whom had a particularly benign disposition toward the Bororo. These events produced an entropic downward spiral of Bororo civilization in three related ways: demographic, economic, and ideological.[16]

Demographically 'he Bororo were confronted with the practical and intellectual necessity of coping with massive population losses. Their system was geared to accommodate villages of a thousand or more; now it had to be made to work for one-half to a tenth of that number. The complex hierarchies of ritual status which maintained order within the clan, and the web of cross-moiety economic and political reciprocities organized by these hierarchies, were eroded and confused. "Suddenly," said an old informant, "there were no chiefs (*emijera*), only men." Furthermore, these losses fell disproportionately among the clans in any one locality. Since the village plan and the ritual cycles demand that each clan be fairly equally represented in a single community, a great deal of inter-village mobility had to be arranged so that traditional forms could be maintained. Of course, this ensured the acceleration of epidemics and the dispersal of the new artifacts.

And then, because every death save those of the very young and unnamed required a complete funeral, the survivors spent much of their time in exhausting symbolic activity, the visiting clans transmitted their sundry germs, more people died who had to be replaced by further infected visitors: the absolute viciousness of the circle derives as much from the prescriptive response of the Bororo to the horrors befalling them, as to those disasters themselves. Indeed, to anticipate my conclusions, it is the very rigidity of the Bororo *aroe*-based structure which condemned its servant, the *aroe etawa-are*, to extinction, not the externally caused dissolution of social forms.

Concomitantly, the indigenous theory of disease and death had to accommodate these cataclysmic losses. The only historically known instance of the interpretations rendered at that time is the episode related in Chapter 2, when a measles epidemic shortly after the turn of the century was found to have been caused by a parent's calamitous dream during childbirth. The significance here of this case is that neither the *aroe* nor the *bope* were credited with malign intent against whole Bororo collectivities. Nor was a shaman-witch blamed. Instead, the only sort of autonomous mystical cause in Bororo cosmology was utilized to explain the afflictions. By its nature neither kind of shaman could prevail against it. Rather than doubting the efficacy of the *aroe* and the *bope*, the Bororo endorsed one of the predicates of these powers' existence: human frailty in achieving the balanced harmony. Since the social response was to kill all children born in the preceding five years, one might even say that the cosmological structure was preserved at the further demographic cost of its believing society.

Contemporary Bororo are apt to interpret a sudden wave of afflictions as due to the *bope*'s successful theft of many souls, as symbolised in the *aroe butu* ("falling star"). I imagine that in the early years of this cen-

Bororo children

tury the Bororo heard numerous meteors crash to earth. This is the *bope*'s most capricious manifestation of their power over humans. It will be remembered that while none of their victims in these raids is ever guilt-less of some offense against the *bope* foods, the offense's character and the victim's relation to it are even more petty and tangential than in the causes of individual affliction, which are certainly vague and circumstantial enough. (For example, most of the robbed persons are the innocent chil-dren or other close relatives of the actual offender.) Further, it is the vic-tims' souls, their transcendent categorical *aroe*, which are taken by the *bope*, who exclusively in this context forego their (and the *aroe*'s) mode of affliction through introjected pathogenic agents. When the *aroe* take a human soul, they do so to awaken its possessor to a new mode of exis-tence, that of intermediary between themselves and human society. The *bope* have no such beneficent motives, but significantly they act here in a way otherwise reserved for the *aroe*. Even the avenue of their attack, through the ornamented bows and baskets which are the material ex-pressions of their owners' *aroe*-defined persona, is appropriate to their symbolic antithesis. By reason of the inversions of shamanistic powers just examined, only the shamans of the *bope* could confront this sort of insidiously oblique attack on the community's integration of form and process. Other threats to Bororo solidarity, especially the novel economic changes, enhanced the *bope*'s strange dominion over the souls.

Material transformations affected both the household's internal dynamics of production and consumption and the total community ecology. As settlers moved into the area and professional hunters appeared to serve the new boomtowns, all kinds of fauna declined, and traditional hunting and fishing techniques became less fruitful. For example, older Bororo claim that in their youth the São Lourenço was limpidly clear so that fish spears and arrows were very productive. But then the mining operations upriver turned the river into its present state of opaque mud. The dry-season treks, a crucial part of the village's ecological cycle, became nearly impossible, owing to presence of Brazilians over parts of the traditional trekking areas and to general ill health. The last in itself posed serious ecological problems. The only time I saw the Bororo's efficient system of differentiated production and distribution break down occurred during an epidemic.[17] Normally, small groups of hunters and fishers can support a largely nonproductive population five times their own number, at least during the prosperous wet season. But when nearly everyone is too sick to work efficiently, the village must fall back on its resources of stored food and readily available plants, meager in the wet season and hardly more adequate in the dry. I think the difficulty of trekking, scarcity of game, and frequent collective ill health led the Bororo to adopt Brazilian cultigens, especially the relatively carefree sweet manioc, and to expand their indigenous maize cultivations. Of course, all their early administrators, military, ecclesiastical, and civil, had urged the delights of pastoral agriculturalism upon them. But the independent villages also began extensive gardens by the 1920s, according to informants. At least among modern Bororo, one of the most frequent topics in the chiefs' nightly harangues is the necessity of assiduous gardening to community prosperity. Their words inspire only reluctant compliance among males.

Bororo men define themselves as hunters, and roundly denounce the tedium of agriculture, even though admitting its economic importance. Traditionally, although labor in the gardens is only lightly sexually differentiated, all cultivated produce belonged to the household's women and was alienable only by decision of its female head. The gathering and distribution of wild plants were and are under exclusive feminine control. Therefore, this shift in Bororo ecology toward increased consumption of vegetable foods had at least two consequences. First, women became more economically and sociologically independent, at least in respect to arrangements in their own households. One of the common domestic quarrels among contemporary Bororo involves the husband's obligation to supply his matrilineal relatives with food, which in the absence of game must come from his wife's garden. At least some women appear to delight in their power to humiliate their spouses by refusing these prestations, or by honoring them in a niggardly, disdainful fashion. Second, meat and fish (above all those of the *bope ure*) are socially prescribed for most formal prestations between households. (A notable exception is the vegetable dishes prepared by women for their *aroe* "sons" in the opposite moiety.) Again, relative lack of game reduces men's capacity to mediate across domestic groups, or, in Bororo terms, to fulfill their obligations as *aroe*, both those of ritual representatives and those deriving from their clans' *aroe* representations.

I must stress that these changes were relative. Game and fish are still astonishingly plentiful in the São Lourenço valley. Men continue to exercise a good deal of authority owing to their control of economic goods, including those of plant origin.[18] Nor have the totemic and ancestral *aroe* lost any of their power to define social organization and the ordering of collective experience. But the domestic group's internal rhythms and the modes of its relationship to analogous units were profoundly troubled in their integration of *bope*-controlled process with *aroe* forms. Socially the collectivity responded more to its external relations, less to its internal *aroe*-generated divisions. The new material goods flooding the system exacerbated these problems.

The utilitarian items (machetes, pots and kettles, guns, cords, fishhooks, and clothes) facilitated the entire adaptive process while upsetting the system's traditional functioning. First, their uneven disposition within and between communities introduced further imbalances in reciprocal exchanges and eroded the prestige of the *aroe*-derived forms of productive wealth, in about equal measure. Second, because of the nature of the contact frontier[19] and Brazilian sexual ideology, only Bororo males were able to have access to procurement of the novel goods. They thus offset their diminishment as procurers of raw protein, but to the further disruption of male-female integration within the basic unit of production and consumption. Women's demands for manufactured items, as explained in Chapter 2, exacerbated the men's conflicting loyalties to their matrilineal and affinal groups. Further, the increase of male wage work led to their daily or weekly, or even seasonal absence from the community, with concomitant disruptions of all relations of common substance. Many young men gave me two reasons for avoiding wage work: the disagreeable character of the labor itself, in its menial nature and association with Brazilians; and their wives' inclination to exploit these opportunities for clandestine adventures. (In fact, as various cases of affliction noted in earlier chapters testify, an individual's regular absence from the village gives rise to all sorts of *bope*- and *aroe*-offending misunderstandings.) In brief, then, the transformations in both ecological and material patterns tended to disrupt further the indigenously fragile domestic group, that center of *bope*-dominated processing of *raka* and integration of beings with antithetical powers of *raka*.

One novel Brazilian good seems to have summarized all the attractive lethality, the irreversible entropic decline, the cancerous blossoming of indigenous social tensions, brought about by sustained contacts between the two societies. This was alcohol, or in the form most commonly known to the Bororo, cachaça, sugar-cane brandy or rum, locally called pinga. While my reconstruction of the varied consequences of pacification upon the Bororo are poor enough, I can only guess at the effect of this substance. It is certain that Bororo chiefs now condemn it roundly. Missionaries and federal agents forbade its presence in areas under their control very early in this century, as they do now. [20] The only contemporary Bororo homicides were committed under its influence, according to informants, and the only times I saw Bororo men deviate notably from their cultural ethos happened when they were thoroughly drunk.

Traditionally the Bororo brewed a palm wine from the sap of the acuri palm (*Attalea* sp.), which was called *iworo*. This is also the title of one sort of *bope*, and, indeed, several shamans of these spirits claimed an Iworo among their familiars. But the lightly fermented *iworo* was also one of the drinks given to the *aroe* through their shaman, and to the human actors after *aroe* representations. *Iworo etawujedu*, "the 'spirit of leaves' representation," described earlier in this chapter, is one of the crucial ceremonies in the funeral cycle. Consistently the Bororo do not class *iworo* with either form of mystical being: "It goes to both sides at once." Its mild effervescence promotes the gay social harmony associated with the *aroe*; it also arouses the blacker passions indulged by the *bope*. When contemporary Bororo condemn alcohol, they do so with a self-righteousness tinged by a longing regret. I suppose that in the early years Brazilian liquor exacerbated all the epidemiological and cultural disasters deriving from the contact situation, but at the same time it provided some temporary surcease from these miseries. As one informant said, "Pinga stirs up *raka*, so even the oldest of men feel their *aroe* young and sound once again." In denying themselves access to it, the Bororo confess their inability to control directly not just this substance but all those processes changing their lives, from within as surely as from without.

# 12

## Dead Souls

When confronted by multitudinous threats to their civilization, the Bororo responded by refusing to accommodate them, even to acknowledge their existence through alterations in the organizational system expressed by the *aroe*. And their conservatism was successful, save in one particular, the disappearance of the shaman of the souls. The issue now is how the particular transformations in indigenous demography and economy led to this result rather than to any other. The Bororo themselves are baffled by the *aroe*'s sudden refusal to manifest themselves through human beings. As I said earlier, several men, paragons of Bororo virtue, grieved repeatedly that they wished fervently to be *aroe etawa-are*, and others were as puzzled as they over the souls' lack of interest in such exemplary potential mediators. My feeling is that the *aroe* are not entirely "real" to these men, nor to the Bororo as a society. I do not mean that the Bororo have ceased to believe in the transcendental categories of truth and order represented by the *aroe*: collective thought rests upon these as unskeptically as the village self-confidently represents refractions of the *aroe* in its ceremonials. Rather, I hypothesize that the domains of social experience most informed by *aroe* symbolism have been impoverished, while the categories themselves have come to be irrelevant to the novel forms of disorder brought about in the past half-century. This new chaos is appropriate to the *bope*, in such a way that only their agents can deal with it. The *aroe*'s refusal to manifest themselves through humans is consequently one way to express the human failure to "feel" their dominion, their character and intrusive presence in this world, and just as much a reflection of the *bope*'s supremacy over "feltness," of their manifest suzerainty over all forms of reality.

I first came to this interpretation when puzzling over another contemporary Bororo phenomenon, the scarcity of children in the general population. At first this seemed reasonable, given the high level of infant mortality. Often middle-aged women, and occasionally men, told me of their desire to have more children, and several younger women were notorious in gossip for their use of plant contraceptives and abortifacients: "The babies just die." I thought this a temporary individual response to the recent death of an infant, until I began to hear about that village, Pobojari, whose inhabitants had decided collectively "to have no more children." I was skeptical until I talked with visitors from that village and then visited it myself.

Pobojari is located on the Rio Vermelho, one of the major tributaries of the São Lourenço and about 170 kilometers upstream from the villages where I did my fieldwork.[21] It is (or was) one of the two remaining "unprotected" Bororo villages: its land and the welfare of its inhabitants were in principle protected by federal law, but only in principle. The community's domain had been eroded by a series of legally dubious transactions, and further usurped by squatters. It was, in 1966, ringed on three sides by Brazilian settlers, of whom at least two had their homesteads within eye- and earshot of the village. A small Brazilian town was only a few kilometers away and provided all sorts of manufactured goods, including rum and beer, to both settlers and Bororo.

Pobojari was laid out in traditional fashion around a large and well-maintained men's house, but its population had no children under six years of age, and only two under twelve. Several residents spontaneously told me that "everyone" had decided to have no more children. That evening, at the men's council meeting, one of the clan chiefs explained this decision to me and my Bororo traveling companions. Pobojari had fallen upon evil times. Little game remained in the forests, the fishing was poor, and the Bororo gardens were constantly invaded by the Brazilians' domesticated animals. Many people had to work for Brazilians in order just to eat. Worst of all, the proximity of their homesteads meant that no ceremony could be conducted without the mocking presence of Brazilian spectators.

"We can no longer live like Bororo, and we will not live like Brazilians. So we have decided not to live at all: we will die in the Bororo way, one by one, and after us there will be nothing." The Bororo with me found this argument entirely persuasive. They urged the residents of Pobojari to move to the protected villages, while tacitly recognizing that, given the profound attachment to native locality, many of them would prefer to die right there, without issue. They also noted the similarity of this decision to that taken in response to the epidemic fifty years ago, to destroy the recently born children to preserve the society. In both cases the transformations in organic nature provoked by *raka* had to be denied, undone, so that the domain of form could be preserved. These collective responses to threatened change mirror the loss of the shaman of the *aroe*: while they are deliberate negations, the latter is an unwilled lack, a lamented absence. But both types of loss are linked by common properties besides their formal structural inversion of each other.

In the inverted division of labor between the two shamans, the *aroe etawa-are* was publicly responsible for regulating the order of social divisions and transactions between them. It should not be forgotten that the domain of the *aroe* extended both to cosmological order and to the competitive divisiveness over categorical rights in the artifacts and status positions defined by that order. The knowledge of the "souls' ways" possessed by their shaman guaranteed his ability to arbitrate these conflicts between and within clans. But over the years of direct confrontation with Brazilian society these internal dissensions had to be suppressed, while at the same time the differentiated social organization also based on the *aroe* had to be preserved and enhanced. The *aroe etawa-are*'s other public responsibility came vitally to the fore: his role in the symbolic processes whereby Bororo society asserts its integrity against those external forces which harm and destroy its members, the institution of the "new soul" and the *marege mori-xe*, the animals of revenge.

But now carnivorous nature had ceased to be the adversary to be conquered to assure the transcendence of a deceased's soul. Henceforth, the ultimate form of *marege mori-xe* would be man himself, in the person of a Brazilian who had to be slain. Further, the shaman of the *aroe* also had to deal with the new material things, and the unique knowledge that accompanied them, flooding in upon the Bororo. He had to categorize them, fix them within the finite order of the *aroe*. I have wondered if the *aroe etawa-are* did not flourish during the first two centuries of contact, even if the whole dyadically balanced system of Bororo shamanism only assumed its "traditional" form during this time. But no matter that, once the dubious benefits of peace with the aliens had been secured, the problems subtly altered so that the shaman of the souls was powerless to confront them.

The mystical functions of the *aroe* shaman involve the provision of *raka*-laden game to the village's hunters, as symbolized in his metamorphosis into a tapir, the prime "food of the *bope*." But as soon as he accomplishes this, his colleague the *bari* takes over, now pragmatically, to ensure the transformation of this substance into a form safe for humans to consume. In this context the *aroe* are "on the outside" of the community, the *bope* very much within the conjugal household. It is in this domain that crises actively threaten, and in two ways. First, there are the disruptions provoked by all the demographic, ecological, and material transformations. Second, there is the *bope*'s haphazard theft of "sleeping souls"— the utter, random suddenness with which affliction falls on first one and then another member of the domestic group, just as meteors flash by in defiance of all celestial rhythm. All at once human beings are unable to accomplish their organic destinies. The rules which integrate individual growth with identity, *raka* with *aroe*, and which provide for the integration of those with complementary selves into harmonious, self-reproducing units, no longer seem to function very well. As we have seen, the *aroe* utilize the generative capacities of human beings to kill their owners when they confound form and process; the *aroe* attack *raka* so that the soul drifts off, easy prey to the devouring *bope*. The shamans of the *bope* are logically the community's only defense against this form of mystical attack; only they and the spirits they serve actively sustain *raka*. The *aroe* and their shamans bring about the nomination of new things and ensure their eternal existence; they have nothing to do with the sustenance of their organic development, with the creations and destructions they accomplish through their natural energies. But in choosing to die as a people the Bororo acknowledge their final helplessness against these *bope*-inspired forces: they assert against them the dominion of the transcendent dead. The *aroe* live in all our memories.

# Reference Material

# APPENDIX A

# Aroe or "Totems" Owned by Bororo Clans

## Iwagudu-doge

aere (urutau, type of water bird)
karao (type of water bird)
kido (parakeet)
xeje (variety of small hawk)
iwaje (turkey-vulture)
pobureu (vulture generally)
aroebai (type of large hawk)
keagu (hawk)
kujibo (cardinal)
maridogareu (small black bird)
piodudu (hummingbird)
piroje (type of swallow)
pogoriwo (other type of swallow)
kuje (curassow)
mokureabu (type of urutau)
kurutui (goatsucker bird)
uwarinogo (scissor-tailed hawk)
tururu (type of goatsucker)
iwagudu (crow)
koxaga (seracura, type of water bird)

jakome (a spirit like a small raccoon)
tugo (a spirit like a large rat)
akiwa (capivara)
arigao (dog)

marido (buriti palm(
beragu (type of resin)
mixori (a thin tough vine)

arori (coral snake)
araru (piraputanga, type of fish)
jarudo (bogre, kind of fish)

aroia (manufactured cloth or beaten bark)
butore (rattles worn around ankle)
buke (fish net)
aria (bowl)
pori (water pot)
mixigu (small "purse" woven from palm)
beto (large mat woven from palm)
joru (fire)

## Arore

bakuguma (type of small hawk)
boro (small spotted moray)
ierarai (jerakambea, small bird)
nabure ("blue" macaw)
reoreo (small finch)
korao (parrot)
metugo (dove)
tamigi (horned screamer)
batagaje xoreu (type of loon)
metugo kujagureu ("red" dove)
barakaia (ocelot)
jugo (caitetu)
jui (quexada)
ipie (otter)
etarigo (large quexada)
jomo (type of small otter)
aokurumodo (another type of small otter)
kudobu (coati)
meridabu (ferret)
merirugo (small ferret)
kudugi (type of small monkey)
moribo (wild dog)
ipoxereu (tayra, type of "weasel")
bokwari (type of large otter)
okwa (small wolf)
aimeareu (ocelot)
aimeareau xoreu (black ocelot)

nonoguje (wild urucu)
mano (round bundle of palm strips used in dances)
botoro (seriva, wood used for bows)
pareriwoe (tree whose bark is used for belts)
kogwaiwoi (another "bark" tree)
baxewoe (tiliacea vine)
kodobi (generic term for vine)

aroro (larva of certain butterfly)
bakorororeu (type of coral snake)

buke (fish net)
arago (large club)

335

bakoreu (woven fan)
muiao bori (termite "honey")
aragioro (type of wild honey)

## Apiborege

aroe exeba (harpy eagle)
kurugugwa (large hawk)
torowa (fish-eating hawk)
parabara (irere, water bird)
tano (quero-quero, water bird)
tudu (type of owl)
beo (type of water bird?)
baxe (heron)
xugui (type of toucan)
baxe kuguio (wood ibis)

bakure (night monkey)
atomoyo (river turtle)
aipobureu (large ocelot)
awagadari (even larger ocelot)

tubore (lambari, small fish)
tubore xoreu (black lambari)
buruwo (sawa, small fish)
akurara (pacupeba, fish)

atu (fresh water mussel)
aturebo (small variety of mussel)

irui (large lizard or iguana)

kueje kurireu (star, Venus)
kueje kujagureu (star, Mars?)

baku (type of palm-woven fan)
bakureu (another kind of fan)
bapu (rattle)

apido (akuri palm)

*Mountains in the Rio Vermelho area*
Ikuieri
Ipareri
Torowari
Tuburari

## Paiwoe

tagae (the great tanager)
tububari (duck)
baxe akorogoreu (heron)
kugu (large owl)
bokururodu (murucututu, type of owl)
tagogo (field owl)

bi (very small owl)
kaikai (owl)
kugoxoreu (a hawk, the quiriquiri)
kugo kigadureu (a "white" hawk)
iwabo (japu, large bird)
kerekere (small parrot)
korao (parrot)
xuru-i (parrot-vulture)
keakorogo (guava)
ore (jandaia, small bird)
kuritaga (trumpet parrot)
makao (macaua, water bird)
koido ("red" macaw)

nonogo (domesticated urucu)
kidoguru (type of resin)
kaidaga (acioma palm)
kuiada (corn)
mixori (imbe vine)

Aturuari (a certain mountain)

meriri (general term for metal)
buke (type of fish net)
mixigu (large woven purse)
juko (monkey, cepus niger)
pai (howler monkey)
buke (anteater)
apogo ("blond" anteater)
ato (jabuti, type of turtle)
jerigigi (cagado, type of turtle)
rie (guara or wolf)
iwe (porcupine)
mea (cutia)
atubo (type of deer)
ru (toad)
baraetaitai (type of tree frog)
uwai xoreu (black alligator)

poru (jau, large fish)
orarije (surubim, large fish)
orari nogurari (pintado)
orari xoreu (other type of pintado)
kudogo (abotoado, fish)
nowareu (bagre, "catfish")
rokoreu (type of lambari)
akoro (jurumpensem)
rekudo (surubim-chicote)
koma (jurupoca)
juireu (cuiu-cuiu)
rureu (palmito)

*Types of spirits all living in or near rivers*
Tori

Butori
Utogaga
Bakagwei

## Bado Jeba Xebegiwuge

pobu (pacu, large fish)

o kujagureu (tiger bittern)
baxe (small heron)
eregejeje (red-black woodpecker)
kadamo (king fisher)
meri (tie-fogo, small bird)
monoko (snipe)
kurege (mythical water bird)

ewo (rattlesnake)
rea (type of armadillo, tatu liso)
uwai akia kigadureu ("white"
   alligator)
ixe (boa constrictor)
pogodo (another type of boa
   constrictor)

bokwadi (jatoba tree)
nonogo (variety of urugu)

kaibori (pestle)

*Varieties of spirits*
Okoge Bakororo
Okoge Kujagureu
Meri (sun spirit)
Ari (moon spirit)
Bokodori
Bokwamo
Iwara-Rege
Paiko
Adugo Oro
Edogodogo
Tabo Kujagureu
Jowari
Butao-doge

bope (nature sprites or demons)
maereboe (sub-variety of bope)

## Kie

porobwe (japuira, bird)
kudoru ("black" macaw)
batara xoreu (black jao pinto)
bai (king vulture)
bai xoreu (black king vulture)
apodo oto xoreu (small black toucan)

kuo (jao, type of quail)
pari (ema)
tuiotorogo (small black bird?)
mudu (juruva)

ki (tapir)
bokodori xoreu ( black armadillo)
aigo (puma)
aipobureu (ocelot)
amo (rabbit)
apu (paca)
baxieje (the male guacuti deer)
pobogo (forest deer)

okoge xoreu (black dourado fish)

jure (red-black anaconda)
jure marido (type of anaconda)

toro (dance skirt)
toro xoreu (black dance skirt)
kugu bari (wind instrument)
bapu xoreu ("black" rattles)
bapu rogu kurireu (type of rattle)
kaia (mortar)
ika xoreu (black wind instrument)
koe xoreu (black necklace)
barae xoreu (Negroes)

*Varieties of spirits*
Bokuwojeba
Kabeo
Merijokimoio
Baparu Kadojebage

## Bokodori Exerae

xinaetautau (big crow)
batara kujagureu (red jao-pinto)
xiwabo (small japu)
agwa (tico-tico rei, type of sparrow)
meriaku (another type of sparrow)
baruwa-are (small black bird)
kadagare (kingfisher)

okoge (dourado fish)
okogearege (small dourado)

iturawori (armadillo)
bokodori (giant armadillo)
ruwo (snail)

ika (wind instrument)
bapu rogu (rattles)
akigu (cotton plant)
boaro (type of earring)

koe (type of necklace)
koereu (another type of necklace)
poiwo (bamboo "cup" for drinking
    palm wine)


Bado Jeba Xobugiwuge

adugo xoreu (black jaguar)
adugo kujagureu (red jaguar)
okwaru (type of armadillo)
rie (type of armadillo)
bokodori (necklace)
o xoreu (type of tiger bittern)

boro (small snail)
aribo ekureu (apara-pedra, bird)

buiogwa (piranha, fish)
bokwari (pagucu, fish)
je kujagureu (red piava, fish)
reko (rubafo, fish)

pana (type of wind instrument)

*Types of spirits all connected with rivers or
    streams*
Tabo Xoreu
Itubore
Iworo

# Plan of Korugedu Paru (Corrego Grande), 1965

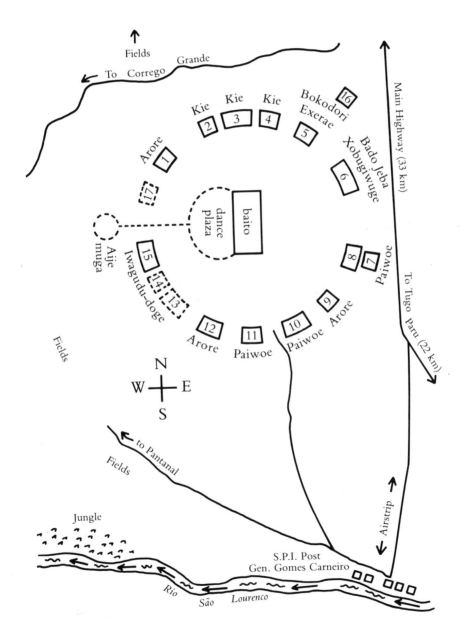

# Plan of Pobojari, 1965

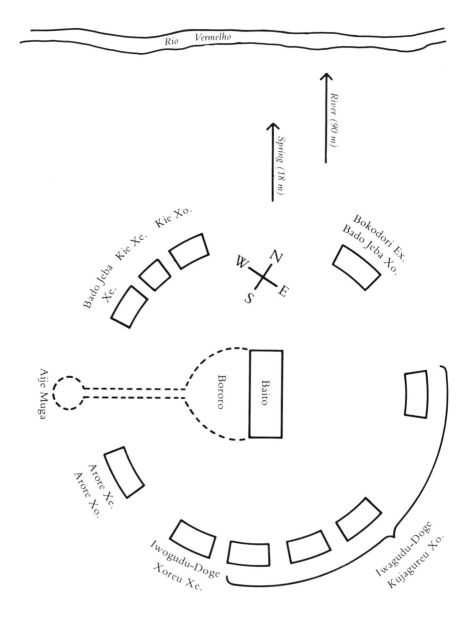

# Notes

## Prologue and Introduction

1. I have in mind particularly those ethnographic classics by Bogoraz (1904, 1910–1912), Rasmussen (1929), Shirokogoroff (1923, 1935), and Nordenskiold (1931). The North European tradition of shamanistic scholarship has continued to present times (Hultkrantz 1963, Edsman 1967) and so represents an exception to the contemporary neglect of the topic.

2. "Pintado" do exist in the Araguaia River, which drains the northeastern quadrant of traditional Bororoland, but informants insisted that this species was far less common there than in the São Lourenço. *Orari* ("pintado") are one of the species subject to elaborate rules governing human relationships with them, including shamanistic mediation, and are the vehicles of other complex symbolisms. See Chapters 2 and 3.

3. Most of the attrition has been due to the advent of such Western diseases as smallpox, measles, and tuberculosis, as well as exceedingly high levels of infant mortality. By no means coincidentally, the surviving (and most traditional) villages are those at the very center of Bororoland, those most insulated by sheer distance from all the repercussive effects of the Western presence.

4. There are differences between villages, such as the placement of the men's house, that cannot be explained in demographic and typographic terms. Furthermore, informants disagree and sometimes contradict themselves on the finer details of the village plan. But all Bororo remain convinced that there is a "perfect" village model, exactly replicated by the villages of the dead. Also, the observed deviations from the plan and disagreements about it seem themselves to be systematic. I treat these problems in the next book on Bororo social organization.

5. Some informants stated that traditionally a third subclan existed between the "upper" and "lower" divisions, termed appropriately enough "Boedadawu," "those of the middle." It was said to have been originally composed of conquered non-Bororo adopted into the tribe, and it owned only a few, very poor ceremonial rights. Other Bororo firmly denied the existence of such a grouping.

6. The Bororo do say that adjacent households are "closer," "more like each other," than spatially distant households of the same clan, and in some contexts this closeness is given a consanguineal connotation. But men knowledgeable in traditional lore make it clear that this relationship reflects the similarity in property, names, ceremonial prerogatives, and ornaments owned by the households. This similarity in turn derives from the particular refraction of the clan's totemic *aroe* associated with the subclan, including the adjacent households. See Crocker (1977b, 1979) for further discussion.

7. In Bororo theory the first person who discovered and named a novel species or other form of being thereby obtained it as an *aroe* for his or her clan. However, in the time of the culture heroes Baitogogo (Bakororo) and Borogei (Itubore) (who are now the *pagimejera,* "chiefs," of all the *aroe*), many men gave certain of their clans' *aroe* to their sons' clans. The point here is that the Bororo do not perceive any unique relationship among all the *aroe* associated with a clan. They are regarded instead as a disordered jumble assembled by historical accident and held together only by their common occupancy of a single cosmological space. This does not mean that an analogic scheme does not order their relationships, and I explore some possible schemes in Chapter 10. But the Bororo themselves reject any such notion of structure in the domain of the *aroe*.

8. Such paths are actually physically rare in contemporary villages, for most of the intermoiety exchanges occur in or just outside the men's house. Informants also make a distinction between "great" and "little" paths according to the relative prestige of the *aroe* representations which generate them.

9. There is a critical exception to this generalization: the *aroe* (here the undifferentiated collectivity of ancestral souls and the totemic essences) are considered to control the reproduction of most species of fish. This indicates the complex associations between the *aroe* and the aquatic domain, which is explored in Chapter 10.

# Part I

## CHAPTER 1: VITAL HUMORS

1. The Bororo have no very precise ideas of the functions of *raka* in vegetable, fish, reptile, and other forms of being which, as they say, "lack balls and breasts." To the extent that these creatures possess blood, they are treated as having *raka,* but consideration for its different nature in them emerges in their ceremonial and symbolic treatment, as shown later in this chapter and in the remainder of the book.

2. This is the Bororo version of the nature-nurture paradox. It extends to issues of individual morality and intelligence, with these qualities being traced to direct inheritance from the parents and their consanguines, to whom these ties of shared blood and character logically extend. Such natural attributes influence but do not determine mature behavior, for reasons discussed in later sections.

3. This figure should be regarded with a certain skepticism, since it reflects the modern tendency to limit birth by the contraceptive and abortifacient methods discussed later in the chapter. Informants claimed, on the other hand, that their contemporaries tended to have infants much more closely spaced in time than their ancestors, but this, in turn, may be only a manifestation of a general tendency to compare a "golden age" with current degenerations.

4. A similar end awaits all birth anomalies. The official murderer is the midwife, whose social and symbolic attributes are discussed later in the chapter and in Crocker (1977c). Twins, among the monstrosities of birth, seem especially anomalous in terms of Bororo logic, for informants refused to discuss the topic, although they freely expressed their views on other types of "wrong births." I believe twins contradict the logic of Bororo rules for the regulation of sibling conduct, which feature the logic of "elder" and "younger."

5. Breech and other awkward presentations are explained by failure to observe this rule.

6. A sensitive and sophisticated review of the ethnographic literature can be found in Rivière (1974); facts comparable to the Bororo situation are found in Maybury-Lewis (1969: 65–66). My general impression is that Rivière's hypothesis tends to hold true for indigenous groups other than Gê-speakers, all of whom stress the name-giving relation as the foundation of social existence and who utilize a parent's cross-sex sibling in the role.

7. One of the most terrible episodes in Bororo history came from failure to obey this rule. Early in the century villages were being decimated by a smallpox epidemic. A shaman of the souls discovered in communicating with the *aroe* that this illness had been dreamed about by a father during his wife's labor, but he failed to tell the *i-maruga* anything about it. The only way to stop the terrible affliction, which was killing dozens of Bororo, was to kill the baby. But the difficulty was that the souls did not know which child was involved, only that it had been born between two and six years before the beginning of the epidemic. The Bororo of the region put to death every child born during this period. My own informants, some of whom had been born shortly after this horrifying episode, often spoke of it with no moral condemnation, only a sense of great tragedy. This seems to have been the first major epidemic after contact; subsequent ones have been otherwise interpreted and treated (see Chapters 3 and 4).

8. Among the verbal formulas was the *aware are,* the formal and sterotyped chant of welcome rendered to visitors personally unknown in the village. It states, among other things, "You have wandered far. Your feet have been bruised by stones. Your flesh has been torn by thorns and stinging vines. You have been bitten by insects, by snakes, by wild animals. You have been attacked by jaguars, anteaters, armadillos, alligators, and they have hurt you very much. But now you are here among us, safe. We will care for you," and so on. I do not think the Bororo are especially sissy, although they certainly spend a great deal of informal time as well as ritual moments complaining of how badly nature hurts them. More crucially, their classification of the natural world and its symbolic associations rest upon a carnivore-noncarnivore duality, which correlates with "harming" and "non-harming" entities. This logic is discussed in Part IV.

9. One should take a thorough bath as soon as possible after intercourse and after killing animals. The Bororo possess a very elaborate classification of smells, discussed in Chapter 6, and associate those deriving from the freshness of nature and from the *aroe* as invigorating and life-sustaining, although I know of no

symbolic acts in which smelling of these things is "deliberately" employed. But water is very clearly an agency imbued with pollution-removing efficacy, and as such is employed in many ritual contexts.

10. Actually, these last entities are included in a somewhat attenuated way among "Foods of the *bope*." Chapter 6 sets out the ethnographic details and provides an analysis of these items.

## CHAPTER 2: THE WHEEL OF LIFE

11. By "more than adequate" I mean that food was abundant enough to nourish not only the human population, which includes a very high number of nonproductive persons, but also to feed a grotesquely large number (in my opinion) of domestic animals, especially pigs, who are fed exclusively on household garbage. Only during epidemics, when most of the adults were physically incapacitated, was daily food scarce.

12. I hope to complete an ethnohistory of the Bororo in the near future, as their past raises some interesting questions concerning the relative influence of general economic and sociological factors in the intrusive civilization upon degree and kind of acculturation. Certainly, Bororo ability to resist the Brazilians, both militarily and culturally, must be related to the unique qualities of their social system.

13. I know of only two Bororo males who are regarded as having definitively left their society, although at least half a dozen, some with Bororo families, work for Brazilian ranchers and farmers. But they will return to indigenous communities after a year or two of wage work. At least two villages in close proximity to Brazilian settlements have been so disturbed that traditional existence is no longer possible in them.

14. The exact proportion of domesticated to nondomesticated foodstuffs (including fish and game) tends to vary seasonally, between villages, and from one household to the next. While in some cases cultigens account for 80 percent of all food consumed during the week, in others they may be less than half. The average amount over the year is about 60 percent. It seems that corn was cultivated aboriginally, and perhaps certain species of squash (Albisetti and Venturelli 1962: 754–55).

15. The Bororo believe that the souls of dead persons, especially children, frequently return invisibly to visit their parents and maternal relatives. These souls enter the domesticated macaws, which are therefore sometimes addressed as the "children" of their owner. Alternately, the souls go into the baskets where duck down and macaw breast feathers are kept (Crocker 1977b).

16. More extended discussions of this complicated subject can be found in Crocker (1969a, 1977b, 1977c, and 1979). It should be mentioned that, while the Bororo are convinced of the precise association between household/name-group and particular *aroe* ornaments and forms, and of the relationships between name-groups within the subclan, in practice the details of the system are confused, even in the minds of single informants. This confusion seems functionally useful in giving flexibility to what is otherwise a very rigid organization.

17. The category of *aroe* includes not just the "souls" of the ancestors but also the divinized nominal essences of categorical forms, to which I usually refer as "totems." The Bororo are rather ambiguous as to which type of *aroe* actually punishes ceremonial infractions, but usually the totemic variety appears to take the most active roles. Specific cases and their treatment are discussed in Part IV. It

should be noted here that in this respect and others the Bororo ancestors' relationships with their descendants are very different from those characterizing, for example, African "ancestor cults."

18. This situation proved invaluable during fieldwork, since I became considered as at least possible heir by several *emijera,* especially by one of the most eminent who, in fact, adopted me as his *i-wagedu* by giving me a name from his own name-group (Noapayepa of the Bado Jeba Xebegiwuge). I carried out some of the social and ritual duties associated with the *emijera* of my subclan. I was also considerably helped by my wife's adopted brothers and mother's brothers, with two of whom I came to have a quasi-filial relationship. After an initial period, in fact, nearly all *emijera* I met were exceedingly cooperative, not so much for personal reasons as because the position of "ritual disciple" is one of the most fundamental of Bororo relationships; it is perfect for an ethnographer. However, my relationship with my adopted *i-edaga* soon came to transcend that of anthropologist-informant. He continues to have considerable moral authority over me and has been a great influence on my life.

## CHAPTER 3: SEXUAL DIALECTICS

19. It may be the prejudice in favor of the society acquired by most ethnologists, but I find Bororo artifacts to be exceedingly well made and to reflect great skills of craftmanship. The acquisition of these skills takes considerable time and careful instruction, so that the father's training of his son is no small matter, especially since ability in craftmanship is a very important element in personal prestige. Certain individuals become renowned for their expertise in a certain area and manage to derive a certain income from their specializations.

20. I suspect that their relationship might include homosexuality, which is certainly known to the Bororo and apparently practiced fairly widely, especially in youth. Information on the subject was as difficult to obtain as that relating to other aspects of sexuality, but I was told by two informants that rules of moiety exogamy pertained to these acts and were almost always observed. I have not been able to discover any information on the character and amount of homosexuality in related societies, and so cannot say what structural factors might explain its occurrence among the Bororo.

21. Eating is regarded as one of the "fleshly appetites," along with copulation and sleeping. As such it must be conducted, publicly at least, with great restraint and even a sort of repugnance. Bororo older men often boast about how little they eat, sleep, and copulate, and how, consequently, very *rakare* they are. That is, excessive eating leads to a diminution of *raka.* One of the traditional health practices involved the induction of vomiting an hour or two after eating, which was thought to have a "cleansing" effect on the entire body. Consistently with these attitudes, culinary symbolism among the Bororo regards only the species to be cooked, not the modalities of their preparation.

# Part II

## CHAPTER 4: THE *BOPE* IN BORORO EPISTEMOLOGY

1. This description, very much a collective representation, may contain elements borrowed from Brazilian folk-Catholic images of the devil. If so, such

loans must have been highly selective, since such critical devilish attributes as a forked tail and horns do not appear in the *bope*'s portrait. Since each detail of the last is echoed throughout the heterogeneous range of practices and beliefs involving all the myriad aspects of the *bope,* I am inclined to accept the entire description as indigenously Bororo.

2. In common with most totemic peoples (Lévi-Strauss 1962b: 228–31), the Bororo account for the original association between a generic *aroe* and a specific clan through the historical chance encounter between that *aroe* and a clan ancestor, who, by naming this hitherto unknown condition of being, acquired certain rights over it for his name-group and clan. More idiosyncratically, the Bororo also hold that many totems were subsequently transferred as prestations from one moiety to the other or by other transfers within the clan or moiety (Albisetti and Venturelli 1962: 100–8). In the present case it is known that a member of the Bokodori Exerae was the first Bororo to meet a Brazilian, "small and dark-skinned as a *bope.*" There seems to be a growing tendency to differentiate categorically between different types of non-Indians and to associate particularly Americans and their unique artifacts (such as airplanes) with one of the Bado Jeba clans. I do not know whether this means that Americans are viewed as a variety of *bope* or simply inventions of the spirits; I suspect the unflattering but internally consistent former view is the correct one.

3. Even to term such structures as termite nests and rocks as their "homes" is misleading, for the *bope* do not "live" in any organic sense within a specific habitat, let alone "dwell" in a place. Rather, the *maereboe* are perceived to radiate out from these loci, as fields of metaphysical power whose strength is diminished with distance from their centers. The usual Bororo attitude toward these *maereboe* sites is a certain heightened awareness of the total surroundings, but certainly it cannot be said to be "animistic." The sites are not tabooed, nor are any of their physical properties ritually used.

4. The evidence of this fear is in various standardized bits of behavior. Commonly a cigarette is lit and smoked and puffed to the four cardinal points, a gesture also constantly employed by shamans to placate their familiars. Children are quickly if calmly removed from the locality of the sign. Very occasionally a young man will dash toward the scene of the *bope*'s apparent manifestation with grotesquely exaggerated vocal and physical threats of violence. The at once uneasy and relieved laughter which follows his buffoonery is itself perhaps the most common reaction to these signs of the *bope.* The social response to omens, events interpreted as volitional communication from *bope* to mankind, is much more complex, and is discussed in detail later in this section.

5. There appears to be a certain ambiguity in Bororo classification of rain spirits, as Lévi-Strauss notes (1969: 50–51, 213–15). According to a myth recorded by Colbacchini and Albisetti (1942: 229–30), the *Butao-doge* bring only gentle, calm rain, whereas violent wind-and-thunder storms are caused by the *Badogebague* class of *bope.* The last could be a variant form of the *Boegabe-doge,* credited by my informants as the bringers of high winds and destructive rains. However, the same Salesian source also cites the *Butao-doge* ("Butaudogue") as the bringers of cold, wet weather which afflicts mankind (Colbacchini and Albisetti 1942: 229), thus agreeing with my informants. Yet the Bororo certainly do contrast in myth and daily life that absolute distinction between two kinds of celestial water, one gentle and beneficent and the other violent and harmful, deduced by Lévi-Strauss (1969: 214). This dichotomy is correlated with that between rapid-flowing terrestrial water and calm streams, river reaches, and lakes, itself linked to

the *bope-aroe* antithesis (see below and Part IV). As absolute masters of all manner of celestial water, the *Butao-doge* must harbor a profound contradiction in their nature, which is manifested in their rather anomalous position among the *bope* and in what might be an imperfectly institutionalized effort to dichotomize conceptually their contradictory powers.

6. This bit of reasoning is something of a folk saying, and more skeptical informants were quite whimsical in repeating it. However, the association between the anaconda and both celestial and terrestrial waters, two forms usually contrasted very sharply, is inflexible and pervades this species' unique position in myth. (See Part IV.)

7. The *o* in this episode seems to be a socó, a type of small heron or perhaps bittern (Ardeideos fam.). These birds tend to be active during the night (Ihering 1968: 639), and their peculiar cry characteristic of the precrepuscular dawn, at least in my experience. However, the general significance of this story derives from the Bororo interpretation of all forms of large, wading water birds as especially associated with the *aroe*. These spirits represent the principle of timeless form, as over against the *bope*'s mastery of organic transformation. I cannot explain why the socó, alone among wading birds, should be credited with the original possession of control over the most minimal manifestation of diachrony, the alteration between day and night, unless in its symmetry this be taken simply as "form" over against "movement." But, then again, why should birds of the Ardeideos family be given a privilege of place in mastering the nexus between cyclic and serial time, unless it be for their "inverted" habits?

8. An important dimension of Bororo masculine rivalry and status involves skill in the construction of material goods, especially ceremonial ones. Ritual bows are particularly regarded as a crucial test of a man's ability. Since these are used infrequently, normatively only during ceremonial hunts dedicated to the killing of "revenge" animals (see Chapter 9), they tend to dry out and, through time, betray faults of craftsmanship. This not only brings shame on the maker, but the *aroe* are extremely offended and likely to punish both him and the user. Vulture feathers and rotten wood are in every way the antithesis of the parrot feathers and heartwood used for a proper bow. Finally, a ritual bow is never made for one's own use but is given as part of a complex series of prestations between a dead man's relatives and his "revenger," or *aroe maiwu*. Meri's behavior is therefore the complete inversion of proper, *aroe*-inspired Bororo moral conduct.

9. The status of the red-necked dove (item 15 in Table 4.1) as *bope* food is open to considerable question. It does not appear in any published list of *bope ure* (see text citations), and, of over forty Bororo asked to name these species, only two cited the red-necked dove. Its attributes, to my knowledge, do not include any of these distinguishing the *bope ure* as a conceptual set. But when I checked with five shamans, each independently said that the bird could be treated as "food of the *bope*," although such action was not necessary to render it fit for human consumption. Since the last is necessary for all the other *bope ure* species, this bird must be regarded as a complete anomaly in this context. I cannot explain why it should be so singled out.

10. The *bope ure* are cited in the body of the myth, which is given interlinearly in Bororo and Portuguese. The only differences between this list and that presented here are the red-necked dove (preceding footnote) and a few plant species. However, the Salesians' account of Bororo shamanistic practices and Bororo attitudes toward the *bope* is somewhat more divergent with my data (1962: 245–48). These differences, such as the generally much greater importance ac-

corded the alligator by the Salesians' informants, might be explained as due to regional variation or historical change.

11. The Bororo attitude toward these species, and the rituals they accord them, are the aspects of Bororo culture most widely known among local Brazilians. There are numerous reasons for this: Bororo refusal to eat *bope* food procured by a Brazilian, their reluctance to pursue one of these species in the absence of a shaman, and their unwillingness to sell or trade *bope ure*. For their part, the Bororo are somewhat ambivalent about the consequences of non-Bororo consumption of the *bope* foods. The most common attitude was that the *bope* did not recognize innocence of the law and fully punished Brazilians who broke the universal dietary laws. Yet many believed that Brazilians (and by extension, other non-Indians), being products of the *bope,* were immune to these regulations. My own afflictions in the field were, on the other hand, attributed by public opinion and shamanistic diagnosis to my consumption, prior to living among the Bororo, of "untreated" *bope ure.* "But then," said one shaman, "you are a kind of *bóe*" ("Bororo").

## CHAPTER 5: FIRST FRUITS, SACRIFICE, AND DANGEROUS FOODS

12. The sort of metonymic logic underlying sacrifice seems intimately associated with societies committed to pastoralism, or otherwise pervaded with the idiom of domesticated animals. At least in South America, sacrifice appears only among the "domesticating" societies of the Andes, with the apparently concomitant association of shamanism with "totemism."

13. Generally Bororo classify animals outside of ritual contexts (when other criteria are applicable) in terms of diet, habitat, and mode of sexual reproduction. But my informants were most uncertain as to details of bats' food and domains. They did insist that they suckled their young, an attribute they find definitional, along with external masculine genitalia, female breasts, and "hair," of mammals.

14. Apparently dolphins very occasionally make their way up the Plate River into the São Lourenço. At least, several informants claimed to have seen these creatures years ago and to have described their visible attributes and habits very accurately. Photographs of dolphins were also unhesitatingly identified by all Bororo who saw them as *jakoreu.* Sea cows, or manatees, also appear, but very rarely, in the São Lourenço. They are categorized as *aije,* a type of *aroe* which is accorded a very special ritual and conceptual position (Crocker 1983). And they, too, are completely inedible.

15. As mentioned earlier, anacondas are intimately associated with the *aroe.* Rattlesnakes are accorded a special symbolic position, owing to their unique blend of lethality, definitive skin markings, and capacity to produce a "communicative" noise. They figure importantly among the *aroe* totems of the Exerae moiety, and their skins' patterns are said to be the basis for design motifs owned by certain clans of this moiety, all of which are used to decorate the rattles sacred to the *aroe.* I discuss the issue of why the former should be an "anomalous animal" and the latter a "transcendental spirit" in later chapters.

16. I mean by "symbolic operator" something very close to what Victor Turner defines as "symbolic article," an entity which as a "member of a configuration of symbols, a selection can be made among its connotations for that one or those few compatible with the 'telos' of the situation" (Turner 1975: 164).

17. Very recently this situation has begun to correct itself, thanks to the efforts of Rodney Needham (1972, 1975). No efforts to extend this perspective to

ethnographic analyses have appeared at the time of writing, at least to my knowledge. My own reading of Wittgenstein with attention to the idea of "family resemblance" was inspired by informal conversations with Needham in the summer of 1968. I first applied his logic in the analysis of *bope ure* in an unpublished paper delivered before the Anthropology Department of New York University in the spring of 1970.

18. Corn is at once among the *bope ure* and the most preferred vegetable dish given by a ritual "mother" to her "son," the ceremonial representative of her own dead child, or that of her matrilateral consanguine. Corn is clearly a "first fruit," in the ritualized circumstances of its presentation to the *bope* and as the only aboriginal cultigen among the *bope ure* plants. Yet it is also one of the most preferred cooked dishes of the *aroe*. I suspect it is just its associations as a "domesticated" vegetable counterpart to the vulnerable wild animals among the *bope ure* which explains its status as a medial dish.

19. This Bororo sentiment is the more incomprehensible, since at least some of the Gê societies and the contiguous tribal groups sheltered in the upper Xingu regard both species of wild pig as most formidable adversaries (personal communication, da Matta, Menget, and T. Turner). And given the Bororo "sissy" sensitivity to the most inconsequential of hurts inflicted by nature, it is also culturally inconsistent. I can merely reassert that no Bororo perceived wild pigs as potential agents of harm, and I can in no way explain why they did not.

20. I have not been able to discover whether these three species commonly and/or exclusively among large fish occupy backwaters and ponds near the São Lourenço, or whether they lack the poisonous barbs common to other catfish, or if they were especially sought during collective hunts. I suspect the answer in each case is affirmative but lack the data to be definitive.

## CHAPTER 6: A *BOPE* BESTIARY

21. I was very pleased, after years of puzzling over this bird's peculiar signification for the Bororo, to find that the directors (or keepers, or some decision-maker) of the Parisian "Parc Zoologique de Vincennes" had caged four caracaras with a group of vulture species, in a very large flight-cage at the extreme northeastern point of the zoo. They were the only nonvultures so included. All the other rapinous birds were meticulously caged by species some distance away. It was gratifying so to encounter "wild thought" in the most civilized circumstances and to witness the easy accommodation between the vultures and caracaras themselves, a double confirmation of both cultural and natural levels of Bororo classification.

22. See note 21. The Bororo seem to classify all small, definitively red-and-black banded snakes as *barororeu,* including (I believe) in this class such harmless genera as *Atractus, Erythrolampus,* and *Pseudoboa* (Ihering 1968: 242–43).

23. This species has a most eerie cry, something comparable to the North American coyote's howl, but still quite different. The reversal of its significance between "seen abnormally" and "unusually heard" is characteristic of omens: the *sense* of their intrusion into human affairs is relatively indifferent to their apparent *signification*. That is, just what social construction is placed upon the meaning of a particular behavior of the signifying species is dependent on a logic independent from that which accorded the beast's communicative importance in the first place.

24. Lévi-Strauss (1962b: 289–95), with his uncanny sense of the ethnographically precise, notes the theoretical implications of such niceties of natural

signification. For a social phenomenology one might explore the way most omens become publicly significant only after the event they herald. Minimal phonetic differences may be most usefully blurred in recall, so that private experience continues to validate social cosmology, at least in retrospect.

# Part III

## CHAPTER 7: BECOMING AND BEING A SHAMAN

1. Both Bororo and local Brazilians set fire to the savannah in the dry season, supposedly to make it at once more fertile and easier for hunting. The grass smoulders and produces clouds of smoke lit from within by the flares of more combustible materials. There is a certain quality of menace in the spectacle, and some real danger that the fire could range out of hand and burn down the village, where all the huts are made from woven palm leaves. Its smoke is a convincing visual image of a "natural affliction" sweeping upon the village.

2. My information on this "dream-copulation" of the new shaman is ambiguous. I could not determine whether the shaman's soul itself was actually thought to have sexual intercourse, or whether it was "taken along with" the familiar while it did so, or whether it was merely told to witness the *bope*'s activities. Shamans themselves claimed that the souls of "good" shamans never copulated with sleeping women, although the *bope* did so at every opportunity.

3. Drowning often appears in stories about offenders against the *bope*. As the Bororo are universally excellent water men, drownings are *ipso facto* mysterious and peculiar events. It is, however, somewhat curious that the *bope* are credited with this form of retribution, because otherwise rivers are the domain of the *aroe*. It may well be that traditionally, when the dual shamanistic system was functioning, drowning was ascribed to the *aroe;* now, in the general eclipse of *aroe* involvement in human affairs, the *bope* are thought to operate in this habitat as well as upon land. It will be noted that all drownings mentioned here followed problems thought by some informants, at least, to concern the *aroe*.

4. Economic considerations, such as proximity to gardens and other natural resources, were never mentioned as affecting the decision to move the community. Informants seemed to regard the physical work involved in clearing the new village site and constructing new homes as far greater and more bothersome than the necessity of walking an extra half-kilometer to their gardens.

5. The utensils' importance in these conflicts explains why the original donor must keep them in good repair, for it would be fatal for the *bari* if his *jota* broke or *batureu* disintegrated during the battle. His familiars "would not wait" to punish the inept craftsman.

6. These same objects are carried by a dead person's ritual representative (*aroe maiwu*) during the funeral's concluding rites. Generally only the best bow, finest basket, or favorite toy is so utilized. All the rest of the deceased's property is burned, including other bows, his or her mats, clothing, and so forth. The "burning up" of the stolen objects in the shooting stars is a very obvious synonym of death's oblivion to the self's material dimension.

7. Discrepancies between different shamans' lists of the victims are easily reconciled, for each shaman knows only the identity of those souls he himself rescued. Furthermore, initial revelations are made informally, in discussion with friends. And adjustments can be made during the period between waking and public meetings.

8. Generally the village should keep as quiet as possible during the initial stages of the trance. Noise inhibits the familiar's arrival and the shaman's recognition of false *bope*. Once the familiar has taken possession of the shaman's body, people can relax and assume their usual activities. But the whole process of trance and the *bope*'s utterances are followed with interest, which contrasts with the casualness and quality of boring routine with which activities relating to the *aroe* are carried out.

9. This carrier nominally should be a male sibling of the deceased, or at least a co-clansman. He receives a precisely designated piece of the game for his service; neither it nor the reward is by any means inconsequential. To carry 20 or 30 kilos of dead weight through the forest or across the hot savannah, sometimes for 10 kilometers or more, is a miserable, exhausting task for which 5 kilos of meat or so is not an unsuitable compensation.

10. This mode of carrying someone is used ritually during the representation of the *aije,* the water-monsters who are the most powerful of the *aroe* spirits. Since this representation is "owned" by clans in the Tugarege moiety, it is males of the Exerae who actually impersonate the *aije*. At one point the Exerae "mount" the Tugarege and are carried about the village, whooping and imitating the cries of the various animals which always accompany the *aije*. Since, as explained earlier, these spirits, and especially the bullroarers which reproduce their calls, are explicitly phallic symbols, the "mounting" has a decided sexual connotation, as well as being a way the Tugarege "honor" the Exerae.

## CHAPTER 8: THE SHAMAN AND MORAL ORDER

11. I and especially my wife tried our limited best to help the ill, and we visited sick people as soon as we heard about their maladies. Only later did we learn how appropriate this conduct was within terms of Bororo social morality and how much it had facilitated our acceptance by the community. This is by no means a blanket recommendation for untrained ethnologists to undertake medical aid for humanitarian and more self-serving motives; we were simply very fortunate, both in the consequences of our actions and our reception.

12. I understand a witch to be credited with malign powers resident in his physical person which require no physical agency or even volition to be efficacious in harming others (Evans-Pritchard 1937).

13. Such public confrontation of two antagonists is the traditional way of handling any "trouble case," when two individuals have broken off all social relations and are threatening one another with extreme violence or slander. Traditionally two male antagonists were ordered to duel with each other by the men's council when there could be no clear determination of the guilt of one party. Usually, informants said, the enemies were so embarrassed by the proceedings that they failed to act at all. I think that very few adult male Bororo are capable of cold-blooded physical aggression. All the actual fights occurring during fieldwork came after great quantities of rum had been consumed and when the participants literally did not know what they were doing. The conclusion of Dita and Kadegare's quarrel was therefore typical of the social resolution of "trouble cases" among the Bororo.

14. I refer here to the association of the *bope* with the Exerae as their *i-edaga,* "mothers' brothers." It is true, however, that, other than the assumption that shamans of the *bope* should be Tugarege, this relationship has no social implications: the *bope* are not less severe with members of that moiety, nor do they favor them in any fashion. In contrast, the *bope*-souls of "good" dead shamans are

credited with assisting members of their clan in the hunt and with intervening for them against the *bope*. These *bope*-souls are thought to favor especially their ritual representatives, necessarily shamans themselves. However, the souls of ordinary defuncts also secure the general assistance of the *aroe* for *their* representatives and try to help their clan members in the hunt; none of this can be credited to unique factors in the shaman's postmortem capacities.

15. The last great shaman was "Cadete," who died in 1953. Simultaneously a *bari* and an *aroe etawa-are*, he exercised great prestige throughout the middle São Lourenço. Many of the details of *bope* and *aroe* cosmology presented here were initially proclaimed by him. His predictions were always very precise, detailed, and accurate.

16. The nature of my own involvement in these complex relationships should be mentioned, for they most certainly bear on this feeling and account for much of the information I received about him. Kano was married into the same name-set into which my wife had been adopted, and he treated me mostly as a WyZH, or *i-medu*, "younger brother," that is, with a certain mixture of moral superiority and concerned responsibility. Ugo, and to a lesser degree Kano himself, were my principal informants at Korugedu Paru, a fact which was resented by various factions in the village and probably by Celilo, since I paid for Ugo's and Kano's services in highly public terms the Bororo regarded as generous. On the other hand, Celilo treated me more consistently as a Bororo than anyone else and was himself an able, frequent, and well-paid informant. He and Manukuje both treated me through the *bope*.

17. Most male informants regarded polygyny as rather stupid; as one informant said, "It is hard enough to live with one woman." If one were so foolish as to want two wives, then the best tactic would be to marry unrelated women living at some distance from each other (i.e., of different clans). Despite the near universality of this folk wisdom, the only two cases of polygyny I found (excluding the alleged case of Kadegare) involved marriage with a mother and daughter. The Bororo seem to regard such unions as indecent and even somewhat obscene, and so as having a certain sexual fillip. Both recorded unions came about circumstantially: the marriage with the mother led eventually to cohabitation with the maturing daughter after the last had divorced once or twice. I think the obscenity involved here comes from that quality of contradiction in woman's roles discussed in the second chapter involving the physical juxtaposition of her sexuality with that of her parents.

18. Such an attitude on the part of the *bope* may appear inconsistent with their gleeful enthusiasm for all forms of incest. But this is not so, for the whole principle governing relations between the spirits and society is that each has its proper normative regulations. The *bope* might delight in abrogating these through causing their agent the *bari* to commit mystical incest. But they are the more incensed when he consciously secures this pleasure for himself.

# Part IV

## CHAPTER 9: THE STENCH OF DEATH

1. This phrase may appear too dramatic, too absolute a contrast, and to imply the possibility of self-conscious decisions. But as the last pages of this chapter show, it is an accurate portrayal of the Bororo situation.

2. For nearly all of the two hundred and fifty years of Bororo contact with European society, its presence in Mato Grosso has been founded upon extractive industries, primarily mineral (gold and diamonds). As Cardoso di Oliveira and his collaborators have shown (1964), this sort of "contact frontier" usually has the least malign consequences for indigenous societies. Further, the Bororo were ably championed by a number of Western protectors. Only in this century, and most of all in the past three decades, have the more lethal forms of capitalism intruded upon the Bororo: settlers on freeholds and sharecroppers, vegetable extractors, cattle raisers, and the like (Crocker 1967; Montenegro 1958).

3. I have addressed the problem of Bororo homological totemism elsewhere (Crocker 1977b, 1978) and take it up in my second monograph. Here I should say that while the scheme of *aroe* division appears arbitrary to the Bororo, it does appear to have certain structural consistencies.

4. These are actually pieces of bamboo, 5 or more meters long, and split for about a third of their length. The butt is rested upon the ground and the stick violently shaken, so that the split ends rapidly clack together. But these "instruments" reproduce even fewer of the attributes of the actual Parabara than do other *aroe* representations.

5. As proof of this informants cite the way the knees of *aroe* bend backward rather than forward, "just like a macaw's." Even the shamans of *aroe,* who could see this and other features of the *aroe,* were not able to discover how often the *aroe* copulated, but all agreed it could not be very often and then "just in play."

6. As explained earlier, in Chapter 6, the representative always belongs to the moiety opposite that of the deceased. Also, he should be normatively (and usually is) a member of the deceased's father's clan, which also provides the formal friend of initiation, the *i-orubadari.* Indeed, the last ideally becomes the *aroe maiwu:* the person who legitimated the individual's full exploitation of his personal *raka,* his procreative and destructive potentials, must also be he who ensures the soul's immortality against the flux of natural transformation.

7. In my records such cases involve the slaying of a man by his uterine brother or by some other near matrilineal relative. The Bororo are most reluctant to involve members of the other moiety in such scandals, and so the revenge was carried out by the genealogically closest *i-mana* ("elder brother") of the murderer. Normally the ritual mother never publicly wore the jawbone, too gruesome a testimony to the act of her clansman.

8. For example, the hunter fasts and abstains from sexual contacts for a week before setting out to kill one of these animals; immediately upon slaying one he cuts out the tongue and addresses a chant to the beast. The jaguar's claws and the eagle's flight feathers must be given to chiefs of the Bado Jeba Xobugiwuge and Bado Jeba Xebegiwuge clans, respectively, and so on.

9. One of my younger informants was a recent *aroe maiwu,* selected over the objections of some in the deceased's clan. He was enterprising but profligate, and far too attuned to Brazilian modes of conduct for traditional tastes. He confirmed the village's worst suspicions when he *bought* a ragged moth-chewed jaguar pelt from a passing trader to fulfill his ritual duties. Although he endured public ridicule for this stupid dodge, it was a meritorious deed in his own eyes: the pelt had cost the equivalent of four months' wages, and so, he rhetorically asked, "Is it not worth far more than just something I managed to kill by accident?"

10. I should stress that while the "new soul" is expected to kill these esteemed "strong foods" for his ritual parents, and the "hunts of the souls" are designed and dedicated to just this end, he is under no normative obligation to do

so. But he *must* kill a *marege mori-xe*. Furthermore, as Chapter 2 demonstrated, such game can only sustain an individual's *raka,* never restore it. The *aroe maiwu*'s sustenance of his "soul parents" is therefore as much if not more symbolic than real.

## CHAPTER 10: INITIATION AND POWERS OF THE *AROE* SHAMAN

11. Bakorokudu plays the role of Bakororo and *emijera* of the *aroe* in major rituals such as funerals, name-givings, and initiations. Bakororo, one of the two culture heroes, is especially associated with death, nomination, and all forms of organic flux—he is the *aroe* counterpart of Meri, the supreme *bope* who reveals one dimension of himself in the sun, and, like Bakororo, is one of the *aroe* totems of the Bado Jeba Xebegiwuge. Bakorokudu/Bakororo must attend every death-bed in the village, and so initiates the funeral cycle. Not surprisingly, many *aroe etawa-are* were also Bakorokudu.

12. Each clan segment, or "name group," is associated with several ornamental patterns for these gourd whistles, which are used only for the segment's dead members. The whistles are a true *memento mori* and may be passed down upon the representative's own death to *his* "new soul."

13. I owe this knowledge to my wife, who was sequestered along with the women of her clan during the public appearances of representatives and of the *aije*. When she responded with simulated alarm to the men's whoops, cries, and assaults against the house, she was assured with laughter, "It's just the game of the men," and told of the ceremony's pragmatics. But no woman actually peeked out to watch the performers.

## CHAPTER 11: THE TWO SHAMANS—DYADIC INVERSIONS

14. The erotic significance of birds is one of those phenomena which has much exercised the imagination of many anthropologists, none of whom have yet, to my knowledge, managed to provide any sort of adequate ethnographic or theoretical exploration of the topic. Among the Bororo, at least, I suspect that the sheer remoteness of birds, at all levels of symbolic classification, is one way of objectifying the other sex, making it into a cultural rather than natural thing. But why birds rather than fish should be so inconographically singled out, I do not know.

15. These have already been mentioned in the second note to Part IV; they center on the economy's domination by mineral-extractive industries. Furthermore, in the early years the Bororo were very curious about this new mode of society—at least they appear to have visited São Paulo in 1714 (Crocker 1967) and certainly accompanied the bandeirantes as guides and perhaps mercenaries throughout most of the eighteenth century.

16. I mean "ideological" here in the restricted sense of "the integrated assertions, theories and aims that constitute a socio-political program" (Webster's Seventh), especially as this program expresses indirectly the vested economic interests of a social group.

17. The epidemic was one of severe colds which in many individuals developed into bronchial infections and pneumonia. It spread after a large group of the village's men returned from Cuiabá, where they had participated in an "Indian festival." The epidemic was treated by all the community's *baire,* working both on individual cases and together in the "mass cure" discussed in the last chapter.

The common explanation given by the *bope* through their shamans was that the men had contacted "unblessed" foods of the *bope* while in the city.

18. Although women have titular rights over cultigens, the general rule is that anyone who worked in the garden has control over the food's distribution in proportion to his or her contribution of labor. Most middle-aged husbands are fairly assiduous gardeners and so come to share rights over the crops with their wives.

19. In recent years the local wage market has sought cattle herders and agricultural laborers for land clearing (but not for harvesting), both exclusively masculine pursuits. One middle-aged bachelor at Korugedu Paru supported himself exclusively by fishing and selling or trading his catch for vegetables and other goods. Most men supplement their income in this way rather than by wage labor.

20. Brazilian federal law prohibits the sale of alcoholic beverages to "Indians," just as American law did until the late sixties. Among the Bororo the law is enforced only by the better of the local agents of the Indian Protection Service and by the Salesians on their missions. In some villages cachaça is daily available; in others it can be procured only through considerable effort.

## CHAPTER 12: DEAD SOULS

1. Pobojari was the principal site of extensive fieldwork carried out by Dr. Zarko Levak, who entered Bororoland just as I was leaving. He has confirmed the absence of children in Pobojari, but has a different explanation for it than the one advanced here.

# Bibliography

Ackernecht, E. H.
 1943a Primitive autopsies and the history of medicine. *Bulletin of the History of Medicine* 13: 334–39.
 1943b Psychopathology, primitive medicine, and primitive culture. *Bulletin of the History of Medicine* 14: 30–67.
 1958 Medical Practices. In *Handbook of South American Indians,* vol. 5, edited by J. S. Steward, pp. 621–43. Washington: Bureau of American Ethnology.
Albisetti, Cesar, and A. J. Venturelli
 1962 *Enciclopedia Bororo,* vol. 1. Campo Grande: Museu Regional de Dom Bosca.
 1969 *Enciclopedia Bororo,* vol. 2. Campo Grande: Museu Regional de Dom Bosca.
 1976 *Enciclopedia Bororo,* vol. 3. Campo Grande: Museu de Dom Bosca.
Allee, W. C., et al.
 1961 *Principles of Animal Ecology.* Philadelphia: Saunders Co.
Ardener, Edwin
 1970 Witchcraft, economics, and the continuity of belief. In *Witchcraft Confessions and Accusations,* edited by Mary Douglas, pp. 141–60. Association of Social Anthropologists Monograph No. 9. London: Tavistock Publications.

Bailey, F. G.
  1969   *Strategems and Spoils: A Social Anthropology of Politics.* Oxford: Basil Blackwell.
Balandier, G.
  1970   *Political Anthropology,* translated by A. M. Sheridan Smith. New York: Random House.
Baldus, H.
  1937   *Ensaios de Etnologia Brasileira.* São Paulo: Companhia editora nacional.
Balikci, A.
  1963   Shamanistic behavior among the Netsilik Eskimos. *Southwestern Journal of Anthropology* 19: 380–96.
Beidelman, T. O.
  1966   The ox and Nuer sacrifice. *Man* 1(n.s.): 453–67.
  1968   Some Nuer notions of nakedness, nudity and sexuality. *Africa* 38: 113–32.
  1970   Towards more open theoretic interpretations. In *Witchcraft Confessions and Accusations,* edited by Mary Douglas, pp. 351–56. Association of Social Anthropologists Monograph No. 9. London: Tavistock Publications.
  1971   *The Kaguru: A Matrilineal People of East Africa.* New York: Holt, Rinehart and Winston.
Berlin, B., D. E. Breedlove, and R. H. Raven
  1968   Covert categories and folk taxonomies. *American Anthropologist* 70: 290–99.
Bogoraz, Waldemar G.
  1904   *The Chukchee.* New York: G. E. Stechert. (Johnson Reprint, 1970.
  1910   *Chukchee Mythology.* New York: G. E. Stechert and Co.
Bourguignon, Erika
  1965   The self, the behavioral environment, and the theory of spirit possession. In *Context and Meaning in Cultural Anthropology,* edited by M. E. Spiro, pp. 39–60. New York: The Free Press.
  1972   Dreams and altered states of consciousness in anthropological research. In *Psychological Anthropology,* edited by F. L. K. Hsu, pp. 403–34. New edition. Cambridge: Schenkman Publishing Company.
  1976   Possession and trance in cross-cultural studies of mental health. In *Culture-Bound Syndromes, Ethnopsychiatry and Alternate Therapies,* edited by William Lebra, pp. 47–55. Vol. IV, Mental Health Research in Asia and the Pacific: An East-West Center Book. Honolulu: The University Press of Hawaii.
Boyer, L. B.
  1964a  Folk psychiatry of the Apaches of the Mescalero Indian Reser-

vation. In *Magic, Faith and Healing,* edited by Ari Kiev, pp. 384–419. New York: The Free Press.

1964b Further remarks concerning shamans and shamanism. *The Israel Annals of Psychiatry* 2: 235–57.

Bulmer, Ralph
    1967 Why is the Cassowary not a bird?: A problem of the zoological taxonomy among the Karam of the New Guinea highlands. *Man* 2: 5–25.

Butt, A. J.
    1961 Symbolism and ritual among the Abawaio of British Guiana. *Nieuwe West-Indische Gids,* No. 2 (December).
    1962 Réalité et idéal dans la pratique chamanique. *L'Homme* II(3): 5–52.
    1965 The shaman's legal role. *Revista do Museu Paulista*(n.s.) 16: 66.

Cardoso de Oliveira, Roberto
    1964 *O Indio e o mundo dos Brancos: a situacão dos Tukivna do alto Solimões.* São Paulo: DiFusão Européia do Livro.

Castaneda, Carlos
    1974 *Tales of Power.* New York: Simon and Schuster.

Clastres, Pierre
    1974 *La société contre l'état: recherches d'anthropologie politique.* Paris: Editions de Minuit.

Colbacchini, A., and C. Albisetti
    1942 *Os Bororos Orientais Orarimogodogue do Planalto Oriental de Mato Grosso.* São Paulo: Companhia editora nacional.

Colby, Benjamin N.
    1966 Ethnographic semantics: A preliminary survey. *Current Anthropology* 7: 3–32.

Colson, Audrey Butt
    1976 Binary oppositions and the treatment of sickness among the Akawaio. In *Social Anthropology and Medicine,* edited by J. B. Loudon, pp. 422–99. London: Academic Press.

Crapanzano, Vincent, and Vivian V. Garrison
    1980 *Case Studies in Spirit Possession.* New York: John Wiley & Sons.

Crocker, J. Christopher
    1967 Social organization of the eastern Bororo. Ph.d. dissertation, Department of Social Relations, Harvard University.
    1969a Reciprocity and hierarchy among the eastern Bororo. *Man* 4: 44–58.
    1969b Men's house associates among the eastern Bororo. *Southwestern Journal of Anthropology* 25: 236–60.
    1971 The dialectics of Bororo social reciprocity. *Verhandlungen des XXVIII Internationalen Amerikanisten Kongress,* pp. 387–91. Stuttgart.

Crocker (*cont.*)

1973    Ritual and the development of social structure. In *The Roots of Ritual,* edited by James Shaughnessy. Grand Rapids, Michigan: Eerdman's Publishing Company.

1977a    The social function of rhetorical forms. In *The Social Use of Metaphor,* edited by J. David Sapir and J. Christopher Crocker, pp. 33–66. Philadelphia: University of Pennsylvania Press.

1977b    My brother the parrot. In *The Social Use of Metaphor,* edited by J. David Sapir and J. Christopher Crocker, pp. 164–92. Philadelphia: University of Pennsylvania Press.

1977c    Les Réflexions du soi. In *L'Identité: Séminaire dirigé par Claude Lévi-Strauss,* edited by Jean-Marie Benoist, pp. 157–79. Discussion (C. Lévi-Strauss, J. C. Crocker, and others), pp. 180–84. Paris: Bernard Grassett.

1978    Why are the Bororo matrilineal? in *Actes du XLII Congres International de Americanists,* vol. 2: 245–58.

1979    Selves and alters among the eastern Bororo. In *Dialectical Societies: The Gê and Bororo of Central Brazil,* edited by David Maybury-Lewis, pp. 249–300. Cambridge: Harvard University Press.

1983    Being and essence: Totemic representation among the eastern Bororo. In *The Power of Symbols: Masks and Masquerade in the Americas,* edited by N. Ross Crumrine and Marjorie Halpin, pp. 154–73. Vancouver: University of British Columbia Press.

Cruz, Manuel

1943    O exorcismo da caca, do peixe e das frutas entre os Bororos. *Revista do Arquivo Municipal* (São Paulo) 89: 151–56.

1945    Aroe codu ou a queda dos bólides. *Revista do Arquivo Municipal* (São Paulo) 55: 71–75.

Devereux, George

1956    Normal and abnormal: The key problem in psychiatric anthropology. In *Some Uses of Anthropology: Theoretical and Applied,* edited by J. B. Casagrande and T. Gladwin. Washington, D.C.: Anthropological Society of Washington.

1957    Dream learning and individual ritual differences in Mohave shamanism. *American Anthropologist* 59: 10–36.

Dixon, R. M. W.

1968    Virgin birth (correspondence). *Man* 3: 653–54.

Dorsey, George A.

1904    *Traditions of the Skidi Pawnee.* Memoirs of the American Folklore Society 8.

Douglas, Mary

1966    *Purity and Danger.* London: Routledge and Kegan Paul, Ltd.

1972    On deciphering a meal. *Daedalus* (winter), *Myth, Symbol and Culture:* 61–81.

1973  Torn between two realities. *The Times Higher Education Supplement*, 15 June 1973. Reprinted in M. Douglas, *Implicit Meanings*, pp. 193–200. London: Routledge and Kegan Paul, 1975.

1975  *Implicit Meanings*. London: Routledge and Kegan Paul.

Driver, Harold E.
1964  *Indians of North America*, Chicago: University of Chicago Press. (Original, 1961.)

Dumont, Jean-Paul
1976  *Under the Rainbow: Nature and Supernature Among the Panare Indians*. Austin: University of Texas Press.

Durkheim, Emile
1968  *Les formes élémentaires de la vie religieuse: le système totemique en Australie*. 5th ed. Paris: Presses Universitaires de France.

Edsman, Carl-Martin, Ed.
1967  *Studies in Shamanism*. Stockholm: Almquist and Wiksell.

Eliade, M.
1951  *Shamanism: Archaic Techniques of Ectasy*. Chicago: University of Chicago Press.

Evans-Pritchard, E. E.
1937  *Witchcraft, Oracles, and Magic Among the Azande*. Oxford: Clarendon Press.

1956  *Nuer Religion*. Oxford: Clarendon Press.

1965  *Theories of Primitive Religion*. Oxford: Clarendon Press.

Fabrega, H., and D. B. Silver
1973  *Illness and Shamanistic Curing in Zinacantan: An Ethnomedical Analysis*. Stanford: Stanford University Press.

Field, M. J.
1960  *Search for Security: An Ethno-Psychiatric Study of Rural Ghana*. Evanston: Northwestern University Press.

Firth, Raymond
1966  Twins, birds and vegetables: Problems of identification in primitive religious thought. *Man* 1: 1–17.

1975  *Symbols: Public and Private*. Ithaca: Cornell University Press. (First printing, 1973.)

Fletcher, Alice C., and Francis La Flesche
1972  *The Omaha Tribe*. Lincoln: University of Nebraska Press.

Fox, Renée
1977  The medicalization of American society. *Daedalus* 106: 9–22.

Fox, Robin
1964  Witchcraft and clanship in Cochiti therapy. In *Magic, Faith and Healing*, edited by Ari Kiev, pp. 174–200. New York: The Free Press.

1971  Religion and North American Indian. In *North America, Historia Religionum*, vol. 2: *Religions of the Present*, edited by C. J. Bleeker and G. Wildengren. Leiden: E. J. Brill and Co.

Frake, Charles O.
1962 The ethnographic study of cognitive systems. In *Anthropology and Human Behavior*. Washington, D.C.: Anthropological Society of Washington.

Frank, Jerome D.
1961 *Persuasion and Healing*. Baltimore: Johns Hopkins University Press.

Furst, Peter T.
1972 *Flesh of the Gods: The Ritual Use of Hallucinogens*. New York: Praeger.

Gill, M., and M. Brenman
1961 *Hypnosis and Related States: Psychoanalytic Studies in Regression*. New York: International Universities Press.

Gillin, John
1948 Magical fright. *Psychiatry* 11: 387–400.

Goldenweiser, A. A.
1910 Totemism: An analytical study. *Journal of American Folklore* 23(88): 179–293 .
1918 Form and content in totemism. *American Anthropologist* 20: 280–95.

Goodenough, Ward H.
1956 Componential analysis and the study of meaning. *Language* 32: 195–216.

Gudeman, S.
1972 The *compadrazgo* as a reflection of the natural and spiritual person. *Proceedings of the Royal Anthropological Institute, 1971*: 45–71.

Hallowell, Irving
1938 Fear and anxiety as cultural and individual variables in a primitive society. *Journal of Social Psychology* 9: 25–47.

Harris, Marvin
1968 *The Rise of Anthropological Theory: A History of Theories of Culture*. New York: Thomas Y. Crowell Co.

Hartmann, Tekia
1967 *A Nomenclatura Botânica dos Bororos*. Publicacão do Instituto de Estudos Brasileiros 6. Sao Paulo.

Hemming, John
1978 *Red Gold: The Conquest of the Brazilian Indians*. Cambridge: Harvard University Press.

Hertz, R.
1960 *Death and the Right Hand*, translated by R. Needham and C. Needham. New York: The Free Press. (Original, 1909).

Heusch, Luc de
1962 Cultes de possession et religions initiatiques de salut en

Afrique. *Annales du Centre d'Etudes des Religions II.* Brussels: Université de Bruxelles.

1964  Possession et chamanisme. In *Les religions africaines tradition-nelles* (Recontres Internationales de Bouake), pp. 133–46. Paris: Seuil.

1971  La folie des dieux et la raison des hommes. In *Pourquoi l'épouser?*, pp. 245–85. Paris: Gallimard.

Hippler, Arthur E.
1976  Shamans, curers and personality: Suggestions toward a theoretical model. In *Culture-Bound Syndromes, Ethnopsychiatry and Alternate Therapies,* edited by William Libra, pp. 103–14. Honolulu: The University of Hawaii Press.

Hultkrantz, Ake
1963  *Les religions des Indiens primitifs de l'Amérique.* Stockholm: Almquist and Wiksell.

Huxley, Francis
1963  *Affable Savages,* 2nd ed. London: Hart-Davis.

Ihering, Rodolpho von
1963  *Da vida dos nossos animais: Fauna do Brasil,* 4th ed. São Leopoldo: Rotermund & Cia., Ltd.

1968  *Dicionaria dos Animais do Brasil.* São Paulo: Editora Universidade de Brasilia.

Jensen, Adolf E.
1948  Das religiose Weltbild einer Fruhen Kultur. *Studien zur Kulturkunde,* vol. 9. Stuttgart.

1951  Mythos und Kult bei Naturvolkern. *Studien zur Kulturkunde,* vol. 10. Wiesbaden.

Kaberry, P. M.
1968  Virgin birth. *Man* 3: 311–13.

Kaplan, Bert, and Dale Johnson
1964  The social meaning of Navaho psychopathology. In *Magic, Faith and Healing,* edited by Ari Kiev, pp. 203–29. New York: The Free Press.

Kluckhohn, Clyde
1944  *Navaho Witchcraft.* Boston: Beacon Press.

La Barre, Weston
1964  Confession as cathartic therapy in American Indian Tribes. In *Magic, Faith and Healing,* edited by Ari Kiev, pp. 36–83. New York: The Free Press.

Langness, Lewis
1976  Hysterical psychoses and possession. In *Culture-Bound Syndromes, Ethnopsychiatry and Alternate Therapies,* edited by William Libra, pp. 56–67. Honolulu: University of Hawaii Press.

Larsen, Stephen
    1976   *The Shaman's Doorway*. New York: Harper & Row.

Leach, Edmund
    1962   *Rethinking Anthropology*. London: Athlone Press.
    1964   Anthropological aspects of language: Animal categories and verbal abuse. In *New Directions in the Study of Language,* edited by E. H. Linneberg, pp. 23–63. Cambridge: M.I.T. Press.
    1967   Virgin birth. *Proceedings of the Royal Anthropological Institute,* 1966: 39–50.
    1968   Virgin birth (correspondence). *Man* 3: 655–56.

Lévi-Strauss, Claude
    1936   Contribution a l'étude de l'organisation sociale des indiens Bororo. *Journal de la Société des Americanistes (Paris)* 28: 269–304.
    1944a  Reciprocity and hierarchy. *American Anthropologist* 46: 266–68.
    1944b  The social and psychological aspects of chieftainship in a primitive tribe: The Nambikuara. *Transactions of the New York Academy of Sciences Ser. 2,* VII, No. 1.
    1949a  Le sorcier et sa magie. *Les Temps Moderne* 41: 3–24.
    1949b  L'efficacité symbolique. *Review de l'Histoire des Religions* 135 (1): 5–27.
    1949c  Les structures élémentaires de la parente. Paris: Presses Universitaires de France.
    1958   *Anthropologie structurale.* Paris: Plon.
    1960   On manipulated sociological models. *Bijdragen tot de Taal-, Land-en Volken Kunde* 116: 45–52.
    1962a  *Le totémisme aujourd'hui.* Paris: Presses Universitaires de France.
    1962b  *La pensée sauvage.* Paris: Plon.
    1963a  The Bear and the Barber. *Man* 93: 1–11.
    1963b  Totemism, translated by Rodney Needham. Boston: Beacon.
    1967   *Structural Anthropology.* Garden City, New York: Anchor Books.
    1968   *L'origine des manières de table.* Paris: Plon.
    1969   *The Raw and the Cooked.* New York: Harper & Row.
    1971   *L'Homme Nu.* Paris: Plon.
    1974   *Compte rendu des cours, 1972–73.* Paris: Collège de France.
    1975   *Tristes Tropiques.* New York: Atheneum.

Levy-Bruhl, L.
    1910   *Les Fonctions Mentales dans Les Sociétés Inférieures.* Paris: F. Alcan.

Lewis, Ioan M.
    1971   *Ecstatic Religion.* Harmondsworth, Middlesex (England): Penguin Books.

Loeb, E. M.
  1924   The shaman of Niue. *American Anthropologist* 26: 393–402.
  1929   Shaman and seer. *American Anthropologist* 31: 60–84.

Lowie, R. H.
  1942   The transition of civilizations in primitive society. *American Journal of Sociology* 47: 527–43.
  1948   *Primitive Religion.* New York: Liverright. (Original, 1924.)
  1961   *Primitive Society.* New York: Harper Torchbooks. (Original, 1920.)

Macfarlane, Alan
  1970   *Witchcraft in Tudor and Sussex England.* London: Routledge and Kegan Paul.

Mair, Lucy
  1969   *Witchcraft.* New York: McGraw-Hill.

Maybury-Lewis, David
  1960   The analysis of dual organizations: A methodological critique. *Bijdragen tot de Taal-, Land-en Volkenkunde* 116: 17–44.
  1967   *Akwē-Shavante Society.* Oxford: Clarendon Press.
  1974   *Akwē-Shavante Society,* 2nd ed. Oxford: Clarendon Press.
  1979   *Dialectical Societies.* Cambridge: Harvard University Press.

Mauss, M., and H. Beuchat
  1906   Essai sur les variations saisonnières des sociétés Eskimos. *L'Année Sociologique, neuvième année* (1904–1905): 39–132.

Mauss, M., and H. Hubert
  1899   Essai sur la nature et la fonction du sacrifice. *L'Année Sociologique, deuxième année* (1897–1898): 29–138.

Metraux, Alfred
  1944   Estudios de etnografia chaquense. In *Anales Instituto Etnografia Americana.* Mendoza: Universidad Nacional de Cuyo.
  1945   Le chamanisme chez les indiens du Gran Chaco. *Sociologia* 7(3): 157–68.
  1967a  Le chaman dans les civilizations indigènes des Guyanes et de l'Amazonie. In *Religions et magies indiennes d'Amérique du Sud,* edited by A. Metraux, pp. 81–101. (Revised from Le chamanisme chez les indiens de l'Amérique du sud tropicale. *Acta Americana* 2(1): 197–219; (2): 320–41.)
  1967b  Le chamanisme Araucan. In *Religions et Magies Indiennes d'Amerique du Sud.* edited by A. Metraux, pp. 179–235. (Revised from Le shamanisme araucan. *Revista del Instituto de Anthropologia de la Universidad nacional de Tucuman* 2(10): 309–62.)
  1967c  *Religions et magies indiennes d'Amérique du Sud.* Edition Posthume Etablie par Simone Dreyfus. Paris: Gallimard.

Michael, H. N., Ed.
  1963   *Studies in Siberian Shamanism.* Toronto: Toronto University Press.

Middleton, John
1960 *Lugbara Religion.* London: Oxford University Press.
Middleton, John, and Edward H. Winter, Eds.
1973 *Witchcraft and Sorcery in East Africa.* London: Routledge and Kegan Paul.
Montenegro, Olman P.
1958 Conservantismo e mudanca na cultura Bororo. Plano de Pesquisa, Curso de Aperfeicoamento de Pesquisadores Sociais, CAPES-CBPE, Rio de Janeiro.
Muller, Werner
1969 North America. In *Pre-Columbian American Religions,* edited by Krickeberg et al., pp. 147–229. New York: Holt, Rinehart and Winston.
Murphy, Jane M.
1964 Psychotherapeutic aspects of shamanism on St. Lawrence Island, Alaska. In *Magic, Faith and Healing,* edited by Ari Kiev, pp. 53–83. New York: The Free Press.
Myerhoff, Barbara G.
1974 *Peyote Hunt: The Sacred Journey of the Huichol Indians.* Ithaca: Cornell University Press.
Nadel, S. F.
1946 A study of shamanism in the Nuba Mountains. *Journal of the Royal Anthropological Institute* 76: 25–37.
Needham, Rodney
1972 *Belief, Language and Experience.* Oxford: Blackwell.
1975 Polythetic classification: Convergence and consequences. *Man* 10: 349–69.
New, Jerome
1975 Lévi-Strauss on shamanism. *Man* 10: 285–92.
Nordenskiold, Erland
1931 Origin of the Indian civilization in South America. *Comparative Ethnological Studies* (Göteborg) 9: 1–153.
Nôvo Michaelis
1961 *Portuguese-Ingles,* vol. II, 2nd ed. São Paulo: Edicoes Melhoramentos.
O'Nell, C. W., and H. A. Selby
1968 Sex differences in the incidence of susto in two Zapotec pueblos: An analysis of the relationships between sex role expectations and a folk illness. *Ethnology* 7(1): 95–105.
Onians, Richard Broxton
1951 *The Origins of European Thought about the Body, the Mind, the Soul, the World, Time and Fate.* Cambridge: Cambridge University Press.
Opler, Morris E.
1936 Some points of comparison and contrast between the treat-

ment of functional disorders by Apache shamans and modern psychiatric practice. *American Journal of Psychiatry* 92: 1371–87.

Opler, M. E., Ed.
1959   *Culture and Mental Health.* New York: Macmillan Company.

Park, Willard Z.
1938   *Shamanism in Western North America.* Evanston: Northwestern University Press.

Parsons, Elsie Clews
1917   Notes on Zuñi: Part II. *Memoirs of the American Anthropological Association* 4, No. 4.

Pfister, O.
1932   Instinctive psychoanalysis among the Navajos. *Journal of Nervous and Mental Disease* 66: 234–54.

Pouillon, J.
1964   La structure du pouvoir chez les Hadjerai (Tchad). *L'Homme* 4 (3): 18–70.

Powell, H. A.
1968   Virgin birth (correspondence). *Man* 3: 651–53.

Radcliffe-Brown, A. R.
1964   *The Andaman Islanders.* Glencoe, Illinois: The Free Press.

Radin, Paul
1957a  *Primitive Religion: Its Nature and Origin.* New York: Dover Publications. (Original, 1937.)
1957b  *Primitive Man as Philosopher.* New York: Dover Publications. (Original, 1927.)
1970   *The Winnebago Tribe,* 2nd ed. Lincoln: University of Nebraska Press. (Original, 1923.)

Rappaport, Roy A.
1968   *Pigs for the Ancestors: Ritual in the Ecology of a New Guinea People.* New Haven: Yale University Press.

Rasmussen, Knud
1929   *Intellectual Culture of the Iglulik Eskimos. Report of the Fifth Thule Expedition,* 1921–24, vol. 7, No. 1. Copenhagen: Glydendalske Boghandel, Nordisk Forlag.
1930   *Observations on the Intellectual Culture of the Caribou Eskimos. Report of the Fifth Thule Expedition,* 1921–24, vol. 7, Nos. 2 and 3. Copenhagen: Glydendalske Boghandel, Nordisk Forlag.

Rivière, Peter
1970   Factions and exclusions in two South American village systems. In *Witchcraft Confessions and Accusations,* edited by Mary Douglas, pp. 245–56. London: Tavistock Publications.
1974   The couvade: A problem reborn. *Man* 9: 423–35.

Roheim, Geza
1971   *The Origin and Function of Culture.* New York: Doubleday.

Romano, O.
    1965   Charismatic medicine, folk healing and folk sainthood. *American Anthropologist* 67: 1151–73.

Sapir, J. David
    1977a  The Anatomy of metaphor. In *The Social Use of Metaphor,* edited by J. D. Sapir and J. C. Crocker, pp. 3–32. Philadelphia: University of Pennsylvania Press.
    1977b  The fabricated child. In *The Social Use of Metaphor,* edited by J. D. Sapir and J. C. Crocker, pp. 193–224. Philadelphia: University of Pennsylvania Press.

Sasaki, Y.
    1969   Psychiatric study of the shaman in Japan. In *Mental Health Research in Asia and the Pacific,* edited by W. Caudill and T. Y. Lin. Honolulu: East-West Center Press.

Schauensee, Rodolphe Meyer de
    1970   *A Guide to The Birds of South America.* Published for the Academy of Natural Sciences of Philadelphia. Wynnewood, Pennsylvania: Livingston Publishing Co.

Schneider, David M.
    1968   *American Kinship: A Cultural Account.* Englewood Cliffs, New Jersey: Prentice-Hall.

Shirokogoroff, Sergei M.
    1923   General theory of shamanism among the Tungus. *Journal of the Royal Asiatic Society, North China Branch (Shanghai)* 62: 123–83.
    1935   *Psychomental Complex of the Tungus.* London: Kegan Paul.

Silverman J.
    1967   Shamans and acute schizophrenia. *American Anthropologist* 69: 21–31.

Siskind, Janet
    1973   *To Hunt in the Morning.* New York: Oxford University Press.

Spiro, Melford E.
    1961   Social systems, personality, and functional analysis. In *Studying Personality Cross-Culturally,* edited by Bert Kaplan, pp. 93–127. Evanston, Illinois: Row, Peterson and Co.
    1968   Virgin birth, parthenogenesis and physiological paternity: An essay in cultural interpretation. *Man* 3: 242–61.

Steinen, Karl von den
    1942   *Entre os Aborigenes do Brasil Central* (Portuguese translation of *Unter den Naturvolkern Zentral-Brasiliens*). São Paulo.

Steiner, Franz
    1956   *Taboo.* London: Cohen and West, Ltd.

Stocking, George
    1974   Introduction: The basic assumptions of Boasian anthropology. In *The Shaping of American Anthropology,* edited by G. Stocking, pp. 1–20. New York: Basic Books.

Swartz, M., V. Turner, and A. Tuden, Eds.
    1966   *Political Anthropology*. Chicago: Aldine.

Tambiah, S. J.
    1968   The magical power of words. *Man* 3: 175–209.
    1969   Animals are good to think and good to prohibit. *Ethnology* 8: 423–59.
    1970   *Buddhism and the Spirit Cults in North-east Thailand.* Cambridge: Cambridge University Press.

Thomas, L.
    1977   On the science and technology of medicine. *Daedalus* 106: 35–46.

Tillyard, E. M. W.
    n.d.   *The Elizabethan World Picture*. New York: Vintage Books.

Tonelli, A.
    1928   Alcune notizie sui Baere e sugli Aroettwarare 'medicistregoni' degli indi Bororo-Orari del Matto Grosso. *Atti del XXII Congresso Internazionale degli Americanisti* II:560–89. Rome.

Turner, Victor W.
    1957   *Schism and Continuity in an African Society.* Manchester: Manchester University Press.
    1964   An Ndembu doctor in practice. In *Magic, Faith and Healing,* edited by Ari Kiev, pp. 230–63. New York: The Free Press.
    1967   *The Forest of Symbols*. Ithaca: Cornell University Press.
    1968   *The Drums of Affliction*. Oxford: The Clarendon Press.
    1969   *The Ritual Process*. Chicago: Aldine.
    1974   *Dramas, Fields and Metaphors: Symbolic Action in Human Society.* Ithaca: Cornell University Press.

Tyler, Stephen A.
    1969   Introduction. In *Cognitive Anthropology,* edited by Stephen Tyler, pp. 1–23. New York: Holt, Rinehart and Winston.

Wagner, Roy
    1972   *Habu*. Chicago: University of Chicago Press.
    1975   *The Invention of Culture*. Englewood Cliffs, New Jersey: Prentice-Hall.

Wagley, Charles
    1943   Tapirapé shamanism. *Boletim do Museu Nacional (Anthropologia)* No. 3: 61–92.

Walker, Ernest P.
    1968   *Mammals of the World,* 2nd ed., 2 vols. Baltimore: Johns Hopkins University Press.

Wallace, Anthony F. C.
    1959   Cultural determinants of response to hallucinatory experience. *Archives of General Psychiatry* 1: 58–69.
    1966   *Religion: Anthropological View*. New York: Random House.

Wallace, Anthony F. C., and J. Atkins
  1960   The meaning of kinship terms. *American Anthropologist* 62: 54–80.

Wilbert, Johannes
  1972   Tobacco and shamanistic ecstasy among the Warao Indians of Venezuela. In *Flesh of the Gods,* edited by Peter T. Furst, pp. 55–83. New York: Praeger.

Wilson, P. J.
  1967   Status ambiguity and spirit possession. *Man* 2: 366–78.

Wittgenstein, Ludwig
  1953   *Philosophical Investigations,* translated by G. E. M. Anscombe. New York: Macmillan Co.

Worsley, Peter
  1967   Groote Eylandt Totemism and *Le Totémisme Aujourd'hui.* In *The Structural Study of Myth and Totemism,* edited by Edmund Leach, pp. 141–59. London: Tavistock Publications.

Young, A.
  1976   Some implications of medical beliefs and practices. *American Anthropologist* 78: 5–23.

Zemplani, Andras
  1980   From symptoms to sacrifice: The story of Khady Fall. In *Case Studies in Spirit Possession,* edited by V. Crapanzano and V. Garrison, pp. 87–140. New York: John Wiley & Sons.

Zerries, Otto
  1968   Primitive South America and the West Indies. In *Pre-Colum-bian American Religions,* edited by W. Kriceberg, H. Trimborn, W. Muller, O. Zerries. New York: Holt, Rinehart and Winston.

Zola, I. K.
  1966   Culture and symptoms: An analysis of patients presenting complaints. *American Sociological Review* 31: 615–16.

# Index

practical aspects of, 224, 230–32
social attitudes toward, 230–32, 256
social and kinship affiliations, 198–
201; *See also* Celilo; Kadegare; Manukuje
and the soul, 211–12
and witchcraft, 237–38, 255, 319,
324
Shaman of the soul (*aroe, etawa-are*),
101, 197, 199, 207, 234–35,
261, 265–68, 343
absence of, 234–35, 305, 329–31
metamorphoses, 299–300, 302
as a "priest," 308–10
recruitment, 292–98
Shame, 53–54, 108, 297
Sherente, 7
Shirokogoroff, Sergei M., 341
Siskind, Janet, 164
Sister (*i-tuie/i-wie*), 75–77, 95–97,
114, 135, 259
Skewer (*joto*), 209, 216, 218, 221, 258,
350
Skullcap (*boe etao bu*), 63–64, 117
Sloth, 155
Smell as a classificatory principle,
160–61
Snakes
edibility of, 156
symbolism of, 183–84, 186, 188–
89, 286, 349
Social ethics, 25–26, 93, 135, 147,
239–40, 249–50, 255–56, 259–
61, 305–7, 311–12
and social emotions, 25–26
Socialization, aggression in, 101–3
Sociology of knowledge, 125
and the *bope,* 128–29
Soul loss, 22–23, 25, 112, 163, 217–
20, 315, 325, 332
*See also* Aroe
Sound, meaning of
in afterlife, 274, 294, 301, 351
in bird calls, 183, 186–88
of falling star, 216–20, 302
in wild animals, 191–92, 349
Sponsor (*i-orubadari*), 106–7, 293, 295,
353
Spouse of sibling (*in-odowu*), 82, 238–
39, 255
Steinen, Karl von den, 9, 192, 284, 285

Stingray, 156
Stork, as *aroe,* 277
Stratification, 7, 138
Subsistence, 29–30, 33, 48, 70–71,
79–81, 87, 94, 99–100, 104,
326–27, 344
*See also* Hunts, collective
Surubim, ("pintado"), 26–27, 341
as food of the *bope,* 141, 249–50
as itself a *bope,* 183
Suya, 9, 10
Swartz, M., V. Turner, and A. Tuden, 237

Taboo, 21, 346
Tambiah, S. J., 25, 162
Tapir
and the *aroe,* 278, 299–300
as a *bope* food, 127, 140, 143–45,
163, 167–69, 170, 177, 203,
221, 243, 253
and shamans, 315, 331
Termites, 127
Theft, 25–26, 260, 307
Tillyard, E. M. W., 21
*Tinamideus,* 52
Tobacco
and the *aroe,* 270, 293
and the *bope,* 133, 202–3, 218, 346
used in curing, 228–29, 233–34
and trance, 218, 221
Tonelli, A., 142
Totemic, 17, 21, 30–31, 33–36, 64–
67, 71–73, 82–86, 87–88, 101,
105–6, 137–38, 198–99, 267,
272, 279, 310, 327, 342, 346,
348
Trance, 17, 18, 19, 22–23, 25, 202–7,
221–24, 228, 298–99
specialists, 19
Transvestism, 47, 103
Triester, 132–33
Tuden, A., 237
Tugarege, 30–31, 126, 198–201, 206–
7, 225, 233, 241, 246, 268, 272,
280, 292–93, 298, 300–1, 310,
311, 314, 318, 351
Tupa-doge, 131, 205, 208, 245, 247,
253, 256
Turner, Victor, 25, 149, 237, 238, 348
Turtle, 62–63, 178
Twins, 49, 343